Fenton Art Glass
Patterns
1939 – 1980
SECOND EDITION

IDENTIFICATION & VALUE GUIDE

Margaret & Kenn Whitmyer

COLLECTOR BOOKS
A Division of Schroeder Publishing Co., Inc.

Front cover:
Top Left to Right — Ruby Overlay Diamond Optic Melon Rib vanity set,
Black Rose hurricane lamp, Cranberry Coin Dot decanter.

Bottom Left to Right — Milk Hobnail 2-piece epergne set, Charleton-
decorated Aqua Crest clock made from a 6" plate.

Back cover:
Top Left to Right — Cameo Opalescent Lily of the Valley fairy light,
Blue Opalescent Diamond Lace 2-piece epergne set, Blue Opalescent
Hobnail vanity bottle.

Bottom Left to Right — Aventurine Green with Blue Vasa Murrhind vase,
Cranberry Spiral Optic basket.

Cover design by Beth Summers
Book design by Joyce A. Cherry

COLLECTOR BOOKS
P.O. Box 3009
Paducah, Kentucky 42002-3009
www.collectorbooks.com

Copyright © 2004 Margaret & Kenn Whitmyer

The current values in this book should be used only as a guide. They are not
intended to set prices, which vary from one section of the country to another.
Auction prices as well as dealer prices vary greatly and are affected by condition
as well as demand. Neither the authors nor the publisher assumes responsibility
for any losses that might be incurred as a result of consulting this guide.

Searching For A Publisher?

We are always looking for people knowledgeable within their fields. If you
feel that there is a real need for a book on your collectible subject and have a
large comprehensive collection, contact Collector Books.

Dedication

*This book is dedicated to all the
collectors of Fenton glassware.
Enjoy your avocation!*

Contents

Introduction

Fenton Art Glass Patterns 1939 – 1980 is an in-depth look at the regular line production of Fenton's major patterns over four decades. In order to accomplish this purpose the book is divided alphabetically into four major chapters covering the specific patterns — Coin Dot, Crests, Hobnail, and Spiral Optic. Each chapter is further subdivided alphabetically by the various colors in which the pattern was produced. An additional chapter is provided to present the miscellaneous patterns that may only consist of a few pieces or were only made in a few colors.

The primary focus of this book is patterns and shapes made for the regular Fenton line. An effort has been made to illustrate some sample items and a few of the more frequently seen pieces that Fenton made for other companies. However, comprehensive coverage of this type of production is beyond the scope of this book. In most instances, examples of sample items and private contract production will be illustrated at the end of each chapter. The Supplemental Patterns chapter illustrates items of this type with the appropriate patterns.

Pattern and Shape Identification ❖

Prior to July 1952, Fenton identified patterns or shapes with a mould number. For example, the number "389" was used to represent the entire Hobnail pattern. All pieces of this pattern were identified by this number and a further description was necessary to identify an individual item. Also, in the Crest pattern and overlay colors, the mould number "711" was used to represent all items with the Beaded Melon shape.

After July 1952, Fenton switched to a ware number system. With this new system each item in regular line production was assigned a four-digit number followed by a two letter code. The numerals represent the pattern and shape and the letters indicate the color or hand-painted decoration. As an example, examine Ware No. 2858-AG:

> The first two numbers — 28 — represent the Wild Rose with Bowknot pattern
> The second two digits — 58 — represent a 7½" vase
> The two letters — AG — represent the cased 1950s color Apple Green

With very few exceptions, each item has a unique ware number. There have been instances where numbers and letters have been reused. Most of the time there has been a significant time gap between the two occurrences and there should not be any confusion about the description.

Identification of items by using the photographs and many of the catalog reprints in this book may be accomplished by referring to the number and description below each item. Generally, if the number is preceded by the letters "No.," the number is a mould number that was used prior to July 1952. This number will be found with the item descriptions in the accompanying price listings — for example — Bowl, 7", #389 flared. If the number accompanying the item has no letter prefix, it is a ware number. Ware numbers are listed in a separate column in the price listings. If a piece was made both before and after the conversion, both numbers will be provided. The mould number will be with the item description and the ware number will be listed in the Ware No. column. An exception to this is the Hobnail pattern where all pieces had the same mould number prior to 1952.

Determining Dates of Production ❖

Columns in the price listing labeled "Introduced" and "Discontinued" provide the date each item entered the regular line and the year that item was no longer listed as available in the price listing. As an example:

Peach Crest	Ware No.	Introduced	Discontinued	Value
Basket, #1924-5" handled	7235-PC	1942	1954	40.00 – 45.00

The Peach Crest basket in the above illustration was introduced in January 1942. It was in production through December 1953, and was no longer available in the price listing issued in January 1954. Also the ware number for this basket is No. 7335-PC and the mould shape is #1924. It is not possible to determine the exact dates for some of the items produced before 1947. For some of these earlier items and patterns we have been fortunate to have inventory records and the recollection of Frank Fenton as our guide. Accurate dates of production are only listed for items introduced and discontinued in the period from 1939 through the end of 1979. Items that entered the line prior to 1980, but which have continued in production will be designated "1980+" in the discontinued column.

Consulting the Price Guide ❖

The prices in this book represent average retail prices for mint condition pieces. Pieces that are chipped, cracked, or excessively worn should only bring a fraction of the listed price. Also, collectors should be aware that certain currently rare items that are now valued at a high dollar amount may prove hard to sell if a large quantity of these items is discovered. A few items that have been found listed in the company catalogs, but are not known to be available, may not be priced in the listings.

A price range is included to allow for some regional differences. This book is intended to be only a guide, and it is not the intention of the authors to set or establish prices.

Prices are for each piece unless a set is indicated in the description. Candleholders are priced each. Salt and pepper shakers were listed in the Fenton price lists as sets and are priced in the price lists in this book as sets. The prices listed are those we have seen collectors pay and prices collectors have told us they would be willing to pay.

A Note Concerning Fenton Reissues ❖

Periodically, when Fenton has determined that market conditions are appropriate, old moulds may be reused to produce items for the regular line. The management of Fenton is well aware of the collectibility of their older glassware. As a result certain steps have been taken to ensure that newer issues will enhance the collectibility of Fenton glassware and preserve the value of the older collectibles.

Many of the older moulds that are brought out of retirement are used for special purposes, such as the "Family Signature Series," the Connoisseur Collection," or the "Historical Collection." These special series usually feature pieces in colors that have not been made previously.

Beginning in 1970, moulds used to produce carnival ware were marked with an oval Fenton logo. This process was completed for Hobnail and other items by about 1974. All items made after this date for the regular line will be marked on the bottom with the oval logo. As production has progressed through each successive decade, a small number has been added to the logo. The 1980s decade has an "8" and the 1990s production bears a "9." Items made in the first decade of the twenty-first century have a small "0" under the Fenton logo.

Additional marks have been used in other special cases. A script capital "F" in a vertical oval has been used on the bottom of pieces made from moulds purchased from other glass companies. This mark began appearing on items in 1983, but was not used on moulds aquired from Verly's. A sandblasted Fenton mark in an oval was used on some blown items or limited edition items where no other mark would be readily visible. This mark was also used on off-hand or paste mould items where no logo could be incorporated into the mould. This mark was used from the 1980s to 1994.

Intentional Omissions ❖

As this book developed it became obvious that Fenton produced too much glass over this forty year span for it all to be included in one book. As a result a decision had to be made as to whether some patterns would be covered more superficially or whether the end result should be a more complete coverage with a division of this time period into two separate books. The latter option was chosen and the division was effected as follows:

The first book, *Fenton Art Glass Patterns 1939 – 1980*, contains all the major patterns such as Coin Dot, Crests, Hobnail, Spiral Optic, and any other patterns with a significant number of pieces.

A subsequent book, *Fenton Art Glass Colors and Hand-Painted Decorations 1939 – 1980*, will contain pieces in colors that do not have enough pieces to warrant grouping them together into a single pattern. It will also include Fenton's later carnival glass production and hand-painted patterns. In addition it will provide additional information on Fenton's production of Olde Virginia Glass.

Also, space limitations do not allow us to include in detail the multitude of special issues, sample items and whimsies that were not a part of the regular line. Numerous items have been made in small numbers for other companies, clubs, organizations, and individuals over the years. In many cases these are regular line items that were made in special color. Some pieces were regular line items that were purchased to be hand decorated by independent decorating companies. In addition, numerous lamps were fashioned by lamp manufacturers from glass lamp parts made by Fenton. A limited number of these examples have been included.

Private mould work commissioned by other companies using non-Fenton moulds has not been covered in depth, but a glimpse at some of the major players such as L. G. Wright and Rubel has been provided.

Acknowledgments

It seems like this second Fenton Art Glass book has been in the research and development stage forever. We would like to express our gratitude to the loyal collectors and dealers who have had the fortitude to bear with us and were gracious enough to share their time and contribute their treasures and knowledge. Without the help of a multitude of dedicated Fenton enthusiasts, this book would not be possible.

It is probably hard for the casual reader to appreciate that producing a volume of this magnitude involves the energies of a virtual army of dedicated people — not just the authors. It is very difficult to give these hard workers the recognition they deserve, but without their efforts this book would not have been possible. Many of these names will be familiar to readers as serious collectors of Fenton glassware and others are close friends and associates who have helped us on previous works. We would like to thank all of them for their patience and co-operation.

Frank Fenton was undoubtedly the most important contributor. Without his knowledge, assistance, and encouragement this book would not exist. He provided us with detailed historical information and interesting antecdotes. We had the freedom to copy company records and catalogs. He also allowed us to photograph at will in the Fenton Art Glass Museum. He graciously assisted by answering our questions and provided anything we needed for our photography and research.

Nancy Fenton, Frank's daughter-in-law, was always available to answer the many questions we had concerning Fenton production from the later years.

Several Fenton employees also deserve special acknowledgment. Among them are Anne Martha, Frank's secretary, who knows all his hiding places. Jennifer Maston, hostess of The Fenton Art Glass Museum, was always most helpful. Tamara Armstrong, an information specialist, saved us countless hours with her organization of the Fenton archives.

Berry Wiggins, a noted author and researcher of early glassware, was often at the Fenton plant. He was very helpful with his knowledge in some areas in which we had little experience. This kind of assistance is invaluable.

Carrie Domitz is an avid collector and enthusiastic Fenton supporter. We were able to persuade her to share her vast knowledge. She was always there to answer our questions and provide the help we needed. Again we would like to extend a special thanks to Gerry Domitz for helping with photography.

The Pacific NW. Fenton Association was extremely hospitable. Their conventions are a great learning experience. Members provided us with valuable information and allowed their treasures to be photographed.

Jackie Shirley also deserves special mention. Her knowledge in the areas of Topaz Opalescent glassware and cologne bottles was extremely valuable.

Michael and Lori Palmer, who have spent years researching and identifying independent hand-painted decorations on Fenton and other contemporary glassware, have produced an authoritative work on this subject. They have identified the Charleton decorations of the Abels, Wasserberg & Co. and also have uncovered examples of various other decorators of the same era. They have graciously allowed us to use the names they have chosen to identify patterns that have not yet been identified with original names. For more information, we encourage interested readers to investigate the informative book produced by this couple. Please see the bibliography for more information.

Others who contributed in a large way include:

Henke and Anne van Bemmelen
Berner's Auction Gallery
Gordon and Darlene Cochran
Randy and Debbie Coe
Sam and Becky Collings
Janice Estrada
Eric and Jay Fralick
Luane French
Lynette and Greg Galusha
Jerry and Connee Hack
Bill Harmon
William Hatchett

Rebecca and Russell Hattal
Heart of Ohio Antique Center
Lorrie Kitchen and Mark Hunter
Kevin Kiley
Lorraine and Dave Kovar
Carolyn Kriner
Debbie Lane
Leora and Jim Leasure
Ed and Shirley Lehew
Nancy Maben
Fred McMorrow
Jacque Metcalfe

Liz Paldanius
Connie Rich
Tom Smith
Jean and Lee Spaulding
Kathy and Bud Stultz
Rick and Ruth Teets
Dan and Geri Tucker
Eddie and Neil Unger
Lynn Welker
Max and Lou Wenger
Jeanne Word

Historical Synopsis

1939

Fenton stepped up production of the No. 289 Hobnail cologne bottle for Wrisley. At times there were as many as eight to ten shops making this piece. Production for the regular line was concentrated on the Spiral pattern in Steigel Blue Opalescent, French Opalescent, Green Opalescent, Blue Ridge, and Cranberry. Demand for the patterns and treatments that were popular in the mid-1930s was tapering off. Thus, most of the pieces in the Daisy and Button, Georgian, Lincoln Inn, and Plymouth patterns were discontinued. Satin finished patterns were also diminishing in popularity and were phased out. Peach Blow — a cased glass with a gold ruby interior and a milk glass exterior layer — also entered the line for a single year.

1940

The outbreak of war, in late 1939, resulted in a desperate scramble among importers to establish new sources of supply to replace their old links which were interrupted. Fenton was able to accommodate this new business and the relationship with the importers continued until about 1947. By that time the war had ended and many of the plants that were damaged by the war had been rebuilt. The importers then re-established their old contacts and abandoned their American suppliers.

Although orders for the No. 289 cologne bottle from Wrisley were diminishing, Fenton made a major commitment to the future of both opalescent colored glassware and the Hobnail pattern. The 1940 general catalog showcases the introduction of the No. 389 Hobnail line in Blue Opalescent, French Opalescent, Green Opalescent, and Cranberry.

Crest patterns were also highlighted. Peach Crest spruced up and replaced the original Peach Blo pattern. Blue Ridge was discontinued, and the new Crest color was Ivory Crest. This new color featured a pale yellow body with a spun crystal edge.

June 29 — the day the stack fell — was among one of the more memorable days around the Fenton plant that year. The disaster left one person dead and several injured. Partial production resumed about three weeks later utilizing the day tanks. These tanks were located in an area of the factory that had only sustained minor damage and could be used to produce certain types of glassware. Meanwhile the stack and the main roof of the plant were undergoing reconstruction. Repairs proceeded quickly and the factory was back in full production by the beginning of September.

1941

Aqua Crest entered the line and was made for two years before production was interrupted. Production of this color resumed in 1948, after the ease of wartime restrictions.

Green Opalescent was discontinued and the new opalescent color was Topaz.

1942

The war years were difficult times for the American glass industry. Fenton, along with the rest of the industry, struggled to maintain an uninterrupted output. Due to the many wartime restrictions, the demand for attractive glassware completely surpassed Fenton's production capability. Although the basic ingredients for making glass were plentiful, there was great difficulty in obtaining essential ingredients for producing colors. Perhaps the greatest changes during these years were the elimination of some colors that could no longer be made and the introduction of new colors that were easier to produce. New colors in the line this year included Mulberry, Crystal Crest, and Ruby Overlay. A major style change was effected with the introduction of the No. 192 Melon Rib shape. Over the next few years, obtaining iron to produce new molds was almost impossible. Therefore, old molds were used throughout the war years with very few changes in the items produced.

1943

In about mid-1942, Crystal Crest was discontinued and production changed to the less labor intensive Silver Crest. The Mulberry color was discontinued after only remaining in the line for a year. The Peach Crest line continued to expand and Gold Crest was added. Also, Ruby Overlay continued in production and the Blue and Rose Overlay colors were implemented.

1944

Rose Crest was initially marketed to Weil Freeman several years before the pattern entered the Fenton catalog. Abels, Wasserberg and Company, a decorating firm from New York became one of Fenton's largest accounts. Many items from the regular Fenton line, especially pieces in the Crest pattern, may be found with the this company's decorations.

1945

As the war ended, boom times continued with strong orders from jobbers who normally bought their products from foreign suppliers. Fenton boasted about a year backlog in orders at the end of the war.

1946

The Fenton plant got some needed repairs and improvements that the wartime shortages had prohibited. Rose Crest was introduced to the regular line. This pattern had been made for Weil Freeman the previous two years.

1947

The Coin Dot pattern was added to the regular line in Blue Opalescent, French Opalescent, and Cranberry colors. On the economic front, the boom resulting from the limited competition of the war years was coming to an end. Increased competition from foreign manufacturers resulted in a sharp decrease in orders from domestic retailers.

1948

Fenton Art Glass co-founder Frank L. Fenton died May 18, at age 68, from complications resulting from a heart attack on April 23. About six months later his older brother, Robert C. Fenton also died. These losses were particularly critical since the younger generation, which included Frank M. and Wilmer C., had a very limited knowledge of company's operations. Also, at this time many glass and pottery companies were having difficulties surviving the challenges of increased foreign competition.

The Diamond Lace pattern was introduced to the line and Coin Dot was added in the Honeysuckle color. Honeysuckle Coin Dot only remained in the line until the end of 1949, although lamp parts in Coin Dot were made in this color during the 1950s.

1949

Paul Rosenthal, Fenton's chief chemist at the time of Frank L. Fenton's death, decided to retire. After his retirement the Rosenthal formulas were acquired by Fenton, and Rosenthal's son-in-law took over the job of glass maker. However, a dispute quickly arose about his lack of record keeping and he soon departed. As a result, a search began for a new chemist who could implement the old formulas and develop new ones. Meanwhile, Frank M. Fenton had the added responsibility of supervising the chemical mixing.

In a style modification, the No. 711 Beaded Melon shape replaced the No. 192 Melon Rib shape. This style change was incorporated into the new crest and overlay colors that also debuted this year. New overlay colors included Ivy, Green Overlay, and Gold Overlay. Emerald Crest also made a debut.

As the never-ending effort to expand the market for Fenton glassware continued, Fenton developed a stronger sales relationship with the A. L. Randall Company of Chicago. The wholesale catalog for florists from the A. L. Randall Company illustrates numerous items made by Fenton in a 20 page layout. Patterns illustrated include Coin Dot, Hobnail, Diamond Lace, and Crests. The introductory message to the trade proclaims, "Because of the many years we have served the Floral Industry, Fenton Art Glass Company felt we were best qualified to handle the Floral end of their business. For this reason they have designated us their sole distributor to the Florist." Over the next several years. the A. L. Randall Company became one of Fenton's largest customers.

1950

Numerous changes were implemented as the new generation became more familiar with the company's operations. Isaac Willard, a young chemical engineering graduate from University of Pittsburgh, came to Fenton to assume duties of chief chemist. The sales organization was revamped to eliminate the role of jobbers in the sale of Fenton glassware. From now on only manufacturers' representatives would handle the sales. Manufacturers' representatives are sales specialists who work on sales commissions and usually represent several companies for specialized products. In addition, to spark interest in Fenton glassware, a national advertising campaign was begun.

However, on the labor front, a 17 day strike during September by members of the national glassworkers union helped to compound problems for the company and its new leaders. One result of this strike and the resulting agreement was the realization that the two different types of manufacturers — hand and machine — could not be represented by the same organization. Over the next several years all of the major hand manufacturing companies withdrew from the national organization. This move allowed them to bargain with the union on an individual basis rather the being forced to accept the national agreement which favored the needs of the larger and more influential machine made operations.

New patterns for the year included Priscilla in Crystal, Green, and Blue and the Spiral Optic shape in various colors with a milk glass crest (Snowcrest).

1951

The advertising budget was sacrificed in favor of putting more money into product design. Industry sales continued to slump and numerous Fenton patterns were not doing well. The recently introduced Tiara line, Priscilla, and Snowcrest items were not selling as well as anticipated. This year's square shape Hobnail entry was a complete failure, although other pieces of Hobnail still sold well.

With the demise of the Paden City Glass Company, Fenton began supplying glass to Rubel. Many of these items were dark green in color. Pieces produced included mustards and heart-shaped bowls that were intended to be placed into metal holders for use as condiment sets. Some pieces were also made in milk glass with an emerald crest. The association with Rubel continued until 1959. At that time Rubel was no longer buying glassware from Fenton, but the molds were still in Fenton's possession. Fenton acquired the molds from Rubel and has used those molds to produce glassware over the years.

1952

Modernistic designer Stan Fistick was hired to implement contemporary design in the company's products. His first creation was a set of cookie canisters which proved difficult to make; thus, they were soon discontinued. Modern style cased glass vases in ruby and dark green were also produced, but did not sell well and were discontinued at the end of the year. He forged ahead to design the New World shapes, but this pattern only enjoyed limited success and Fenton's experiment with contemporary style was put on hold. Fistick became disillusioned and moved on to academia.

On the more traditional side, a few select pieces of Hobnail were introduced in Peach Blo and new items were introduced in milk glass Hobnail. Plates and bowls were drilled and combined with metal parts to provide useful items such as planters and tidbits.

The Diamond Optic and Rib Optic patterns from the past were revived with new shapes appearing in satin opalescent colors. The first three of Fenton's Lacy Edge shapes entered the line in milk glass at mid-year. This pattern was expanded over the next few years and many of the shapes were also made in Blue Pastel, Green Pastel, Rose Pastel, and Turquoise during the mid-1950s.

1953

The Daisy and Button pattern re-entered the Fenton line in mid year in milk glass and Fenton's new pastel colors — Blue Pastel, Green Pastel, and Rose Pastel. New Hobnail and Lacy Edge shapes in milk glass were featured in the catalog supplement and these opaque shapes began to outdistance the sales of opalescent glassware. Black Rose was the new crest color. The Swirled Feather pattern debuted in satin opalescent colors. Notable among the pieces included in this pattern was the introduction of Fenton's first fairy light.

New novelty items such as the fish vase, Happiness bird, Madonna vase, chicken egg server, and hen on nest covered boxes were designed to appeal to a market that was eagerly seeking decorative accessories.

New World was finally introduced, but the modernistic styles and colors did not sell well. Items in Dusk were discontinued before the end of the year, but the opalescent colors fared somewhat better and remained in the line for several years. Georgian tumblers like those appearing in the 1930s were brought back into the line in several sizes and colors.

1954

Fenton introduced the new Swirl and Lamb's Tongue patterns in opaque pastel colors. Also several Cranberry Spiral vases reminiscent of ware from the late 1930s returned for another showing. The tall footed cake plate made its appearance in the Fenton line. This piece in a variety of patterns would eventually become one of Fenton's most popular pieces. The Spanish Lace pattern also made its debut in the Fenton line. The first item in this pattern was the footed cake plate. This pattern was reproduced from an old Northwood butter dish that Frank M. Fenton bought at an antique show. Also new in the catalog were two sizes of free form ashtrays made in amber and dusk from old Rubel molds. An interesting item made during this year was the No. 7302 bathroom set. The set included three bath bottles with ground stoppers and a matching rectangular tray. Some of these sets may be found with the Abels, Wasserberg Charleton decoration.

1955

A noteworthy event for this year was the production of the first catalog with full-color photographs. Milk glass Hobnail became the leading seller as more pieces were added to that line. The Polka Dot pattern was introduced in Cranberry, but sales for this pattern were less than spectacular. New colors in the general line included Cased Lilac and the opaque Turquoise and Rose Pastel colors. Block and Star, Fenton's interpretation of the old Hobbs, Brockunier, and Company Block pattern made its debut in Turquoise and milk glass. A Teardrop mustard in Fenton's Turquoise and milk glass colors entered the line in January. More pieces in these same colors followed in the July supplement. Fenton began to investigate the possibilities of supplying glassware to catalog wholesalers and small retail outlets. In order to serve this market, a secondary line that was separate from the regular Fenton line was developed. Thumbprint in milk glass was the first pattern created for this line that later became known as Olde Virginia Glass.

1956

New items in the January catalog supplement included a punch set, salt and pepper shakers, and a large 12" vase in Silver Crest. Although others had been using the term "petticoat glass" for Silver Crest for some time, the first Fenton references for this terminology began to appear in catalogs. Over time "petticoat glassware" has evolved as a general term that includes all Crest colors. The regular line included Crest shapes in which the color selection was expanded to include items in Silver Turquoise and Silver Rose. Last year's new pattern, Polka Dot in Cranberry, did not sell as well as expected and was discontinued at the end of June. However new shapes in Polka Dot were introduced in Ruby Overlay at this time. The Wave Crest style No. 6080 candy box was also featured in Ruby Overlay. A bold new color was Goldenrod — a brilliant yellow overlay — that was implemented with the Teardrop pattern and several other bowls and vases.

1957

The Jamestown Blue color was introduced in both transparent and overlay versions. Fenton's Teardrop pattern was expanded in milk glass, but the Turquoise and Goldenrod colors were discontinued. Fenton entered into an agreement with Michael Lax for the design of contemporary style glassware. However, Fenton's regular line of traditional glassware was selling so well that plans for the introduction of this bold new contemporary ware were temporarily shelved.

1958

Cranberry Spiral Optic returned to the line in seven new shapes. Ten different Polka Dot shapes were introduced in transparent Jamestown Blue. These pieces joined a Polka Dot barber bottle in this color which made its debut the year before.

1959

The Cactus pattern, a reproduction of an earlier Greentown pattern with both original shapes and Fenton creations from new moulds, made an appearance in the line in Topaz Opalescent and milk at the start of the year. Cactus appeared just in time for use with Fenton's more dense milk glass formula. This denser formula was developed as a response to complaints from customers that Fenton's milk glass was too transparent. Pieces also often had a sandy appearance or an objectionable gray ring. The new denser formula eliminated these problems and was used for all patterns of milk glass produced after this date. New colors in Hobnail included Green Opalescent and Plum Opalescent. The new green color was much more of a blue-green than any of the earlier Green Opalescent colors. The plum color came about as a result of trying to produce pressed items in Cranberry.

The Michael Lax contemporary creation officially dubbed "Horizon" was finally introduced in the July catalog supplement. The assortment was comprised of hanging bowls with leather thongs, candleholders with inserts, salt and pepper shakers, nut dishes, and various other accessory pieces. The candleholders were fitted with porcelain inserts and bases and other pieces such as sugar bowls and shakers were graced with walnut tops.

1960

Two Jacqueline vases entered the line in Blue, Pink, and Yellow Opaline colors. Apple Blossom Crest was the new entry in the Crest line, and Waffle made a short appearance in Green Opalescent, Blue Opalescent, and milk glass.

Fenton made glass for Rubel and Company in the 1950s after the demise of the Paden City Glass Company. Fenton was able to buy the Rubel moulds after they stopped purchasing glass. Several ashtrays from these moulds were put into the regular Fenton line.

1961

Fenton's new overlay colors included Powder Blue Overlay, Coral, Apple Green, Wild Rose, and Opaque Blue. New patterns that utilized some of these unique colors were Jacqueline, Wild Rose with Bowknot, and Bubble Optic.

1962

Thumbprint and Diamond Optic were introduced in Colonial Blue and Colonial Amber. The history of Diamond Optic with Fenton goes back over 30 years. Diamond Optic first appeared in the Fenton line in 1927. The pattern was made in overlay colors during the 1940s and appeared in opalescent colors in the early 1950s. Now, in 1962 it had come full circle and was back in the line in transparent colors.

1963

Gold Crest returned to the line with new shapes after a 20 year rest. Blue Crest — with a much more vibrant crest than the earlier Aqua Crest — and Flame Crest were also new entries. None of these colors was carried over into 1964. The number of pieces of the Thumbprint pattern was expanded and Diamond Optic was made in Orange.

1964

Vasa Murrhina made an appearance in Rose Mist, Blue Mist, Rose with Aventurine Green, and Aventurine Green with Blue. Vasa Murrhina is a special type of cased glassware that has colored glass or mica frit embedded in one layer. The resulting pattern is varied and colorful. The Rose pattern made a seemingly reluctant entry with only a single item — the No. 9222 tall footed comport appearing in Amber, Blue, Green, and Pink. The July catalog supplement displayed wrought iron holders for Hobnail planters and candles. These holders were designed by Dave Ellies, Inc., of Columbus, Ohio. The Silver Crest footed salt and pepper set was in the line briefly before the mould was enhanced with the Spanish Lace design.

1965

After numerous record setting years for sales, the cramped facilities were in much need of expansion and repair. The plant could no longer keep up with the orders and office space was cramped. Renovation of the hot metal department began in late 1964 and was completed by mid-1965. Construction of new offices was completed by the end of 1965. The entire year was a time of renovation and expansion.

The oval candy box was added to the Rose pattern, but this piece only remained in production for one year. Novelty items included the high button shoe and the Leaf pattern plate which was one of the few pieces remaining in the line from the 1930s.

1966

Fenton is continually searching for new ideas to expand its product base. As a result, when moulds from defunct companies become available, the possibility of purchasing them is usually explored. Frank Fenton was able to purchase the Verly's of America moulds from Holophane of Newark, Ohio, after agreeing that the Verly's name would not be used. Some of these moulds had been used previously by the Heisey Glass Company of Newark.

Fenton explored the possibility of entering the lamp business. Previously, Fenton had made lamp parts for many years for numerous companies who then assembled and marketed the finished product. Recently, milk Hobnail lamps had been successfully tested in the Fenton gift shop. Also, other test market results indicated a strong possibility that a line of lamps could be successfully marketed. After this short but successful test marketing period, Fenton entered the lamp business with an initial offering of 18 lamps. Lamp patterns included Rose, Poppy, and a large Coin Dot style that Fenton dubbed Thumbprint. Pieces of the Thumbprint pattern made their debut in Ruby.

1967

Fenton separated lamps from the regular catalog by issuing a special lamp supplement. The Rose pattern allocation of the new regular catalog was three pages compared to a mere one piece two years ago.

1968

Fenton began utilizing the Verly's moulds by offering an assortment of items in milk glass, orange, and opalescent colors. However, production problems resulted in an early discontinuance of these items. Thumbprint entered the line in ebony and was quite popular in this color. In the early 1970s ebony was spruced up with a white daisies hand-painted decoration. One of the few setbacks in Hobnail occurred with the new entry for 1968. Crystal Hobnail never approached its expected sales projections. On the brighter side, Louise Piper's Violets in the Snow hand-painted decoration, which first appeared in the July supplement, proved to be one of the more popular introductions.

1969

A totally new entry for 1969 was Fenton's Valencia pattern. Anthony Rosena's design was adapted from a Czechoslovakian Moser piece bought at an antique show by Frank M. Fenton. The line was expanded considerably in 1970, but no new items were created in the following years. The pattern was well received, but production problems greatly hindered Fenton's ability to produce this pattern. The line dwindled to only two items in the 1972 – 1973 catalog.

A marketing attempt to promote a candle bowl as the "creative candle bowl" was met with stiff resistance. A threatened lawsuit over the registered trademark name "creative" forced the elimination of that word and the description was shortened to simply candle bowl.

1970

Fenton ventured into the 1970s with a brightly iridized new line of wares. This reintroduction of carnival glass was the first small step in the development of a major new line of glassware. These new pieces were marked with an embossed Fenton logo and all came complete with a descriptive tag attached. The first in a series of annual carnival glass collectible plates in the Craftsman series appeared in the January catalog supplement. The July supplement announced the first plate of an annual limited edition Christmas in America series of plates in Blue Satin, White Satin, and carnival. A new light blue color with opal swirls called Blue Marble appeared in the Hobnail and Rose patterns.

Fenton began the process of affixing a molded identifying logo onto the bottom of each piece. Moulds were modified as time permitted and the process of incorporating the logo into all the moulds was completed by 1974.

1971

Selected lamps were marketed with cloth shades to department and furniture stores. These did not sell well and this experiment was abandoned after a few years. Later, all Fenton lamps were made with glass shades and were marketed through normal retail outlets. Louise Piper's first hand-painted decoration on Burmese, the popular Rose Burmese pattern, was introduced the year after the development of the Burmese color. Another annual series of plates was introduced for Mother's Day.

In the July supplement Orange Carnival made a comeback with a limited assortment of 14 different items before the color was retired in 1973. Holly decorated milk glass Hobnail was available for the Christmas season.

1973

Separate lamp supplements were discontinued; from this time on lamps have been listed in the general catalog. Candle arrangements were the feature of the July supplement and the Santa fairy light was offered in Lime Sherbet, Custard, and milk glass for the Christmas season.

1974

In preparation for America's celebration, the first Bicentennial pieces appeared in Independence Blue. Satin colors were gaining appeal and popularity as the lineup of items in Custard and Lime Sherbet was expanded and the Rose Satin color was added.

1975

Robert Barber developed a relationship as a resident artist at Fenton. He was given the freedom to develop his ideas and express them in the glass medium. In April, four of his creations were selected for production and offered to Fenton customers as a limited-edition collectible. Fenton dealers responded enthusiastically, therefore, another six shapes of vases were commissioned and put into production. Unfortunately, these items did not sell as well as expected and dealers began to use their special return option. As a result this experiment with a new version of off-hand art glass was abruptly halted.

The July supplement featured Bicentennial items in Valley Forge White, Patriot Red, and Independence Blue. Included in the series were a collectible plate, a large 14 ounce stein, a bell, and a large covered Jefferson comport.

With Louise Piper at the helm of the decorating department, lines of hand-painted glassware had been steadily expanding and maturing. New decorations were developed and implemented and individual artists also began to include their signature on their work.

1976

The Hanging Hearts pattern developed by Robert Barber was a new but short-lived addition to the Fenton line. The last of the Barber designs, a collection of colorfully variegated egg paperweights, appeared in the July catalog supplement.

A new opaque rose color with opal swirls called Rosalene was created. The early production of this color is bright. However, this formula proved to be too corrosive for the equipment. The formula was altered to make it easier to work with and later production has a lighter color. Fenton commemorated the past by reviving its historical Red Carnival color. This new version of the color was called Ruby Iridescent. Ten shapes were introduced in this color in the first year. In 1977, five more shapes were added to the line. The color was discontinued at the end of 1977. Chocolate glass also returned and was used with the American Bicentennial items.

1977

Hobnail with the milk glass color at the forefront, was still the prevailing pattern in the line. Other Hobnail colors included Colonial Blue, Cranberry, Colonial Amber, and Ruby. New to the Hobnail line was the bright Springtime Green color which replaced Colonial Green in the Fenton array of colors. Ruby was the color for the assortment of carnival glass whose main attraction was the 24" Poppy Gone with the Wind lamp. The ultimate in lamps was the three lamp Candy Stripe assortment in Rosalene Satin. For some reason this style of lamp was not an overwhelming favorite with the public.

1978

The January supplement offered numerous new items in the popular satin Crystal Velvet color. Satin was a popular look for this period. Other satin colors included Lime Sherbet, Custard, Lavender Satin, and Blue Satin. Blue Opalescent returned to the line with pieces of Hobnail especially prominent. The Hobnail footed candle bowl appeared in the line in Blue Opalescent and milk glass. Fenton's Lily of the Valley pattern was introduced in Cameo Opalescent and carnival colors.

Left to right: Natalie Fenton is the granddaughter of Frank M. Fenton and the second daughter of Mike and Kathy Fenton. Ben Fenton, son of George and Nancy Fenton, is the grandson of Frank M. Fenton. Lynn Fenton, the eldest grandchild of Frank M. Fenton, is the daughter of Frank R. Fenton. She is the first fourth generation Fenton to work full-time for the Fenton Art Glass Company. Danielle Fenton, granddaughter of W.C. (Bill) Fenton, is the daughter of Randy and Debbie Fenton.

Left to right: David Fenton, grandson of Frank M. Fenton, is the second son of George and Nancy Fenton. Meredith Fenton, daughter of Mike and Kathy Fenton, is the granddaughter of Frank M. Fenton. Scott Fenton is the son of Thomas K. Fenton and the grandson of Frank M. Fenton.

HOW IT'S MADE

The basic pattern mold for all Coin Dot pieces is called a spot mold. By skillful construction of this mold, the pattern is formed in the glass. Feel the inside of a Coin Dot piece, and you will find there is a hollow at each transparent area. Look through it, and you'll see an interesting optical effect—six dots on the far side making a daisy pattern inside each near dot.

Certain kinds of glass, when allowed to cool slightly, will turn white or cloudy if reheated. This is the "secret" of Coin Dot—the parts which you see as white are cooled briefly and warmed again at the "glory hole" in an operation requiring about as much instinctive skill and judgment as anything you can imagine.

French Opalescent and Blue Opalescent glass can be made to turn Opaque. To make Cranberry and Lime Coin Dot, a colored bubble of Gold Ruby or Green is blown inside a gather of French Opalescent, giving you a piece that is actually two layers of glass fused together—clear glass on the inside, opaque glass on the outside. This is called cased ware.

Fenton is the only manufacturer in America making gold ruby glass. This is the glass used on the inside of all Cranberry pieces, and it requires the addition of coin gold to the glass batch. When first made, gold ruby glass is a pale green in color—like magic, reheating turns it to a rich ruby red. Blowing stretches it thin, until it takes on the soft glow you see in Cranberry and Peach Crest.

Coin Dot

Fenton's Coin Dot Pattern

Coin Dot Colors and Shapes

Fenton's Coin Dot design, patterned after an old Victorian polka dot pattern, was introduced in 1947. The original colors that entered the regular line in that year were Blue Opalescent, Cranberry, and French Opalescent. Fenton's Cranberry color during this period consisted of Gold Ruby cased with French Opalescent to produce an opalescent color. Coin Dot in Blue Opalescent was discontinued by the end of 1954. French Opalescent remained in the line slightly longer — until the end of 1956. Cranberry, which was the bestselling color, remained in the regular line until the end of 1964.

Coin Dot is sometimes confused by novice collectors and dealers with another opalescent Fenton pattern called Dot Optic. The Coin Dot pattern consists of glassware with colored dots. Areas between the dots are opalescent. In the case of the French Opalescent color, the dots are clear. Dot Optic has dots that are opalescent and the areas between the dots are colored.

In 1948, Coin Dot was introduced into the line in Honeysuckle, a cased glass with amber on the inside and French Opalescent on the outside. Honeysuckle only remained in the line for two years — until the end of 1949. Later, from the mid-1950s through the 1960s, Fenton made lamp parts that were sold to other companies for use in the production of lamps. Also, during this same period some new shapes may have been sampled in this color.

The next color to enter the line in Coin Dot was Lime Opalescent. This yellow-green cased color was made by casing dark green inside French Opalescent. Lime Opalescent was produced from January 1952 through December 1955. Coin Dot pattern lamps parts, made in the mid-1960s, may also be found in a light green opalescent color called Honeydew. This color was made by casing Colonial Green with French Opalescent.

Later, in 1959, Coin Dot was introduced in Topaz Opalescent. Some pieces continued to be made in this color through July 1961.

Later, some items in the Coin Dot pattern were also produced in transparent and cased colors, without opalescence. Also in the late 1980s and during the 1990s, Coin Dot items were made in various opalescent colors. All of these pieces will bear the oval Fenton logo.

In addition to regular production items in the Coin Dot line, Fenton also made lamp parts and other special order pieces for various companies. Among their better customers were Quoizel, DeVilbiss, and L. G. Wright. Numerous items sold by these companies are pictured at the end of this chapter.

It is also interesting to note that parts of regular line items, such as candy jar bottoms, were sometimes adapted for other purposes. As an example, the 1949, A. L. Randall florist's wholesale catalog pictures the No. 1522 candy jar bottom for use as a vase. This use may explain the number of bottoms available in collector's hands that are begging for lids.

Supplemental issues include:

1948

Several Coin Dot shapes were sold to Quoizel for use in the manufacture of lamps, The No. 61 fount was sold in Blue Opalescent, Cranberry, and French Opalescent. The No. 894-10" vase in French Opalescent was drilled and used as a lamp part. Also, the No. 194-6" special vase with the neck cut off was sold in Blue Opalescent, Cranberry, and French Opalescent for use in the production of lamps.

1949

Quoizel began buying the No. 91 candy bottom which was incorporated into their new line of lamps. The colors used were Blue Opalescent, Cranberry, and French Opalescent. Virtually the entire line of Coin Dot in all the available colors was featured in the A. L. Randall florists wholesale catalog. The price of the Cranberry 12" basket in that catalog was $3.25. Blue Opalescent and French Opalescent 12" baskets were priced at $2.75 each.

1950

The No. 7 fount was purchased by Quoizel in French Opalescent and Cranberry for used in the manufacture of lamps.

1966

In the January catalog supplement, Fenton introduced two sizes of Coin Dot lamps, which they called Thumbprint. The lamps, No. 1410-20½" and No. 1408-19½" were made in Colonial Amber, Colonial Green, and Ruby Overlay.

1976

Two different Coin Dot lamps with cased Honey Amber parts were introduced in the July 1976 catalog supplement. These lamps were also pictured in the 1977 – 78 catalog. For more information see the photo at the end of this chapter.

1982

The No. 1432-32 oz pitcher was in the line in Country Cranberry (CC), Country Peach (RT), Forget-Me-Not Blue (KL), Ruby (RU), and Glacier Blue (BB).

The following pieces were also available in Country Cranberry:

Basket	1434-CC	Vase, 9½"	1433-CC
Lamp, 20"	1400-CC		

J. C. Penney also carried the Country Cranberry versions of the pitcher and vase.

The eight items in the list below were produced in Cranberry Opalescent for Levay Distributing Company in late 1982:

Basket	1439-CR	Fairy light, 3-piece	1403-CR
Basket, 7"	1446-CR	Rose bowl, 4½"	1436-CR
Bottle Vase	1483-CR	Vase, 7" Jack in Pulpit	1489-CR
Ewer	1493-CR	Vase, DC	1479-CR

The baskets and the ewer featured applied candy stripe handles and all the pieces have the oval Fenton logo on the bottom.

1983

The No. 1432-32 oz. pitcher was in the line in Country Peach (RT), Cobalt (KB), and Forget-Me-Not Blue (KL).

1986

The regular line catalog listed the following Coin Dot pieces in the popular Country Cranberry (CC) color:

Basket	1434-CC	Pitcher, 32 oz.	1432-CC
Lamp, 20"	1400-CC	Vase, 9½"	1433-CC

1988

Greenish blue Teal Royale (OC) and cobalt blue Blue Royale (KK) were the featured colors for the following items in Coin Dot:

Basket, 8"	1434	Pitcher, 32 oz.	1432
Lamp, 20"	1400	Vase, 11"	1443

The following items were also available in Country Cranberry:

Basket, 10½"	1445-CC	Vase, 8½"	1478-CC
Lamp, 22"	1400-CC	Vase, 10½"	1443-CC

1989

Several pieces in Coin Dot were made in Persian Blue Opalescent (XC) as part of an assortment grouped with other patterns. Coin Dot items bear the Fenton logo and include:

Basket, 5" top hat	1435-XC	Top hat	1492-XC
Creamer	1461-XC	Water set, 7-piece	1404-XC
Lamp, 22"	1413-XC		

Also available in Mulberry this year were a No. 1415-MG 34" lamp, a No. 1432-MG 32 oz. pitcher, and the No. 1434-MG 8" basket.

1990 – 91

The No. 1432 pitcher was introduced in Ruby (RU) and still continued in the line in Blue Royale. The No. 1434-8" basket and 1432 pitcher were offered in Mulberry (MG). Cranberry Opalescent made a reappearance in the Coin Dot pattern with the introduction of the No. 1413-21" lamp with prisms in that color.

The Country Cranberry collection was modified to include:

Basket, 8"	1434-CC	Pitcher, 32 oz.	1432-CC
Lamp, 20"	1400-CC	Vase, 10½"	1443-CC

1992 – 93

The Cranberry Opalescent No. 1413-CR 21" lamp with prisms continued to be available in the new catalog. The old No. 893 rose jar was revived. It was made in Cranberry Opalescent. Hand decoration and a black lid and base were added. The resulting product with the Ware No. CV007 8C was called a ginger jar and was sold through QVC.

The No. 1400 lamp was discontinued and the assortment of Country Cranberry (CC) continued as follows:

Basket, 8"	1434-CC	Vase, 8½"	1478-CC
Pitcher, 32 oz.	1432-CC	Vase, 10½"	1443-CC

In 1994, the No. 1498-8½" pinch vase was added to the above Country Cranberry pieces in the line. This vase was discontinued in 1996, but the other pieces were still in production. The No. 1443-10½" vase was discontinued in 1997. The other three items still remained in the line. In 1999 the No. 1432 pitcher was discontinued. The No. 1434-8" basket and the No. 1478-8½" vase remained in production, but Cranberry Coin Dot disappeared from Fenton's regular line at the end of this year.

2003

Coin Dot returned to the general line in four different colors. The No. 2435-9" basket, No. 2469-6½" pitcher and the No. 2463-5" vase were made in Blue Topaz Opalescent, Willow Green Opalescent, Violet Opalescent, and Rosemilk Opalescent. In addition, a No. 2460-8½" vase and a No. 2101-18" lamp were made in Violet Opalescent.

The three different styles of Coin Dot candy jars are illustrated in the photo below. The two jars on the left are the No. 91 shape. This jar was made in Cranberry, Blue Opalescent, and Cranberry. The large candy jar on the right is the No. 1522 style. This jar was made in Blue Opalescent, Cranberry, and French Opalescent between 1947 and 1951. The low candy jars in the center represent the possibilities for the No. 93 shape. This jar is not illustrated, but is listed in the Fenton catalogs for two years — 1948 and 1949. We have found these jars with two different lids, and either or both could be correct. The lid on the jar to the left matches the style of the other two candy jars in the pattern. A satin version of the other style lid is used by the Swirled Feather pattern. Swirled Feather is the pattern to which this candy jar mould was converted in the mid-1950s.

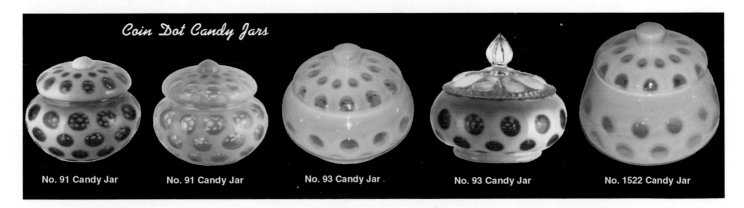

Coin Dot Candy Jars

| No. 91 Candy Jar | No. 91 Candy Jar | No. 93 Candy Jar | No. 93 Candy Jar | No. 1522 Candy Jar |

Blue Opalescent Coin Dot

The Blue Opalescent color of Coin Dot was first offered with the introduction of the Coin Dot pattern in 1947. The initial production period of Coin Dot in Blue Opalescent included pieces which were made until 1955, when Blue Opalescent was discontinued. Production of a few vases in Blue Opalescent resumed for a brief time in 1960. This later production consisted of shapes which had not been made earlier.

The #1522 epergne and block listed in 1947 was sold with the #1522-10" bowl and a pair of #1524 candles as a five-piece set. The #1353 ice lip jug was sold with six #1353-12 oz. tumblers as a seven-piece beverage set. The ware number of this set after 1952 was 1407-BO. Two colognes and a puff box were also sold as a vanity set. The ware number for this combination was 1405-BO.

In addition to items found in the regular line, a cylindrical shape atomizer may be found in Blue Opalescent Coin Dot. In 1948, Fenton made the glass parts for DeVilbiss of Toledo, Ohio. The DeVilbiss Company attached the metal fittings and marketed the atomizers. See the atomizers shown on the pages at the end of this section for more information.

Elusive Coin Dot items in this color include all the candy jars, the epergne horn, the 12" handled basket, the No. 814-8" handled bottle, the decanter, and the cruet with the smooth top.

Blue Opalescent Coin Dot	Ware No.	Introduced	Discontinued	Value
Basket, #203-7" handled	1437-BO	1947	1955	85.00 – 95.00
Basket, #1353-12" handled		1947	1950	500.00 – 600.00
Basket, #1522-10" handled	1430-BO	1947	1951	250.00 – 275.00
Basket, #1523-13" handled		1947	1949	500.00 – 550.00
Basket, #1924-5" handled	1435-BO	1948	1955	110.00 – 125.00
Basket, #1925-6" handled		1948	1951	300.00 – 340.00
Bottle, #814-8" handled	1469-BO	1948	1954	225.00 – 250.00
Bowl, #203-7"	1427-BO	1947	1953	40.00 – 50.00
Bowl, #1522-10" double crimped	1424-BO	1947	1951	90.00 – 110.00
Bowl, #1523-13" double crimped		1947	1949	140.00 – 160.00
Candleholder, #1524	1470-BO	1947	1953	85.00 – 95.00
Candy jar, #91 covered		1948	1951	275.00 – 325.00
Candy jar, #93 crystal cover		1948	1950	250.00 – 350.00
Candy jar, #93 dome cover		1948	1950	300.00 – 350.00
Candy jar, #1522 covered		1947	1951	325.00 – 375.00
Cologne bottle, #92	1465-BO	1948	1955	140.00 – 150.00
Creamer, #33		1948	1949	70.00 – 85.00
Creamer, #1924 handled	1461-BO	1948	1955	60.00 – 70.00
Cruet, #208 (crimped top)	1463-BO	1948	July 1953	185.00 – 195.00
Cruet (smooth top)	1473-BO	July 1953	1955	195.00 – 225.00
Decanter, #894 handled		1947	1950	450.00 – 500.00
Epergne and block, #1522		1948	1949	350.00 – 400.00
Epergne set, #1522/1524 5-pc.		1948	1949	610.00 – 700.00
Jug, #201 squat		1947	1950	175.00 – 200.00
Jug, #1353-70 oz. crimped		1947	1952	225.00 – 275.00
Jug, #1353-70 oz. ice lip	1467-BO	1948	1955	225.00 – 275.00
Jug, #1934 handled		1947	1950	185.00 – 200.00
Powder jar, #92	1485-BO	1948	1955	150.00 – 200.00
Rose jar, #893		1947	1949	430.00 – 500.00
Sugar, #33		1948	1949	70.00 – 85.00
Top hat, #1924-5"	1492-BO	1948	1955	50.00 – 65.00
Tumbler, #1353-9 oz. straight	1449-BO	1948	1953	35.00 – 40.00
Tumbler, #1353-10 oz. barrel		1947	1952	35.00 – 40.00
Tumbler, #1353-12 oz.	1447-BO	1948	1955	40.00 – 45.00
Vanity set, #92 3-pc.	1405-BO	1948	1955	420.00 – 500.00
Vase, #189-10"		1947	1952	175.00 – 190.00

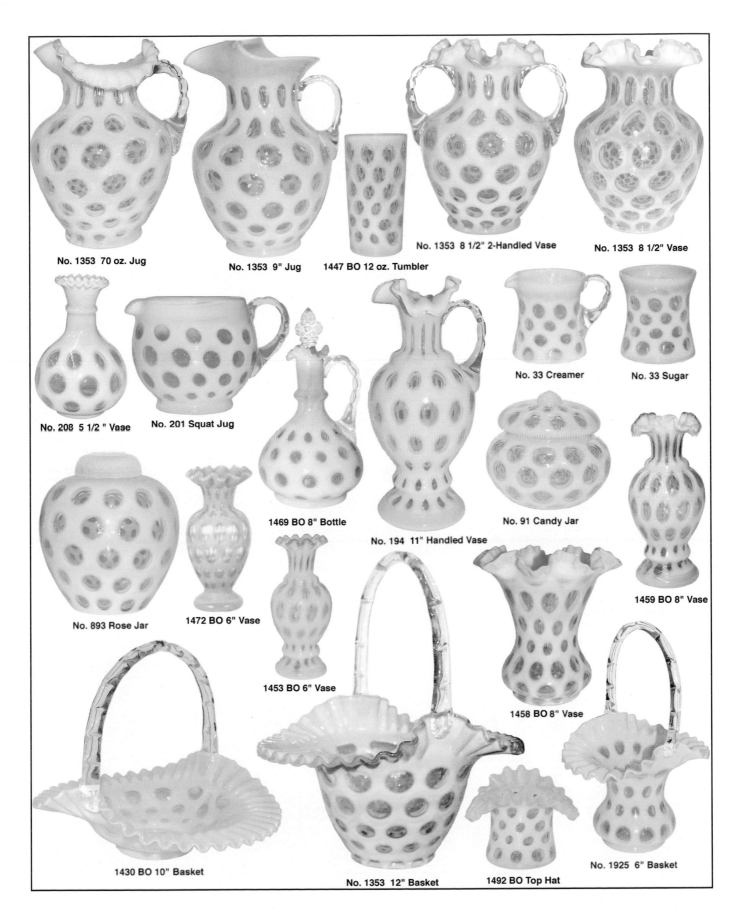

No. 1353 70 oz. Jug

No. 1353 9" Jug

1447 BO 12 oz. Tumbler

No. 1353 8 1/2" 2-Handled Vase

No. 1353 8 1/2" Vase

No. 208 5 1/2 " Vase

No. 201 Squat Jug

No. 33 Creamer

No. 33 Sugar

1469 BO 8" Bottle

No. 194 11" Handled Vase

No. 91 Candy Jar

No. 893 Rose Jar

1472 BO 6" Vase

1453 BO 6" Vase

1459 BO 8" Vase

1458 BO 8" Vase

1430 BO 10" Basket

No. 1353 12" Basket

1492 BO Top Hat

No. 1925 6" Basket

Blue Opalescent Coin Dot	Ware No.	Introduced	Discontinued	Value
Vase, #194-6" crimped	1453-BO	1948	1953	50.00 – 60.00
Vase, #194-6" triangular		1948	1952	55.00 – 65.00
Vase, #194-6" handled		1948	1951	80.00 – 90.00
Vase, #194-8"	1459-BO	1947	1955	70.00 – 80.00
Vase, #194-8" handled		1947	1952	120.00 – 140.00
Vase, #194-11" double crimped		1947	1951	120.00 – 140.00
Vase, #194-11" handled		1947	1950	200.00 – 225.00
Vase, #194-11" 2-handled		1947	1950	220.00 – 240.00
Vase, #194-13" double crimped		1947	1950	185.00 – 225.00
Vase, #194-13" handled		1947	1950	220.00 – 275.00
Vase, #194-13" 2-handled		1947	1950	250.00 – 300.00
Vase, #201-5"	1450-BO	1947	1952	45.00 – 55.00
Vase, #203-4½"	1454-BO	1948	1953	45.00 – 55.00
Vase, #208-5½" crimped, triangular		1948	1950	60.00 – 70.00
Vase, #894-10"		1947	1949	200.00 – 225.00
Vase, #1353-8½" double crimped		1947	1952	225.00 – 250.00
Vase, #1353-8½" 2-handled		1947	1949	225.00 – 265.00
Vase, #1924-5" double crimped	1455-BO	1948	1953	50.00 – 65.00
Vase, #1925-6"	1456-BO	1948	1955	60.00 – 80.00
Vase, #1925-8"	1458-BO	1947	1954	150.00 – 175.00
Vase, #1934-7" double crimped		1947	1950	80.00 – 100.00

The vases listed below were produced in 1960 and 1961. The #1425-4" rose bowl and #1472-6" vase were in the catalog for a year starting in January 1960. The #1466-6" vase and #1477-8" vase were first offered in January 1960, and were discontinued by July 1961.

Blue Opalescent Coin Dot	Ware No.	Introduced	Discontinued	Value
Rose bowl, 4"	1425-BO	1960	1961	45.00 – 50.00
Vase, 6" wheat sheaf	1466-BO	1960	July 1961	60.00 – 70.00
Vase, 6"	1472-BO	1960	1961	55.00 – 65.00
Vase, 8"	1477-BO	1960	July 1961	85.00 – 100.00

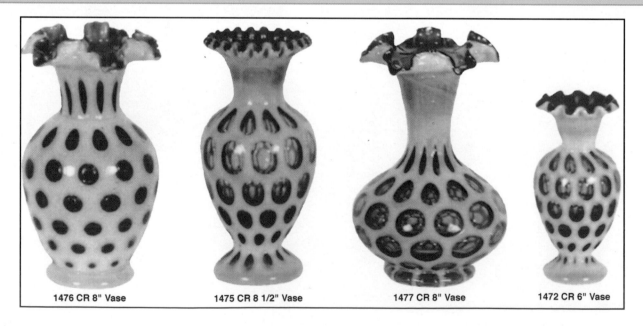

1476 CR 8" Vase   1475 CR 8 1/2" Vase   1477 CR 8" Vase   1472 CR 6" Vase

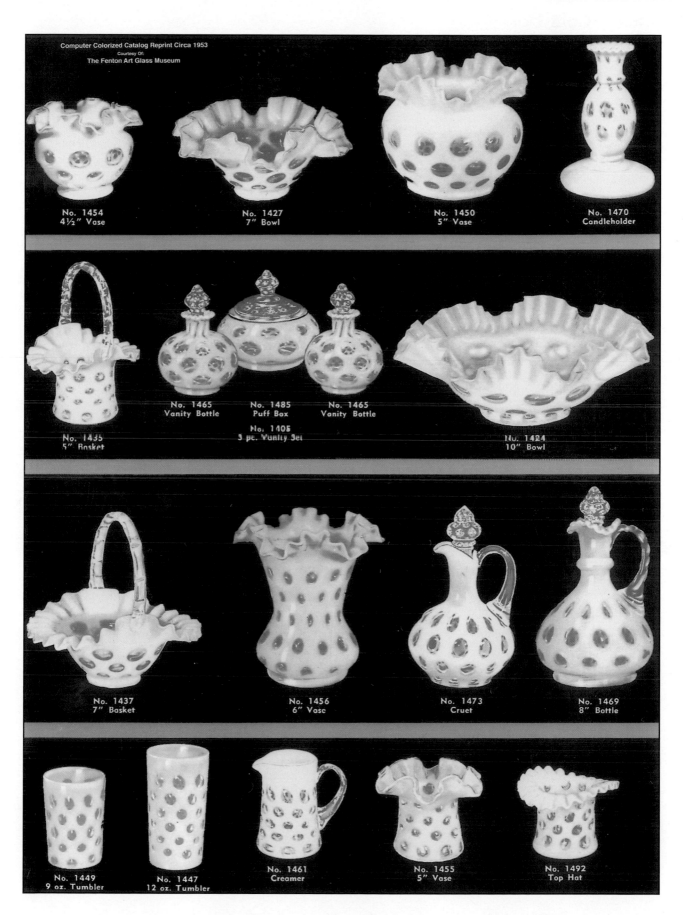

Computer Colorized Catalog Reprint Circa 1953
Courtesy Of:
The Fenton Art Glass Museum

No. 1454
4½" Vase

No. 1427
7" Bowl

No. 1450
5" Vase

No. 1470
Candleholder

No. 1435
5" Basket

No. 1465
Vanity Bottle

No. 1485
Puff Box

No. 1465
Vanity Bottle

No. 1405
3 pc. Vanity Set

No. 1424
10" Bowl

No. 1437
7" Basket

No. 1456
6" Vase

No. 1473
Cruet

No. 1469
8" Bottle

No. 1449
9 oz. Tumbler

No. 1447
12 oz. Tumbler

No. 1461
Creamer

No. 1455
5" Vase

No. 1492
Top Hat

Cranberry Coin Dot

Fenton's Coin Dot pattern was introduced in opalescent cranberry and other colors in 1947. Opalescent cranberry, called Cranberry by Fenton, was the bestselling color in Coin Dot and remained in the line for almost two decades. The last pieces of Coin Dot in Cranberry were discontinued at the end of 1964. Cranberry Opalescent glassware was produced by casing a layer of Gold Ruby glass with a layer of French Opalescent glass.

Several combinations of beverage sets were sold in Coin Dot. In 1947, a 70 oz. jug and either six or eight tumblers were sold as seven-piece and nine-piece beverage sets. In 1948, the 70 oz. jug was listed in a set with both 10 oz. and 12 oz. tumblers. In the same year, Fenton marketed the No. 1522/1524 five-piece epergne set. The set consisted of the 10" double crimped bowl, an epergne and block, and a pair of candleholders. The No. 92 vanity set was comprised of a puff box and two colognes.

Two different styles of cruet may be found. One style has a ruffled top and the other has a smooth top with a pour spout. Also, some of the vases that were produced in the early years may be found with different shapes of crimping around the top edge. Although they were not listed as a set in the Fenton catalogs, the top hat was originally intended to be used as a sugar bowl to complement the No. 1924 cream pitcher. A matching handleless sugar was made for a private company and may sometimes be found in a set with the creamer. This style sugar did not appear in the Fenton catalog. Elusive items include the 13" basket, the 12" basket, the epergne horn, the rose jar, and the #33 sugar and creamer. Finding the decanter, any of the candy jars, and the large two-handle vase is also challenging for many collectors.

The listing below reflects the transition in the Fenton numbering system. Line numbers for the items are included in the description and ware numbers are also included for pieces that continued in production after July 1952. A separate listing is provided on the next page for items introduced in the 1950s.

In the 1990s Fenton was still producing opalescent cranberry glassware. The old color code is still being used for this color and the name Cranberry Opalescent is now associated with the color. The old term cranberry is now being used to designate a cased color which is similar to Fenton's old Ruby Overlay. A Coin Dot item made recently for QVC is the Cranberry Opalescent rose jar with hand-painted decoration. Another item shown in the 1993 catalog is a Cranberry Opalescent 21" lamp with a metal base and crystal prisms.

Cranberry Coin Dot	Ware No.	Introduced	Discontinued	Value
Basket, #203-7" handled	1437-CR	1947	1965	115.00 – 125.00
Basket, #1353-12" handled		1947	1950	600.00 – 650.00
Basket, #1522-10" handled	1430-CR	1947	1954	325.00 – 350.00
Basket, #1523-13" handled		1947	1949	600.00 – 650.00
Basket, #1924-5" handled	1435-CR	1948	1958	125.00 – 145.00
Basket, #1925-6" handled		1948	1951	320.00 – 350.00
Bottle, #814-8" handled	1469-CR	1948	1956	300.00 – 340.00
Bowl, #203-7"	1427-CR	1947	1965	50.00 – 65.00
Bowl, #1522-10" double crimped	1424-CR	1947	1957	120.00 – 140.00
Bowl, #1523-13" double crimped		1947	1949	170.00 – 190.00
Candleholder, #1524	1470-CR	1947	1954	125.00 – 150.00
Candy jar, #91 covered		1948	1951	300.00 – 350.00
Candy jar, #93 crystal cover		1948	1950	250.00 – 350.00
Candy jar, #93 dome cover		1948	1950	300.00 – 375.00
Candy jar, #1522 covered		1947	1951	400.00 – 450.00
Cologne bottle, #92	1465-CR	1948	1956	160.00 – 180.00
Creamer, #33		1948	1949	90.00 – 110.00
Creamer, #1924 handled	1461-CR	1948	1957	70.00 – 80.00
Cruet, #208 (crimped top)	1463-CR	1948	July 1953	220.00 – 250.00
Decanter, #894 handled		1947	1950	700.00 – 750.00
Epergne and block, #1522		1948	1949	400.00 – 500.00
Epergne set, #1522/1524 5-pc.		1948	1949	845.00 – 940.00
Jug, #201 squat		1947	1950	200.00 – 225.00
Jug, #1353-70 oz. crimped		1947	1952	295.00 – 325.00

No.1925 6" Basket

No. 1353 12" Basket

No. 1522 Candy Jar

No. 33 Creamer

1430 CR 10" Basket

1405 CR 3-Piece Vanity Set

No. 33 Sugar

1437 CR 7" Basket

No. 208 Cruet

1469 CR 8" Bottle

No. 1934 Handled Jug

No. 1353 Tumbler (Straight)

No. 1353 Tumbler (Barrel)

No. 201 Squat Jug

No. 1353 9" Jug

1471 CR Barber Bottle

1452 CR 11" Vase

No. 194 11" Handled Vase

No. 1353 8 1/2" Vase

Cranberry Coin Dot	Ware No.	Introduced	Discontinued	Value
Jug, #1353-70 oz. ice lip	1467-CR	1948	1958	295.00 – 325.00
Jug, #1934 handled		1947	1950	225.00 – 250.00
Powder jar, #92	1485-CR	1948	1956	200.00 – 225.00
Rose jar, #893 (old)		1947	1949	350.00 – 400.00
Sugar, #33		1948	1949	90.00 – 110.00
Top hat, #1924-5"	1492-CR	1948	1954	70.00 – 80.00
Tumbler, #1353-9 oz. straight	1449-CR	1948	1952	40.00 – 47.00
Tumbler, #1353-10 oz. barrel		1947	1952	40.00 – 47.00
Tumbler, #1353-12 oz.	1447-CR	1948	1957	40.00 – 47.00
Vanity set, #92 3-pc.	1405-CR	1948	1956	520.00 – 585.00
Vase, #189-10"		1947	1951	200.00 – 240.00
Vase, #194-6" crimped, triangular		1948	1952	55.00 – 65.00
Vase, #194-6" handled	1453-CR	1948	1954	85.00 – 100.00
Vase, #194-8"	1459-CR	1947	1959	75.00 – 85.00
Vase, #194-8" handled		1947	1952	125.00 – 150.00
Vase, #194-11" double crimped	1452-CR	1947	1954	140.00 – 170.00
Vase, #194-11" handled		1947	1950	250.00 – 275.00
Vase, #194-11" 2-handled		1947	1950	250.00 – 275.00
Vase, #194-13" double crimped		1947	1950	235.00 – 260.00
Vase, #194-13" handled		1947	1950	300.00 – 325.00
Vase, #194-13" 2-handled		1947	1950	325.00 – 350.00
Vase, #201-5"	1450-CR	1947	1962	70.00 – 80.00
Vase, #203-4½"	1454-CR	1948	1965	55.00 – 65.00
Vase, #208-5½" crimped, triangular		1948	1950	85.00 – 95.00
Vase, #894-10"		1947	1949	225.00 – 250.00
Vase, #1353-8½" double crimped		1947	1952	240.00 – 260.00
Vase, #1353-8½" 2-handled		1947	1949	250.00 – 285.00
Vase, #1924-5" double crimped	1455-CR	1948	1955	55.00 – 65.00
Vase, #1925-6"	1456-CR	1948	1965	90.00 – 110.00
Vase, #1925-8"	1458-CR	1947	1962	180.00 – 210.00
Vase, #1934-7" double crimped		1947	1950	115.00 – 135.00

Cranberry Coin Dot Shapes Introduced in the 1950s	Ware No.	Introduced	Discontinued	Value
Barber bottle	1471-CR	1957	1959	275.00 – 325.00
Bowl, 8½"	1438-CR	1957	1959	200.00 – 245.00
Cruet (smooth top)	1473-CR	July 1953	1961	200.00 – 225.00
Rose bowl, 4"	1425-CR	1960	1962	50.00 – 65.00
Vase, ivy	1448-CR	1956	1960	125.00 – 150.00
Vase, 6" wheat sheaf	1466-CR	1956	1965	75.00 – 95.00
Vase, 6"	1440-CR	1958	1960	125.00 – 150.00
Vase, 6"	1472-CR	1960	1962	80.00 – 90.00
Vase, 7"	1441-CR	1958	1962	85.00 – 95.00
Vase, 7½"	1457-CR	1952	1965	115.00 – 135.00
Vase, 8"	1476-CR	1960	1962	170.00 – 200.00
Vase, 8"	1477-CR	1960	1962	165.00 – 185.00
Vase, 8½"	1475-CR	1960	1962	155.00 – 185.00
Vase, 10"	1442-CR	1958	1960	200.00 – 225.00
Vase, 11" double crimped	1451-CR	1952	1962	160.00 – 180.00

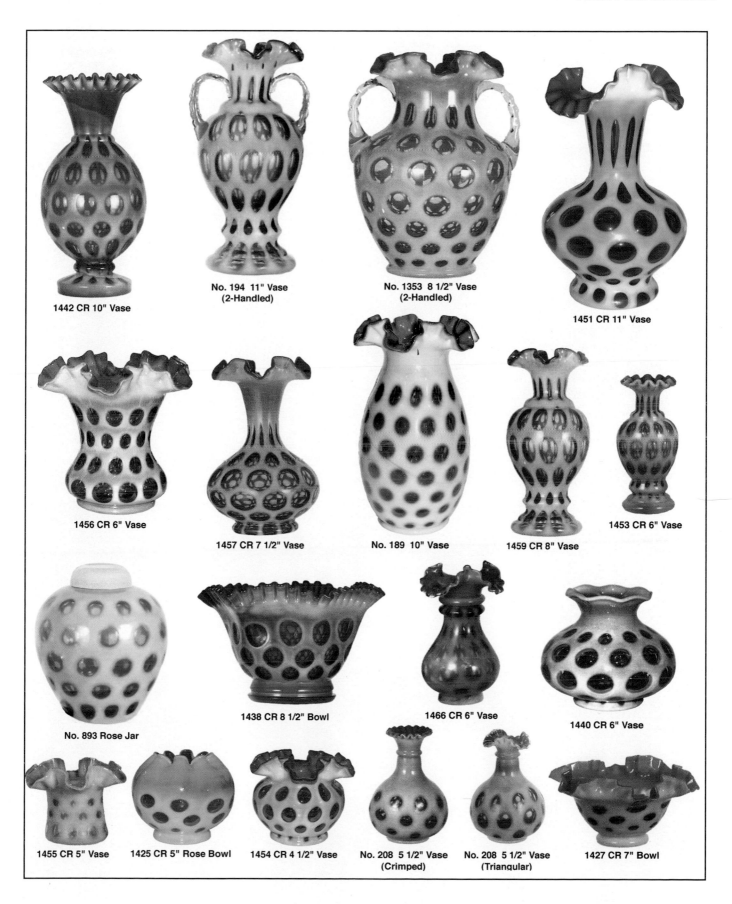

1442 CR 10" Vase

No. 194 11" Vase
(2-Handled)

No. 1353 8 1/2" Vase
(2-Handled)

1451 CR 11" Vase

1456 CR 6" Vase

1457 CR 7 1/2" Vase

No. 189 10" Vase

1459 CR 8" Vase

1453 CR 6" Vase

No. 893 Rose Jar

1438 CR 8 1/2" Bowl

1466 CR 6" Vase

1440 CR 6" Vase

1455 CR 5" Vase

1425 CR 5" Rose Bowl

1454 CR 4 1/2" Vase

No. 208 5 1/2" Vase
(Crimped)

No. 208 5 1/2" Vase
(Triangular)

1427 CR 7" Bowl

French Opalescent Coin Dot

   Coin Dot in the crystal with opal color that Fenton called French Opalescent entered the Fenton line in 1947. Most items were discontinued by the early 1950s. However, a few pieces remained in the line for a few more years. The No. 1425-6" vase, ice lip pitcher, and 12 oz. tumblers were made through the end of 1956. Six tumblers and the pitcher were marketed as a No. 1407 seven-piece ice tea set. Hard-to-find items include the large baskets, all the candy jars, the rose jar, and the epergne horn.

French Opalescent Coin Dot	Ware No.	Introduced	Discontinued	Value
Basket, #203-7" handled	1437-FO	1947	1953	55.00 – 65.00
Basket, #1353-12" handled		1947	1950	350.00 – 400.00
Basket, #1522-10" handled	1430-FO	1947	1951	180.00 – 200.00
Basket, #1523-13" handled		1947	1949	350.00 – 400.00
Basket, #1924-5" handled	1435-FO	1948	1953	75.00 – 85.00
Basket, #1925-6" handled		1948	1951	150.00 – 175.00
Bottle, #814-8" handled	1469-FO	1948	1953	160.00 – 180.00
Bowl, #203-7"	1427-FO	1947	1953	30.00 – 40.00
Bowl, #1522-10" double crimped	1424-FO	1947	1955	55.00 – 65.00
Bowl, #1523-13" double crimped		1947	1949	85.00 – 100.00
Candleholder, #1524	1470-FO	1947	1954	45.00 – 55.00
Candy jar, #91 covered		1948	1951	190.00 – 225.00
Candy jar, #93 crystal cover		1948	1950	150.00 – 225.00
Candy jar, #93 dome cover		1948	1950	200.00 – 250.00
Candy jar, #1522 covered		1947	1951	250.00 – 300.00
Cologne bottle, #92	1465-FO	1948	1952	90.00 – 110.00
Creamer, #33		1948	1949	45.00 – 55.00
Creamer, #1924 handled	1461-FO	1948	1954	40.00 – 50.00
Cruet, #208 (crimped top)	1463-FO	1948	1952	115.00 – 135.00
Decanter, #894 handled		1947	1950	300.00 – 350.00
Epergne and block, #1522		1948	1949	150.00 – 200.00
Epergne set, #1522/1524 5-pc.		1948	1949	335.00 – 375.00
Jug, #201 squat		1947	1950	75.00 – 100.00
Jug, #1353-70 oz. crimped		1947	1952	150.00 – 200.00
Jug, #1353-70 oz. ice lip	1467-FO	1948	1957	150.00 – 200.00
Jug, #1934 handled		1947	1950	95.00 – 125.00
Powder jar, #92	1485-FO	1948	1952	100.00 – 125.00
Rose jar, #893		1947	1949	225.00 – 250.00
Sugar, #33		1948	1949	45.00 – 55.00
Top hat, #1924-5"	1492-FO	1948	1954	30.00 – 45.00
Tumbler, #1353-9 oz. straight	1449-FO	1948	1953	20.00 – 22.00
Tumbler, #1353-10 oz. barrel		1947	1952	22.00 – 25.00
Tumbler, #1353-12 oz.	1447-FO	1948	1957	25.00 – 27.00
Vanity set, #92 3-pc.	1405-FO	1948	1952	215.00 – 275.00
Vase, #189-10"		1947	1952	150.00 – 170.00
Vase, #194-6" crimped	1453-FO	1948	1953	40.00 – 45.00
Vase, #194-6" triangular		1948	1952	42.00 – 42.00
Vase, #194-6" handled		1948	1951	50.00 – 60.00
Vase, #194-8"	1459-FO	1947	1954	55.00 – 65.00
Vase, #194-8" handled		1947	1952	95.00 – 110.00
Vase, #194-11" double crimped	1452-FO	1947	1952	90.00 – 110.00
Vase, #194-11" handled		1947	1950	120.00 – 140.00
Vase, #194-11" 2-handled		1947	1950	140.00 – 160.00
Vase, #194-13" double crimped		1947	1950	130.00 – 150.00
Vase, #194-13" handled		1947	1950	140.00 – 160.00
Vase, #201-5"	1450-FO	1947	1954	40.00 – 45.00

French Opalescent Coin Dot	Ware No.	Introduced	Discontinued	Value
Vase, #203-4½"	1454-FO	1948	1953	30.00 – 35.00
Vase, #208-5½" crimped, triangular		1948	1950	40.00 – 45.00
Vase, #894-10"		1947	1949	125.00 – 150.00
Vase, #1353-8½" double crimped		1947	1952	90.00 – 110.00
Vase, #1353-8½" 2-handled		1947	1949	120.00 – 150.00
Vase, #1924-5" double crimped	1455-FO	1948	1953	30.00 – 40.00
Vase, #1925-6"	1456-FO	1948	1957	45.00 – 55.00
Vase, #1925-8"	1458-FO	1947	1954	75.00 – 95.00
Vase, #1934-7" double crimped		1947	1950	50.00 – 65.00

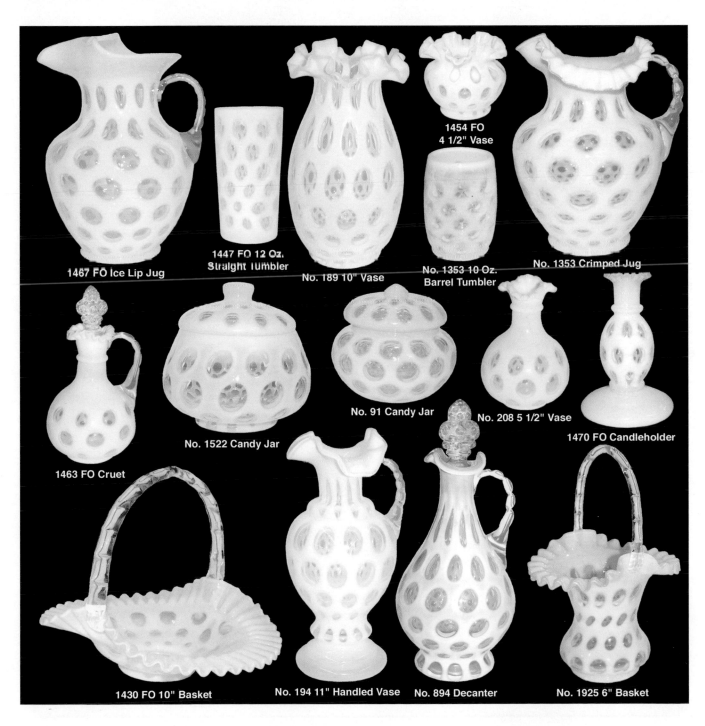

1467 FO Ice Lip Jug

1447 FO 12 Oz. Straight Tumbler

No. 189 10" Vase

1454 FO 4 1/2" Vase

No. 1353 10 Oz. Barrel Tumbler

No. 1353 Crimped Jug

1463 FO Cruet

No. 1522 Candy Jar

No. 91 Candy Jar

No. 208 5 1/2" Vase

1470 FO Candleholder

1430 FO 10" Basket

No. 194 11" Handled Vase

No. 894 Decanter

No. 1925 6" Basket

Honeysuckle Coin Dot

Coin Dot was made in a Honeysuckle Opalescent color in 1948 and 1949. Fenton's Honeysuckle Opalescent color consists of an interior layer of amber glass cased with an outside layer of French Opalescent.

Beverage sets were sold using the 70 oz. jug in combination with either six or eight 9 oz. or 12 oz. tumblers. Both the ice lip and crimped top jugs were made in this color.

Due to the limited production period, many of the items in the listing below are not easily found. Other Fenton Coin Dot Honeysuckle Opalescent items which are seen more often include lamps and lamp shades. For more information on the lamps produced by Fenton in this color, see pages 36, 43, and 44 at the end of this section.

Honeysuckle Coin Dot	Value
Basket, #203-7" handled	145.00 – 165.00
Basket, #1925-6" handled	300.00 – 325.00
Bowl, #203-7"	50.00 – 65.00
Jug, #1353-70 oz. crimped	375.00 – 425.00
Jug, #1353-70 oz. ice lip	375.00 – 425.00
Tumbler, #1353-9 oz. straight	40.00 – 45.00
Tumbler, #1353-10 oz. barrel	40.00 – 50.00
Tumbler, #1353-12 oz	50.00 – 55.00
Vase, #194-6" crimped, triangular	60.00 – 70.00
Vase, #194-6" handled	75.00 – 85.00
Vase, #194-8"	75.00 – 85.00
Vase, #194-8" handled	110.00 – 120.00
Vase, #194-11" double crimped	150.00 – 185.00
Vase, #194-11" handled	200.00 – 225.00
Vase, #194-11" 2-handled	225.00 – 240.00
Vase, #201-5"	70.00 – 80.00
Vase, #203-4½"	60.00 – 65.00
Vase, #1925-6"	110.00 – 125.00

No. 1353 70 oz. Ice Lip Jug   No 1925 6" Handled Basket   No. 203 7" Handled Basket   No. 194 8" Handled Vase   No. 194 8" Vase

No. 1353 12 oz. Straight Tumbler   No. 1353 10 oz. Barrel Tumbler   No. 203 7" bowl   No. 203 4 1/2" Vase   No. 1925 6" Vase

Lime Opalescent Coin Dot

Fenton's Lime Opalescent color was introduced into the Coin Dot line in January 1952. This color is produced by casing dark green inside French Opalescent.

The 1925-8" vase is listed in inventory records for 1951 but does not appear on the January 1952 price list or any later price lists. It is possible this vase may not have been put into production. Production of Coin Dot in Lime Opalescent was discontinued by the end of 1954. This short production period virtually assures collectors that most pieces will be elusive.

Lime Opalescent Coin Dot	Ware No.	Introduced	Discontinued	Value
Basket #203-7" handled	1437-LO	1952	1954	150.00 – 185.00
Bowl, #203-7"	1427-LO	1952	1954	70.00 – 80.00
Creamer, #1924	1461-LO	1952	1955	100.00 – 110.00
Top hat, #1924	1492-LO	1952	1954	120.00 – 140.00
Vase, #194-8"	1459-LO	1952	1955	100.00 – 145.00
Vase, #203-4½"	1454-LO	1952	1954	60.00 – 70.00
Vase, #1925-6"	1456-LO	1952	1955	120.00 – 140.00
Vase, #1925-8"	1458-LO	1951	1952	220.00 – 245.00
Vase, #3005-7½"	1457-LO	1952	1955	125.00 – 150.00
Vase, #3005-11"	1451-LO	1952	1955	220.00 – 250.00

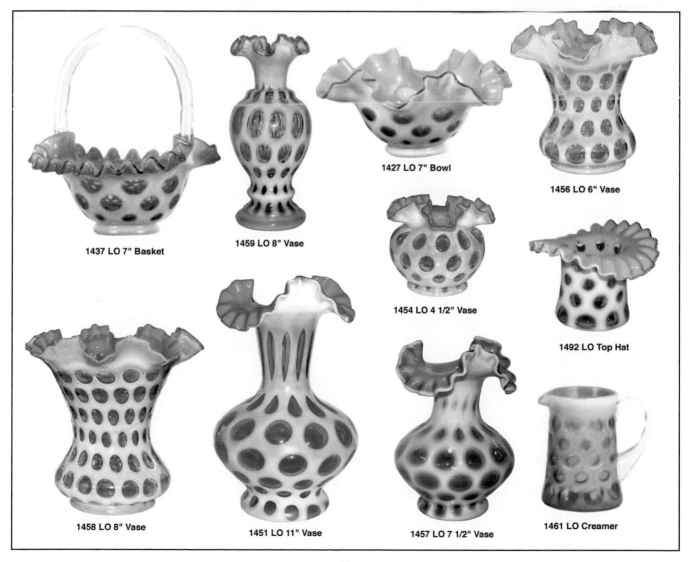

1437 LO 7" Basket

1459 LO 8" Vase

1427 LO 7" Bowl

1456 LO 6" Vase

1454 LO 4 1/2" Vase

1492 LO Top Hat

1458 LO 8" Vase

1451 LO 11" Vase

1457 LO 7 1/2" Vase

1461 LO Creamer

Topaz Opalescent Coin Dot

Coin Dot was introduced in the Topaz Opalescent color in 1959. Topaz is a bright yellow color which is produced by using uranium oxide.

From the initial offering of 15 different pieces, the only remaining Topaz Opalescent Coin Dot item remaining in the line after July 1960 was the No. 1427-7" bowl. This final item disappeared from production by the end of June 1961.

Topaz Opalescent Coin Dot	Ware No.	Introduced	Discontinued	Value
Basket, 7" handled	1437-TO	1959	July 1960	175.00 – 185.00
Bowl, 7"	1427-TO	1959	July 1961	60.00 – 70.00
Cruet	1473-TO	1959	July 1960	280.00 – 325.00
Ivy vase	1448-TO	1959	July 1960	170.00 – 210.00
Rose bowl, 4"	1425-TO	1959	July 1960	70.00 – 80.00
Vase, 4½"	1454-TO	1959	July 1960	70.00 – 80.00
Vase, 5"	1450-TO	1959	July 1960	90.00 – 110.00
Vase, 6"	1440-TO	1959	July 1960	180.00 – 200.00
Vase, 6"	1456-TO	1959	July 1960	90.00 – 110.00
Vase, 6"	1466-TO	1959	July 1960	80.00 – 90.00
Vase, 7"	1441-TO	1959	July 1960	120.00 – 140.00
Vase, 7½"	1457-TO	1959	July 1960	110.00 – 130.00
Vase, 8"	1458-TO	1959	July 1960	225.00 – 250.00
Vase, 11"	1451-TO	1959	July 1960	220.00 – 250.00
Vase, 10"	1442-TO	1959	July 1960	210.00 – 225.00

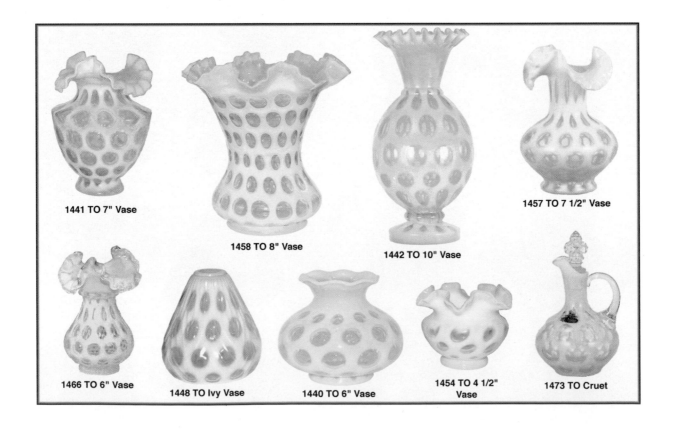

1441 TO 7" Vase

1458 TO 8" Vase

1442 TO 10" Vase

1457 TO 7 1/2" Vase

1466 TO 6" Vase

1448 TO Ivy Vase

1440 TO 6" Vase

1454 TO 4 1/2" Vase

1473 TO Cruet

Unusual Coin Dot, Sample Items, or Special Order Pieces

Numerous Coin Dot items may appear on the secondary market that were never offered in the regular Fenton line. There are several explanations for the existence of these pieces. Items were sometimes sampled to test the feasibility of future production. Certain items were made under contract with other companies using molds supplied and owned by that company. For example, Fenton produced pieces for L. G. Wright in a pattern called Eye Dot that is similar to Coin Dot. Many different lamp parts were also made for various companies. These parts were then combined with metal or other glass pieces to produce a finished lamp. Atomizer blanks were made for the DeVilbiss Company of Toledo, Ohio. These glass bases were fitted with metal parts and squeeze bulbs by DeVilbiss to produce the finished atomizer.

The pieces pictured in the photo below include two different Coin Dot atomizers in the Coin Dot pattern marketed by DeVilbiss and unusual pieces from the Fenton regular line that were only made for a short time.

Most of the items on the next page were made by Fenton for L. G. Wright in a pattern somewhat similar to Coin Dot. L. G. Wright called this pattern Eye Dot. Notice that with the exception of the lamps, the dots are arranged uniformly, in vertical columns. Some of the items were also available in a satinized version.

The photo on page 36 features lamps, lamp parts, and sample items in the Coin Dot pattern.

Coin Dot Item	Value
1. Blue Opalescent Coin Dot Model No. S350-37 atomizer made for DeVilbiss in 1948	100.00 – 125.00
2. Cranberry Opalescent ashtray made from the puff box bottom for use in the DeVilbiss vanity set pictured in #7	175.00 – 225.00
3. No. 170 Hurricane lamp in Cranberry Coin Dot was a sample item	250.00 – 275.00
4. Cranberry Opalescent No. 1522 rose bowl or small vase	150.00 – 180.00
5. Small bud vase in Blue Opalescent Coin Dot fashioned from the epergne and a domed candy lid used as the base	200.00 – 250.00
6. Blue Opalescent Coin Dot lamp made with a Coin Dot puff box lid	85.00 – 95.00
7. Cranberry Opalescent Model No. S 1500-1 three-piece vanity set made for DeVilbiss in 1952	600.00 – 700.00
8. Epergne set in Blue Opalescent Coin Dot made in 1948	350.00 – 400.00
9. Cranberry Opalescent pinch decanter or large cologne bottle	500.00 – 600.00
10. Blue Opalescent lamp base fashioned from a DeVilbiss atomizer bottom	80.00 – 110.00

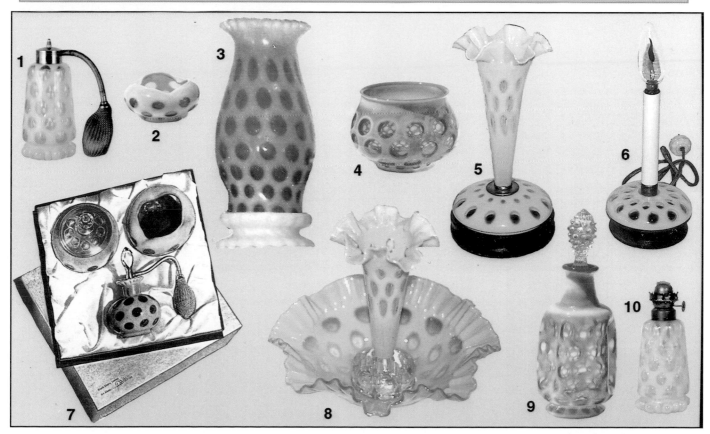

Photo on Page 35:

   Most of the items on this page are examples of private mould items that were made for L. G. Wright by Fenton. These are Coin Dot–style pieces in a pattern that Wright called Eye Dot. Notice the dots in this pattern are aligned in vertical rows.

Coin Dot-Style item	Value
1. Blue opalescent Eye Dot 10" tankard-style water pitcher	280.00 – 320.00
2. Cranberry opalescent Beaded Curtain miniature oil lamp made for L. G. Wright	400.00 – 450.00
3. Cranberry opalescent Eye Dot small nappy and underplate	125.00 – 150.00
4. Cranberry opalescent Eye Dot small rose bowl	60.00 – 70.00
5. Cranberry opalescent Eye Dot tall cream pitcher	130.00 – 150.00
6. Blue opalescent tankard – style Eye Dot 10" vase	125.00 – 150.00
7. Cranberry opalescent satin Eye Dot small rose bowl	60.00 – 70.00
8. Cranberry opalescent satin small crimped Eye Dot vase	60.00 – 70.00
9. Cranberry opalescent satin Eye Dot tall cream pitcher	120.00 – 150.00
10. Cranberry opalescent Eye Dot 8 oz. water tumbler	70.00 – 90.00
11. Cranberry opalescent miniature oil lamp with an original label that reads "Alice Minster Original Little Lamp"	200.00 – 250.00
12.. Cranberry opalescent miniature oil lamp made for L. G. Wright	275.00 – 325.00
13. Blue opalescent Eye Dot cruet	60.00 – 70.00
14. Cranberry opalescent Coin Dot miniature oil lamp made for L. G. Wright	320.00 – 360.00
15. Cranberry opalescent Eye Dot cream pitcher	110.00 – 125.00
16. Cranberry opalescent Eye Dot 6" jug	225.00 – 250.00
17. Blue opalescent Eye Dot square crimped water pitcher	250.00 – 300.00
18. Cranberry opalescent Eye Dot barber bottle	200.00 – 240.00
19. Cranberry opalescent Eye Dot cruet	175.00 – 190.00
20. Blue opalescent Eye Dot barber bottle	190.00 – 220.00
21. Cranberry opalescent Eye 10" tankard-style water pitcher	320.00 – 350.00

Photo on Page 36:

   Most of the lamps in this photo were assembled by independent lamp manufacturers from the glass lamp parts supplied by Fenton.

Coin Dot–Style item	Value
1. Cranberry opalescent Coin Dot lamp with a 6" glass fount and a 7" diameter shade	300.00 – 350.00
2. Honey Amber Coin Dot lamp from the regular Fenton line in 1977	150.00 – 175.00
3. Honey Amber Coin Dot wheat sheaf shape vase sampled by Fenton and now residing in the Fenton Art Glass Museum	N.D.
4. Cranberry opalescent Coin Dot lamp with a gold decorated 8" vase used for the shade	300.00 – 350.00
5. Cranberry opalescent Coin Dot vase made from a shade that was not cut off	140.00 – 160.00
6. Honey Dew Coin Dot large lamp shade	200.00 – 225.00
7. Orange opalescent Coin Dot No. 7451-6" vase made as a sample	N.D.
8. French opalescent Coin Dot lamp made by combining a gold-decorated 8" vase with a metal base; was probably made for Max, Horn, Zoerner and Lewis of New York	225.00 – 250.00
9. Cranberry opalescent Coin Dot lamp	500.00 – 600.00
10. Honey Amber Coin Dot lamp from the regular Fenton line in 1977	225.00 – 250.00
11. Blue opalescent Coin Dot large 10" lamp shade–style vase	170.00 – 225.00
12. Topaz opalescent cupped crimped small rose bowl	90.00 – 110.00

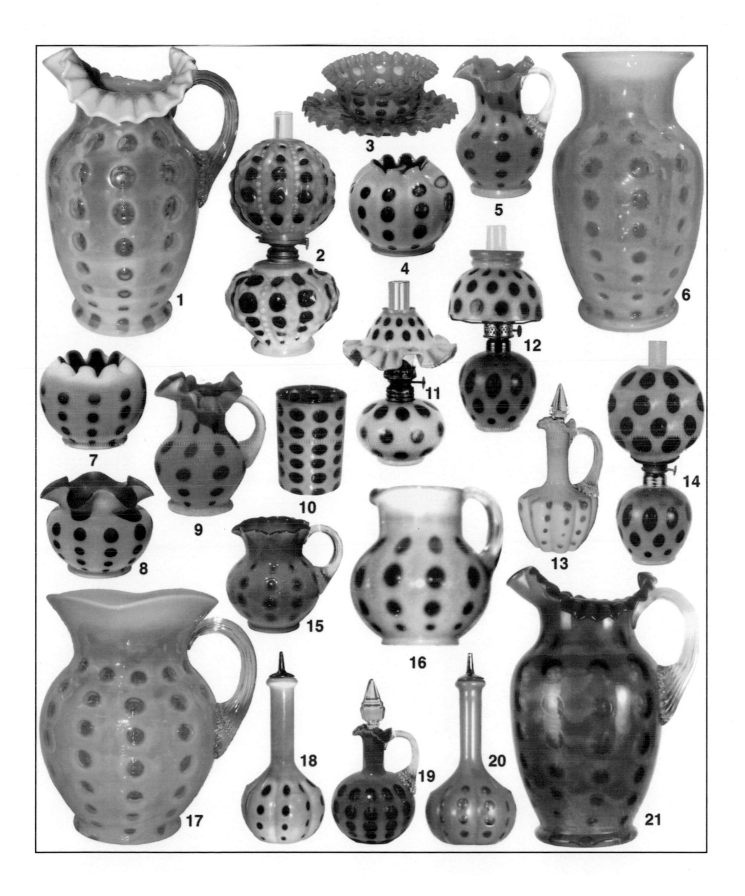

Charleton-Decorated Coin Dot

Abels, Wasserberg & Company was founded in New York City during the mid-1920s. In the early years, the company concentrated on importing lamps, lamp parts, and gift items for use in interior decoration. When sources for these items were cut off during World War II, the company established a decorating shop and began buying undecorated lamp parts and accessory pieces from domestic sources such as the Fenton Art Glass Company. The hand-painted Charleton decoration found most frequently on Fenton's Coin Dot pattern consists of pink roses. This pattern is generally referred to as "Charleton Roses," and the decoration may vary slightly from one piece to another.

Photo Below:
All pieces have the "Charleton Roses" decoration.

Item	Value
1. Cranberry No. 893 rose jar	400.00 – 450.00
2. Cranberry No. 92 3-piece vanity set	600.00 – 700.00
3. Blue Opalescent No. 201 squat jug	225.00 – 250.00
4. Cranberry No. 1454-4½" vase	125.00 – 145.00

Photo to the Right:

Item	Value
French opalescent 14" lamp with "Charleton Roses" decoration	240.00 – 260.00

Blue Opalescent Coin Dot Lamps

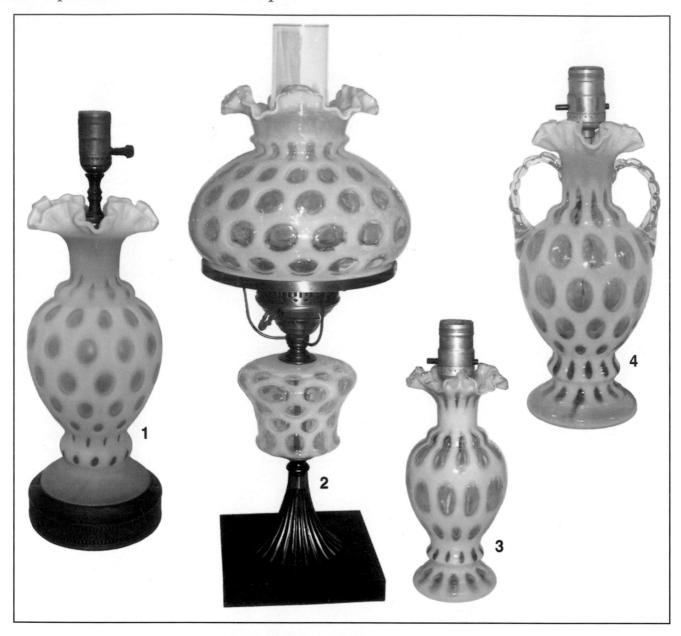

Numerous shapes of Coin Dot lamps were assembled by independent lamp manufacturers from parts made by the Fenton Art Glass Company during the late 1940s and early 1950s. The photos here and on the following pages illustrate some examples of these creations.

Photo Above:

Coin Dot Lamp	Value
1. Blue opalescent satin Coin Dot lamp made from a No. 194-11" vase	150.00 – 180.00
2. Blue opalescent Coin Dot 22" student lamp on a painted wood base	300.00 – 350.00
3. Blue opalescent Coin Dot lamp produced from an 8" No. 194 vase	100.00 – 125.00
4. Blue opalescent Coin Dot lamp made by using a No. 194-11" 2-handled vase	175.00 – 200.00

Cranberry Coin Dot Lamps

Photo to the Left:

Coin Dot Lamp	Value
1. Cranberry Coin Dot lamp made from a No. 1458-8" flared vase drilled for hanging prisms and decorated with gold fleur-de-lis	325.00 – 375.00
2. Cranberry Coin Dot lamp produced by using a No. 1456-6" vase as the shade and an inverted No. 1427 7" bowl as the base	250.00 – 290.00
3. Cranberry Coin Dot 7½" miniature lamp	290.00 – 325.00
4. Cranberry Coin Dot 12" lamp	80.00 – 110.00
5. Cranberry Coin Dot 16" lamp (glass fount is 6½")	150.00 – 175.00
6. Cranberry Coin Dot lamp assembled using a No. 1353-9" pitcher	200.00 – 250.00

Photo to the Right:

Coin Dot Lamp	Value
Cranberry Coin Dot pole light consisting of three Coin Dot shades and a floor-to-ceiling adjustable height pole held in place with a tension spring	250.00 – 300.00

Cranberry Coin Dot Lamps, Cont.

Shown in the picture below are three different styles of student lamps made with Cranberry Coin Dot parts. The lamps on either end were made with 10" diameter Coin Dot shades. The lamp in the center has an 8" diameter Coin Dot shade. The lamp to the left also has a Coin Dot glass fount.

Coin Dot Lamp	Value
1. Cranberry Coin Dot lamp with glass fount	350.00 – 400.00
2. Cranberry Coin Dot lamp with 8" diameter shade	250.00 – 275.00
3. Cranberry Coin Dot lamp with burnished brass base	275.00 – 325.00

French Opalescent Coin Dot Lamps

A variety of different styles of French Opalescent Coin Dot lamps may be found. Included in the selection are student lamps, hanging chandeliers, and ceiling fixtures.

Coin Dot Lamp	Value
1. French opalescent Coin Dot lamp with 6" high glass fount	75.00 – 100.00
2. French opalescent Coin Dot ceiling fixture with 10" diameter shade	100.00 – 125.00
3. French opalescent Coin Dot lamp with 6" diameter fount and clambroth color glass base	125.00 – 150.00
4. French opalescent Coin Dot hanging light with 10" diameter shade	225.00 – 250.00
5. French opalescent Coin Dot lamp with a 6" diameter glass fount and a 10" diameter shade	240.00 – 275.00
6. French opalescent Coin Dot 18" lamp with glass fount and glass shade	325.00 – 375.00

French Opalescent Coin Dot Lamps, Cont.

The French Opalescent chandelier has six arms. Each arm is accented with an inverted candy jar lid that has been drilled to fit over the end of the arm. These Coin Dot pieces are fashioned as candle cups for the candle-style lights. The center post is also decorated with two lids. In the center of the post is a symmetrically uniform glass ornament that was created from the top part of the Coin Dot candle. Glass beads have also been strung between the arms and from the top of the lamp to the arms. The Coin Dot lamp on the left is also shown on page 37 with a Charleton Roses decoration.

Coin Dot Lamp	Value
1. French opalescent Coin Dot chandelier	500.00 – 600.00
2. French opalescent Coin Dot lamp with 6" tall fount	110.00 – 125.00
3. French opalescent Coin Dot lamp	150.00 – 170.00

Honeysuckle Coin Dot Lamps

Judging from the number of lamps seen on the resale market, Fenton's Honeysuckle color must have been popular with decorators and lamp manufacturers of the era. Lamps and ceiling fixtures of many different shapes and sizes may be found in this color.

Coin Dot Lamp	Value
1. Honeysuckle Coin Dot 18" lamp	225.00 – 250.00
2. Honeysuckle Coin Dot 12" diameter lamp base	150.00 – 175.00
3. Honeysuckle Coin Dot lamp with 6" diameter fount and 7" diameter shade	225.00 – 250.00
4. Honeysuckle Coin Dot lamp made by using a No. 894-10" vase	125.00 – 150.00
5. Honeysuckle Coin Dot lamp made with a 6" fount and a 10" diameter shade	175.00 – 200.00

Honeysuckle and Honey Dew Coin Dot Lamps

The photo to the left pictures a Honeysuckle color floor lamp. Floor lamps in any color are harder to find than the tabletop varieties. The lamp shown in the lower left of the photo on the right is Fenton's Honey Dew color. Lamps made from parts in this color are seldom found today.

Photo to the Right:

Coin Dot Lamp	Value
1. Honeysuckle Coin Dot lamp with 7" diameter shade	190.00 – 210.00
2. Honeysuckle Coin Dot 12" diameter hanging shade	150.00 – 175.00
3. Honey Dew Coin Dot lamp	275.00 – 325.00
4. Honeysuckle Coin Dot 7" diameter hanging shade	80.00 – 100.00
5. Honeysuckle Coin Dot lamp made with a 5" fount and a 10" diameter shade	175.00 – 200.00
6. Honeysuckle Coin Dot lamp made using a 6" diameter vase	80.00 – 90.00

Photo to the Left:

Coin Dot Lamp	Value
Honeysuckle Coin Dot floor lamp	225.00 – 250.00

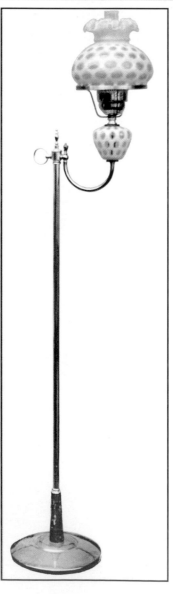

Fenton's Crest Pattern

Crest Colors and Shapes

Fenton's Crest pattern consists of glassware made with applied colored or crystal trim. Most of the pieces have trim around the edge, but pitchers, sugar, creamers, and some baskets may have matching colored handles. Many of the patterns were made with a milk glass base using colored trim, but during the early 1950s the procedure was inversed and transparent colored pieces were also decorated with milk glass trim. Early examples of crests date back to the 1920s and 1930s when cobalt edges were added to Topaz Iridescent and Persian Pearl bowls, plates, vases, and a few other select items. Beginning in 1939, Fenton began to concentrate on the production of milk glass ware with applied colored trim. The first Crest pattern, Blue Ridge, was French Opalescent Spiral Optic decorated with a cobalt trim. This pattern only remained in the line one year. The next two Crest patterns, Peach Crest and Ivory Crest, entered the line in 1940. Peach Crest replaced Peach Blow, the same color of cased glassware that lacked a crest, which was in the Fenton line during 1939.

1941

Aqua Crest was made in 1941 and 1942. This color disappeared from the line until 1948, when some of the old shapes reappeared and new shapes were added.

1942

Fenton introduced a new Crest pattern called Crystal Crest. The crests on these pieces were formed by applying two different colored layers of glass on a milk glass body. The first layer of glass applied was crystal, which was followed by an outer layer of opal. Thus, pieces of Crystal Crest have a thin crystal ribbon encased between two layers of opal. About mid-year, Silver Crest, Fenton's longest running and most popular Crest pattern, was created by modifying the Crystal Crest pattern. The demise of Crystal Crest and the evolution of Silver Crest were the result of the elimination of the outer opal layer of trim from the former. Ivory Crest was discontinued at the end of the year. Early examples of Snowcrest were made with a jade body and an opal crest.

1943

Fenton introduced milk glass pieces with a spun transparent amber crest this year. This new Crest color was called Gold Crest and was continued through the end of 1944. Both Silver Crest and Peach Crest were produced through World War II.

1946

Milk glass pieces with a transparent rose-colored crest entered the line. Other Rose Crest pieces had been made the previous few years under a contract with Weil Freeman, but the new shapes introduced this year with this color crest were the first ones in the regular Fenton line. Rose Crest was discontinued at the end of 1947.

1949

Fenton began using transparent green glass to produce crests on glassware with an opal body. At first this pattern was called Green Crest, but the name later evolved into Emerald Crest. This pattern was discontinued at the end of 1955. Some items in dark green Crest were also produced for Rubel during this period. For more information on these pieces, see the pages at the end of this chapter.

Crest shapes underwent a major style change. The No. 192 Melon Rib shape was replaced by new No. 711 Beaded Melon shape. Also, the No. 680 dinnerware shape became a prominent part of the line.

1950

Selected Spiral Optic shapes in transparent blue, ruby, ivy, and amber were trimmed with an opal crest. Resulting pieces formed Fenton's new Snowcrest line. Production of Amber and Blue Snowcrest was discontinued by the end of 1951. Numerous pieces of green and ruby were made through 1953 and one green vase was in the line until the end of 1954.

1953

Black Rose, a cased Peach Blow style glassware with a black crest, entered the line. Black Rose remained in the line for two years and was made in nine different shapes. Aqua Crest was discontinued at the end of 1953.

1956

Beginning in January 1956, Fenton offered seven different shapes of opaque pink milk glass trimmed with a spun crystal crest. The pattern was called Silver Rose and was only available until the end of 1957. At the same time, 16 pieces of turquoise milk glass with a silver crest were introduced. This pattern was called Silver Turquoise, and most pieces were made through June 1959.

1957

A spun crystal crest was added to seven cased Jamestown pieces. The resulting pattern was named Silver Jamestown. On five of the pieces the Jamestown Blue color is on the inside with opal on the outside. On the other two shapes this blue color is on the outside and opal is on the inside. This pattern was discontinued at the end of 1959.

1958

A more dense milk glass formula replaced opal as the base color. Pieces made during and after this year appear less translucent than the items made prior to this time.

1960

Apple Blossom was introduced. This pattern is composed of milk glass pieces trimmed with an opaque rose crest. Some pieces only remained in production for a year and the entire pattern was discontinued by July 1961.

1963

Fenton used their Colonial Blue color to form a crest with eight different milk glass shapes to produce a pattern called Blue Crest. This pattern was discontinued at the end of the year. Flame Crest, another milk glass pattern with a Colonial Orange crest utilizing the same eight shapes, was only made during 1963. The orange crest was heat sensitive. This resulted in crests ranging in color from bright red to yellow-orange.

1968

Hand-painted decorations were introduced to the Crest line with the introduction of Louise Piper's Violets in the Snow decoration on Silver Crest shapes in July 1968. The Silver Crest trim was introduced to four new pieces of milk glass with the Spanish Lace design. More pieces of Spanish Lace were trimmed in Silver Crest over the next few years and the resulting pattern continued into the 1980s.

1969

The last five remaining pieces in Fenton's popular and long running Peach Crest pattern were discontinued. The hand-painted Apple Blossom decoration was used on nine different Silver Crest shapes between July 1969 and December 1970. The identical nine shapes were also decorated with Fenton's hand-painted Yellow Rose pattern during the same period.

1974

The hand-painted Violets in the Snow decoration was expanded to include items in the Spanish Lace with Silver Crest pattern. New shapes were added with this decoration in 1975 and production of pieces with this decoration continued into the early 1980s.

1979

The Valentine's Day assortment included two sizes of heart-shaped bonbons with milk glass bodies and transparent ruby crests. These bonbons were also made with transparent ruby bodies and milk glass crests.

1985

The June catalog supplement heralded the return of Blue Ridge to celebrate Fenton's 80th anniversary. New shapes were used with this deep blue crest and the pieces have the Fenton logo on the base.

1986

The regular catalog still showed 14 pieces of Silver Crest and Spanish Lace with Silver Crest remaining in the line, but the end was drawing near. Of the items remaining, eight had the embossed Spanish Lace design.

A Blue Ridge four-piece vanity set was made as part of the Connoisseur Collection. Pieces included a cologne bottle with stopper, a puff box, and a crystal satin tray. Production was limited to 1000 sets.

1987

New softer colors were the focus of the general catalog, and for the first time since 1939, no Crest items were included in the regular line.

1988

Two items with a teal crest were made as a part of the 1988 Connoisseur Collection. A teal crest was applied to a No. 2065-16 oz. pitcher made with a layer of opalescent glass cased over gold ruby. The teal crest No. 2556-ZI 6" vase was produced in the same fashion. As a final touch the vase was iridized. Both items had a production limit of 3500 pieces.

1989

Silver Crest returned to the Fenton line as a part of the newly created Elizabeth Collection. Some pieces were available with a hand-painted Blue Floral (ES) decoration. The following pieces of decorated Silver Crest were made:

Basket, 9" "Melon"	7532-ES		Pitcher, 6" "Beaded Melon"	7692-ES
Bell, 7" "Paisley"	6761-ES		Vase, 4" "Basket Weave"	9357-ES
Comport, 6½" "Empress"	9229-ES		Vase, 6" "Beaded Melon"	7693-ES
Lamp, 20" "Classic"	9308-ES		Vase, 6½" "Rose"	9252-ES

Pieces made in Silver Crest without the Blue Floral decoration included:

Basket, 8½" "Paisley"	6730-SC		Epergne set, 4-pc. "Diamond Lace"	4801-SC
Bell, 7" "Paisley"	6761-SC		Lamp, 23" "Rose" Gone with	
Bowl, 11" "Paisley"	6721-SC		the Wind	9219-SC
Cake plate, 12¼" "Paisley"	6710-SC		Vase, 7¾" "Daffodil"	9752-SC

These same pieces remained in the line in the 1990 – 91 catalog.

1993

The No. 6730-PJ hand-painted Lilacs basket with plum trim was included in the first Fenton Family Signature Series. The basket was inscribed with the signature of Bill Fenton, chairman of the board and past president. This first edition of the Family Signature Series was limited to pieces sold through April 30, 1993. The hand-painted Lilacs assortment in the regular line also included three other pieces with plum trim.

Two sizes of French Opalescent Hobnail baskets with blue and rose crests and handles were offered as a part of Fenton's Easter collection.

1994

The Fenton Family Signature Series included the No. 2738 hand-painted Lilacs milk glass basket with a plum crest and handle. The basket was inscribed with the signature of assistant sales manager, Shelley Fenton, a member of Fenton's third generation. Seven other pieces with plum crests were included in the hand-painted Lilacs assortment offered in the regular line.

Three baskets — No. 3834-4½", No. 1158-7½", and No. 3638-8½" — were made in French Opalescent Hobnail with Autumn Gold crests and handles.

1995

The signature of Fenton fourth generation sales and marketing specialist, Lynn Fenton, was inscribed on the special hand-painted Trellis basket with Dusty Rose trim that was produced for the 1995 Family Signature Series.
Three other items in the Trellis pattern with Dusty Rose trim made their debut and the hand-painted Lilacs assortment from 1994 remained in the line.

French Opalescent Hobnail baskets continued to be offered with colored trim. Three different baskets were available in three different colors, French Opalescent with Sea Mist Green trim (IM), French Opalescent with Dusty Rose trim (IH), and French Opalescent with Cobalt trim (IQ):

Basket, 6"	1159-IM	1159-IH	1159-IQ
Basket, 8½"	1160-IM	1160-IH	1160-IQ
Basket, 10½"	3830-IM	3830-IH	3830-IQ

1996

Two special series included items with colored crests. The Family Signature Series sported a hand-painted Meadow Beauty 11" No. 1563 vase with a Sea Mist Green crest. This piece was inscribed with the signature of Fenton's director of design Nancy Fenton, a member of the third generation. Also included in this series was the No. 5585 puff box in the Pansies pattern with a plum lid. This special piece was signed by Shelley Fenton. The Designer Series featured two bells with crests. Frances Burton designed the No. 4568-EB Gilded Berry bell with a plum crest. Another bell, No. 4564-IN Floral Medallion, was designed by Martha Reynolds. The color used for the crest on this bell was Dusty Rose.

The regular line included six other items with the Meadow Beauty decoration trimmed with Sea Mist Green crests. The hand-painted Trellis pattern was expanded to include a total of seven items with Dusty Rose crests. The hand-painted Pansies decoration replaced Lilacs as the pattern accented with plum trim. Besides the puff box, six other shapes were made with plum trimmed crests or handles.

1997

The 1997 Designer Series included three hand-painted bells. The No. 9862 Whitton bell with hand-painted Feathers design had a Dusty Rose crest. The No. 4629 bell featured the Roses on Ribbons decoration with Sea Mist Green trim and the No. 1145 bell had a hand-painted Butterflies decoration with a plum ring.

The Meadow Beauty pattern in the regular line featured hand-painted pink floral French Opalescent Spiral Optic pattern pieces with Sea Mist Green trim. Dusty Rose trim was used to accent the hand-painted French Opalescent Diamond Optic Trellis pattern pieces. Eight different pieces with a Dusty Rose crest are highlighted in this pattern. Milk glass is trimmed with a plum crest on five different pieces of Fenton's hand-painted Pansies pattern.

1998

The Designer Bell Series was graced with a transparent Misty Blue Hibiscus–decorated bell with a milk glass edge. The Family Signature Series included a hand-painted French Opalescent Trellis-design 9½" hat-shaped basket with Empress Rose trim, signed by Tom Fenton. Seven other floral-decorated French Opalescent Trellis pieces with Empress Rose crests were included in an assortment offered in the regular catalog. Seven hand-painted milk glass items with a plum crest were also in the catalog. Additionally, seven pieces with Meadow Beauty decoration, a hand-painted floral French opalescent rib optic design with Sea Mist Green trim, were in the regular line.

1999

The Designer Bell Series included a Fuchsia-decorated bell trimmed with a milk glass ring. Morning Mist, a new line with hand-painted leaves on white included six pieces with a crystal ring. Another hand-painted new offering, called Martha's Rose, was detailed on French opalescent Rib Optic blanks trimmed with Aquamarine handles and rings. Pieces of hand-painted Trellis with Empress Rose trim were still in the regular line.

2000

Frances Burton's creation for the Designer Bell Series included a hand-painted bell with Empress Rose trim. Six items in the new Lavender Petals hand-painted decoration on French Opalescent Spiral Optic were trimmed with a violet ring. A few new items were added to the hand-painted Trellis line, and some of the earlier pieces were discontinued. Several pieces of a new, undecorated assortment called Tranquility were accented with cobalt trim.

2001

The Designer Bell Series included a hand-painted Rose Court bell with a milk glass ring. A Topaz Opalescent Drape pitcher and a hand-painted Lily Trail on a topaz opalescent vase were decorated with a black crest. A Violet Iridescent 3-piece fairy light with a milk glass ring was included in a Violet-colored assortment created to coordinate with the Lavender Petals items. Production of Violet-trimmed Lavender Petals items continued. A new-style small pitcher was substituted for a shape that was discontinued. Daisy Lane was introduced as a new hand-painted floral pattern on a French Opalescent Trellis background. Seven decorated and two undecorated pieces were accented with Pink Chiffon trim.

2002

Frances Burton's hand painted Pink Chiffon Butterfly Breeze bell in the Designer Bell Series was trimmed with a violet ring. The Daisy Lane pattern continued to be produced for the regular line. Two new undecorated French Opalescent items trimmed with Pink Chiffon rings included a 7½" Daffodil-embossed vase and a Daisy and Button bell. The Lavender Petals pattern was also still in the line. In the 2003 catalog, Lavender Petals was the only crest-decorated pattern remaining in the regular line. An impressive 28" Gone with the Wind lamp was added to the pattern.

206—6" Footed Comport, Double Crimped   206—6" Footed Comport Plate   206—Footed Covered Candy Jar   206—6" Footed Comport, Flared   206—6" Footed Comport, Triangle

HOW  "PETTICOAT GLASS" IS MADE

An excellent name for Fenton milk glass with sparkling clear edges of handspun crystal is "Petticoat Glass." Many of the bowls and vases on the following pages begin their lives as gobs of molten glass gathered on the end of a hollow blow pipe by the "gatherer" who passes it on to the blower for further shaping.

The edge is put on the basic form by our most skilled craftsman whose ticklish job requires that he apply an equal amount of molten glass all the way around the edge, using only his sure hand and eye.

After spinning the clear crystal "ring" of glass, the piece is turned over to a "warming-in boy" who reheats it in the "glory-hole", shown at left. In hand-forming of glass it is necessary to frequently reheat the glass piece to keep it hot enough for further shaping. The "glory-hole" is a small reheating furnace kept at a temperature of 2500°.

When the glass piece is again almost molten the warming-in boy gives it back to the skilled finisher who uses his wooden buffer to flare it out flat for further shaping with a foot crimp. After foot crimping which gives the lovely fluted edge, he moulds it to its final shape, completely by hand.

Catalog Reprint   Courtesy Of: The Fenton Art Glass Museum

PETTICOAT GLASS in APPLE BLOSSOM

Milk Glass fluted with edges ranging from
light pink to deeper reds of handspun opaline
glass. Now, anytime is Apple Blossom Time!

*7258 AB
8'' DC Vase

*7336 AB
6½'' Hdl. Basket

*7228 AB
Ftd. Comport

*7254 AB
4½'' Vase

*7428 AB
8'' Bonbon

*7262 AB
12'' Vase

*7308 AB
4 Pc. Epergne Set

*7271 AB
Candleholder

*7224 AB
10'' Bowl

*7271 AB
Candleholder

*7377 AB
Ash Tray

*7213 AB
Ftd. Cake Plate

*7333 AB
Handled Relish

Catalog Reprint   Courtesy Of: The Fenton Art Glass Museum

Apple Blossom Crest

Twelve different pieces of Apple Blossom were made in 1960 and 1961. The pattern consists of milk glass pieces trimmed with an opaque pink crest. By January 1961 the 7428-8" bonbon, the 7254-4½" vase, the 7258-8" vase, and the 7262-12" vase were discontinued. The July 1961 price list reveals that all of the pieces of Apple Blossom were removed from the line. The limited production period practically assures collectors most items will not be easy to find.

Notice in the catalog reprint that Fenton ads referred to this type of glassware as "petticoat glass."

The Apple Blossom name was also used for a hand-painted floral decoration on Silver Crest in 1969 and 1970. The same AB code designation was used for these pieces.

Apple Blossom	Ware No.	Introduced	Discontinued	Value
Ashtray	7377-AB	1960	1961	35.00 – 45.00
Basket, 6½" handled	7336-AB	1960	1961	150.00 – 185.00
Bonbon, 8"	7428-AB	1960	1961	40.00 – 50.00
Bowl, 10"	7224-AB	1960	1961	95.00 – 110.00
Bowl, heart-shape relish	7333-AB	1960	1961	85.00 – 90.00
Cake plate, ftd.	7213-AB	1960	1961	180.00 – 200.00
Candleholder	7271-AB	1960	1961	45.00 – 50.00
Comport, ftd.	7228-AB	1960	1961	55.00 – 65.00
Epergne set, 4-pc.	7308-AB	1960	1961	350.00 – 450.00
Vase, 4½"	7254-AB	1960	1961	40.00 – 45.00
Vase, 8" double crimped	7258-AB	1960	1961	80.00 – 90.00
Vase, 12"	7262-AB	1960	1961	250.00 – 280.00

7258 AB
8" DC Vase

7213 AB
Ftd. cakeplate

7308 AB
4 Pc. Epergne Set

7354 AB
4 1/2" Vase

7333 AB
Handled Relish

7271 AB
Candleholder

Aqua Crest

Aqua Crest pieces feature spun clear turquoise trim around the edges of opal glassware. This color of crest was initially made in 1941 and 1942. The color then disappeared from the line until 1948, when it reappeared in a wide assortment of shapes that were much different from the earlier issue. Therefore the listing below is split into two separate sections. The first listing features the shapes made in 1941 and 1942 and the second represents shapes made after the pattern was revived in 1948 until it was discontinued at the end of 1953.

In the early years the edges of most of the bowls and vases were crimped in four or five different styles to produce assortments for wider appeal. After 1948, both the number of different items produced and shapes they were molded into were more limited.

Fenton often combined individual pieces to produce sets. Their No. 1522/951 epergne set was comprised of six pieces — one No. 1522-10" bowl, one flower block, one 5½" epergne, two No. 951 cornucopia candles, and one base for the 10" bowl. The nymph figure was also listed in a four-piece set combination with this bowl. This set was composed of the nymph, a 10" No. 1522 bowl, a flower block, and a base for the bowl. The base for the bowl is the same as the one used for the No. 751 hurricane lamp. A three-piece console set was also produced by combining the No. 1522-10" bowl with a pair of No. 951 cornucopia candles.

In 1949, shortly after Aqua Crest reentered the line, the three following large assortments were available. The prices listed are the cost for Fenton's distributors. Actual retail prices would have been about double.

1. A 27-piece service for 6:
   sugar and cream, 6 cups and saucers, 6-8½" plates, 1-12" plate, and 6 sherbets for $16.25.
2. A 10-piece Bridge Set:
   sugar and cream, 4 cups and saucers, 4-8½" plates, 1-12" plate, 4 desserts and 1 nut dish for $11.80.
3. A 61-piece dinner service:
   sugar and cream, 8 cups and saucers, 8-6½" plates, 8-8½" plates, 8-10" plates, 2-12" plates, 1-10" salad bowl, 8 soups, and 8 sherbets for $39.25.

The No. 680-10" bowl and the 12" plate were offered in a combination as a two-piece salad set. Also, the No. 680-8½" flared bowl and a pair of No. 680 candles were sold as a three-piece console set. The No. 1353 jug was combined with six plain opal tumblers and offered as a seven-piece beverage set. After July 1952, the ware number for the sugar and creamer set was 7201 and the opal cup and aqua trimmed saucer were sold together using the 7208 ware number.

Two styles of cups are listed on the 1948 price list. The cup may be found with either an aqua handle or an opal handle.

Seven pieces in the No. 1948 Diamond Lace pattern in French Opalescent color were also made with an aqua crest during the early 1950s. For more information, see page 284.

Aqua Crest (1941 – 1942)	Introduced	Discontinued	Value
Basket, #36-6¼" handled	1942	1943	95.00 – 120.00
Basket, #37-2½" fan, flared, oval, square	1942	1943	145.00 – 165.00
Basket, #192-10½" handled	1942	1943	160.00 – 180.00
Basket, #192-7" handled	1942	1943	95.00 – 125.00
Basket, #201-10" handled	1941	1943	160.00 – 180.00
Basket, #203-7" handled	1941	1943	90.00 – 110.00
Basket, #203-7" special handled	1941	1943	165.00 – 185.00
Basket, #1502-8" handled (Diamond Optic int.)	July 1941	1942	225.00 – 250.00
Basket, #1523-13 " handled	1941	1943	300.00 – 350.00
Basket, #1923-6" handled	1941	1943	90.00 – 110.00
Basket, #1924-5" handled	1942	1943	80.00 – 90.00
Basket, #1925-7" handled	1941	1943	180.00 – 200.00
Bonbon, #36, 4½" flared, oval	1941	1943	22.00 – 27.00
Bonbon, #36, 5½" double crimp, oval,	1941	1943	22.00 – 27.00
Bonbon, #36, 5½" plate	1941	1943	22.00 – 27.00
Bonbon, #36, 5½" square, triangular	1941	1943	22.00 – 27.00
Bottle, #192 squat cologne	1942	1943	90.00 – 110.00
Bottle, #192-5½" (Blue Hobnail stopper)	1942		110.00 – 120.00
Bottle, #192-7"	1942	1943	120.00 – 140.00
Bottle, #192-A vanity bottle (Blue Hobnail stopper)	1942		90.00 – 100.00
Bowl, #192-10½" double crimped	1942	1943	65.00 – 70.00
Bowl, #201-9½" special triangular	1941	1943	55.00 – 65.00
Bowl, #202 finger	1941	1943	25.00 – 30.00
Bowl, #203-4½" special cupped flared	1941	1943	22.00 – 27.00

7298 AC 3-Tier Tidbit

No. 1353 10 1/2" Vase

No. 193 11" Hand Vase

No. 184 10" Vase

7220 AC 10" Salad Bowl
7210 AC 10" Plate

7269 AC Oil Bottle

No. 37 2 1/2" Basket

7217 AC 8 1/2" Plate

No. 192-A Vanity Bottle

No. 835 6" Tulip Vase

No. 187 6" Vase

No. 1924 Creamer

No. 186 8" Tulip Vase

No. 203 7" Basket

7226 AC Sherbet

7236 AC 5" Basket

7320 AC 5 1/2" Soup

7356 AC 6 1/4" DC Vase

No. 1522 10" Crimped Bowl

7222 AC Dessert

Aqua Crest (1941 – 1942)	Introduced	Discontinued	Value
Bowl, #203-7" flared, oval square	1941	1943	30.00 – 40.00
Bowl, #205-8½" double crimped	1942	1943	40.00 – 45.00
Bowl, #205-8½" flared, square, triangular	1942	1943	40.00 – 45.00
Bowl, #682-9½" regular	1941	1943	55.00 – 70.00
Bowl, #1522-10" double crimped	1941	1943	75.00 – 85.00
Bowl, #1522-10" oval, triangular	1941	1943	75.00 – 85.00
Bowl, #1523-13½" double crimped, triangular	1941	1943	110.00 – 125.00
Bowl, #1523-13" special rolled rim	1942	1943	115.00 – 145.00
Candleholder, #192	1942	1943	40.00 – 50.00
Candleholder, #192 squat	1942		40.00 – 50.00
Candleholder, #1523	1941	1943	40.00 – 48.00
Candy jar, #206 ftd.	1942	1943	185.00 – 200.00
Comport, #206-6" ftd. double crimped, flared, plate, triangular			35.00 – 45.00
Cornucopia, #951	1941	1943	45.00 – 55.00
Creamer, #1924 aqua handle	1942	1943	47.00 – 52.00
Epergne and base	1941	1943	175.00 – 215.00
Epergne set, #1522 4-pc.	1941	1943	300.00 – 325.00
Hand vase, #193-11"	1942		290.00 – 325.00
Jug, #37-2" miniature handled	1942	1943	125.00 – 135.00
Jug, #192 squat	1942	1943	225.00 – 250.00
Jug, #192-6" handled	1942	1943	55.00 – 65.00
Jug, #192-8" handled	1942	1943	95.00 – 110.00
Jug, #1353-70 oz.	1942	1943	400.00 – 450.00
Lamp base, #192-6" handled	1942	1943	200.00 – 250.00
Plate, #680-6½"	1942	1943	14.00 – 16.00
Plate, #681-9"	1941	1943	25.00 – 30.00
Plate, #682-10"	1942	1943	55.00 – 85.00
Plate, #682-12"	1941	1943	65.00 – 80.00
Puff box, #192-A	1942		65.00 – 75.00
Salver, #600-12"	1941	1943	45.00 – 65.00
Top hat, #1923-6"	1943		85.00 – 110.00
Top hat, #1924-5"	1942	1943	55.00 – 65.00
Tumbler, #1353-10 oz. (opal only)			14.00 – 16.00
Vanity set, #192 3-pc.	1942	1943	285.00 – 315.00
Vanity set, #192-A 3-pc.	1942		245.00 – 275.00
Vase, #36-4½" double crimped, fan, square	1941	1943	24.00 – 28.00
Vase, #36-4½" triangular, tulip	1941	1943	24.00 – 28.00
Vase, #36-6¼" double crimped	1942	1943	28.00 – 32.00
Vase, #36-6¼" fan, square, triangular	1942	1943	28.00 – 32.00
Vase, #37-2" miniature fan, flared	1942	1943	100.00 – 125.00
Vase, #37-2" miniature oval, square	1942	1943	100.00 – 125.00
Vase, #37-2" miniature triangular, tulip	1942	1943	100.00 – 125.00
Vase, #186-8" double crimped	1941	1943	50.00 – 60.00
Vase, #186-8" square, triangular, tulip	1941	1943	50.00 – 60.00
Vase, #187-6" double crimped	1941	1943	50.00 – 60.00
Vase, #187-6" square, triangular, tulip	1941	1943	50.00 – 60.00
Vase, #189-10" double crimped, triangular	1941	1943	125.00 – 145.00
Vase, #190-10½" double crimped	1941	1943	N.D.
Vase, #190-10½" triangular	1941	1943	N.D.
Vase, #191-12" double crimped, triangular	1941	1943	N.D.
Vase, #192-5" cupped flared, flared, square	1942	1943	38.00 – 42.00
Vase, #192-5" double crimped, triangular	1942	1943	40.00 – 45.00
Vase, #192-6" double crimped, regular	1942	1943	55.00 – 60.00
Vase, #192-6" square, triangular, tulip	1942	1943	55.00 – 60.00

No. 680 Cup & Saucer

No. 37 2"
Miniature Jug

No. 37 2"
Miniature Vase

No. 192 5"
Vase

No. 1353 70 Oz. Jug

No. 1523 13" Basket

No. 203 4 1/2"
Tulip Vase

No. 36 5 1/2" Oval Bonbon

No. 680 Creamer & Sugar

No. 36 5 1/2" Square Bonbon

No. 201 5" Triangle Vase

No. 1924 5" Top Hat

No. 186 8" DC Vase

No. 951 Cornucopia Candleholder

No. 1523 Candleholder

No. 36 4 1/2" Ftd. Vase

No. 36 4 1/2" Ftd. Fan Vase

Aqua Crest (1941 – 1942)	Introduced	Discontinued	Value
Vase, #192-8" double crimped	1942	1943	65.00 – 75.00
Vase, #192-8" square, triangular, tulip	1942	1943	65.00 – 75.00
Vase, #192-9½" regular	1942	1943	80.00 – 90.00
Vase, #201-5" double crimped, square, triangular	1941	1943	40.00 – 45.00
Vase, #203-4½" cupped flared, triangular	1941	1943	38.00 – 42.00
Vase, #203-4½" double crimped, tulip	1941	1943	38.00 – 42.00
Vase, #835-5½" double crimped, triangular, tulip	1941	1943	95.00 – 125.00
Vase, #1353-10" double crimped, triangular	1942	1943	200.00 – 225.00
Vase, #1502-8" double crimped (Diamond Optical int.)	1941	1942	75.00 – 85.00
Vase, #1923-6½" double crimped	1941	1943	45.00 – 50.00
Vase, #1923-6½" triangular, tulip	1941	1943	45.00 – 50.00
Vase, #1924-5" double crimped, square	1942	1943	25.00 – 30.00
Vase, #1924-5" triangular, tulip	1942	1943	30.00 – 32.00
Vase, #1925-6" double crimped, triangular	1941	1943	65.00 – 75.00

Aqua Crest (1948 – 1953)	Ware No.	Introduced	Discontinued	Value
Basket, #680-5" handled	7236-AC	1949	1953	100.00 – 125.00
Basket, #711-7"		1950	1951	145.00 – 165.00
Bonbon, #36-5½" double crimped	7225-AC	1948	1954	22.00 – 27.00
Bowl, #680 deep dessert	7221-AC	1948	1954	25.00 – 30.00
Bowl, #680 dessert (low)	7222-AC	1948	1954	28.00 – 35.00
Bowl, #680-5½" soup	7320-AC	1949	1954	35.00 – 45.00
Bowl, #680-10" salad	7220-AC	1948	1954	75.00 – 85.00
Bowl, #680-8½" flared		1949	1951	65.00 – 75.00
Bowl, #1522-10"		1949	1952	75.00 – 85.00
Cake plate, #680-13" footed	7213-AC	1951	1954	120.00 – 140.00
Candleholder, #680		1949	1951	55.00 – 65.00
Candleholder, #1523		1948	1951	40.00 – 48.00
Comport, #680 ftd. double crimped	7228-AC	1949	1954	35.00 – 40.00
Creamer, #680-3¼"	7261-AC	1948	1954	45.00 – 50.00
Cup, #680 (aqua handle)		1948	1952	35.00 – 45.00
Cup (opal)		1948	1956	28.00 – 32.00
Nut dish, #680 ftd.	7229-AC	1948	1954	32.00 – 37.00
Oil, #680	7269-AC	1949	1954	185.00 – 200.00
Plate, #680-6½"	7219-AC	1948	1954	14.00 – 16.00
Plate, #680-8½"	7217-AC	1948	1954	25.00 – 30.00
Plate, #680-10"	7210-AC	1948	1954	55.00 – 85.00
Plate, #680-12"	7212-AC	1948	1954	65.00 – 80.00
Planter, #680 2-tier		Sept. 1950	1952	75.00 – 90.00
Planter, #680 3-tier		Sept. 1950	1952	145.00 – 185.00
Saucer, #680-5½"	7218-AC	1948	1954	12.00 – 15.00
Sherbet, #680 ftd.	7226-AC	1948	1954	25.00 – 27.00
Sugar, #680-3"	7231-AC	1948	1954	45.00 – 50.00
Top hat, #1924		1948	1949	55.00 – 65.00
Tray, #680 2-tier tidbit	7297-AC	1948	1954	65.00 – 85.00
Tray, #680 3-tier tidbit	7298-AC	1948	1954	90.00 – 110.00
Vase, #36-4½" double crimped	7354-AC	1948	1954	24.00 – 28.00
Vase, #36-4½" fan	7355-AC	1948	1954	24.00 – 28.00
Vase, #36-6¼" double crimped	7356-AC	1948	1954	28.00 – 32.00
Vase, #36-6¼" fan	7357-AC	1948	1954	25.00 – 32.00
Vase, #1924-5" double crimped, square		1948	1949	25.00 – 30.00
Vase, #1924-5" triangular, tulip		1948	1949	30.00 – 32.00
*Vase, #4517-6½"				55.00 – 75.00
*Vase, #4517-11"				175.00 – 200.00

* Made for Weil Ceramics, not in the regular line.

Black Crest

Items in Black Crest have a milk glass body with a spun black trim around the edge. Numerous pieces of Black Crest were made by Fenton, but this color of Crest was never placed in the regular line. Most of the pieces shown below were made for a special order placed by a Cleveland, Ohio, firm. It also has been reported that some Black Crest items were available through the Fenton gift shop in the early 1970s.

Black Crest	Ware No.	Value	Black Crest	Ware No.	Value
Ashtray	7377-BC	40.00 – 50.00	Plate, 8¼"	7217-BC	25.00 – 30.00
Basket, small	7436-BC	125.00 – 145.00	Relish, heart-shape	7333-BC	80.00 – 100.00
Basket, 7"	7237-BC	145.00 – 165.00	Tidbit, 8½" (metal handle)	7498-BC	80.00 – 90.00
Basket, 6½" crimped	7336-BC	130.00 – 150.00	Tidbit, 2-tier	7294-BC	85.00 – 110.00
Bowl, 11½" crimped	7321-BC	120.00 – 140.00	Vase, fan	7357-BC	50.00 – 60.00
Candle, 3½"	7271-BC	50.00 – 60.00	Vase, 6"	7256-BC	150.00 – 180.00
Comport, ftd. DC	7228-BC	70.00 – 75.00	Vase, 6" Melon Rib	7451-BC	55.00 – 65.00
Comport, ftd. flared	7429-BC	90.00 – 120.00	Vase, 6¼" fan	7356-BC	85.00 – 100.00
Fairy light	7392-BC	200.00 – 250.00	Vase, 7¾" Daffodil	9752-BC	125.00 – 150.00
Plate, 6"	7219-BC	14.00 – 16.00			

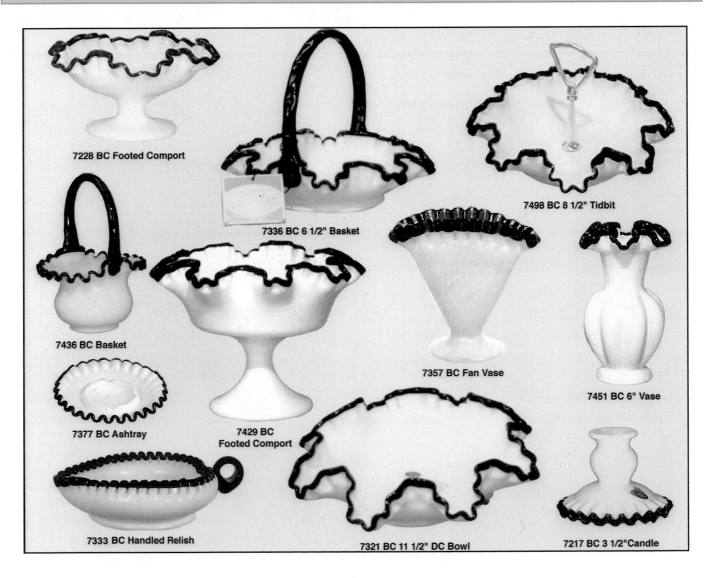

7228 BC Footed Comport

7336 BC 6 1/2" Basket

7498 BC 8 1/2" Tidbit

7436 BC Basket

7357 BC Fan Vase

7451 BC 6" Vase

7377 BC Ashtray

7429 BC Footed Comport

7333 BC Handled Relish

7321 BC 11 1/2" DC Bowl

7217 BC 3 1/2"Candle

Black Rose

When Black Rose was introduced in 1953, Fenton described the pattern as "Peach Blow with a black crest." Black Rose is a cased glass. Gold Ruby forms an inner layer which is fused with an opal exterior layer. The January supplement revealed five pieces and made promises of additional pieces later that year. More items were added in July and a few additional items were added in 1954 before the pattern was discontinued at the end of the year. There were ten different pieces made during the two years Black Rose remained in the line. The No. 7277 two-piece candleholder was only in the line for one year. It is comprised of the No. 7227-7" bowl fitted with a crystal votive style candleholder. Notice the color code (BR) is the same as the one used later for Burmese.

Collectors should be aware the hand vase was produced in 1992 for QVC with an iridescent milk exterior. This hand vase was also sold in 1997 through QVC with an iridescent milk exterior accented with a hand-painted vining floral decoration.

Black Rose	Ware No.	Introduced	Discontinued	Value
Basket, 7" handled	7237-BR	July 1953	1955	145.00 – 185.00
Bowl, 10"	7224-BR	July 1953	1954	200.00 – 225.00
Bowl, 7"	7227-BR	1953	1955	90.00 – 110.00
Candleholder, 2-pc.	7277-BR	1954	1955	95.00 – 120.00
Hand vase	5155-BR	1954	1955	475.00 – 550.00
Hurricane lamp	7398-BR	1953	1955	300.00 – 375.00
Vase, 8" tulip	7250-BR	1953	1955	150.00 – 170.00
Vase, 4½"	7254-BR	July 1953	1955	55.00 – 60.00
Vase, 5"	7350-BR	1953	1955	60.00 – 75.00
Vase, 6"	7256-BR	1953	1955	145.00 – 165.00

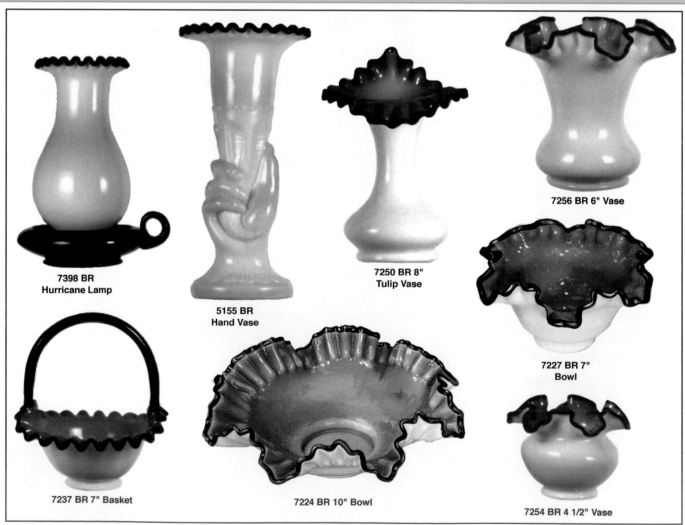

7398 BR
Hurricane Lamp

5155 BR
Hand Vase

7250 BR 8"
Tulip Vase

7256 BR 6" Vase

7227 BR 7"
Bowl

7237 BR 7" Basket

7224 BR 10" Bowl

7254 BR 4 1/2" Vase

Blue Crest

Fenton made eight items in Blue Crest in 1963, using the Colonial Blue color for the crest. This blue is deeper and much more vivid than the blue used with Aqua Crest. All of the Blue Crest pieces are shown in the catalog reprint below. Blue Crest was discontinued at the end of 1963.

Blue Crest	Ware No.	Value
Bonbon, 8"	7428-BC	45.00 – 55.00
Bowl, 11½" double crimped	7321-BC	85.00 – 90.00
Cake plate, 13" ftd.	7213-BC	140.00 – 160.00
Candleholder	7474-BC	55.00 – 65.00
Comport, ftd.	7228-BC	45.00 – 55.00
Comport, low ftd.	7329-BC	40.00 – 45.00
Comport, ftd.	7429-BC	60.00 – 70.00
Tidbit, 2-tier	7294-BC	110.00 – 135.00

Catalog Reprint   Courtesy Of: The Fenton Art Glass Museum

Blue Crest

7428 BC
8" Bonbon

7329 BC
Low Ftd. Comport

7228 BC
Ftd. Comport

7429 BC
Ftd. DC Comport

7474 BC
6" Candleholder

7321 BC
11 1/2" DC Bowl

7294 BC
2 Tier Tidbit

7213 BC
Ftd. Cakeplate

Blue Ridge Crest

Pieces in the Blue Ridge pattern have a French Opalescent Spiral body with an accenting dark blue trim on the edges and on the handles of baskets. Old inventory records and price lists show this pattern was produced in 1939. There is no mention of this color on available price lists or in inventory records after 1939, therefore, the remaining inventory was sold and the line was probably discontinued by 1940.

Price lists indicate the pitcher was sold with both the 9 ounce and 12 ounce tumblers as a seven-piece beverage set. The hurricane shade was available with a crystal, milk, or crystal satin base. Bowls are pictured in the catalog reprint with dark blue bases. The milk glass nymph was sold with this pattern as a four-piece set — the nymph, a white block, a 9" flared or 10" crimped #1522 bowl, and a base for the bowl.

The #201 vase or rose bowl may also be found listed as a bowl in some catalog references. See the Spiral Optic chapter to help identify shapes not shown in this section.

Blue Ridge, using all new shapes, was revived in 1985 as part of Fenton's 80th Anniversary celebration. These later items include:

Basket, #2362	Fairy Lamp, #2604
Basket, #2635	Lamp, #2603 with metal base
Bowl, #2624	Pitcher, #2664

The pitcher was sold as part of a water set using the #2640 French Opalescent tumbler to complement the pitcher.

In 1986, a Blue Ridge four-piece vanity set was made as part of the Connoisseur Collection. Pieces included a cologne bottle with stopper, a puff box, and a crystal satin tray. Production was limited to 1000 sets.

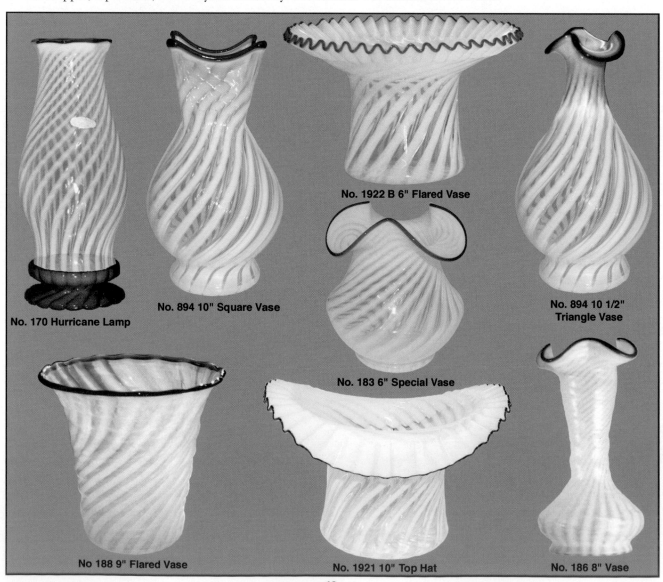

No. 170 Hurricane Lamp

No. 894 10" Square Vase

No. 1922 B 6" Flared Vase

No. 183 6" Special Vase

No. 894 10 1/2" Triangle Vase

No 188 9" Flared Vase

No. 1921 10" Top Hat

No. 186 8" Vase

Blue Ridge Crest	Value
Basket, #1923-6"	150.00 – 160.00
Basket, #201-9"	160.00 – 185.00
Basket, #1922-10"	290.00 – 325.00
Basket, #1921-11"	325.00 – 350.00
Bowl, #1522-9" flared	75.00 – 85.00
Bowl, #1522-10" crimped, oval, square, triangular	85.00 – 95.00
Bowl, #1522-A-10" crimped	85.00 – 95.00
Bowl, #1523-12" flared	125.00 – 150.00
Candle holder, #1523	75.00 – 80.00
Hurricane lamp, #170 w/base	190.00 – 220.00
Pitcher, #187	325.00 – 425.00
Rose bowl, #201 crimped	70.00 – 80.00
Rose bowl, #201 special	70.00 – 80.00
Top hat, #1924-4"	70.00 – 80.00
Top hat, #1923-6"	100.00 – 120.00
Top hat, #1922-8"	145.00 – 185.00
Top hat, #1921-10"	200.00 – 250.00
Top hat, #1920-12"	275.00 – 325.00

Blue Ridge Crest	Value
Tumbler, #187-9 oz.	45.00 – 60.00
Tumbler, #187-12 oz.	65.00 – 75.00
Vase, #201-6" cupped, crimped; cupped, flared	80.00 – 90.00
Vase, #183-6"	80.00 – 90.00
Vase, #187-7" crimped, flared, triangular	110.00 – 120.00
Vase, #188-7½" cupped	120.00 – 140.00
Vase, #188-7" flared	120.00 – 140.00
Vase, #186-8" crimped, flared, square, triangular, tulip	90.00 – 110.00
Vase, #1922-B-6" flared	100.00 – 125.00
Vase, #1922-8" flared, square, triangular	125.00 – 150.00
Vase, #188-9½" flared	130.00 – 150.00
Vase, #183-10" flared, regular, special, square, triangular	150.00 – 175.00
Vase, #894-10" flared, triangular, tulip	170.00 – 190.00
Vase, #895-10" flared	150.00 – 175.00

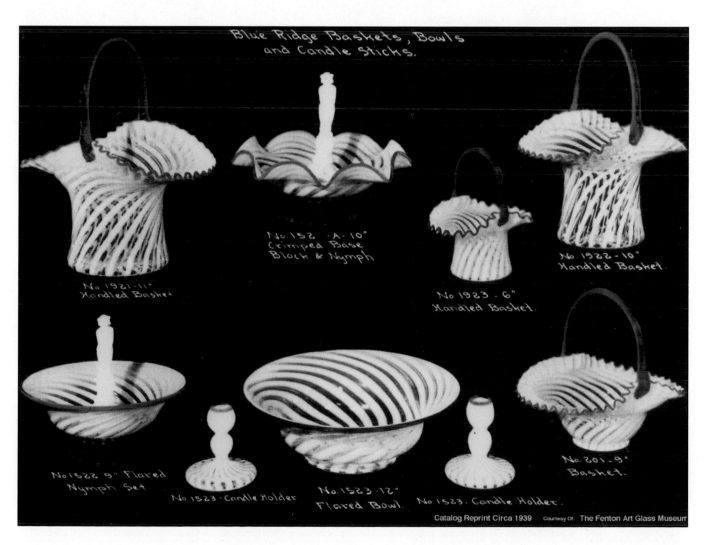

Crystal Crest

Crystal Crest is an opal glassware with a clear spun glass edge which also has an outer layer of opal trim. Fenton's Crystal Crest pattern was only made for about the first half of 1942. Sometime after mid-year, the opal trim was dropped and the similar Silver Crest pattern was born. This pattern was much easier to produce and proved to be one of Fenton's most popular. Although the listing of Crystal Crest items made is extensive, the short period of time this pattern was in production has resulted in a very short supply of items on the secondary market.

Crystal Crest	Value
Basket, #36-6¼" handled	125.00 – 150.00
Basket, #36-8" cone shape	145.00 – 165.00
Basket, #37-2½" handled fan	125.00 – 150.00
Basket, #37-2½" handled flared	125.00 – 150.00
Basket, #37-2½" handled oval	125.00 – 150.00
Basket, #37-2½" handled square	125.00 – 150.00
Basket, #192-10½" handled	250.00 – 275.00
Basket, #192-7" handled	125.00 – 140.00
Basket, #1924-5" handled	95.00 – 125.00
Basket, #201-10" handled	250.00 – 275.00
Basket, #203-7" handled	125.00 – 140.00
Basket, #1523-13 " handled	300.00 – 350.00
Bonbon, #36-4½" double crimped, oval	25.00 – 35.00
Bonbon, #36-4½" square, triangle	25.00 – 35.00
Bonbon, #36-5½" double crimped, oval	25.00 – 35.00
Bonbon, #36-5½" square, triangle	25.00 – 35.00
Bonbon, #36-5½" tulip	25.00 – 35.00
Bottle, #192 squat cologne	125.00 – 150.00
Bottle, #192-5½"	125.00 – 150.00
Bottle, #192-7"	125.00 – 150.00
Bottle, #192-A cologne or vanity bottle	125.00 – 150.00
Bowl, #192-10½" double crimped	75.00 – 95.00
Bowl, #203-7" double crimped	40.00 – 50.00
Bowl, #203-7" flared	40.00 – 50.00
Bowl, #203-7" square	40.00 – 50.00
Bowl, #203-7" triangle	40.00 – 50.00
Bowl, #203-8½" double crimped	45.00 – 55.00
Bowl, #203-8½" flared	45.00 – 55.00
Bowl, #203-8½" square	45.00 – 55.00
Bowl, #203-8½" triangle	45.00 – 55.00
Bowl, #205-8½" double crimped	45.00 – 55.00
Bowl, #205-8½" flared	45.00 – 55.00
Bowl, #205-8½" square	45.00 – 55.00
Bowl, #205-8½" triangle	45.00 – 55.00
Bowl, #682-9½" regular	60.00 – 70.00
Bowl, #1522-10" double crimped	75.00 – 85.00
Bowl, #1522-10" oval	75.00 – 85.00
Bowl, #1522-10" triangle	75.00 – 85.00
Bowl, #1523-13½" double crimped	80.00 – 100.00
Bowl, #1523-13" special rolled rim	80.00 – 100.00
Candleholder, #192	70.00 – 80.00
Candleholder, #951 cornucopia	75.00 – 85.00
Candleholder, #1523	50.00 – 60.00
Candlestick, #192 squat	70.00 – 80.00
Candy jar, #206 ftd.	140.00 – 175.00

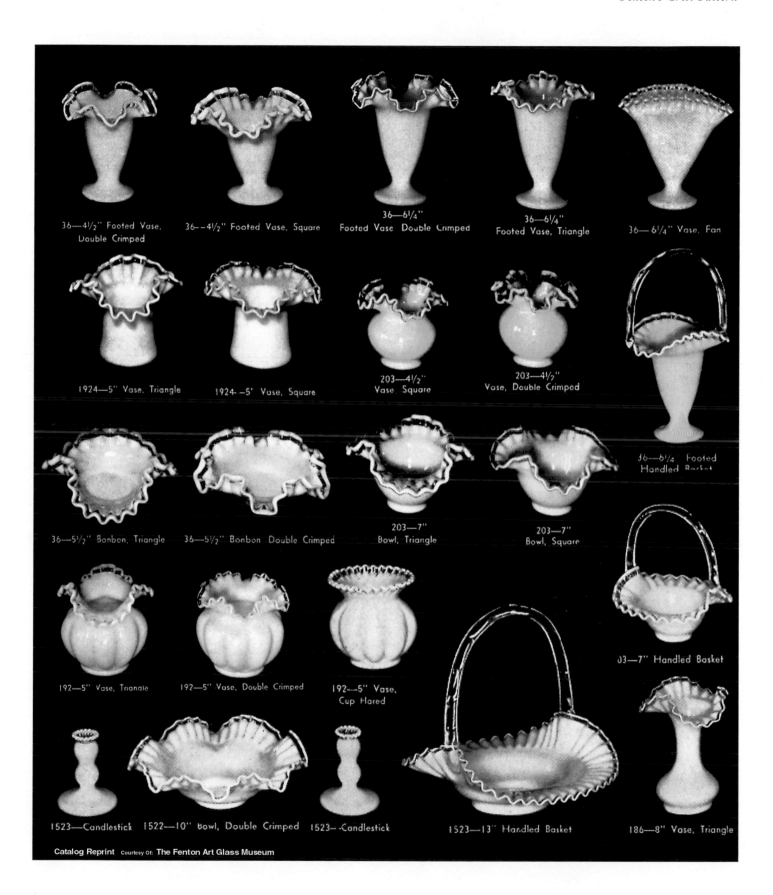

36—4½" Footed Vase, Double Crimped

36—4½" Footed Vase, Square

36—6¼" Footed Vase Double Crimped

36—6¼" Footed Vase, Triangle

36—6¼" Vase, Fan

1924—5" Vase, Triangle

1924—5' Vase, Square

203—4½" Vase, Square

203—4½" Vase, Double Crimped

36—6¼ Footed Handled Basket

36—5½" Bonbon, Triangle

36—5½" Bonbon Double Crimped

203—7" Bowl, Triangle

203—7" Bowl, Square

192—5" Vase, Triangle

192—5" Vase, Double Crimped

192—5" Vase, Cup Flared

03—7" Handled Basket

1523—Candlestick

1522—10" Bowl, Double Crimped

1523—Candlestick

1523—13" Handled Basket

186—8" Vase, Triangle

Crystal Crest	Value
Comport, #206-6" ftd. double crimped, flared, plate, triangular	35.00 – 40.00
Creamer, #1924 opal handled	42.00 – 47.00
Epergne set, #1522-4-pc.	300.00 – 350.00
Finger bowl, #202	30.00 – 35.00
Jug, #37-2" miniature handled	110.00 – 125.00
Jug, #192 squat	150.00 – 175.00
Jug, #192-6" handled	95.00 – 125.00
Jug, #192-8" handled	100.00 – 130.00
Jug, #192-A-9" handled	110.00 – 145.00
Jug, #1353-70 oz.	400.00 – 500.00
Plate, #680-6½"	35.00 – 45.00
Plate, #681-9"	45.00 – 65.00
Plate, #682-10"	65.00 – 85.00
Plate, #682-12"	65.00 – 85.00
Puff box, #192-A	30.00 – 35.00
Top hat, #1924-5"	70.00 – 80.00
Tumbler, #1353-10 oz. opal	14.00 – 16.00
Vanity set, #192 3-pc.	220.00 – 275.00
Vanity set, #192-A 3-pc.	220.00 – 275.00
Vase, #36-4½" double crimped, square	30.00 – 32.00
Vase, #36-4½" fan, triangle	30.00 – 35.00
Vase, #36-6¼" Double crimped, square	30.00 – 40.00
Vase, #36-6¼" fan, triangle	35.00 – 45.00
Vase, #37-2" miniature fan	85.00 – 120.00
Vase, #37-2" miniature flared	85.00 – 120.00
Vase, #37-2" miniature oval	85.00 – 120.00
Vase, #37-2" miniature square	85.00 – 120.00
Vase, #37-2" miniature triangle	85.00 – 120.00
Vase, #37-2" miniature tulip	85.00 – 120.00
Vase, #186-8" double crimped, square	45.00 – 55.00
Vase, #186-8" triangular, tulip	45.00 – 55.00
Vase, #192-5" cupped flared, double crimped	32.00 – 37.00
Vase, #192-5" square, triangle	32.00 – 37.00
Vase, #192-6" double crimped, regular	40.00 – 50.00
Vase, #192-6" square, triangle, tulip	40.00 – 50.00
Vase, #192-8" double crimped, square	50.00 – 70.00
Vase, #192-8" triangle, tulip	50.00 – 70.00
Vase, #192-9½" regular	85.00 – 100.00
Vase, #201-5" double crimped, square, triangle	35.00 – 45.00
Vase, #203-4½" cupped flared, flared	30.00 – 40.00
Vase, #203-4½" double crimped, square	30.00 – 40.00
Vase, #1353-10" double crimped, triangle	70.00 – 80.00
Vase, #1923-6"	100.00 – 125.00
Vase, #1924-5" double crimped, square	50.00 – 60.00
Vase, #1924-5" triangle, tulip	50.00 – 60.00

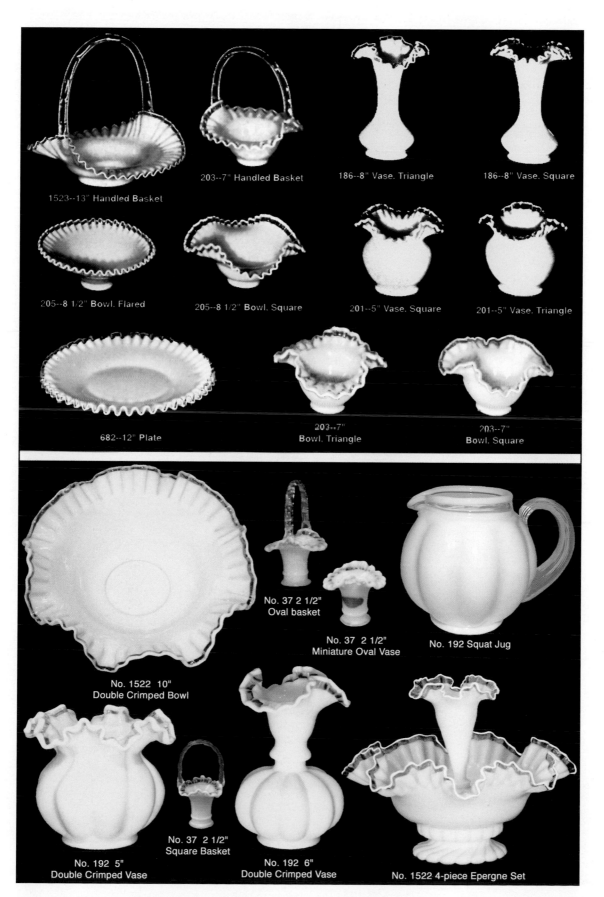

1523--13" Handled Basket

203--7" Handled Basket

186--8" Vase. Triangle

186--8" Vase. Square

205--8 1/2" Bowl. Flared

205--8 1/2" Bowl. Square

201--5" Vase. Square

201--5" Vase. Triangle

682--12" Plate

203--7"
Bowl. Triangle

203--7"
Bowl. Square

No. 1522 10"
Double Crimped Bowl

No. 37 2 1/2"
Oval basket

No. 37 2 1/2"
Miniature Oval Vase

No. 192 Squat Jug

No. 192 5"
Double Crimped Vase

No. 37 2 1/2"
Square Basket

No. 192 6"
Double Crimped Vase

No. 1522 4-piece Epergne Set

Emerald Crest

The pattern collectors know as Emerald Crest today was introduced as Green Crest in January 1949. By the October 1949 price list, this pattern was renamed Emerald Crest. The pattern consists of milk glass pieces with a spun transparent Emerald Green edge. The creamer, sugar, and early cups have an Emerald Green handle. After 1951, cups were only available with Opal handles. Numerous pieces were introduced and discontinued through the years until the production of the pattern was discontinued at the end of December 1955.

In addition to selling individual items, Emerald Crest was marketed in assortments and sets. Some set combinations and dealer costs in 1949 were as follows:

10 pc. Bridge Set: sugar, creamer, 4 cups and saucers, 4-8½" plates, 1-12" plate, 4 desserts, 1 nut dish — $11.80

27-pc. service for 6: sugar, creamer, 6 cup and saucer; 6-8½" plate, 1-12" plate, 6 sherbets — $16.25

61 pc. dinner service: sugar, creamer, 8 cups and saucers, 8-6½" plates, 8-8½" plates, 8-10" plates, 2-12" plates, 10" salad bowl, 8 soups, 8 sherbets — $39.25.

Several pieces were also frequently combined to produce attractive sets. The No. 680-10" bowl was sold with the 12" plate as a 2-piece salad set, and the No. 680-8½" bowl was marketed with a pair of No. 680 candles as a 3-piece console set. Two- and three-tier tidbits and planters were produced by placing metal rods between drilled plates and bowls. The plates used with the earlier No. 680 2-tier tidbit differ in size from the ones used to make the later No. 7296 tidbit. The No. 680 2-tier tidbit consists of a lower 12" plate and an upper 8½" plate. The No. 680 planter tidbit combinations were only made for a short time. They were introduced in September 1950 and were discontinued by January 1952.

After July 1952, Fenton changed to a numbering system in which each shape was identified by a number, and colors were given a two-letter code. Thus, the number and color code would identify each piece. Ware numbers were also used for combinations of items that were sold as sets. The sugar and creamer set used Ware No. 7201 and the cup and saucer set (with the Opal cup only) was Ware No. 7208. In the listing below, items that were made after 1952 also are shown with their identifying ware numbers.

For other pieces with an Emerald crest, see the Diamond Lace pattern on page 284.

Emerald Crest	Ware No.	Introduced	Discontinued	Value
Basket, #203-7"	7237-EC	1952	1955	120.00 – 140.00
Basket, #680-5" handled	7236-EC	1949	1954	100.00 – 125.00
Basket, #711-7" handled		1949	1952	145.00 – 160.00
Bonbon, #36-5½" double crimped	7225-EC	1949	1956	24.00 – 28.00
Bowl, #203-7"	7227-EC	1949	1956	35.00 – 40.00
Bowl, #680 deep dessert	7221-EC	1949	1956	24.00 – 28.00
Bowl, #680 dessert (low)	7222-EC	1949	1956	24.00 – 28.00
Bowl, #680-5½" soup	7320-EC	1949	1956	35.00 – 40.00
Bowl, #680-8½" flared		1949	1952	50.00 – 60.00
Bowl, #680-10" salad	7220-EC	1949	1956	70.00 – 90.00
Bowl, #711-7"		1950	1952	45.00 – 55.00
Bowl, 7" serving	7335-EC	1955	1956	35.00 – 45.00
Bowl, square ftd.	7330-EC	1955	1956	290.00 – 325.00
Bowl, #1522-10"		1950	1952	75.00 – 85.00
Cake plate, low ftd.	5813-EC	1954	1956	90.00 – 125.00
Cake plate, #680-13" ftd.	7213-EC	1952	1956	125.00 – 145.00
Candleholder, #680		1949	1952	60.00 – 80.00
Candlestick, #1523		1950	1952	60.00 – 75.00
Comport, #680 ftd. double crimped	7228-EC	1949	1956	35.00 – 45.00
Comport, low ftd.	7329-EC	1954	1956	50.00 – 55.00
Creamer, #680	7261-EC	1949	1956	40.00 – 50.00
Cup, #680 (green handle)		1949	1952	35.00 – 45.00
Cup, (opal)		1948	1956	28.00 – 32.00
Jug, #711-5½" handled		1949	1952	85.00 – 110.00
Jug, #711-6" handled	7166-EC	1949	1954	90.00 – 125.00
Mayonnaise set	7203-EC	1953	1956	75.00 – 90.00
Nut dish, #680 ftd.	7229-EC	1949	1956	35.00 – 40.00
Oil, #680	7269-EC	1950	1955	185.00 – 200.00

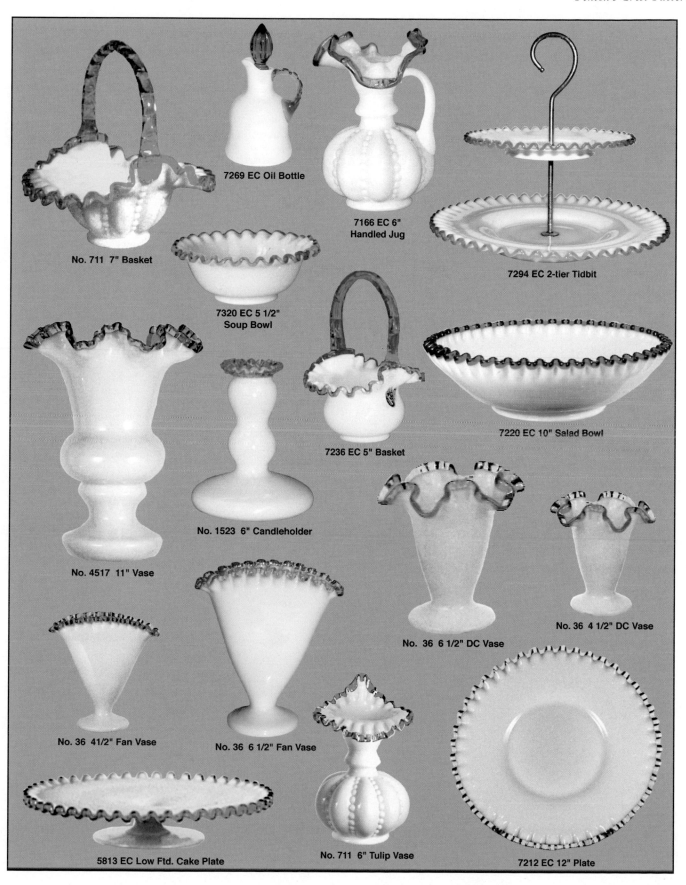

No. 711 7" Basket

7269 EC Oil Bottle

7166 EC 6"
Handled Jug

7294 EC 2-tier Tidbit

7320 EC 5 1/2"
Soup Bowl

7236 EC 5" Basket

7220 EC 10" Salad Bowl

No. 4517 11" Vase

No. 1523 6" Candleholder

No. 36 6 1/2" DC Vase

No. 36 4 1/2" DC Vase

No. 36 41/2" Fan Vase

No. 36 6 1/2" Fan Vase

No. 711 6" Tulip Vase

7212 EC 12" Plate

5813 EC Low Ftd. Cake Plate

Emerald Crest	Ware No.	Introduced	Discontinued	Value
Planter, #680-2-tier	7297-EC	1949	1954	100.00 – 125.00
Planter, #680-3-tier	7298-EC	1949	1954	145.00 – 185.00
Plate, #680-6½"	7219-EC	1949	1956	14.00 – 16.00
Plate, #680-8½" dessert	7217-EC	1949	1956	25.00 – 30.00
Plate, #680-10" dinner	7210-EC	1949	1954	60.00 – 90.00
Plate, #680-12" serving	7212-EC	1949	1956	50.00 – 60.00
Plate, 12" low ftd.	7312-EC	1954	1956	75.00 – 80.00
Plate, 16" torte	7216-EC	1954	1956	65.00 – 85.00
Pot and saucer, #401	7299-EC	1952	1956	90.00 – 110.00
Relish, handled	7333-EC	1955	1956	75.00 – 90.00
Rose bowl, #203-4½"	7254-EC	1949	1956	40.00 – 50.00
Saucer, #680-5½"	7218-EC	1949	1956	10.00 – 12.00
Sherbet, #680 ftd.	7226-EC	1949	1956	25.00 – 30.00
Sugar, #680	7231-EC	1949	1956	50.00 – 55.00
Tray, 2-tier	7294-EC	1954	1956	60.00 – 80.00
Tray, 2-tier	7296-EC	1954	1956	60.00 – 80.00
Tray, 3-tier	7295-EC	1954	1956	90.00 – 125.00
Vase, #36-4½" double crimped	7354-EC	1949	1955	30.00 – 35.00
Vase, #36-4½" fan	7355-EC	1949	1956	32.00 – 35.00
Vase, #36-6½" double crimped	7356-EC	1949	1956	32.00 – 37.00
Vase, #36-6½" fan	7357-EC	1949	1956	40.00 – 45.00
Vase, #186-8" double crimped		1949	1952	60.00 – 65.00
Vase, #186-8" tulip		1950	1952	65.00 – 75.00
Vase, #203-4½"	7254-EC	1950	1956	27.00 – 32.00
Vase, #711 miniature		1950	1952	55.00 – 65.00
Vase, #711-5"		1949	1952	42.00 – 47.00
Vase, #711-5½" double crimped		1949	1952	42.00 – 47.00
Vase, #711-5½" tulip		1949	1952	47.00 – 50.00
Vase, #711-6" double crimped		1949	1952	50.00 – 55.00
Vase, #711-6" tulip		1949	1952	65.00 – 85.00
*Vase, #4517-6½"				65.00 – 85.00
*Vase, #4517-11"				175.00 – 200.00

* Not in the regular line.

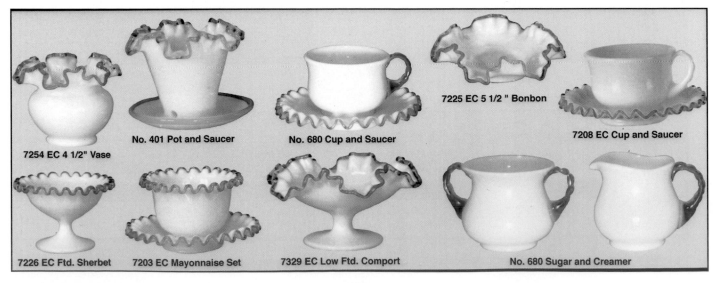

7254 EC 4 1/2" Vase   No. 401 Pot and Saucer   No. 680 Cup and Saucer   7225 EC 5 1/2" Bonbon   7208 EC Cup and Saucer

7226 EC Ftd. Sherbet   7203 EC Mayonnaise Set   7329 EC Low Ftd. Comport   No. 680 Sugar and Creamer

Flame Crest

Flame Crest is milk glass with a spun transparent Colonial Orange edge. Due to the heat sensitive nature of this color, the color of the edge on some pieces may vary from a bright orange to a deep red. Fenton's line of Flame Crest was only made in 1963 and the entire line consisted of eight items. As may be expected, the short period of production has resulted in a lack of any quantity of these items on the secondary market.

In the mid-1970s Fenton made two sizes of heart-shaped bonbons with red crests for Valentine's Day. For examples of these bonbons, see page 112 at the end of the Crest chapter.

Flame Crest	Ware No.	Value
Bonbon, 8"	7428-FC	50.00 – 60.00
Bowl, 11½" double crimped	7321-FC	90.00 – 110.00
Cake plate, 13" ftd.	7213-FC	145.00 – 185.00
Candleholder	7474-FC	60.00 – 65.00
Comport, ftd.	7228-FC	45.00 – 55.00
Comport, low ftd.	7329-FC	40.00 – 50.00
Comport, ftd.	7429-FC	80.00 – 90.00
Tidbit, 2-tier	7294-FC	125.00 – 135.00

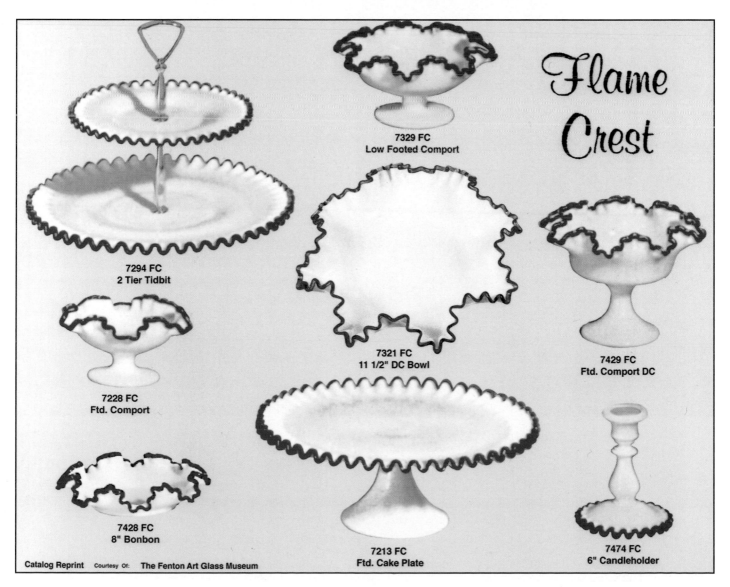

7329 FC
Low Footed Comport

Flame Crest

7294 FC
2 Tier Tidbit

7321 FC
11 1/2" DC Bowl

7429 FC
Ftd. Comport DC

7228 FC
Ftd. Comport

7428 FC
8" Bonbon

7213 FC
Ftd. Cake Plate

7474 FC
6" Candleholder

Catalog Reprint   Courtesy Of: The Fenton Art Glass Museum

Gold Crest

Fenton's Gold Crest pattern consisted of items made in milk glass with a spun amber trim applied to the edge. The original items with this color crest were produced in 1943 and 1944. Notice the various styles of crimping on many of the bowls and vases in the listing below.

In 1963, Gold Crest, with a Colonial Amber edge, again appeared in the Fenton line with the introduction of eight items. This new edition of Gold Crest only remained in the line until the end of 1964.

Gold Crest	Value
Basket, #36-4½" ftd. cone-shaped	40.00 – 60.00
Basket, #36-6½" ftd. cone-shaped	55.00 – 67.00
Basket, #37-2½" miniature fan, square	110.00 – 125.00
Basket, #37-2½" miniature flared, oval	115.00 – 125.00
Basket, #192-10½" handled	150.00 – 175.00
Basket, #1924-5" handled	45.00 – 50.00
Basket, #201-10" handled	95.00 – 125.00
Basket, #203-7" handled	60.00 – 70.00
Basket, #1523-13" handled	95.00 – 225.00
Basket, #1923-7" handled	100.00 – 125.00
Bonbon, #36-5½" double crimped, oval, square, triangle	14.00 – 18.00
Bottle, #192 squat cologne	55.00 – 65.00
Bottle, #192-5½"	65.00 – 75.00
Bottle, #192-7"	75.00 – 85.00
Bottle, #192-A cologne or vanity bottle	55.00 – 65.00
Bowl, #192-10½" double crimped	65.00 – 85.00
Bowl, #203-7" double crimped, flared, square, triangle	25.00 – 30.00
Bowl, #203-8½" double crimped, flared, square, triangle	25.00 – 30.00
Bowl, #682-9½" regular	35.00 – 40.00
Bowl, #1522-10" double crimped	55.00 – 60.00
Bowl, #1523-13" double crimped	70.00 – 80.00
Candleholder, #192 squat	20.00 – 25.00
Candleholder, #192/1943	75.00 – 85.00
Candleholder, #951 cornucopia	35.00 – 45.00
Candleholder, #1523	30.00 – 35.00
Epergne and block, #1522	65.00 – 75.00
Hand vase, #193-11"	225.00 – 250.00
Jar, #192 covered candy or bath powder	55.00 – 65.00
Jug, #192-32 oz. squat	85.00 – 110.00
Jug, #192-5" handled	35.00 – 45.00
Jug, #192-5½" handled	40.00 – 50.00
Jug, #192-6" handled	45.00 – 55.00
Jug, #192-A-9" handled	85.00 – 95.00
Plate, #680-6½"	8.00 – 10.00
Plate, #681-9"	30.00 – 35.00
Plate, #682-12"	35.00 – 40.00
Puff box, #192-A	40.00 – 45.00
Top hat, #1924-5"	25.00 – 32.00
Vanity set, #192-A 3-pc.	150.00 – 175.00
Vase, #36-4½" double crimped, fan, square, triangle	20.00 – 25.00
Vase, #36-6¼" double crimped, fan, square, triangle	25.00 – 30.00
Vase, #37-2" miniature fan, flared, oval, square, triangle, tulip	90.00 – 120.00
Vase, #186-8" double crimp, square, triangle, tulip	45.00 – 55.00
Vase, #192-10" double crimped, square, triangle, tulip	85.00 – 90.00
Vase, #192-5½" double crimped, square, triangle, tulip	25.00 – 30.00
Vase, #192-5" double crimped, oval, square, triangle	20.00 – 25.00

Gold Crest	Value
Vase, #192-6" double crimped, regular	25.00 – 30.00
Vase, #192-6" square, triangle tulip	25.00 – 30.00
Vase, #192-8" double crimped, square, triangle, tulip	35.00 – 40.00
Vase, #192-A-9" double crimped, square	40.00 – 45.00
Vase, #192-A-9" triangle, tulip	40.00 – 45.00
Vase, #201-5" cupped oval, double crimped	40.00 – 45.00
Vase, #201-5" square, triangle	40.00 – 45.00
Vase, #203-4½" cupped flared, double crimped	20.00 – 25.00
Vase, #203-4½" square, triangle	20.00 – 25.00
Vase, #573-8" flared crimped	50.00 – 60.00
Vase, #1924-5" double crimped, square, triangle, tulip	25.00 – 30.00

Gold Crest (1963)	Ware No.	Introduced	Discontinued	Value
Bonbon, 8"	7428-GC	1963	1965	20.00 – 27.00
Bowl, 11½" double crimped	7321-GC	1963	1965	55.00 – 60.00
Cake plate, ftd.	7213-GC	1963	1965	55.00 – 85.00
Candleholder	7474-GC	1963	1965	35.00 – 40.00
Comport, ftd.	7228-GC	1963	1965	28.00 – 32.00
Comport, low ftd.	7329-GC	1963	1965	28.00 – 30.00
Comport, ftd	7429-GC	1963	1965	42.00 – 50.00
Tidbit, 2-tier	7294-GC	1963	1965	65.00 – 85.00

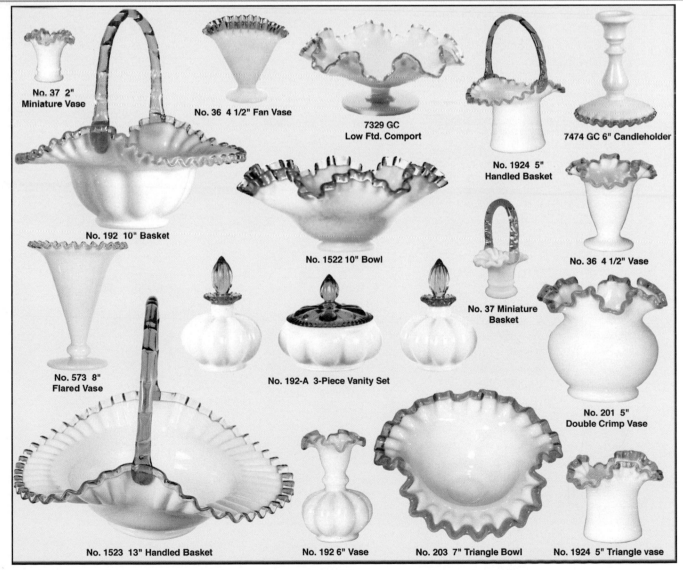

No. 37 2" Miniature Vase

No. 36 4 1/2" Fan Vase

7329 GC Low Ftd. Comport

7474 GC 6" Candleholder

No. 1924 5" Handled Basket

No. 192 10" Basket

No. 1522 10" Bowl

No. 36 4 1/2" Vase

No. 573 8" Flared Vase

No. 192-A 3-Piece Vanity Set

No. 37 Miniature Basket

No. 201 5" Double Crimp Vase

No. 1523 13" Handled Basket

No. 192 6" Vase

No. 203 7" Triangle Bowl

No. 1924 5" Triangle vase

Ivory Crest

Ivory Crest pieces feature a silver crest on a pale yellow body. This line was introduced in 1940 with an exciting array of shapes. However, due to wartime shortages of critical raw materials this color was discontinued by the end of 1941.

The epergne set consisted of four pieces — a No. 1522-10½" bowl, an epergne, a base for the bowl, and a block for the epergne. This set was sometimes sold as a six-piece set with the addition of two No. 951 cornucopia candles. The No. 1522 bowls were also sold as a console set with the No. 951 cornucopia candles and the No. 1523 bowl was listed with the No. 951 candles to produce a console set.

Ivory Crest	Introduced	Discontinued	Value
Basket, #201-10" handled	1940	1942	120.00 – 160.00
Basket, #203-7" handled	1940	1942	80.00 – 90.00
Basket, #1502-8" handled (Diamond Optic int.)	1941	1942	125.00 – 150.00
Basket, #1523-13" handled	1940	1942	250.00 – 275.00
Basket, #1922-10" handled	1940	1941	150.00 – 175.00
Basket, #1923-7" handled	1941	1942	55.00 – 70.00
Basket, #1925-7" handled	1940	1942	100.00 – 120.00
Bowl, #202 finger	1941	1942	22.00 – 25.00
Bowl, #682-9½" regular	1940	1942	30.00 – 40.00
Bowl, #1522-10½" double crimped	1940	1942	45.00 – 50.00
Bowl, #1522-10½" oval, triangle	1940	1942	45.00 – 50.00
Bowl, #1523-13" crimp A or B	1940	1942	70.00 – 85.00
Candlestick, #1523	1940	1942	50.00 – 60.00
Candlestick, #951 cornucopia	1940	1942	40.00 – 45.00
Epergne set, #1522 4-pc.	1940	1942	175.00 – 195.00
Plate, #680-6½"	1941	1942	12.00 – 15.00
Plate, #681-9"	1940	1942	35.00 – 45.00
Plate, #682-12"	1940	1942	50.00 – 60.00
Rose bowl, #201-5"	1940	1942	35.00 – 45.00
Rose bowl, #204	1940	1942	35.00 – 45.00
Top hat, #1922-8"	1940	1941	80.00 – 100.00
Top hat, #1923-6"	1940	1941	35.00 – 45.00
Vase, #36-4½"	1940	1942	18.00 – 20.00
Vase, #183-10" double crimped	1940	1941	85.00 – 100.00
Vase, #183-10" square, triangle	1940	1941	85.00 – 100.00
Vase, #186-7½" special, triangle	1940	1942	27.00 – 35.00
Vase, #186-8½" crimped, DC	1940	1942	27.00 – 35.00
Vase, #186-8½" square, triangle	1940	1942	27.00 – 35.00
Vase, #186-8½" tulip	1940	1942	30.00 – 40.00
Vase, #191-12" double crimped, triangle	1941	1942	N.D.
Vase, #201-5" double crimped	1940	1942	28.00 – 30.00
Vase, #201-5" flared, square, triangle	1940	1942	28.00 – 30.00
Vase, #210-6" double crimped	1940	1942	32.00 – 35.00
Vase, #894-10" flared, square, triangle	1940	1941	85.00 – 90.00
Vase, #894-10" tulip	1940	1941	85.00 – 90.00
Vase, #1502-8" double crimped	1941	1942	40.00 – 50.00
Vase, #1523 cornucopia	1941	1942	80.00 – 95.00
Vase, #1922-10" flared, square, triangle	1940	1941	90.00 – 100.00
Vase, #1923-6½" double crimped	1940	1942	28.00 – 32.00
Vase, #1923-6½" square	1940	1942	28.00 – 32.00
Vase, #1923-7" triangular, tulip	1940	1942	32.00 – 37.00

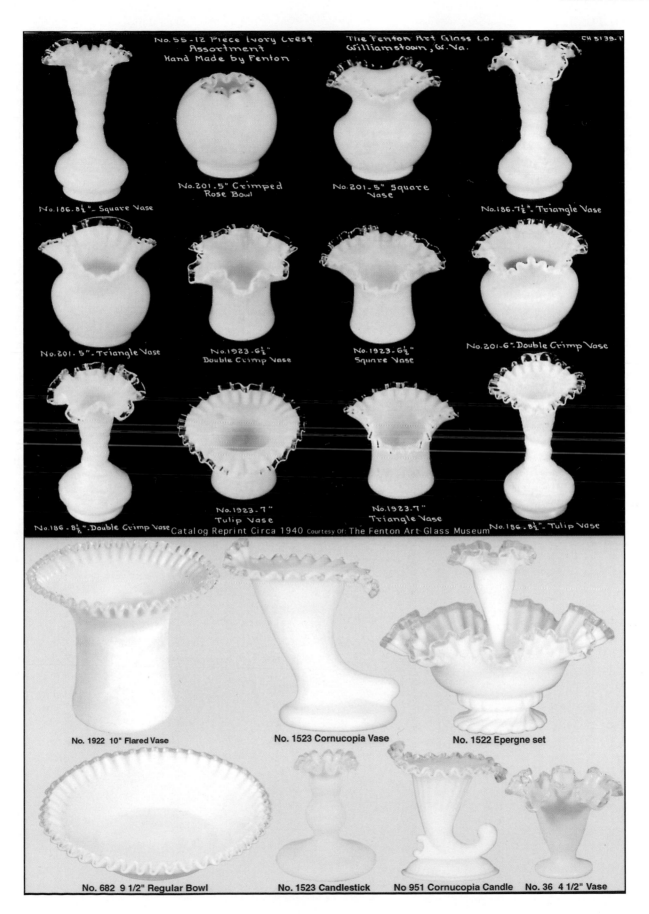

No. 55-12 Piece Ivory Crest Assortment Hand Made by Fenton

The Fenton Art Glass Co. Williamstown, W. Va.

CH 5139-1"

No. 201 - 5" Crimped Rose Bowl

No. 201 - 5" Square Vase

No. 186 - 8¼" - Square Vase

No. 186 - 7½" - Triangle Vase

No. 201 - 5" - Triangle Vase

No. 1923 - 6½" Double Crimp Vase

No. 1923 - 6½" Square Vase

No. 201 - 6" - Double Crimp Vase

No. 186 - 8¼" - Double Crimp Vase

No. 1923 - 7" Tulip Vase

No. 1923 - 7" Triangle Vase

No. 186 - 8¼" - Tulip Vase

Catalog Reprint Circa 1940 Courtesy Of: The Fenton Art Glass Museum

No. 1922 10" Flared Vase

No. 1523 Cornucopia Vase

No. 1522 Epergne set

No. 682 9 1/2" Regular Bowl

No. 1523 Candlestick

No 951 Cornucopia Candle

No. 36 4 1/2" Vase

Peach Crest

In 1940, Fenton's Peach Blow assortment was transformed into the fancier Peach Crest pattern. Peach Crest consists of glassware with an opal exterior layer cased with a Gold Ruby interior layer. After the piece is blown and shaped, a thin crystal edge is added to form the crest. Peach Crest quickly became a popular line and numerous new shapes were added. In 1942, various sizes of handled jugs, the vanity set, different sizes of the No. 192 shape vases, and several shapes of baskets were introduced.

In 1949 the No. 192 shape was discontinued and the No. 711 shape was introduced. This new shape featured many of the same pieces as the old No. 192 shape. The major difference in the two styles was the addition of decorative embossed beads to the No. 711 shape. Peach Crest remained very popular through the 1940s and 1950s. However, as sales began to decline during the early 1960s, the number of different pieces being made began to decrease, and no new shapes were introduced after 1959. Limited production continued until the end of 1969. At this time, only five of the more popular pieces remained in the line.

Collectors have the opportunity of finding two different styles of hand vases in this pattern. Early examples have the traditional single crimped top. Later vases made from 1953 through 1954 have a narrow crimped top. The No. 1925-6½" vase was originally produced in the early 1940s. This vase was made again from 1954 through 1958. Other desirable pieces include the 70 oz. jug, the large 13" basket, the vanity set, and the hurricane lamp. A seven-piece beverage set was listed in 1942. The set included the No. 1353-70 oz. jug and six No. 1353-10 oz. tumblers. After 1942, no reference can be found for either the pitcher or the tumblers. The 7277-PC two-piece candleholder was introduced in January 1954. This item was only in the line for one year. It was produced by fitting the No. 7227-7" bowl with a crystal votive style candleholder. The No. 192-A three-piece vanity set consists of the puff box and two small round vanity bottles. The No. 192 vanity set was comprised of the puff box and two 5" squat cologne bottles. The No. 192 covered candy or bath jar was also listed as a covered ornamental comport during 1946.

Numerous pieces may be found with hand-painted decorations. One of the more famous hand decorated lines used with Peach Crest shapes was the Charleton Roses decoration marketed by Abels, Wasserberg Inc. of New York. For more information see page 116. A Peach Crest atomizer made for DeVilbiss is also shown on page 112.

The listing below has been separated into three sections. The first section lists and prices items introduced into the line prior to 1949. The second grouping features pieces in the No. 711 shape that were introduced in 1949. The last section lists shapes added to the Peach Crest line after the introduction of ware numbers in July 1952. Items made earlier and continued through this numbering transition are not repeated. Instead the ware numbers for these items are listed along with the original line number in the initial listing.

Peach Crest	Ware No.	Introduced	Discontinued	Value
Basket, #192-10½" handled		1942	1949	160.00 – 185.00
Basket, #192-7" handled		1942	1944	70.00 – 80.00
Basket, #201-10" handled		1940	1947	145.00 – 165.00
Basket, #203-7" handled		1940	1949	60.00 – 80.00
Basket, #203-7" special handled		1941	1943	90.00 – 110.00
Basket, #1523-13" handled		1940	1952	240.00 – 250.00
Basket, #1922-10" handled		1940	1941	165.00 – 185.00
Basket, #1923-7" handled		1940	1948	85.00 – 100.00
Basket, #1924-5" handled	7235-PC	1942	1954	55.00 – 65.00
Basket, #1925-7" handled		1940	1943	175.00 – 185.00
Bottle, #192 squat cologne		1942	1948	80.00 – 90.00
Bottle, #192-A vanity		1942	1948	80.00 – 90.00
Bottle, #192-5½"		1942	1948	80.00 – 100.00
Bottle, #192-7"		1942	1949	90.00 – 100.00
Bowl, #192-10½" double crimped		1942	1949	65.00 – 75.00
Bowl, #203-4½" special flared cupped		1941	1943	14.00 – 18.00
Bowl, #203-5" double crimped, tulip		1940	1943	16.00 – 18.00
Bowl, #203-5" oval, square, triangle		1940	1943	16.00 – 18.00
Bowl, #203-5" square cup, oval cup		1940	1944	16.00 – 18.00
Bowl, #203-5" cup flared		1940	1944	16.00 – 18.00
Bowl, #203-7" double crimped		1942	1949	20.00 – 25.00
Bowl, #203-7" oval, square		1942	1949	20.00 – 25.00
Bowl, #1522-10" eight point		1940	1941	75.00 – 85.00

1523 PC 13" Handled Basket

5155 PC Hand Vase

No. 170 Hurricane Lamp

No. 894-10" Flared Vase

1523 PC Cornucopia Vase

6056 PC 6" Vase

7237 PC 7" Basket

7292 PC 5" Top Hat

9020 PC 10 1/4" Shell Bowl

No. 194-13" Handled Vase

1523 PC 13" Bowl

No.192-8" Vase

No. 186-8" Vase

No. 192 A-9" Handled Jug

Peach Crest	Ware No.	Introduced	Discontinued	Value
Bowl, #1522-10" double crimped	7224-PC	1940	1970	75.00 – 80.00
Bowl, #1522-10" oval, triangular		1940	1952	80.00 – 90.00
Bowl, #1523-13" crimp A or B	7223-PC	1940	1968	90.00 – 110.00
Bowl, #1523-13" special rolled rim		1942	1943	125.00 – 145.00
Candleholder, #192 squat		1942	1949	30.00 – 35.00
Candleholder, #1523	7270-PC	1940	1954	35.00 – 40.00
Creamer, #1924 handled		1942	1948	42.00 – 50.00
Hand vase, #193-11"		1942	1948	250.00 – 300.00
Hurricane lamp, #170 w/base		1940	1942	125.00 – 140.00
Jar, #192 covered candy or bath		1943	1949	65.00 – 85.00
Jug, #192 squat		1942	1948	85.00 – 95.00
Jug, #192-5½" handled		1943	1949	30.00 – 35.00
Jug, 192-6" handled		1942	1949	35.00 – 40.00
Jug, 192-8" handled		1942	1949	45.00 – 55.00
Jug, #192-A-9" handled		1943	1949	70.00 – 90.00
Jug, #1353-70 oz.		1942	1943	400.00 – 475.00
Puff box, #192-A		1943	1948	60.00 – 70.00
Rose bowl, #201-5"		1940	1948	50.00 – 60.00
Rose bowl, #203-4"		1940	1949	40.00 – 50.00
Rose bowl, #204		1940	1943	40.00 – 50.00
Top hat, #1922-8"		1940	1941	125.00 – 150.00
Top hat, #1923-6"		1940	1943	55.00 – 65.00
Top hat, 1924-5"	7292-PC	1942	1954	40.00 – 50.00
Tumbler, #1353 10 oz.		1942	1943	14.00 – 16.00
Vanity set, #192 3-pc.		1942	1948	220.00 – 279.00
Vanity set, #192-A 3-pc.		1943	1948	220.00 – 250.00
Vase, #183-10" double crimped		1940	1942	100.00 – 125.00
Vase, #183-10" square, triangular		1940	1942	110.00 – 135.00
Vase, #186-7½" special		1940	1943	40.00 – 50.00
Vase, #186-8" double crimped	7258-PC	1940	1963	35.00 – 45.00
Vase, #186-8" tulip	7250-PC	1940	1963	40.00 – 50.00
Vase, #186-8" triangular, square		1940	1949	35.00 – 45.00
Vase, #187-6½" double crimped	7251-PC	1940	1962	37.00 – 42.00
Vase, #187-6½" triangle, tulip		1940	1952	37.00 – 42.00
Vase, #189-10" double crimped		1940	1943	85.00 – 95.00
Vase, #189-10" triangular		1940	1943	85.00 – 95.00
Vase, #190-10½" double crimped		1940	1943	N.D.
Vase, #190-10½" triangular		1940	1943	N.D.
Vase, #192-10" double crimped		1943	1944	65.00 – 75.00
Vase, #192-10" square, triangular		1943	1944	65.00 – 75.00
Vase, #192-10" tulip		1943	1944	75.00 – 85.00
Vase, #192-5½" double crimped		1943	1949	22.00 – 27.00
Vase, #192-5½" flared, square		1943	1949	22.00 – 27.00
Vase, #192-5½" triangular, tulip		1943	1949	28.00 – 32.00
Vase, #192-5" cupped flared		1942	1949	25.00 – 30.00
Vase, #192-5" double crimped		1942	1949	27.00 – 32.00
Vase, #192-5" square, triangular		1942	1949	30.00 – 35.00
Vase, #192-6" double crimped		1942	1949	30.00 – 35.00
Vase, #192-6" regular, square		1942	1949	30.00 – 35.00
Vase, 192-6" triangular, tulip		1942	1949	30.00 – 35.00
Vase, 192-8" double crimped		1942	1949	40.00 – 45.00
Vase, 192-8" square, triangular		1942	1949	40.00 – 45.00
Vase, 192-8" tulip		1942	1949	40.00 – 50.00
Vase, #192-9½" regular		1942		35.00 – 45.00

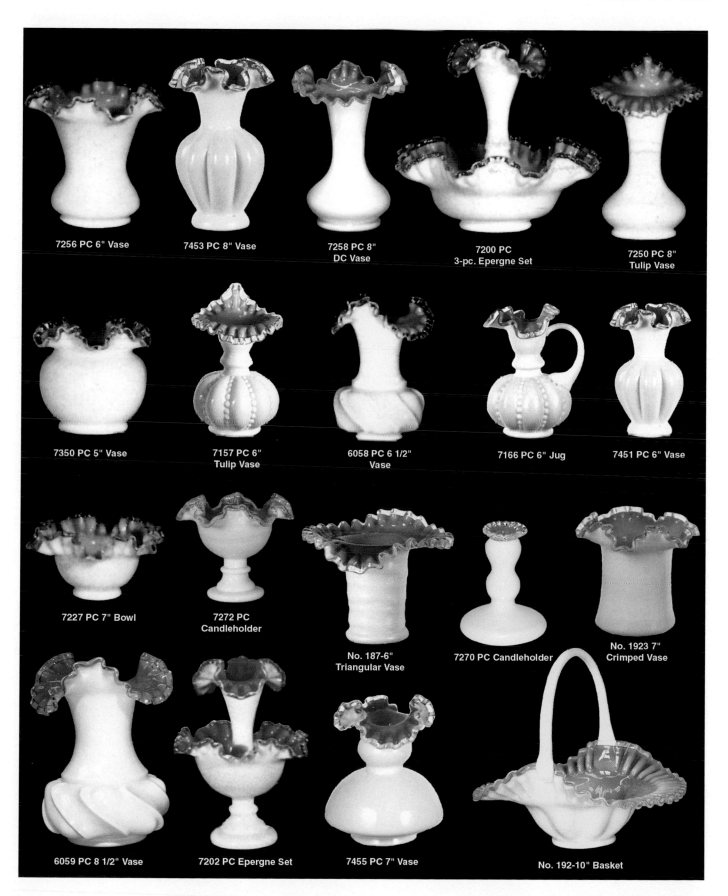

7256 PC 6" Vase

7453 PC 8" Vase

7258 PC 8"
DC Vase

7200 PC
3-pc. Epergne Set

7250 PC 8"
Tulip Vase

7350 PC 5" Vase

7157 PC 6"
Tulip Vase

6058 PC 6 1/2"
Vase

7166 PC 6" Jug

7451 PC 6" Vase

7227 PC 7" Bowl

7272 PC
Candleholder

No. 187-6"
Triangular Vase

7270 PC Candleholder

No. 1923 7"
Crimped Vase

6059 PC 8 1/2" Vase

7202 PC Epergne Set

7455 PC 7" Vase

No. 192-10" Basket

Peach Crest	Ware No.	Introduced	Discontinued	Value
Vase, #192-A-9" double crimped		1943	1949	45.00 – 50.00
Vase, #192-A-9" triangular, tulip		1943	1949	45.00 – 50.00
Vase, #194-11" double crimped		1947	1948	65.00 – 85.00
Vase, #194-13" double crimped		1947	1948	80.00 – 95.00
Vase, #194-11" handled		1947	1948	100.00 – 125.00
Vase, #194-13" handled		1947	1948	120.00 – 155.00
Vase, #201-5" double crimped		1940	1948	20.00 – 25.00
Vase, #201-5" flared, square		1940	1948	20.00 – 25.00
Vase, #201-5" triangular		1940	1948	22.00 – 28.00
Vase, #203-5" cupped flared		1940	1943	20.00 – 25.00
Vase, #203-5" cupped oval		1940	1943	20.00 – 25.00
Vase, #203-5" cupped square		1940	1943	20.00 – 25.00
Vase, #203-5" cupped tulip		1940	1943	25.00 – 28.00
Vase, #203-5" double crimped		1940	1943	20.00 – 25.00
Vase, #203-5" oval, triangular		1940	1943	20.00 – 25.00
Vase, #894-10" flared, square		1940	1943	80.00 – 95.00
Vase, #894-10" triangular, tulip		1940	1943	80.00 – 95.00
Vase, #1353-10" double crimped		1942	1943	100.00 – 125.00
Vase, #1353-10" triangular		1942	1943	100.00 – 125.00
Vase, #1523 cornucopia		1940	1943	80.00 – 90.00
Vase, #1922-10" flared, square		1940	1941	85.00 – 100.00
Vase, #1922-10" triangular		1940	1941	85.00 – 100.00
Vase, #1923-7" double crimped		1940	1943	35.00 – 45.00
Vase, #1923-7" square, triangular		1940	1943	35.00 – 45.00
Vase, #1923-7" tulip		1940	1943	38.00 – 47.00
Vase, #1925-6½" double crimped		1940	1943*	28.00 – 32.00
Vase, #1925-6½" triangular		1940	1943	25.00 – 28.00

*Also made from 1954 to 1958 using Ware No. 7256.

The following items were introduced in the No. 711 shape in 1949:

Peach Crest	Ware No.	Introduced	Discontinued	Value
Basket, #711-10½" handled		1949	1952	175.00 – 200.00
Basket, #711-7" handled	7137-PC	1949	1954	85.00 – 95.00
Bowl, #711-7"	7127-PC	1949	1954	35.00 – 40.00
Candy jar, #711 covered		1949	1950	100.00 – 125.00
Creamer, #711-4" handled		1949	1950	35.00 – 45.00
Jug, #711-5½" handled		1949	1952	40.00 – 50.00
Jug, #711-6" handled	7166-PC	1949	1970	45.00 – 55.00
Jug, #711-8" handled		1949	1950	60.00 – 65.00
Jug, #711-9" handled		1949	1952	90.00 – 110.00
Rose bowl, #711-4"		1949	1950	55.00 – 65.00
Vase, #711 miniature crimped		1949	July 1952	37.00 – 42.00
Vase, #711 miniature triangular		1949	July 1952	37.00 – 42.00
Vase, #711 miniature tulip		1949	July 1952	40.00 – 45.00
Vase, #711-4" double crimped	7154-PC	1949	1954	25.00 – 30.00
Vase, #711-4" cupped crimped		1949	1951	25.00 – 30.00
Vase, #711-5½" crimped, tulip		1949	1952	35.00 – 40.00
Vase, #711-5½" triangular		1949	1950	35.00 – 40.00
Vase, #711-5" double crimped	7155-PC	1949	1954	30.00 – 35.00
Vase, #711-6" double crimped	7156-PC	1949	1970	40.00 – 45.00
Vase, #711-6" tulip	7157-PC	1949	1967	40.00 – 45.00

No. 192 A 3-piece Vanity Set

No. 193-11" Hand Vase

No 203-7" Special Basket

No. 192 Squat Cologne

No. 1925-7" Basket

7155 PC 5" Vase

No. 1924 Creamer

No. 1923-6" Top Hat

7137 PC 7" Basket

7154 PC 4" DC Vase

No. 192-8" Handled Jug

7224 PC 10" Bowl

No 1353-10" Vase

Peach Crest	Ware No.	Introduced	Discontinued	Value
Vase, #711-8" double crimped		1949	1952	50.00 – 60.00
Vase, #711-8" tulip		1949	1952	50.00 – 60.00
Vase, #711-9" double crimped		1949	1952	70.00 – 80.00
Vase, #711-9" tulip		1949	1952	80.00 – 85.00

The following new shapes were created after the introduction of ware numbers in July 1952:

Peach Crest	Ware No.	Introduced	Discontinued	Value
Basket, 7" handled	7237-PC	1954	1970	70.00 – 80.00
Bowl, 7"	7227-PC	1954	1970	45.00 – 47.00
Candleholder	7272-PC	1956	1962	45.00 – 50.00
Candleholder, 2-pc.	7277-PC	1954	1955	47.00 – 55.00
Epergne set, 3-pc.	7200-PC	1956	1959	150.00 – 180.00
Epergne set, 2-pc.	7202-PC	1955	1962	110.00 – 125.00
Hand vase, 10"	5155-PC	July 1953	1955	225.00 – 250.00
Shell bowl	9020-PC	July 1955	1965	125.00 – 135.00
Vase, 5"	9055-PC	July 1955	1956	45.00 – 55.00
Vase, 6"	6056-PC	1955	1963	37.00 – 42.00
Vase, 6½"	6058-PC	1955	1962	45.00 – 50.00
Vase, 8½"	6059-PC	1956	1960	75.00 – 85.00
Vase, 4½"	7254-PC	1954	1957	27.00 – 30.00
Vase, #1925-6"	7256-PC	1954	1958	45.00 – 55.00
Vase, 5"	7350-PC	1953	1963	25.00 – 30.00
Vase, 6"	7451-PC	1959	1962	30.00 – 35.00
Vase, 8"	7453-PC	1959	1962	40.00 – 45.00
Vase, 7"	7455-PC	1959	1960	55.00 – 65.00
Vase, 9"	7459-PC	1959	1962	75.00 – 85.00

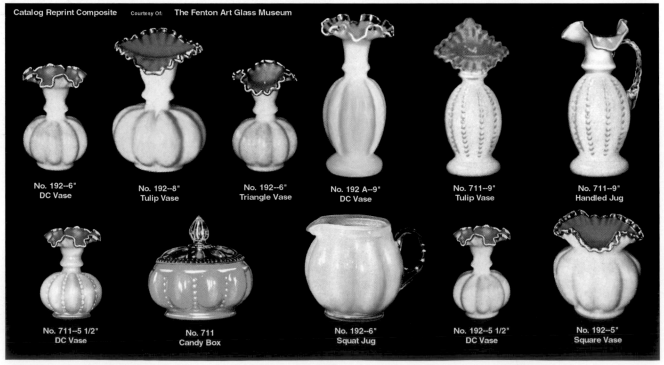

Catalog Reprint Composite   Courtesy Of: The Fenton Art Glass Museum

No. 192--6" DC Vase

No. 192--8" Tulip Vase

No. 192--6" Triangle Vase

No. 192 A--9" DC Vase

No. 711--9" Tulip Vase

No. 711--9" Handled Jug

No. 711--5 1/2" DC Vase

No. 711 Candy Box

No. 192--6" Squat Jug

No. 192--5 1/2" DC Vase

No. 192--5" Square Vase

The Fenton Art Glass Co.,
Williamstown, W.Va.

Open Stock in Peach Crest
Hand Made by Fenton

203.7" Handled Basket

1523.7" Hd'ld. Basket

1523.13" Handled Basket

1923.6" Crimp Top Hat

1523 Cornucopia

1922.10" Hd'ld. Basket

1922.10" Square Vase

1523 Candleholder

1523.13" Double Crimp Bowl

1523 Candleholder

201.10" Hd'ld. Basket

— 1523.3 Pc. D. Crimp Console Set —

1922.10" Crimp Top Hat

1522.10" Triangle Bowl

1522.10" Oval Bowl

1922.10" Fld. Vase

186.7½" Triangle Vase

1522.10" Double Crimp Bowl

No.203.7" Oval Bowl

No.203.7" Square Bowl

No.203.5" Cupped Square Vase

No.187.6" Triangle Vase

No.203.5" Cupped Flared Vase

No.203.4" Rose Bowl

No.203.5" Cup'd. Triangle Vase

No.203.5" Cupped Tulip Vase

No.1923.7" Triangle Vase

No.187.6" Tulip Vase

No.203.5" Double Crimp Vase

No.201.5" Crimped Rose Bowl

No.186.8¼" Double Crimp Vase

No.1923.6½" Square Vase

No.201.5" Triangle Vase

No.201.5" Square Vase

No.186.8½" Square Vase

No.203.5¼" Cupped Oval Bowl

No.187.6" Crimped Vase

No.1923.6½" Double Crimp Vase

No.201.6" Double Crimp Vase

No.1923.7" Tulip Vase

No.186.8½" Tulip Vase

Catalog Reprint
Composite Circa 1940

Courtesy Of:
The Fenton Art Glass Museum

81

Rose Crest

Pieces of Rose Crest were initially produced for Weil Freeman in 1944 and 1945. Due to the favorable reception for this color, Fenton added it to the regular line in 1946. Rose Crest continued in the line for two years before it was discontinued at the end of 1947. After the departure of Rose Crest, new shapes in Aqua Crest were added to the regular line in 1948.

The #1522 bowl was used with an epergne set. This set included the bowl, a block, the epergne, and a base. It was sold with a pair of #951 candles as a six-piece epergne set. The #1522 bowl was also sold with a pair of #951 candles as a three-piece console set.

Rose Crest	Introduced	Discontinued	Value
Basket, #36-4½" handled	1946	1947	75.00 – 85.00
Basket, #36-6½" handled	1946	1947	85.00 – 110.00
Basket, #192-10½" handled	1946	1947	160.00 – 180.00
Basket, #201-10" handled	1946	1947	160.00 – 180.00
Basket, #203-7" handled	1946	1948	85.00 – 100.00
Basket, #1523-13" handled	1946	1948	250.00 – 300.00
Basket, #1924-5" handled	1946	1947	75.00 – 80.00
Bonbon, #36-5½" double crimped, oval, square, triangle	1946	1948	18.00 – 22.00
Bowl, #192-10½" double crimped	1946	1948	75.00 – 80.00
Bowl, #203-7" double crimped, flared, square, triangle	1946	1948	45.00 – 50.00
Bowl, #205-8½"			45.00 – 55.00
Bowl, #680 deep dessert	1946	1948	22.00 – 25.00
Bowl, #1522-10"	1946	1948	75.00 – 85.00
Bowl, #1523-13"	1946	1948	110.00 – 125.00
Candleholder, #192 squat	1946	1948	35.00 – 45.00
Candleholder, #951 cornucopia	1946	1948	45.00 – 50.00
Candlestick, #1523	1946	1948	40.00 – 45.00
Comport, #680-6" ftd. double crimped			35.00 – 45.00
Creamer, #1924 handled	1947	1948	50.00 – 60.00
Cup, #680			40.00 – 50.00
Epergne, #1522 with block	1946	1948	110.00 – 130.00
Jug, #192-32 oz. squat	1947	1948	125.00 – 150.00
Jug, #192-5½" handled	1946	1948	40.00 – 45.00
Jug, #192-6" handled	1946	1948	45.00 – 55.00
Jug, #192-8" handled	1946	1948	90.00 – 125.00
Jug, #192-A-9" handled	1946	1948	125.00 – 150.00
Plate, #680-6"			16.00 – 18.00
Plate, #680-8"			35.00 – 40.00
Plate, #680-10"			75.00 – 85.00
Plate, #680-12"			65.00 – 75.00
Saucer, #680-5½"			10.00 – 12.00
Top hat, #1924-5"	1946	1948	45.00 – 50.00
Vase, #36-4½" double crimped, fan, square, triangular	1946	1948	24.00 – 26.00
Vase, #36-6¼" double crimped, fan, square, triangular	1946	1948	32.00 – 35.00
Vase, #186-8" double crimped, square, triangular, tulip	1946	1948	50.00 – 65.00
Vase, #192-5½" double crimped, square, triangular, tulip	1946	1948	45.00 – 55.00
Vase, #192-5" double crimped, oval, square, triangular	1946	1948	45.00 – 55.00
Vase, #192-6" double crimped, regular	1946	1948	40.00 – 50.00
Vase, #192-6" square, triangular tulip	1946	1948	40.00 – 50.00
Vase, #192-8" double crimped, square, triangular, tulip	1946	1948	65.00 – 85.00
Vase, #573-8" fan			75.00 – 85.00
Vase, #192-A-9" double crimped, square	1946	1948	75.00 – 90.00
Vase, #192-A-9" triangular, tulip	1946	1948	75.00 – 90.00
Vase, #201-5" cupped oval, double crimped	1946	1948	40.00 – 45.00
Vase, #201-5" square, triangular	1946	1948	40.00 – 45.00
Vase, #203-4½" cupped flared, double crimped	1946	1948	25.00 – 35.00
Vase, #203-4½" square, triangular	1946	1948	25.00 – 35.00
Vase, #1924-5" double crimped, square, triangular, tulip	1946	1948	25.00 – 30.00
*Vase, #4517-6½"			65.00 – 85.00
*Vase, #4517-11"			200.00 – 225.00

* Made for Weil Ceramics, not in the regular line.

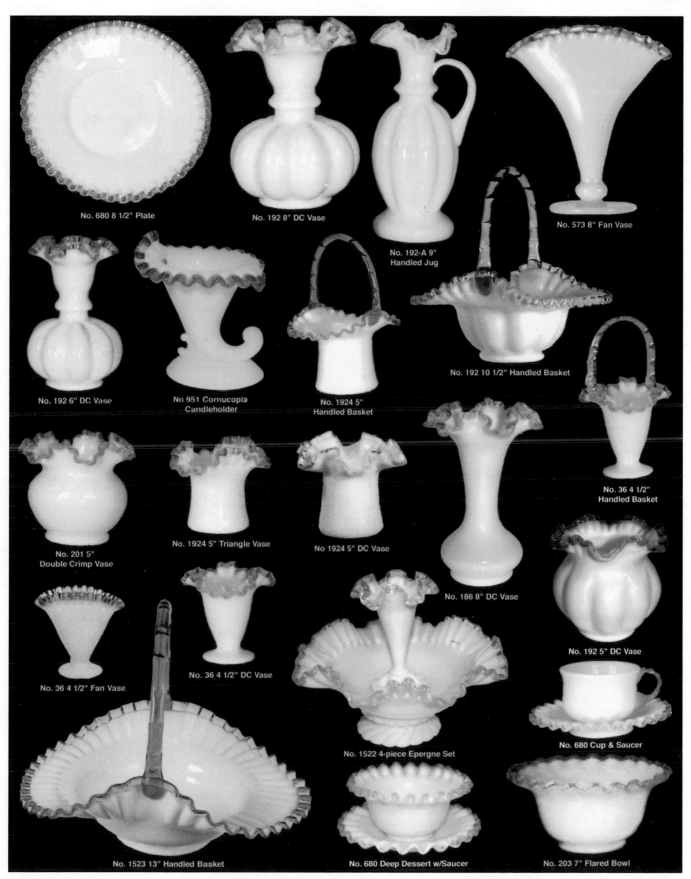

No. 680 8 1/2" Plate

No. 192 8" DC Vase

No. 192-A 9" Handled Jug

No. 573 8" Fan Vase

No. 192 6" DC Vase

No 951 Cornucopia Candleholder

No. 1924 5" Handled Basket

No. 192 10 1/2" Handled Basket

No. 36 4 1/2" Handled Basket

No. 201 5" Double Crimp Vase

No. 1924 5" Triangle Vase

No 1924 5" DC Vase

No. 186 8" DC Vase

No. 192 5" DC Vase

No. 36 4 1/2" Fan Vase

No. 36 4 1/2" DC Vase

No. 1522 4-piece Epergne Set

No. 680 Cup & Saucer

No. 1523 13" Handled Basket

No. 680 Deep Dessert w/Saucer

No. 203 7" Flared Bowl

Silver Crest

Silver Crest replaced Crystal Crest in the Fenton line during mid-1942. Silver Crest is similar in appearance to items in the Crystal Crest pattern. The difference in the two patterns is Silver Crest pieces lack the outer opal edge that Crystal Crest pieces have. Silver Crest was easier and more economical to produce since it only required the addition of a single spun glass layer around the edge of the finished piece.

Fenton's sales of Silver Crest were excellent through the late 1940s. At the end of 1948, the No. 192 shape was discontinued. In January 1949 pieces of Silver Crest were introduced in the new No. 711 shape. This new shape is sometimes referred to as Beaded Melon. Production of Silver Crest diminished during the 1950s when producing milk glass Hobnail was the priority. However, during the early 1960s there was a renewed interest in Silver Crest. Production of Silver Crest peaked during the 1960s. Many pieces of this pattern were discontinued in the late 1960s and early 1970s, but a few pieces were made into the 1980s. By the mid-1980s the emphasis began to shift away from traditional shapes and patterns. Thus, only six plain and eight Spanish Lace Silver Crest shapes appeared in the 1985 – 1986 catalog. No Silver Crest items were listed in the 1987 – 1988 catalog.

Generally, dating pieces of Silver Crest that were made over a long period of time is done in the following manner by veteran collectors. To identify older items — those produced before 1958 — look for a fiery opal glow when the piece is held to a light. Pieces produced before 1958 were made with Fenton's opal formula and are translucent compared to the later issues. Production after 1958 used the more dense milk glass formula and there is no opalescence. Starting in 1970, Fenton began using an embossed "Fenton" logo in an oval ring. Later, in the 1980s, a small "8" was inserted below the Fenton logo. This small number is often difficult to distinguish and may be entirely missing on some pieces.

Through the many years of production, Fenton made a number of similar items. Hopefully, the accompanying photos will solve many of the mysteries, but a few items may need further clarification. The original No. 1522 epergne set was sold as a four-piece set with a 10" double crimped bowl, a base, a small flower block, and the epergne vase. This item was in the line through 1950 and was also listed as a six-piece set when sold with a pair of No. 951 cornucopia candles. This six-piece set retailed for $5.50 in a 1944 Montgomery Ward catalog. Later, beginning in the mid-1950s, numerous other epergne sets were introduced. These sets used bowls with molded holes for the accompanying vases. The 4804-SC epergne set is Diamond Lace with Silver Crest. All the two, three, four, and five piece epergne sets in the listing below include only the bowl and vases. Candles are listed and priced separately.

Starting in the late 1940s, Fenton began drilling plates and bowls to be used in combination with metal handles to form tidbits and servers. Most early tidbits, produced through 1955, are pictured in the catalogs with an open "C" style handle. Beginning with the January 1954 catalog, servers are pictured with both the open and closed style handles. Later, tidbits were made using chrome metal parts with a closed handle. The early No. 680 two and three tier bowl combinations were referred to as planters in the Fenton catalogs. These planters were made from 1950 through 1952.

Silver Crest vanity sets made an appearance with the introduction of the pattern in 1943. Several combinations of vanity sets may be found. The original No. 192-A vanity sets appeared in the catalog with two small cologne bottles and the puff box. This set was sold by Montgomery Ward for $3.95 in 1944. Two squat cologne bottles were also sold in combination with this same puff box as a No. 192 vanity set. The squat cologne bottle is shaped like the small round colognes. However, it is slightly larger. The squat cologne was also sold without a stopper for use as a candleholder. The opening of the candleholder is slightly larger to fit a candle and is not ground to fit a stopper. The 5½" tall cologne bottles were also used with the small puff box to form a vanity set. The larger 7" bottle may sometimes be found used in sets with the large No. 192 bath salts or candy box. These larger types of sets are more commonly found in hand-decorated vanity sets that were decorated by another company. The No. 711 Beaded Melon style vanity set replaced the No. 192 shapes in 1949. There were no squat colognes or 7" bottles in this shape.

The No. 711 seven-piece juice set was comprised of the No. 711 squat jug and six No. 711-5 oz. tumblers. This set was introduced in 1949 and was listed as discontinued in the 1950 catalog. Collectors should expect to have a great deal of difficulty finding both the squat jug and the tumblers.

The No. 680 cup and sugar and creamer were introduced in 1948. Catalogs show these pieces underwent significant style changes by the next year. The creamer initially had a reeded handle and a silver crest around the top edge. The sugar was handleless and had a crest around the top. It looked much like a mayo. By 1949, both pieces were redesigned to look more like a traditional sugar and creamer. The sugar appeared with two crystal handles and the crest around the top was missing. The crest also disappeared from the top of the creamer and the reeded handle was changed to the regular style applied handle. The reeded handle of the cup was also changed to a regular style applied crystal type.

The No. 680-10" salad bowl was sold in combination with the No. 680-12" plate to form a salad set. A 3-piece console set was formed by combining the No. 1522-10" bowl with a pair of No. 951 cornucopia candles. The punch set was sold as a 15-piece set. Items in the set included a large punch bowl, pedestal base, 12 cups, and a No. 9522 large crystal ladle. Other desirable and hard-to-find items include both styles of salt and pepper shakers, the punch set, the large epergnes, hurricane lamp, "Poppy" Gone with the Wind lamp, and 70 oz. jug.

An embossed Spanish Lace design in Silver Crest was added to the line in 1962 with the introduction of an 11" footed cake plate. Beginning in 1965, other pieces were added in Spanish Lace. Other additions occurred to this line throughout the 1970s and most of the 12-item line continued in production into the early 1980s. For more information, see page 104.

One of Fenton's most popular hand-painted decorations — Decorated Violets (DV) — called "Violets in the Snow" by collectors, was introduced on numerous Silver Crest pieces in July 1968. This famous Louise Piper design continued in the line into the 1980s. For more information on this decoration see page 97.

Decorated Silver Crest reappeared in the Fenton January 1989 supplement and continued into the 1990 – 1991 catalog. The following 12 items from the Elizabeth Collection are decorated with a blue floral sprig:

#5151 ES bear cub figure	#9357 ES Basket Weave vase
#6780 ES candy box	#7693 ES Beaded Melon 6" vase
#9295 ES Rose slipper	#5165 ES cat figure
#9252 ES 6½" Embossed Rose vase	#6761 ES Paisley bell
#7692 ES Beaded Melon pitcher	#9229 ES Empress bell
#7694 ES 7" Aurora vase	#9266 ES 4½" Bow and Drape bell

In 1950 and 1951, Fenton began using a silver crest on a few items in the Diamond Lace pattern. The four items below were made with a silver crest in Diamond Lace. For more information on this pattern, see the Diamond Lace section of this book.

Diamond Lace pattern in Blue Opalescent w/Silver Crest

#1948-12" 4-pc. epergne set	#1948-14" cake plate
#1948-12" bowl w/plain bottom	#1948 footed comport, double crimped

The price guide below is divided into two separate sections. The first listing includes items made using the early numbering system from the introduction of Silver Crest in 1943 through the transition to the new No. 711 shape in 1949 and ends with the introduction of ware numbers in July 1952. The second table includes new pieces of Silver Crest placed in the line after July 1952 and continues through 1979. Earlier items that remained in continuous production through the numbering transition are only listed in the first table. These pieces are listed with both the old and new identifying numbers to make their identification easier.

Silver Crest	Ware No.	Introduced	Discontinued	Value
Base, #1522 (opal)		1946	1951	30.00 – 35.00
Basket, #36-4½" cone shape		1943	1947	28.00 – 32.00
Basket, #36-6¼" cone shape		1943	1947	35.00 – 40.00
Basket, #36-8" cone shape		1943	1947	60.00 – 75.00
Basket, #37-2½" miniature fan, flared, oval, square		1943	1948	100.00 – 125.00
Basket, #192-10½" handled		1943	1948	100.00 – 125.00
Basket, #201-10" handled		1946	1947	100.00 – 125.00
Basket, #203-7" handled	7237-SC	1943	1980+	45.00 – 55.00
Basket, #680-5" handled	7236-SC	1949	1954	35.00 – 45.00
Basket, #711-7" handled		1949	1952	80.00 – 90.00
Basket, #1523-13" handled	7233-SC	1943	1971	165.00 – 185.00
Basket, 1924-5" handled		1943	1952	65.00 – 85.00
Bonbon, #36-5½" double crimped	7225-SC	1943	1980+	10.00 – 12.00
Bonbon, #36-5½" oval, square, triangle		1943	1952	10.00 – 12.00
Bottle, #192 squat cologne		1943	1949	55.00 – 60.00

Silver Crest	Ware No.	Introduced	Discontinued	Value
Bottle, #192-5½"		1943	1949	50.00 – 60.00
Bottle, #192-7"		1943	1949	60.00 – 75.00
Bottle, #192-A cologne or vanity bottle		1943	1949	45.00 – 50.00
Bottle, #711 vanity		1949	1952	55.00 – 65.00
Bottle, #711-5½"		1949	1952	55.00 – 65.00
Bowl, #192-10½" double crimped		1943	1949	45.00 – 55.00
Bowl, #202 dessert or finger bowl		1943	1948	16.00 – 19.00
Bowl, #203-7" double crimped	7227-SC	1943	1980+	18.00 – 20.00
Bowl, #203-7" cupped flared, square, triangle		1943	1952	18.00 – 20.00
Bowl, #205-8½"		1943	1948	40.00 – 45.00
Bowl, #680 deep dessert	7221-SC	1948	1962	15.00 – 18.00
Bowl, #680 low dessert	7222-SC	1948	1966	15.00 – 18.00
Bowl, #680-5½" soup	7320-SC	1949	1956	30.00 – 35.00
Bowl, #680-8½" flared		1949	1952	30.00 – 40.00
Bowl, #680-10" salad	7220-SC	1948	1956	55.00 – 65.00
Bowl, #682-9½" regular		1943	1948	35.00 – 40.00
Bowl, #711-7"		1949	1952	30.00 – 35.00
Bowl, #1522-10" double crimped	7224-SC	1943	1971	45.00 – 55.00
Bowl, #1522-10" triangle		1943	1952	45.00 – 55.00
Bowl, #1523-13"	7223-SC	1943	1971	65.00 – 85.00
Cake plate, #680-13" ftd.	7213-SC	1952	1980	45.00 – 55.00
Candleholder #192 squat		1943	1949	25.00 – 28.00
Candleholder, #680		1949	1952	35.00 – 45.00
Candleholder, #951 cornucopia	7274-SC	1946	1966	25.00 – 32.00
Candleholder, #1523	7270-SC	1943	1954	32.00 – 35.00
Comport, #680 ftd. double crimped	7228-SC	1949	1980+	25.00 – 30.00
Creamer, #680 original style		1948	1949	75.00 – 85.00
Creamer, #680-3¼"	7261-SC	1948	1967	25.00 – 30.00
Creamer, #711-4" handled		1949	1950	30.00 – 35.00
Creamer, 1924-5" handled		1947	1949	25.00 – 32.00
Cup, #680		1948	1952	28.00 – 32.00
Epergne and block, #1522		1946	1951	60.00 – 70.00
Hand vase, #193-11"		1943	1948	200.00 – 250.00
Jar, #192 covered candy or bath powder		1943	1949	60.00 – 75.00
Jar, #711 covered candy		1949	1952	85.00 – 95.00
Jug, #192 squat		1943	1949	65.00 – 75.00
Jug, #192-5" handled		1943	1946	28.00 – 32.00
Jug, #192-5½" handled		1943	1949	32.00 – 35.00
Jug, #192-6" handled		1943	1949	35.00 – 37.00
Jug, #192-8" handled		1943	1949	55.00 – 60.00
Jug, #192-A-9" handled		1943	1949	60.00 – 75.00
Jug, #711 squat		1949	1950	85.00 – 95.00
Jug, #711-5½" handled		1949	1950	30.00 – 35.00
Jug, #711-6" handled		1949	1950	32.00 – 40.00
Jug, #711-8" handled		1949	1950	55.00 – 60.00
Jug, #711-9" handled		1949	1950	75.00 – 90.00
Nut dish, #680 ftd.	7229-SC	1948	1980+	22.00 – 27.00
Oil, #680	7269-SC	1950	1955	85.00 – 125.00
Planter, #680 2-tier		1950	1952	55.00 – 65.00
Planter, #680 3-tier		1950	1952	60.00 – 80.00
Plate, #680-6½"	7219-SC	1943	1965	8.00 – 10.00
Plate, #680-8½"	7217-SC	1948	1971	12.00 – 15.00
Plate, #681-9"		1943	1949	25.00 – 30.00
Plate, #680-10"	7210-SC	1948	1967	40.00 – 50.00
Plate, #680-12"	7212-SC	1948	1960	40.00 – 45.00

7233 SC 13" Basket

No. 1924 5" DC Vase

No. 192 10 1/2" Basket

No. 192-A 3-Piece Vanity Set

No. 186 8" Triangle Vase

7339 SC Divided Basket

No. 186 8 1/2" Tulip Vase

No. 192 Candy or Bath Powder Jar

No. 192 Squat Candleholder

No. 192 Squat Cologne Bottle

No. 192 7" Bottle

No. 192 5 1/2" Bottle

No. 1924 5" Basket

7247 MI Punch Cup

7313 SC Punch Bowl
7378 SC Pedestal Base

7247 MI Punch Cup

7202 SC Epergne Set

No. 1522 Epergne Set

Silver Crest	Ware No.	Introduced	Discontinued	Value
Plate, #682-12"		1943	1949	40.00 – 45.00
Puff box, #192-A covered		1943	1949	30.00 – 35.00
Puff box, #711 covered		1949	1952	40.00 – 55.00
Rose bowl, #711-4"		1949	1950	30.00 – 35.00
Saucer, #680-5½"	7280-SC	1948	1965	8.00 – 10.00
Sherbet, #680 ftd.	7226-SC	1948	1965	15.00 – 18.00
Sugar, #680 original style		1948	1949	75.00 – 85.00
Sugar, #680	7231-SC	1948	1967	25.00 – 30.00
Top hat, 1924-5"		1943	1952	25.00 – 28.00
Tray, #680 2-tier tidbit	7297-SC	1948	1955	30.00 – 40.00
Tray, #680 3-tier tidbit	7298-SC	1948	1955	40.00 – 60.00
Tumbler, #711-5 oz.		1949	1950	55.00 – 65.00
Vanity set, #192 3-pc.		1943	1949	130.00 – 152.00
Vanity set, #192-A 3-pc.		1943	1949	120.00 – 132.00
Vanity set, #711		1949	1952	150.00 – 175.00
Vase, #36-4½" double crimped	7354-SC	1943	1967	14.00 – 16.00
Vase, #36-4½" fan	7355-SC	1943	1958	18.00 – 20.00
Vase, #36-4½" square, triangle		1943	1952	14.00 – 16.00
Vase, #36-6¼" double crimped	7356-SC	1943	1967	16.00 – 18.00
Vase, #36-6¼" fan	7357-SC	1943	1958	20.00 – 22.00
Vase, #36-6¼" square, triangle		1943	1952	16.00 – 18.00
Vase, #37-2" miniature fan, flared, oval		1943	1948	65.00 – 75.00
Vase, #37-2" miniature square, triangle, tulip		1943	1949	65.00 – 7.00
Vase, #186-8" double crimped	7258-SC	1943	1967	25.00 – 30.00
Vase, #186-8" square, triangle, tulip		1943	1952	28.00 – 32.00
Vase, #192-5" double crimped, flared, oval, square, triangle		1943	1949	18.00 – 20.00
Vase, #192-5½" double crimped, oval, square, triangle, tulip		1943	1949	20.00 – 22.00
Vase, #192-6" double crimped, oval, regular, square		1943	1949	22.00 – 25.00
Vase, #192-6" triangle, tulip		1943	1949	22.00 – 25.00
Vase, #192-8" double crimped, square, triangle, tulip		1943	1949	25.00 – 30.00
Vase, #192-10" double crimped, square, triangle, tulip		1943	1948	35.00 – 40.00
Vase, #192-A-9" double crimped, square		1943	1949	28.00 – 35.00
Vase, #192-A-9" triangle, tulip		1943	1949	28.00 – 35.00
Vase, #201-5" cupped oval, double crimped		1943	1948	20.00 – 25.00
Vase, #201-5" square, triangle		1943	1948	20.00 – 25.00
Vase, #203-4½" double crimped	7254-SC	1943	1973	15.00 – 18.00
Vase, #203-4½" cupped flared, square, triangle		1943	1952	18.00 – 20.00
Vase, #573-8" fan				45.00 – 55.00
Vase, #711 miniature crimped, triangle, tulip		1949	1952	30.00 – 35.00
Vase, #711-4" cupped crimped, double crimped		1949	1952	22.00 – 27.00
Vase, #711-5" double crimped		1949	1952	22.00 – 27.00
Vase, #711-5½" crimped, triangle, tulip		1949	1950	22.00 – 27.00
Vase, #711-6" double crimped	7156-SC	1949	1972	28.00 – 30.00

7430 SC Flared
Footed Comport

7269 SC Oil

7429 SC Footed DC Comport

No. 36 4 1/2" Basket

7436 SC 6 1/2" Basket

7272 SC
Candleholder

7333 SC Handled Relish

7329 SC Low Footed Comport

7425 SC 7 1/2" Bowl

7228 SC Footed Comport

7204 SC 12" Basket

7227 SC 7" Bowl

7203 SC Mayonnaise Set

7271 SC Candleholder

7321 SC 11 1/2" DC Bowl

7434 SC 11"
Deep Basket

7305 SC 5-Pc. Epergne Set

7308 SC 4-Pc. Epergne Set

7232 SC Footed Ivy Ball

7223 SC 13" Bowl

5824 SC Banana Bowl

7474 SC 6"
Candleholder

5823 SC 11" Bowl

Silver Crest	Ware No.	Introduced	Discontinued	Value
Vase, #711-6" tulip	7157-SC	1949	1958	28.00 – 35.00
Vase, #835-5½" double crimped				85.00 – 100.00
Vase, #4517-6½"		1951	1952	25.00 – 30.00
Vase, #711-8" double crimped, tulip		1949	1950	35.00 – 45.00
Vase, #711-9" double crimped, tulip		1949	1952	45.00 – 55.00
Vase, 1924-5" double crimped, square, triangle, tulip		1943	1952	40.00 – 45.00
Vase, #4517-10"		1951	1952	75.00 – 90.00

Silver Crest Shapes Introduced After July 1952

The following tidbit servers were made during this era.

Tidbit	Ware No.	Introduced	Discontinued	Plate Sizes
Tidbit, 2-tier	7294-SC	1954	1980+	12½", 8½"
Tidbit, 2-tier	7296-SC	1954	1979	8½", 6"
Tidbit, 2-tier	7394-SC	1958	1976	11½", 8"
Tidbit, 3-tier	7295-SC	1954	1978	12½", 8½", 5½"
Tidbit, 3-tier	7397-SC	1956	1960	16½", 11½", 8½"

Other items with metal handles made during this period include the No. 7498-SC bonbon and the 7497-SC two-tier bonbon.

Early versions of the No. 680 cup were made with an applied crystal handle. This cup became the 7248-MI cup starting in July 1952 when the company changed to the ware number system. Another style milk glass cup — 7249-MI — with a foot was introduced to the line in 1956. The 7248-MI cup was discontinued at this time.

Ware number set designations reserved for combinations of individual items after July 1952 included:

7201-SC — 7231-SC sugar and 7261-SC creamer (No. 680 restyled).

7204-SC 3-piece console set — 1-7224-SC-10" bowl & 2-7274 cornucopia candles.

7208-SC cup and saucer set — 7248-MI cup and 7218-SC saucer (prior to 1956).

7209-SC cup and saucer set — 7249-MI cup and 7218-SC saucer (after 1956).

7306-SC 15-piece punch set — 1-7317-SC punch bowl, 12-7247-MI punch cup, 1-7378 pedestal, and 1-9522-CY ladle. (The ladle may be either milk glass or crystal, and the punch cups are entirely milk glass.)

The 7458-SC 11" vase was made in 1971. It has the same ware number as an earlier 8½" vase made during the 1960s. The following items were introduced after the introduction of ware numbers in July 1952:

Silver Crest	Ware No.	Introduced	Discontinued	Value
Ashtray	7377-SC	1960	1965*	35.00 – 45.00
Ashtray	7377-SC	1970	1971	35.00 – 45.00
Basket, small	7436-SC	1970	1977	45.00 – 50.00
Basket, 6½" handled	7336-SC	1957	1980+	27.00 – 38.00
Basket, divided	7339-SC	1958	1960	75.00 – 90.00
Basket, 11" deep	7434-SC	1975	1978	100.00 – 125.00
Basket, 12" handled	7234-SC	1958	1980+	100.00 – 125.00
Bonbon, 8"	7428-SC	1958	1980	18.00 – 22.00
Bonbon, with metal handle	7498-SC	1968	1980+	25.00 – 28.00
Bonbon, 2-tier	7497-SC	1979	1980+	35.00 – 42.00

*Was not listed in the line between January 1965 and December 1969.

7427 SC Footed Bowl

7377 SC Ashtray

7342 SC Footed Tumbler

7467 SC 70 oz. Jug

7334 SC Divided Relish

7324 SC Banana Bowl

7226 SC Sherbet

7229 SC Nut Dish

No. 192-5" Vase

7293 SC 8" Top Hat

7454 SC 9" Vase

No. 680-8 1/2" Flared Bowl

7316 SC Shallow Bowl

7211 SC 12 1/2" Plate

7450 SC 10" Vase

7336 SC 6 1/2" Handled Basket

7237 SC 7" Basket

No. 680 Candleholder

Silver Crest	Ware No.	Introduced	Discontinued	Value
Bowl, banana	5824-SC	1957	1969	38.00 – 42.00
Bowl, banana	7324-SC	1956	1967	45.00 – 60.00
Bowl, divided relish	7334-SC	1958	1967	28.00 – 35.00
Bowl, ftd.	7427-SC	1960	1976	45.00 – 60.00
Bowl, ftd. square	7330-SC	1955	1965	125.00 – 150.00
Bowl, heart-shape relish	7333-SC	1955	1980+	20.00 – 26.00
Bowl, shallow	7316-SC	1956	1971	40.00 – 48.00
Bowl, 7" serving	7335-SC	1955	1956	25.00 – 30.00
Bowl, 7½"	7425-SC	1961	1978	25.00 – 30.00
Bowl, 8½"	7338-SC	1957	1962	40.00 – 45.00
Bowl, 9½"	7423-SC	1969	1976	25.00 – 35.00
Bowl, 11"	5823-SC	1958	1969	50.00 – 60.00
Bowl, 11½" double crimped	7321-SC	1958	1980+	45.00 – 55.00
Bowl, 14"	7323-SC	1958	1963	55.00 – 65.00
Cake plate, low ftd.	5813-SC	1954	1980+	35.00 – 40.00
Candleholder	7272-SC	1956	1963	30.00 – 35.00
Candleholder, 3½"	7271-SC	1956	1980+	14.00 – 16.00
Candleholder, 6"	7474-SC	1963	1978	20.00 – 22.00
Candy box	7280-SC	1956	1965	45.00 – 55.00
Chip 'n Dip	7303-SC	1957	1967	65.00 – 85.00
Chip 'n Dip	7402-SC	1975	1976	70.00 – 85.00
Comport, low ftd.	7329-SC	1954	1978	25.00 – 28.00
Comport, ftd. flared	7429-SC	1961	1980+	25.00 – 35.00
Comport, ftd. flared	7430-SC	1961	1967	35.00 – 45.00
Cup	7248-MI	1952	1956	28.00 – 30.00
Cup	7249-MI	1956	1965	22.00 – 27.00
Cup and saucer	7208-SC	1952	1956	32.00 – 35.00
Cup and saucer	7209-SC	1956	1965	25.00 – 32.00
Epergne set	7202-SC	1955	1965	65.00 – 90.00
Epergne set, 2-pc.	7402-SC	1963	1965	100.00 – 125.00
Epergne set, 2-pc.	7301-SC	1957	1959	100.00 – 125.00
Epergne set, 3-pc.	7200-SC	1956	1960	85.00 – 125.00
Epergne set, 4-pc.	7308-SC	1956	1980+	125.00 – 145.00
Epergne set, 5-pc.	7305-SC	1956	1978	145.00 – 185.00
Hurricane lamp	7290-SC	1956	July 1956	100.00 – 125.00
Ivy Ball, ftd.	7232-SC	1956	1959	40.00 – 45.00
Jug, 70 oz.	7467-SC	1960	1965	300.oz – 325.00
Lamp, "Poppy" Gone w/the Wind	3509-SC	July 1976	1980+	300.00 – 350.00
Mayonnaise set, 3-pc. with ladle	7203-SC	1954	1978	35.00 – 45.00
Pedestal, for punch bowl	7378-SC	1956	1963	75.00 – 85.00
Plate, low ftd.	7312-SC	1954	1956	35.00 – 45.00
Plate, 12½"	7211-SC	1956	1972	40.00 – 45.00
Punch bowl	7317-SC	1956	1963	300.00 – 400.00
Punch cup	7247-MI	1956	1963	18.00 – 20.00
Punch set, 15 pc.	7306-SC	1956	1963	590.00 – 725.00
Salt & pepper	7206-SC	1956	1959	85.00 – 90.00
Salt & pepper, ftd.	7406-SC	1964	July 1964	150.00 – 185.00
Saucer, 5½"	7218-SC	1952	1965	8.00 – 10.00
Shrimp and dip, with toothpick holder	7403-SC	1963	1975	65.00 – 85.00
Tidbit, 2-tier	7294-SC	1954	1980+	40.00 – 45.00
Tidbit, 2-tier	7296-SC	1954	1979	35.00 – 45.00
Tidbit, 2-tier	7394-SC	1958	1976	40.00 – 45.00
Tidbit, 3-tier	7295-SC	1954	1978	55.00 – 65.00
Tidbit, 3-tier	7397-SC	1956	1960	65.00 – 75.00
Top hat, 5"	7292-SC	1968	1970	40.00 – 45.00

7498 SC Handled Bonbon

7303 SC Chip 'n Dip

7394 SC 2 Tier Tidbit

7213 SC Footed Cake Plate

7323 SC 14" Bowl

7296 SC 2 Tier Tidbit

7295 SC 3 Tier Tidbit

7291 SC Sandwich Tray

5813 SC Low Footed Cake Plate

7294 SC 2 Tier Tidbit

Silver Crest	Ware No.	Introduced	Discontinued	Value
Top hat, 8"	7293-SC	1968	1969	100.00 – 145.00
Torte plate, 16"	7216-SC	1954	1971	50.00 – 65.00
Tray, sandwich (chrome handle)	7291-SC	1957	1980+	40.00 – 45.00
Tumbler, ftd.	7342-SC	1957	1963	55.00 – 65.00
*Vase, #36-4½" fan	7355-SC	1970	1971	18.00 – 20.00
Vase, 6"	7451-SC	1959	1980+	22.00 – 25.00
*Vase, #36-6¼" fan	7357-SC	1970	1971	20.00 – 22.00
Vase, 7"	7455-SC	1959	1960	28.00 – 35.00
Vase, 8"	5859-SC	1961	1965	35.00 – 45.00
Vase, 8"	7453-SC	1959	1965	25.00 – 30.00
Vase, 8½"	7458-SC	1959	1960	50.00 – 55.00
Vase, 9"	7454-SC	1959	1962	65.00 – 75.00
Vase, 9"	7459-SC	1959	1961	35.00 – 45.00
Vase, 10"	7450-SC	1959	1960	90.00 – 100.00
Vase, 11"	7458-SC	1971	1972	100.00 – 125.00
Vase, 12"	7262-SC	1956	1967	100.00 – 145.00

*Reintroduced

No. 680 Cup & Saucer (1948)
No. 680 Sugar & Cream (1948)
No. 680 Cup & Saucer (1949-1952)
7208 SC Cup & Saucer
7209 SC Cup & Saucer

No. 192 A 9"
Handled Jug

7450 SC 10" Vase

7262 SC 12" Vase

7459 SC 9" Vase

7458 SC 8" Vase

7224 SC 10" Bowl

7225 SC 5 1/2"
Bonbon

7455 SC 7"
Vase

7356 SC 6 1/4"
DC Vase

7274 SC Cornucopia
Candleholder

7280 SC Footed
Candy Box

7338 SC 8 1/2" Bowl

7453 SC 8"
Vase

5859 SC 8"
Vase

7156 SC 6"
Vase

7451 SC 6"
Vase

7221 SC
Deep Dessert

7406 SC
Salt & Pepper

7354 SC 4 1/2"
DC Vase

7201 SC Sugar & Cream

7206 SC
Salt & Pepper

7254 SC 4 1/2"
Vase

7320 SC Soup

7258 SC 8"
DC Vase

7256 SC 6"
Vase

7357 SC 6 1/4"
Fan Vase

7270 SC
Candleholder

7222 SC Low
Dessert

7220 SC 10" Salad Bowl

Silver Crest with Apple Blossom Decoration

Following the success of Violets in the Snow the previous year, Fenton introduced Louise Piper's Apple Blossom decoration in July 1969. The Apple Blossom decoration consists of a pink hand-painted floral pattern on pieces of Silver Crest. This decoration was created especially for the 1969 Christmas season and was only produced for 18 months — from July 1969 through December 1970.

Apple Blossom	Ware No.	Introduced	Discontinued	Value
Basket, small	7436-AB	July 1969	1971	65.00 – 75.00
Basket, 6½" handled	7336-AB	July 1969	1971	85.00 – 95.00
Bonbon, 5½" DC	7225-AB	July 1969	1971	20.00 – 25.00
Bowl, 9½"	7423-AB	July 1969	1971	55.00 – 65.00
Candleholder	7271-AB	July 1969	1971	25.00 – 32.00
Comport, low ftd.	7329-AB	July 1969	1971	35.00 – 40.00
Comport, ftd.	7429-AB	July 1969	1971	55.00 – 70.00
Vase, 6"	7451-AB	July 1969	1971	30.00 – 35.00
Vase, 8"	7258-AB	July 1969	1971	50.00 – 60.00

7329 AB
Low Footed Comport

7429 AB
Footed Comport

7336 AB 6 1/2"
Handled Basket

7258 AB 8" Vase

7225 AB 5 1/2"
Bonbon

7271 AB Candleholder

7436 AB Small Basket

7423 AB 9 1/2" Bowl

7451 AB 6" Vase

Silver Crest with Violets in the Snow Decoration

Decorated Violets (DV), introduced in July 1968 was the first Louise Piper decoration developed for Fenton. Inspiration for the decoration came from Carl Voigt, a Fenton sales representative from New York. The decoration consists of small hand-painted violets on a milk glass background. This pattern later became more popularly known as Violets in the Snow.

The initial offering consisted of an assortment of 16 different pieces. The popularity of the pattern resulted in the addition of numerous other pieces with this design through the 1970s. Many items chosen for decorating came from Fenton's Silver Crest line. Other popular items were animal figures and small novelty items such as baskets, vases, and candy boxes. Note the listing below includes these items. It is not limited to decorated Silver Crest pieces. Since the pattern was produced over a number of years, used on pieces of various sizes, and hand painted by a number of different artists, the violets decoration may vary slightly in size and shape. Even two items of the same type may be found with slightly different decorations. This pattern was discontinued at the end of 1984.

Collectors should note several items were only decorated with this pattern for a very short time. The No. 7377 ashtray, No. 3580 candy box, No. 7357-6¼" fan vase, No. 7404-33" table lamp, and the No. 9307 Classic lamp were only decorated for one year. Decoration of the No. 7464 pitcher and No. 8494 square planter only continued two years.

Beginning in January 1974, this hand-painted violet decoration was also used with Spanish Lace Silver Crest pieces. For more information, see page 109.

In January 1982, four pieces from Fenton's Basketweave pattern were selected for decoration with this pattern. These items consisted of a basket, a bell, a candlelight, and a chamberstick.

Other items in addition to those in the listing below will sometimes be found. Fenton produced samples, whimsies, or limited edition pieces that were sold through the Fenton Gift Shop or were made for one of the collectors' clubs. Also, Martin House, a former gift and antique shop in Williamstown, West Virginia, bought milk glass and Silver Crest blanks to decorate with a violets pattern.

Violets in the Snow	Ware No.	Introduced	Discontinued	Value
Ashtray	7377-DV	1970	1971	45.00 – 55.00
Basket, small	7436-DV	July 1968	1980+	65.00 – 85.00
Basket	7437-DV	July 1968	1980	75.00 – 85.00
Basket, 6½" handled	7336 DV	July 1968	1978	85.00 – 95.00
Basket, 7"	7237-DV	1978	1980+	125.00 – 135.00
Bell, Medallion	8267-DV	1978	1980+	55.00 – 60.00
Bird, Happiness	5197-DV	1976	1980+	40.00 – 45.00
Bird, small	5163-DV	1978	1980+	30.00 – 37.00
Bonbon, 5½" DC	7225-DV	July 1968	1978	20.00 – 25.00
Bonbon w/metal handle	7498-DV	July 1968	1978	50.00 – 60.00
Bowl, heart-shape relish	7333-DV	July 1968	1972	55.00 – 60.00
Bowl, 9½"	7423-DV	July 1968	1976	65.00 – 75.00
Bunny	5162-DV	1978	1980+	40.00 – 45.00
Cakeplate, 13" ftd.	7213-DV	July 1968	1972	100.00 – 145.00
Candleholder	7271-DV	1969	1973	35.00 – 40.00
Candleholder, 6"	7474-DV	July 1968	1972	37.00 – 45.00
Candy box	6080-DV	July 1968	1971	125.00 – 155.00
Candy box	7484-DV	1979	1980+	65.00 – 75.00
Candy box, Medallion	8288-DV	1976	1979	125.00 – 145.00
Cat	5165-DV	1979	1980+	40.00 – 45.00
Comport, ftd.	7429-DV	July 1968	1980+	45.00 – 55.00
Comport, low ftd.	7329-DV	July 1968	1978	40.00 – 50.00
Fairy light, 2-pc.	7300-DV	1976	1980	55.00 – 65.00
Frog	5166-DV	1979	1980+	35.00 – 45.00
Lamp, 19" Mariner's	7400-DV	1969	1972	275.00 – 325.00
Lamp, 19½" student	9308-DV	1973	1980+	225.00 – 275.00
Lamp, 21" Classic	9307-DV	1978	1979	250.00 – 350.00
Lamp, 33" table	7404-DV	1971	1972	225.00 – 250.00
Pitcher	7464-DV	1969	1971	55.00 – 65.00
Planter, square	8494-DV	1978	1980	60.00 – 70.00
Swan	5161-DV	1978	1980+	40.00 – 42.00

Violets in the Snow	Ware No.	Introduced	Discontinued	Value
Top hat, 5"	7292-DV	July 1968	1970	50.00 – 60.00
Tidbit, 2-tier	7294-DV	July 1968	1972	85.00 – 95.00
Vase, bud	9056-DV	1976	1980+	30.00 – 35.00
Vase, 4½"	7254-DV	1975	1980+	30.00 – 35.00
Vase, 4½" fan	7355-DV	1970	1972	30.00 –35.00
Vase, 6"	7451-DV	July 1968	1980+	35.00 – 45.00
Vase, 6"	7256-DV	1976	1978	90.00 – 125.00
Vase, 6"	7258-DV	1969	1972	55.00 – 65.00
Vase, 6¼" fan	7357-DV	1970	1971	60.00 – 70.00
Vase, 7"	7252-DV	1969	1971	65.00 – 85.00
Vase, 10"	7450-DV	July 1968	1974	150.00 – 185.00
Vase, 11"	7458-DV	1969	1972	140.00 – 160.00

5166 DV Frog

6080 DV Candy Box

8267 DV Medallion Bell

7258 DV 8" Vase

7458 DV 11" Vase

7252 DV 7" Vase

7464 DV Pitcher

7484 DV Candy Box

5163 DV Small Bird

5197 DV Happiness Bird

5161 DV Swan

7377 DV Ashtray

7333 DV Heart-shape Relish

7237 DV 7" Basket

7474 DV Candleholder

7355 DV 4 1/2" Fan Vase

7271 DV Candleholder

5162 DV Bunny

7256 DV 6" Vase

7437 DV Basket

7254 DV 4 1/2" Vase

7225 DV 5 1/2" Bonbon

7450 DV 10" Vase

7329 DV Low Fld. Comport

8288 DV Medallion Candy Box

7292 DV 5" Top Hat

7429 DV Footed Comport

7300 DV Fairy Light

7436 DV Small Basket

7451 DV 6" Vase

9056 DV Bud Vase

7498 DV Handled Bonbon

9308 DV 19 1/2" Student Lamp

7336 DV 6 1/2" Basket

Silver Crest with Yellow Rose Decoration

Fenton's Yellow Rose pattern, a Louise Piper design, was introduced in July 1969. Therefore, these pieces do not bear the Fenton logo and are not artist signed. The pattern consisted of nine items, hand painted on Silver Crest blanks. The decoration was discontinued at the end of 1970, after a period of production of only 18 months.

In July 1969, selected pieces from Fenton's Roses pattern were hand painted for distribution by Sears. This hand-painted design was called Talisman Rose (TR). The embossed rose was painted yellow with a slightly pink tint and the leaves were trimmed in green.

Other yellow rose decorations on Silver Crest may also be found. A hand-painted rose pattern, called Country Rose Bouquet, was produced for Sears in 1977 and 1978. Roses in this pattern were painted on milk glass and Silver Crest blanks which are signed with the Fenton logo. Hand-painted rose colors include blue, yellow, pink, and reddish-brown. For more information on this pattern, see page 114.

Yellow Rose	Ware No.	Introduced	Discontinued	Value
Basket, small	7436-YR	July 1969	1971	45.00 – 55.00
Basket, 6½" handled	7336-YR	July 1969	1971	80.00 – 90.00
Bonbon, 5½" DC	7225-YR	July 1969	1971	20.00 – 25.00
Bowl, 9½" DC	7423-YR	July 1969	1971	50.00 – 60.00
Candleholder	7271-YR	July 1969	1971	25.00 – 30.00
Comport, low ftd.	7329-YR	July 1969	1971	35.00 – 40.00
Comport, tall ftd.	7429-YR	July 1969	1971	55.00 – 65.00
Vase, 6"	7451-YR	July 1969	1971	30.00 – 35.00
Vase, 8"	7258-YR	July 1969	1971	50.00 – 60.00

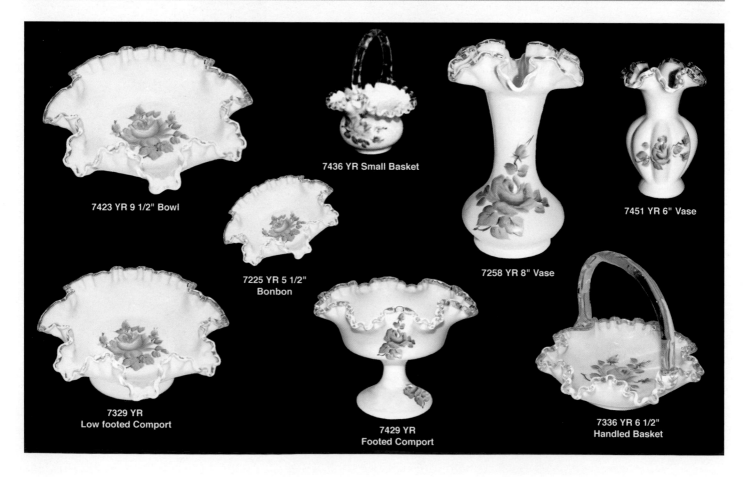

7423 YR 9 1/2" Bowl

7436 YR Small Basket

7451 YR 6" Vase

7225 YR 5 1/2" Bonbon

7258 YR 8" Vase

7329 YR Low footed Comport

7429 YR Footed Comport

7336 YR 6 1/2" Handled Basket

Silver Jamestown

Silver Jamestown was made in seven shapes. Fenton made items in this color from the beginning of 1957 until the end of 1959. All pieces in this pattern were discontinued by the end of December 1959. Therefore, collectors may experience a little difficulty finding examples of this crest color.

The Silver Jamestown pattern consists of pieces in the Jamestown Blue color, cased in white and trimmed with a spun silver edge. On five shapes the blue color is on the inside and on the other two shapes — the #7350-5" vase and the #7262-12" vase — the blue color is on the outside.

Silver Jamestown	Ware No.	Introduced	Discontinued	Value
Basket, 7" handled	7237-SJ	1957	July 1959	125.00 – 135.00
Bowl, 7"	7227-SJ	1957	1960	45.00 – 55.00
Vase, 6"	6056-SJ	1957	1960	55.00 – 65.00
Vase, 6½"	6058-SJ	1957	1960	55.00 – 65.00
Vase, 8" tulip	7250-SJ	1957	1959	115.00 – 130.00
Vase, 12"	7262-SJ	1957	July 1959	185.00 – 200.00
Vase, 5"	7350-SJ	1957	1959	45.00 – 55.00

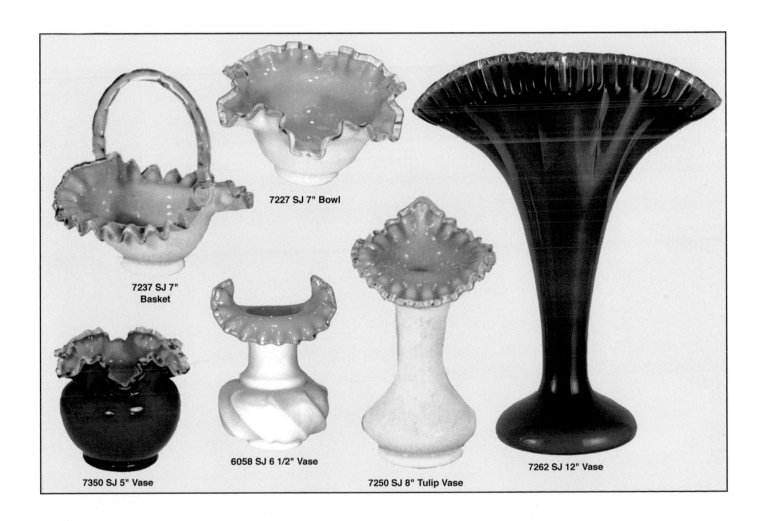

7227 SJ 7" Bowl

7237 SJ 7" Basket

7350 SJ 5" Vase

6058 SJ 6 1/2" Vase

7250 SJ 8" Tulip Vase

7262 SJ 12" Vase

Silver Rose

The Silver Rose pattern consists of pieces with a Rose Pastel body spun with a crystal edge. This pattern was introduced in January 1956 and was discontinued by January 1958. Only seven different shapes were produced.

Silver Rose	Ware No.	Introduced	Discontinued	Value
Basket, 7" handled	7237-SR	1956	1958	100.00 – 125.00
Bonbon, 5½"	7225-SR	1956	1958	20.00 – 25.00
Bowl, 7"	7227-SR	1956	1958	35.00 – 45.00
Bowl, ftd. square	7330-SR	1956	1958	110.00 – 130.00
Cake plate, ftd.	7213-SR	1956	1958	125.00 – 185.00
Comport, ftd.	7228-SR	1956	1958	40.00 – 45.00
Relish, heart-shaped, handled	7333-SR	1956	1958	50.00 – 60.00

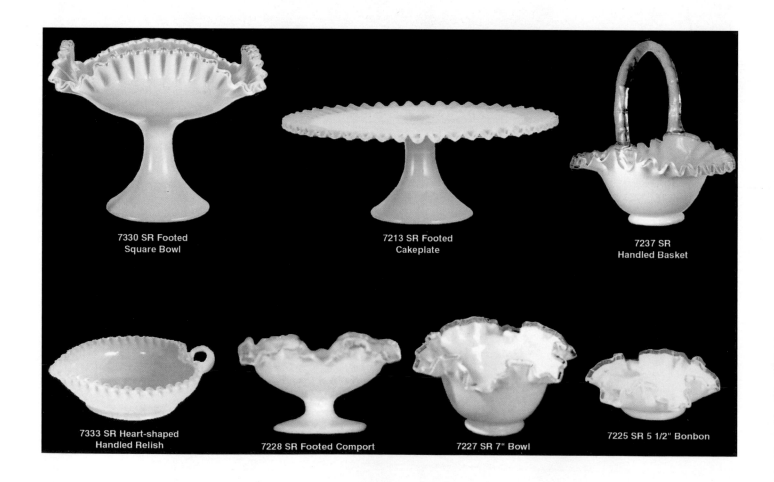

7330 SR Footed
Square Bowl

7213 SR Footed
Cakeplate

7237 SR
Handled Basket

7333 SR Heart-shaped
Handled Relish

7228 SR Footed Comport

7227 SR 7" Bowl

7225 SR 5 1/2" Bonbon

Silver Turquoise

Fenton's Silver Turquoise pattern was produced from January 1956 through June 1959. This pattern consists of 16 different pieces that have a solid opaque turquoise body decorated with a spun silver edge. All the pieces were introduced in January 1956. By January 1957, the hurricane lamp and the 8½" plate had been discontinued. Collectors should expect to experience considerable difficulty when trying to acquire these pieces. Some pieces of this pattern had been discontinued by January 1959. However, most items, as indicated in the listing below, were produced through June 1959.

Silver Turquoise	Ware No.	Introduced	Discontinued	Value
Basket, 7" handled	7237-ST	1956	July 1959	100.00 – 125.00
Basket, 13" handled	7233-ST	1956	1959	220.00 – 240.00
Bonbon, 5½"	7225-ST	1956	July 1959	15.00 – 20.00
Bowl, 13"	7223-ST	1956	July 1959	75.00 – 87.00
Bowl, 10"	7224-ST	1956	July 1959	50.00 – 60.00
Bowl, 7"	7227-ST	1956	July 1959	32.00 – 35.00
Bowl, footed square	7330-ST	1956	July 1959	125.00 – 145.00
Cake plate, 13" ftd.	7213-ST	1956	July 1959	125.00 – 140.00
Candleholder	7271-ST	1956	July 1959	20.00 – 25.00
Candleholder	7272-ST	1956	1959	40.00 – 45.00
Comport, ftd.	7228-ST	1956	July 1959	30.00 – 35.00
Epergne set, 3-pc.	7200-ST	1956	1959	170.00 – 190.00
Epergne set	7202-ST	1956	1959	100.00 – 125.00
Hurricane lamp	7290-ST	1956	1957	165.00 – 185.00
Plate, 8½"	7217-ST	1956	1957	25.00 – 35.00
Relish, handled, heart-shaped	7333-ST	1956	July 1959	45.00 – 55.00

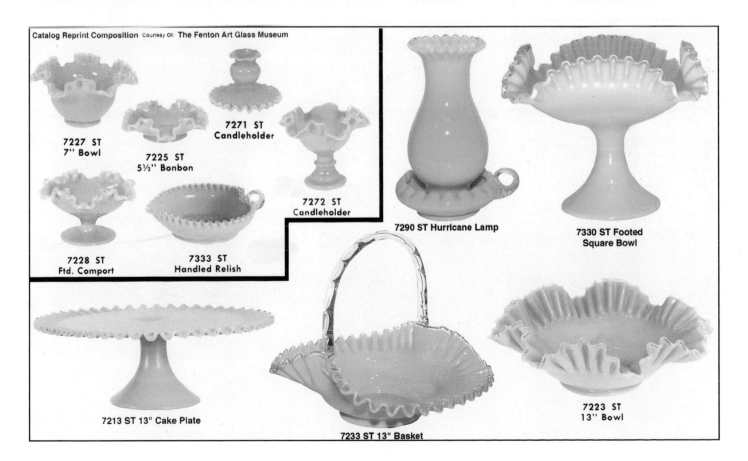

Catalog Reprint Composition Courtesy Of: The Fenton Art Glass Museum

7227 ST 7" Bowl

7225 ST 5½" Bonbon

7271 ST Candleholder

7272 ST Candleholder

7228 ST Ftd. Comport

7333 ST Handled Relish

7290 ST Hurricane Lamp

7330 ST Footed Square Bowl

7213 ST 13" Cake Plate

7233 ST 13" Basket

7223 ST 13" Bowl

Silver Crest with Spanish Lace

Introduction of an 11" footed cake plate with an embossed Spanish Lace design in 1962, sparked the beginning of a new line of pieces with the Silver Crest trim. A few years later, in 1965, other pieces were added to the regular line in Spanish Lace. Other additions occurred to this line throughout the 1970s and most of the 12-item line continued in production into the early 1980s.

Spanish Lace pieces do not appear in the 1974 price lists, but they reappear in 1975. The salt and pepper shakers were produced by adding the Spanish Lace design to the footed Silver Crest shaker moulds. As a result of this conversion, the regular Silver Crest shakers were only made for a very short time. Desirable items that many collectors are seeking include the Gone with the Wind lamp and the salt and pepper shakers. Most of the other items were made for a lengthy period and are in ample supply.

Items from the Spanish Lace with Silver Crest assortment were also selected for hand painting. For more information about the Violets in the Snow decoration used with this pattern, see page 109.

In 1988, two White Carnival Spanish Lace items with a Teal Crest (TC) were made for QVC. Included in this issue were the No. C3522-TC footed comport and the No. C3538-TC 8½" basket. Also, in 1988, a Teal with milk glass crest (TX) console set was sold through QVC. This set consisted of a pair of No. C3570-TX candleholders and a No. C3524-TX 9" console bowl. In 1994 and 1995, the No. 3559-7" vase and No. 3538-8½" basket in Spanish Lace with a plum crest were decorated with hand-painted lilacs. Items were also made in the Spanish Lace pattern without a crest. In the early 1980s the No. 3539-8½" basket and the No. 3527 footed comport were made in carnival (CN). The No. 3567 bell with the Spanish Lace design without a crest was made in Persian Pearl (XV) as part of Fenton's historic collection in 1993.

The No. 3538-8½" basket and No. 3559-7" vase were made in 1995 with Lilacs hand-painted decoration and a plum crest. The No. 3504-23" Gone with the Wind lamp was made in Fenton's Country Cranberry during 1995 and 1996. Also, during 1995 and 1996, the No. 3559-7" vase and the No. 3522-7½" comport were hand painted with Kristen's Floral design on Ivory Satin (YB). In 1996, the No. 1231-7½" basket was made in red carnival.

The Spanish Lace pattern continued to be produced without a crest. The Cranberry Gone With the Wind lamp continued in production through 1999. In these later years, it was joined in the line by the Cranberry No. 3559-8" vase without hand-painted decoration. A Spanish Lace No. 3500-30" lamp was made in Spruce Green Carnival in 2000. In 2002, a fairy light was made in the Violet and Pink Chiffon colors.

Spanish Lace with Silver Crest	Ware No.	Introduced	Discontinued	Value
Basket, 10" handled	3537-SC	1968	1980	125.00 – 145.00
Basket, 8½" handled	3538-SC	1973	1980+	65.00 – 85.00
Bell	3567-SC	1973	1980+	40.00 – 45.00
Bowl, 9"	3524-SC	1968	1980+	45.00 – 55.00
Cake plate, 11" ftd.	3510-SC	1962	1980+	60.00 – 70.00
Candleholder	3570-SC	1968	1980+	20.00 – 22.00
Candy Box, ftd.	3580-SC	1965	1980	65.00 – 75.00
Comport, ftd.	3522-SC	1975	1980+	30.00 – 40.00
Lamp, 24" Gone with the Wind	3509-SC	1976	1980+	275.00 – 340.00
Shaker, ftd.	3508-SC	1965	1970	40.00 – 45.00
Vase, 4"	3554-SC	1973	1980	20.00 – 25.00
Vase, 8"	3551-SC	1968	1980+	50.00 – 60.00

3850 SC Footed Candy Box

3508 SC Footed Shakers

3570 SC Candleholder

3554 SC 4" Vase

3509 SC 24" Gone with the Wind Lamp

3551 SC 8" Vase

3567 SC Bell

3524 SC 9" Bowl

3510 SC 11" Footed Cakeplate

3537 SC 10" Basket

3522 SC Footed Comport

3538 SC 8 1/2" Basket

Snowcrest

An early version of a Snowcrest glassware in jade with an opal trim was introduced into the Fenton line in 1942. This jade colored glassware with a Snowcrest edge must not have sold very well since examples are seldom seen. Also at the same time, essentially the same pieces were made in the reverse colors — opal with a jade crest.

The pattern that later became known as Snowcrest was originally introduced in the fall of 1950 as Spiral with Opal Ring. Fenton used the Spiral pattern mold with Ruby, Blue, and dark green colors to produce pieces with an opal crest. Amber Snowcrest replaced Blue Snowcrest in the line in January 1951.

The No. 1721 vase may be found with either a six-point crimp or a fine crimp. Two different sizes of top hat were made in Snowcrest. The No. 1921 top hat is 7" high and 9½" wide and the smaller No. 1923 top hat is 4½" high and 5½" wide. Hand-painted examples of Snowcrest may also be found. Blanks in Blue, Green, and Ruby made without the spiral optic were sold to outside decorating companies.

The No. 170 hurricane and the No. 1721-8½" pinch vase were sold to Quoizel in 1951 to be used in the manufacture of lamps. In the process the top was removed from the pinch vase which eliminated the white crest.

Two sizes of heart-shaped handled Ruby Snowcrest bonbons were marketed as part of the 1979 Valentine's Day promotion. For more information about these pieces, see the additional Crest items at the end of this chapter.

Amber Snowcrest	Ware No.	Introduced	Discontinued	Value
Bowl, #1522-11"		1951	1952	60.00 – 70.00
Hurricane lamp, #170		1951	1952	90.00 – 110.00
Top hat, #1923-4½"		1951	1952	35.00 – 40.00
Top hat, #1921-7"		1951	1952	100.00 – 125.00
Vase, #194-8"		1951	1952	30.00 – 40.00
Vase, #203-4½"		1951	1952	20.00 – 25.00
Vase, #1721-8½" pinch		1951	1952	40.00 – 45.00
Vase, #1925-5"		1951	1952	25.00 – 30.00
Vase, #1925-6"		1951	1952	40.00 – 45.00
Vase, #1925-8"		1951	1952	50.00 – 55.00
Vase, #3004-9½"		1951	1952	45.00 – 55.00
Vase, #3005-7½"		1951	1952	27.00 – 32.00
Vase, #3005-11"		1951	1952	55.00 – 60.00
Vase, #4516-8½"		1951	1952	40.00 – 45.00

Blue Snowcrest	Ware No.	Introduced	Discontinued	Value
Vase, #194-8"		Sept. 1950	1951	65.00 – 75.00
Vase, #203-4½"		Sept. 1950	1951	35.00 – 40.00
Vase, #1925-5"		Sept. 1950	1951	40.00 – 50.00
Vase, #1925-6"		Sept. 1950	1951	60.00 – 70.00
Vase, #3004-9½" spiral		Sept. 1950	1951	100.00 – 125.00
Vase, #3005-11" spiral		Sept. 1950	1951	100.00 – 125.00
Vase, #4516-8½"		Sept. 1950	1951	55.00 – 65.00

Dark Green Snowcrest	Ware No.	Introduced	Discontinued	Value
Bowl, #1522-11"	3124-GS	1951	1953	90.00 – 100.00
Hurricane lamp, #170	3109-GS	1951	1953	90.00 – 140.00
Pot and saucer	7299-GS	1952	1954	75.00 – 85.00
Top hat, #1923-4½"	3191-GS	1951	1954	50.00 – 60.00
Top hat, #1921-7"	3192-GS	1951	1953	175.00 – 225.00
Vase, #194-8"	3159-GS	Sept. 1950	1954	65.00 – 85.00
Vase, #203-4½"	3154-GS	Sept. 1950	1954	35.00 – 45.00
Vase, #1721-8½" pinch	3152-GS	1951	1954	75.00 – 95.00*
Vase, #1925-5"	3155-GS	Sept. 1950	1953	35.00 – 45.00
Vase, #1925-6"	3156-GS	Sept. 1950	1954	50.00 – 60.00
Vase, #1925-8"	3158-GS	1951	1953	65.00 – 85.00
Vase, #3004-9½"	3150-GS	Sept. 1950	1953	110.00 – 135.00
Vase, #3005-7½"	3157-GS	Sept. 1950	1953	80.00 – 85.00

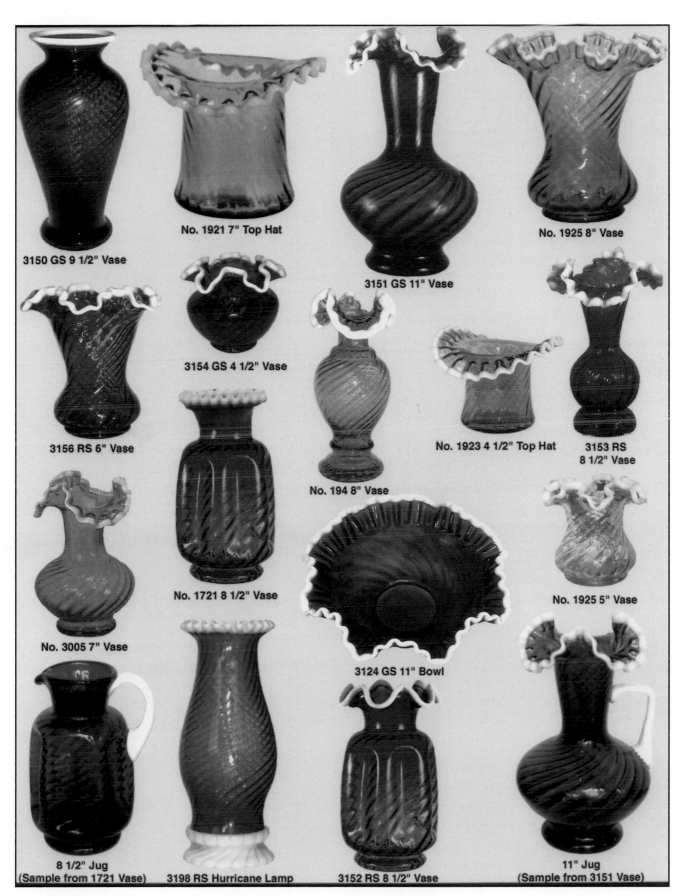

3150 GS 9 1/2" Vase

No. 1921 7" Top Hat

3151 GS 11" Vase

No. 1925 8" Vase

3156 RS 6" Vase

3154 GS 4 1/2" Vase

No. 194 8" Vase

No. 1923 4 1/2" Top Hat

3153 RS
8 1/2" Vase

No. 3005 7" Vase

No. 1721 8 1/2" Vase

3124 GS 11" Bowl

No. 1925 5" Vase

8 1/2" Jug
(Sample from 1721 Vase)

3198 RS Hurricane Lamp

3152 RS 8 1/2" Vase

11" Jug
(Sample from 3151 Vase)

Emerald Snowcrest	Ware No.	Introduced	Discontinued	Value
Vase, #3005-11"	3151-GS	Sept. 1950	1955	110.00 – 135.00
Vase, #4516-8½"	3153-GS	Sept. 1950	1954	75.00 – 85.00

*With narrow crimp 100.00 – 125.00

Jade Snowcrest & Opal w/Jade Crest	Ware No.	Introduced	Discontinued	Value
Bowl, #680 dessert		1942		35.00 – 45.00
Bowl, #680-8½" salad		1942		100.00 – 125.00
Bowl, #1522-10"		1942		140.00 – 170.00
Candleholder, #951 cornucopia		1942		75.00 – 100.00
Plate, #680-6½"		1942		20.00 – 25.00
Plate, #680-8½"		1942		40.00 – 50.00
Plate, #680-10"		1942		85.00 – 95.00
Plate, 12"		1942		100.00 – 125.00

Ruby Snowcrest	Ware No.	Introduced	Discontinued	Value
Bowl, #1522-11"	3124-RS	1951	1954	100.00 – 125.00
Hurricane lamp, #170	3198-RS	1951	1954	150.00 – 185.00
Top hat #1923-4½"	3191-RS	1951	1953	55.00 – 65.00
Top hat, #1921-7"	3192-RS	1951	1953	200.00 – 225.00
Vase, #194-8"	3159-RS	Sept. 1950	1954	60.00 – 75.00
Vase, #203-4½"	3154-RS	Sept. 1950	1954	35.00 – 40.00
Vase, #1721-8½" pinch	3152-RS	1951	1954	85.00 – 100.00
Vase, #1925-5"	3155-RS	Sept. 1950	1953	45.00 – 50.00
Vase, #1925-6"	3156-RS	Sept. 1950	1954	60.00 – 65.00
Vase, #1925-8"	3158-RS	1951	1953	85.00 – 95.00
Vase, #3004-9½"	3150-RS	Sept. 1950	1953	95.00 – 110.00
Vase, #3005-7½"	3157-RS	Sept. 1950	1954	85.00 – 95.00
Vase, #3005-11"	3151-RS	Sept. 1950	1954	110.00 – 140.00
Vase, #4516-8½"	3153-RS	Sept. 1950	1954	75.00 – 85.00

No. 680 6 1/2" Plate

No. 680 8 1/2" Plate

No. 680 8 1/2" Salad Bowl

No. 951 Cornucopia Candleholder

No. 680 Dessert

No. 680 8 1/2" Salad Bowl
No. 680 8 1/2" Plate

Violets in the Snow on Spanish Lace

Louise Piper's Violets in the Snow decoration was expanded to include items from the Spanish Lace pattern beginning in 1974. A few additional pieces were added to the line in 1975. All items were made into the early 1980s with the exception of the candy box. This piece was discontinued after only three years and will prove to be the most difficult item of the decorated Spanish Lace line for collectors to find on the secondary market.

Violets in the Snow	Ware No.	Introduced	Discontinued	Value
Basket, 8½"	3538-DV	1974	1980+	125.00 – 140.00
Bell	3567-DV	1974	1980+	50.00 – 60.00
Bowl, 9"	3524-DV	1975	1980+	55.00 – 65.00
Candleholder	3570-DV	1975	1980+	30.00 – 40.00
Candy box	3580-DV	1974	1977	100.00 – 125.00
Comport, ftd.	3522-DV	1975	1980+	50.00 – 60.00
Vase, 4"	3554-DV	1974	1980+	25.00 – 30.00
Vase, 8"	3551-DV	1974	1980+	65.00 – 85.00

3551 DV 8" Vase

3538 DV 8 1/2" Basket

3522 DV Footed Comport

3567 DV Bell

3580 DV Candy Box

3524 DV 9" Bowl

3570 DV Candleholder

3554 DV 4" Vase

Unusual Crests, Sample Items, or Special Order Pieces

Fenton made a number of items for Rubel and Company during the early 1950s. Some of these items are pictured in Emerald Crest on the next page. The Rose Crest vases were made for Weil Ceramics during the 1940s.

Photo on page 111:

Crest Items	Value
1. Emerald Snowcrest sherbet made in the early 1950s	35.00 – 40.00
2. Emerald Crest 10½" bowl made for Rubel	85.00 – 95.00
3. Emerald Crest relish set made for Rubel	110.00 – 130.00
4. Emerald Crest jam set made for Rubel	120.00 – 140.00
5. Emerald Crest No. 4517-11" vase made as a special order item	175.00 – 200.00
6. Emerald Crest 5-piece condiment set made for Rubel	180.00 – 200.00
7. Ruby with Silver Crest No. 835-6" vase made as a special order item	100.00 – 125.00
8. Emerald Snowcrest flower pot No. 7299 GS; was part of the regular line from 1952 through 1953	75.00 – 85.00
9. Emerald Crest heart-shaped bowl made for Rubel	125.00 – 145.00
10. Emerald Crest small bonbon converted to a finger lamp	50.00 – 60.00
11. Rose Crest No. 4517-6½" vase made for Weil Ceramics during the 1940s	65.00 – 85.00
12. Ruby with Silver Crest 8" vase made as a special order item	100.00 – 125.00
13. Jade No. 1522-10" bowl with Snowcrest	140.00 – 170.00
14. Rose Crest No. 4517-11" vase made for Weil Ceramics during the 1940s	200.00 – 225.00
15. No. 1522/951 console set in Ivory Crest with metal filigree holders	185.00 – 200.00

Photo on page 112:

Crest Items	Value
1. Silver Crest 9½" bowl with narrow crimp	90.00 – 120.00
2. Peach Crest 9½" bowl with narrow crimp	100.00 – 125.00
3. Topaz Crest No. 7336 basket made about 1970 (not in the line)	100.00 – 125.00
4. Ivory Crest 5" basket	45.00 – 65.00
5. Rose Crest 14" epergne set made for L. G. Wright	400.00 – 450.00
6. Rose Swirl 7" basket with Silver Crest	N.D.
7. Blue Ridge Barcelona vase	190.00 – 210.00
8. Peach Crest Thumbprint 8" vase	90.00 – 100.00
9. Heart-shaped No. 7333 handled bonbon in opal with ruby crest made as a part of the Valentine's Day assortment in 1979	75.00 – 85.00
10. Peach Crest rose bowl whimsey	75.00 – 85.00
11. Silver Crest No. 7252-7" vase with hand-painted Louise Piper Bluebirds decoration	N.D.
12. Ruby Snowcrest heart-shaped No. 7333 handled bonbon made in 1979 for Valentine's Day	75.00 – 85.00
13. Opal with Ruby crest small bonbon made for Valentine's Day in 1979	40.00 – 50.00
14. Blue with Silver crest 14" epergne set made for L. G. Wright	500.00 – 550.00
15. Ruby Snowcrest heart-shaped small heart bonbon made for Valentine's Day 1979	40.00 – 50.00
16. Topaz Opalescent 14" epergne set made for L. G. Wright	450.00 – 500.00
17. Peach Crest atomizer made for DeVilbiss in 1948	120.00 – 140.00
18. Amethyst with Opal crest 14" epergne set made for L. G. Wright	450.00 – 500.00

Photo on page 113:

Crest Items	Value
1. Aqua Crest experimental 9" jug	N.D.
2. Aqua Crest No. 192 melon rib squat jug	225.00 – 250.00
3. Aqua Crest experimental milk jug	180.00 – 210.00
4. Rose Overlay No. 192-8" vase with Silver Crest	N.D.
5. Jade shell-shaped bowl with Silver Crest	N.D.
6. Rose Overlay No. 1924-5" tulip-shaped top hat vase with Silver Crest	N.D.
7. Peach Blow Melon Rib No. 192-6" vase with Crystal Crest edge	125.00 – 150.00
8. Small Jade top hat with Silver Crest	N.D.
9. Flared 7" bowl with deep Red Crest	125.00 – 140.00
10. Melon Rib No. 192-6" vase with Ruby and Opal Crest	125.00 – 150.00
11. Large 10" Jade hat with Silver Crest	N.D.
12. Amber Spiral Optic large hat with a Cobalt Crest	N.D.
13. Rose Satin large crimped console bowl with a Snowcrest edge	N.D.
14. Melon Rib Peach Blow 6" jug with a Crystal Crest edge	125.00 – 150.00

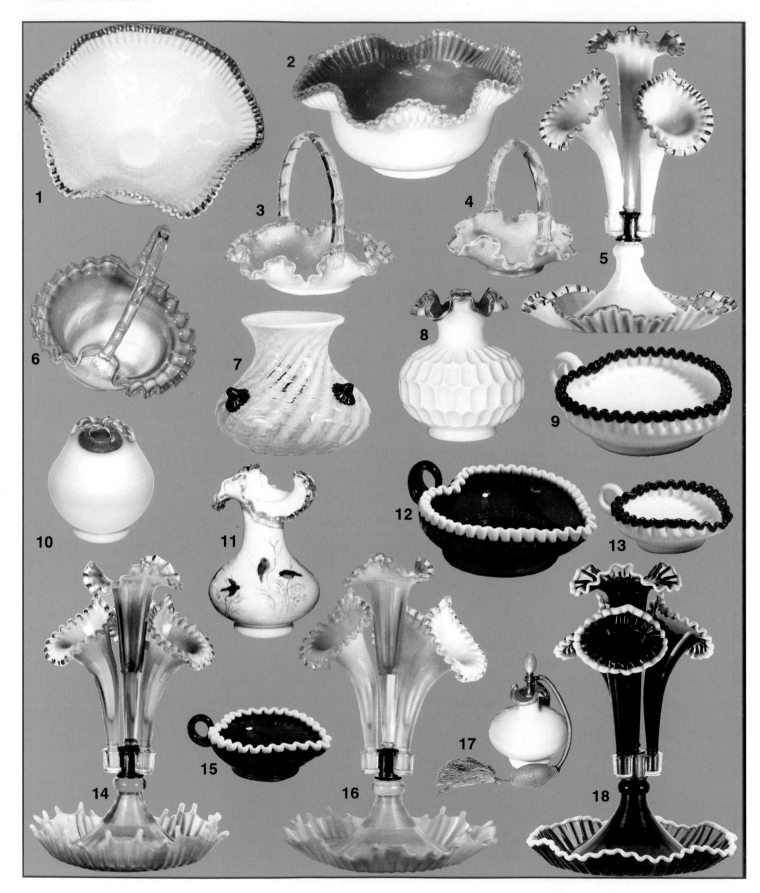

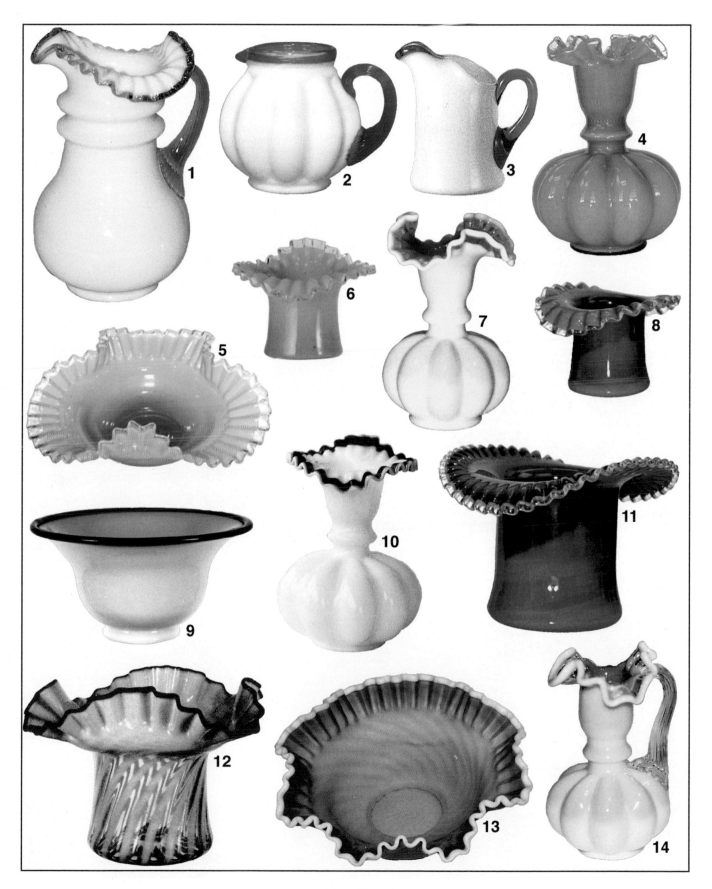

Silver Crest with Sears Country Rose Bouquet

A Fenton-decorated colored rose decoration was made for Sears in 1977 and 1978. This Country Rose Bouquet design was intended to match Sears' French Bouquet line of towels and pillow cases. The Rose decoration was hand painted on eight selected Silver Crest and milk glass shapes. Items were available decorated with blue (QB), pink (QP), or yellow (QY) roses. These pieces will have the Fenton logo on the bottom.

Country Rose Bouquet	Ware No.	Blue	Pink	Yellow
Basket, 7"	7237	55.00 – 65.00	60.00 – 65.00	55.00 – 60.00
Bell, Medallion	8267	30.00 – 35.00	35.00 – 40.00	30.00 – 35.00
Candy box, Medallion	9288	70.00 – 80.00	70.00 – 80.00	70.00 – 80.00
Comport, footed	7429	50.00 – 55.00	50.00 – 55.00	45.00 – 50.00
Happiness Bird	5197	35.00 – 40.00	35.00 – 40.00	30.00 – 35.00
Vase, bud	9056	22.00 – 27.00	25.00 – 30.00	22.00 – 27.00
Vase, 4½"	7254	30.00 – 35.00	30.00 – 33500	28.00 – 32.00
Vase, 7"	7252	50.00 – 55.00	50.00 – 55.00	45.00 – 55.00

7429 QP Footed Comport

7237 QB 7" Basket

8288 QY Medallion
Candy Jar

5197 Happiness Bird

7254 QB 4 1/2" Vase

8267 QP Medallion Bell

7254 QY 4 1/2" Vase

Decorated Aqua Crest and Emerald Crest

Most of the decorations found on Emerald Crest and Aqua Crest pieces are the Charleton designs of the Abels, Wasserberg & Company. Like several other importers, the Abels, Wasserberg relationship with Fenton was spurred by the onset of World War II in Europe. Most of the Charleton-decorated Fenton items were produced from the early 1940s through the mid-1950s. All of the items in the photo below have Charleton decorations except for the Emerald Crest basket. Small vases, bonbons, and comports are found most often with these hand-painted decorations. Hand-decorated clocks, made from a 6½" plate, are the only items in Aqua Crest being found with any regularity.

Item	Decoration	Value
1. Aqua Crest Clock from Ware No. 7219-6½" plate	Charleton Roses	115.00 – 140.00
2. Emerald Crest Ware No. 7229 nut dish	Charleton Pegged Roses	45.00 – 55.00
3. Emerald Crest Ware No. 7219-6½" plate	Charleton Green Mist Rococo	20.00 – 30.00
4. Emerald Crest Ware No. 7225-5½" DC bonbon	Charleton Green Sprig	30.00 – 40.00
5. Emerald Crest Ware No. 7236-5" basket	Unknown Gold Floral	120.00 – 130.00
6. Aqua Crest Clock from Ware No. 7219-6½" plate	Charleton Roses	115.00 – 140.00

Decorated Peach Crest

Peach Crest vases, jugs, and baskets were popular with decorating companies. Notice the different styles of hand painting associated with the Charleton Roses pattern.

Photo Below:

Item	Decoration	Value
1. Peach Crest Mould No. 192-8" handled jug	Charleton Ivy	150.00 – 175.00
2. Peach Crest Mould No. 192-8" handled jug	Tyndale Gold Rose transfer	120.00 – 140.00
3. Peach Crest Mould No. 192-8" handled jug	Charleton Open Rose	170.00 – 195.00

Photo to the Right:

Item	Decoration	Value
1. Peach Crest Mould No. 192-6" DC Vase	Charleton Roses	65.00 – 75.00
2. Peach Crest Mould No. 192-5½" DC Vase	Charleton Roses	60.00 – 70.00
3. Peach Crest Mould No. 192-5½" DC Vase	Charleton Roses	60.00 – 70.00
4. Peach Crest Mould No. 192-5½" DC Vase	Charleton Blue Mist and Blue Roses	80.00 – 90.00
5. Peach Crest Ware No. 7258-8" DC vase	Charleton Roses and Bows	85.00 – 100.00
6. Peach Crest Ware No. 7235-5" basket	Tyndale Gold Rose transfer	75.00 – 95.00
7. Peach Crest Ware No. 7327-7" basket	Tyndale Gold Rose transfer	90.00 – 110.00
8. Peach Crest Ware No. 7256-6" DC vase	Charleton Pink Mist with Roses and Bows	140.00 – 160.00

Decorated Rose Crest and Silver Crest

Photo Above:

Item	Decoration	Value
1. Silver Crest Ware No. 7213-13" footed cake plate	Charleton Roses and Gold Spatter	140.00 – 160.00
2. Silver Crest Ware No. 7219-6½" plate	Charleton Strawberry	22.00 – 27.00
3. Silver Crest Ware No. 7212-12" plate	Charleton Blue Mist with Inlaid Roses	80.00 – 90.00
4. Silver Crest Ware No. 7212-12" plate	Charleton Roses	60.00 – 70.00
5. Rose Crest Mould No. 203-7" flared bowl	Charleton Arched Roses	60.00 – 75.00
6. Silver Crest Mould No. 680-8½" flared bowl	Charleton Roses	60.00 – 70.00

Photo to the Right:

Item	Decoration	Value
1. Silver Crest Mould No. 192-6" DC vase	Charleton Roses	45.00 – 55.00
2. Silver Crest Ware No. 7228-6" comport	Charleton Gold Roses	60.00 – 70.00
3. Silver Crest Ware No. 7280 candy	Charleton Gold Roses	100.00-125.00
4. Silver Crest Ware No. 7329 comport	Unknown Rose	70.00 – 80.00
5. Silver Crest Ware No. 7357-6¼" fan vase	Charleton Red Sunburst and Roses	60.00 – 70.00
6. Silver Crest Ware No. 7225-5½" DC bonbon	Charleton Roses and Bows	25.00 – 30.00
7. Silver Crest Ware No. 7228 comport	Charleton Roses	45.00 – 55.00
8. Silver Crest Mould No. 1928" vase	Charleton Roses	80.00 – 90.00
9. Rose Crest Mould No. 951 cornucopia vase	Charleton Arched Roses	90.00 – 110.00
10. Silver Crest Ware No. 7329 comport	Charleton Roses and Bows	75.00 – 90.00

Decorated Silver Crest and Snowcrest

The Beth Weissman Company was a decorator and distributor of lamps and giftware. The company was head-quartered in New York and operated as a contemporary of the Abels, Wasserberg & Company.

Photo Above:

Item	Decoration	Value
1. Silver Crest Mould No. 192-6" candy jar	Unknown Blue floral	75.00 – 85.00
2. Silver Crest Ware No. 7237-7" basket	Wheeling Decorating Gold Rose transfer	65.00 – 75.00
3. Silver Crest Ware No. 7228 comport	Charleton Pink Mist and Roses	75.00 – 85.00
4. Silver Crest Mould No. 192-5½" vase	Unknown Pink Rose	30.00 – 40.00
5. Silver Crest Mould No. 203-7" bowl	Charleton Blue Roses	45.00 – 55.00
6. Silver Crest Ware No. 7228 comport	Charleton Green Mist and Roses	60.00 – 70.00

Photo to the Right:

Item	Decoration	Value
1. Silver Crest Mould No. 192-6" DC vase	Charleton Roses and Bows	50.00 – 60.00
2. Silver Crest Ware No. 7212-12" plate	Unknown Pink Rose	75.00 – 85.00
3. Silver Crest Ware No. 7270 candleholders ea.	Beth Weissman Roses and Bows	50.00 – 60.00
4. Amber Satin Snowcrest Ware No. 3198 hurricane lamp	Unknown White Sailing Ship	100.00 – 125.00
5. Silver Crest Mould No. 1924-5" basket	Charleton Blue Latticed Roses	80.00 – 90.00
6. Silver Crest Ware No. 7219-6½" plate	Unknown Pink Rose	25.00 – 30.00
7. Silver Crest Ware No. 7270 candleholders ea.	Charleton Turquoise Band and Roses	60.00 – 70.00
8. Silver Crest Mould No. 192-8" vase	Unknown Rose and Gold	70.00 – 80.00
9. Silver Crest Mould No. 192-6" vase	Beth Weissman Roses and Bows	50.00 – 60.00
10. Silver Crest Ware No. 7356-6¼" vase	Wheeling Decorating Gold Rose transfer	40.00 – 50.00
11. Emerald Snowcrest Ware No. 3151-11" vase	Charleton Camellias	200.00 – 225.00

Lamps and Miscellaneous Decorated Crests

Photo Above:

Item	Value
1. Aqua Crest Mould No. 192-6" oil lamp base	180.00 – 200.00
2. Silver Crest nite lite made from epergne	75.00 – 85.00
3. Ivory Crest lamp made from a No. 183-10" vase	150.00 – 175.00
4. Silver Crest lamp made from a No. 192-7" bottle	90.00 – 110.00
5. Silver Crest lamp made from a No. 192-6" candy	90.00 – 110.00
6. Emerald Crest lamp made from a No. 711-6" vase	75.00 – 85.00

Photo to the Right:

Item	Decoration	Value
1. Silver Crest Ware No. 7354-4½" DC vase	Unknown Violets	25.00 – 30.00
2. Silver Crest Ware No. 7355-4½" fan vase	Unknown Violets	30.00 – 40.00
3. Crystal Crest Mould No. 206-7" DC comport	Charleton Roses	85.00 – 95.00
4. Aqua Crest mould No. 1924-5" basket	Unknown Roses	120.00 – 140.00
5. Silver Crest Ware No. 7274 cornucopia candle	Unknown Roses	30.00 – 40.00
6. Silver Crest Ware No. 7356 – 6¼" DC vase	Unknown Violets	30.00 – 40.00
7. Silver Crest Mould No. 36 – 6¼" vase	Unknown Gold	90.00 – 110.00
8. Silver Crest Ware No. 7354-4½" DC vase	Unknown Violets	30.00 – 35.00
9. Silver Crest Ware No. 7229 nut dish	Unknown Violets	40.00 – 45.00
10. Silver Crest Mould No. 573-8" fan vase	Unknown Violets	90.00 – 110.00

Decorated Silver Crest Vanity Sets

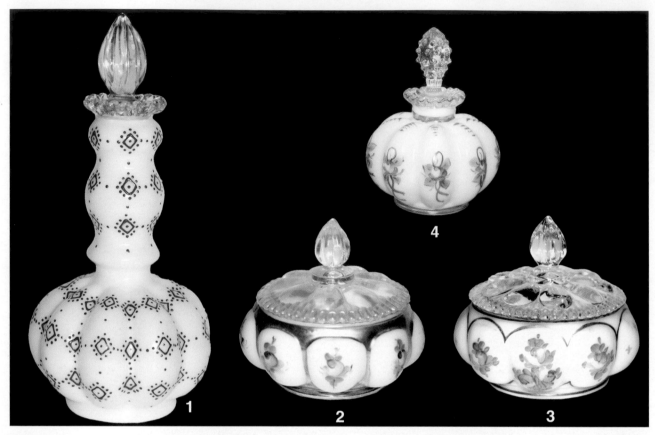

Vanity sets were one of the favorite subjects of the decorating companies. Note the very heavy gold decoration on the puff box in the center of the picture above. The vanity sets at the top of the photo to the right are a turned-out, retooled, smooth-sided variation of Fenton's No. 192 Melon Rib mould.

Photo Above:

Item	Decoration	Value
1. Silver Crest Mould No. 192-7" bottle	Charleton Red Geometric	180.00 – 200.00
2. Silver Crest Mould No. 192 puff box	Charleton Roses	75.00 – 85.00
3. Silver Crest Mould No. 192 puff box	Tyndale Blue Roses	75.00 – 85.00
4. Silver Crest Mould No. 192 squat cologne	Charleton Roses and Bows	80.00 – 95.00

Photo to the Right:

Item	Decoration	Value
1. Silver Crest turned-out Mould No. 192-5" vanity bottles and 4¼" puff box		300.00 – 340.00
2. Silver Crest turned-out Mould No. 192-5" vanity bottles and 4¼" puff box	Charleton Pink Mist and Roses	325.00 – 375.00
3. Silver Crest Mould No. 192-5" vanity bottles and 4¼" puff box	Charleton Blue Mist and Roses	325.00 – 375.00
4. Silver Crest Mould No. 192-5" vanity bottle and 4¼" puff box	Unknown Roses and Leaves	110.00 – 130.00
5. Silver Crest Mould No. 192-5" vanity bottles and 4¼" puff box	Charleton Roses	310.00 – 350.00
6 Silver Crest Mould No. 192-7" vanity bottle and 6" puff box	Unknown Enameled Blue and Gold	250.00 – 300.00

1

2

3

4

5

6

Fenton's Hobnail Pattern

Hobnail Colors and Shapes

Fenton began its long romance with the Hobnail pattern with the introduction of a lamp font in 1935. Over the next several years, from 1936 to 1938, reproductions of Hobnail barber bottles from old moulds were made for L. G. Wright. Starting in 1938, a modified barber bottle with a shorter neck and a wider opening was fitted with a wooden stopper and sold to Wrisley of Chicago for use as a perfume bottle. Later, the greater economies of mass-produced machine-made glassware caused Fenton to lose this contract. Close examination of the bottle will reveal the maker. Fenton bottles were produced with a 6-part mould. The machine-made bottles were made using a four part mould. The earlier Fenton bottles were fitted with a wooden stopper. The later machine-made bottles were sold with a cork-encased glass stopper. Examples of the two colors of colognes and the puff box that Fenton made for Wrisley are shown below.

Item	French Opalescent	Cranberry Opalescent
Cologne with wooden stopper	18.00 – 25.00	85.00 – 100.00
Puff box with wooden lid	22.00 – 27.00	

No. 289
Colognes & Puff Box
Made for
Wrisley

FO Puff Box with
Original Wooden Lid

FO Cologne with Original Stopper

CR Cologne with Original Stopper

FO Cologne Filled
with Original Cologne

HOW IT'S MADE

To make Hobnail pieces, the glass is blown or pressed into a mold like the one in the sketch. Each "hobnail" shows in the mold as a deep dimple, which becomes the raised part of the finished glass.

The picture shows the blower placing the gather into the mold which stands on the floor at the edge of his platform. An apprentice will close the mold around the blob of glass, the blower will judge the exact amount of air pressure needed to fill the mold. Here again is a skill hard to analyse. Too much glass in the mold would make a thick, clumsy piece.

Hobnail, like Coin Dot, uses two different processes, depending on the colors. French Opalescent, Blue Opalescent, and Milk Glass are single layers of glass. Skillful cooling and re-warming brings out the opacity of the edges and the hobs in French and Blue Opalescent. Cranberry and Lime Hobnail are cased glass, using a layer of French Opalescent outside, and colored glass inside. Peach Blow uses gold ruby glass inside, Milk Glass outside . . . Crimped edges are made with the foot operated crimper this finisher is using.

Hobnail

Brief synopsis of Hobnail colors made between 1939 and 1980

Color	Composition	Introduced	Discontinued
Amber	Transparent amber	1959	1982
Apple Green Overlay	Light green exterior cased over an opal interior layer	1961	1962
Black	Ebony milk glass	1962	1975
Blue Marble	Opal added to molten light opaque blue glass producing white swirls	1970	1974
Blue Opalescent	Blue transparent glass with opalescence	1939	1955*
Blue Pastel	Light blue milk glass	1954	1955
Blue Satin	Medium blue satin milk glass	1971	1981
Burmese	Pale opaque yellow accented with red trim	1971	1972
Cameo Opalescent	Transparent amber glass with opalescence	1979	1982
Colonial Blue	Transparent deep electric blue	1962	1980
Colonial Green	Transparent olive green	1963	1967
Colonial Pink	Transparent light rose	1967	1968
Coral	Colonial pink cased over opal	1961	1962
Cranberry	Ruby glass with opalescence	1940	1980+
Crystal	Clear transparent glass	1968	1969
Custard	Opaque beige	1972	1978
French Opalescent	Crystal glass with opalescence	1939	1965
Green Opalescent	Transparent green with opalescence	1940	1941**
Green Pastel	Shiny light green milk glass	1954	1956
Honey Amber	Transparent amber cased over opal	1961	1967
Pekin Blue II	Bright opaque blue jade color similar to Pekin Blue	1968	1968
Jonquil Yellow	Bright opaque yellow jade color similar to Chinese Yellow	1968	1968
Lime Green Opalescent	French Opalescent cased over transparent green	1952	1955
Lime Sherbet	Green satin milk glass	1973	1980
Milk Glass	Opaque white glass	1950	1980+
Opaque Blue Overlay	Colonial Blue cased over opal	1962	1964
Orange	Transparent orange	1964	1978
Orchid Opalescent	Transparent violet glass with opalescence	1942	1943
Peach Blo	Opal cased over gold ruby	1951	1958
Plum Opalescent	Transparent purple with opalescent hobs	1959	1963
Powder Blue Overlay	Transparent light blue cased over opal	1961	1962
Rose Overlay	Transparent pink cased over opal	1941	1944
Rose Pastel	Pink milk glass	1954	1958
Ruby	Transparent deep red glass	1972	1980+

Ruby Overlay	Crystal cased over Gold Ruby	1941	1944
Springtime Green	Light transparent green	1977	1979
Topaz Opalescent	Transparent yellow with opalescent hobs	1941	1944***
Turquoise	Deep blue-green milk glass	1955	1959
Wild Rose	Gold Ruby cased over milk glass	1961	1963

*Blue Opalescent was initially discontinued at the end of 1954. Blue Opalescent was made again between July 1959 and 1964. Later, after 1980, other shades of Blue Opalescent Hobnail were made, but these will be marked with the Fenton logo.
**Hobnail was made in a new darker green opalescent color that was introduced in July 1959. This color was in the regular Fenton line through July 1961.
***The original issue of Topaz Opalescent Hobnail was made from 1941 through the end of 1943. This color again became a part of the Fenton line from 1959 through 1962.

Transparent amber was called Antique Amber prior to 1963. After 1963, this same color was called Colonial Amber. Hobnail in amber was generally made between 1959 and 1982. However, the rectangular ashtray set was also made in 1954. Custard (CU) glassware was normally sold satinized. However, Fenton did produce the candle bowl in glossy custard. The most frequently found items in crystal Hobnail are the ones produced in the late 1960s. In addition Fenton made a few pieces of Hobnail in crystal in the early 1940s. For more information see the section on Crystal Hobnail.

Identification of Early Shapes

One of the more confusing aspects of collecting Fenton's Hobnail pattern is identifying the shapes of pieces made prior to the introduction of ware numbers in July 1952. Ware numbers standardized Fenton's product line with each ware number representing a specific shape in a pattern. Prior to that time all items in the Hobnail pattern were identified by using the No. 389 pattern number. Adding to the confusion is the slight differences in size for the same item that may have been listed in the Fenton catalogs over the period of years. For example the 8½" flat double crimped vase from the early 1940s is listed at 8" in the late 1940s. Also, terminology changed over the years. A shallow bowl listed as a nappy one year might be listed as a bonbon the next year. It is therefore, sometimes difficult to differentiate numerous shapes of the same type of item that were made during this period. The shapes of the various covered candy jars, bowls, and vases seem to be the most confusing. The accompanying catalog reprints from the early 1940s on the next page have been used to help illustrate the differences among the similar items. Remember that many of the pieces made during this era from the same mould were often finished with a different crimping. Therefore, pieces from the same mould that are finished in a different fashion may vary considerably in size.

Bowls listed in the 1940 catalog:
Small shallow bowls were also called nappies
Bonbon, 6" double crimped, flared, plate, oval, square, triangle
Bonbon, 7" double crimped, flared, plate, oval, square, triangle
Bowl, 7" flared, oval
Bowl, 9" flared, 7" special, rose bowl
Bowl, 11" double crimped, flared, oval, triangle

1942 additions:
Bonbon (nappy), 5" 2-handled oval, square
Bowl, 7½" flared
Bowl, 11" ftd. shallow
Bowl, 12" ftd, double crimped

1943 additions:
Bonbon (nappy), 6" 2-handled oval, square

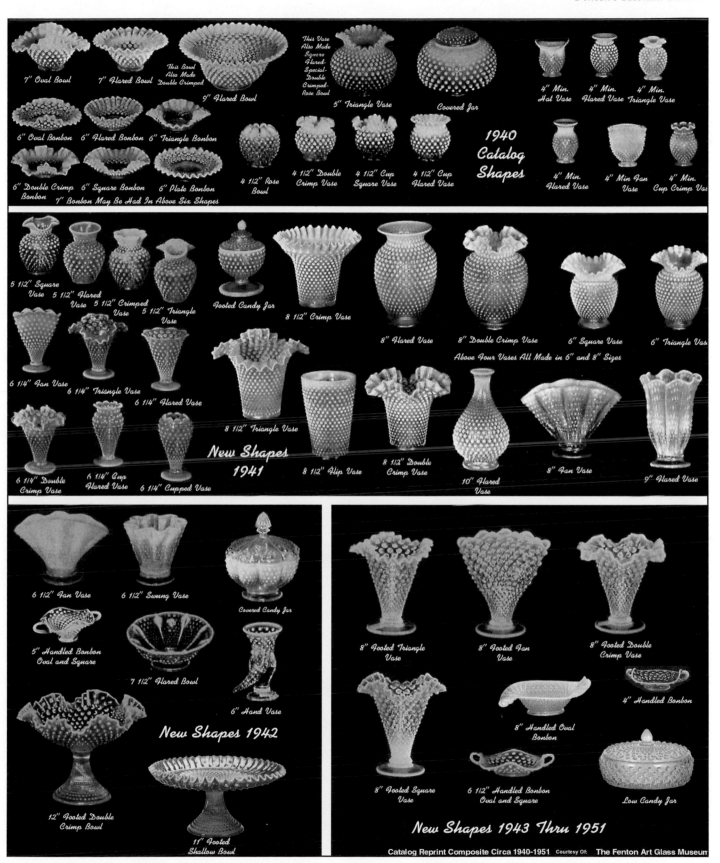

7" Oval Bowl

7" Flared Bowl

This Bowl Also Made Double Crimped

9" Flared Bowl

6" Oval Bonbon

6" Flared Bonbon

6" Triangle Bonbon

6" Double Crimp Bonbon

6" Square Bonbon

6" Plate Bonbon

7" Bonbon May Be Had In Above Six Shapes

This Vase Also Made Square-Flared-Special-Double Crimped-Rose Bowl

5" Triangle Vase

Covered Jar

4 1/2" Rose Bowl

4 1/2" Double Crimp Vase

4 1/2" Cup Square Vase

4 1/2" Cup Flared Vase

4" Min. Hat Vase

4" Min. Flared Vase

4" Min. Triangle Vase

4" Min. Flared Vase

4" Min Fan Vase

4" Min. Cup Crimp Vase

1940 Catalog Shapes

5 1/2" Square Vase

5 1/2" Flared Vase

5 1/2" Crimped Vase

5 1/2" Triangle Vase

Footed Candy Jar

8 1/2" Crimp Vase

8" Flared Vase

8" Double Crimp Vase

6" Square Vase

6" Triangle Vase

Above Four Vases All Made in 6" and 8" Sizes

6 1/4" Fan Vase

6 1/4" Triangle Vase

6 1/4" Flared Vase

8 1/2" Triangle Vase

8 1/2" Hip Vase

8 1/2" Double Crimp Vase

10" Flared Vase

8" Fan Vase

9" Flared Vase

6 1/4" Double Crimp Vase

6 1/4" Cup Flared Vase

6 1/4" Cupped Vase

New Shapes 1941

6 1/2" Fan Vase

6 1/2" Swung Vase

Covered Candy Jar

5" Handled Bonbon Oval and Square

7 1/2" Flared Bowl

6" Hand Vase

New Shapes 1942

12" Footed Double Crimp Bowl

11" Footed Shallow Bowl

8" Footed Triangle Vase

8" Footed Fan Vase

8" Footed Double Crimp Vase

4" Handled Bonbon

8" Handled Oval Bonbon

8" Footed Square Vase

6 1/2" Handled Bonbon Oval and Square

Low Candy Jar

New Shapes 1943 Thru 1951

1946 addition:
Bonbon, 4" handled

1951 additions:
Bonbon, 7" handled — a reintroduction of the 6½" handled bonbon from the early 1940s listed in the catalog at a slightly larger size

Bonbon, 8" oval handled

Covered Candy Jars listed in the 1940 catalog:
Covered jar, 5" — This is a small bulbous jar that takes the dome-shaped puff jar lid.

1941 addition:
Candy jar, ftd. — This is the original footed candy jar in the Hobnail line. The size of the base was reduced by about one half inch in diameter about 1943. Later, in about 1947, the stem on the base was eliminated to produce the forerunner of the shape that finally evolved into the No. 3980 candy jar.

1942 addition:
Candy jar, ftd. with scalloped base. The lid has been found with two different styles of finials.

1951 addition:
Candy jar, low covered — became the No. 3880 candy after July, 1952

Vases listed in the 1940 catalog:
Vase, 4" miniature, cup, crimped, cup flared, fan, flared, hat, triangle

Vase, 4½" cupped flared, cupped square double crimped

Vase, 5" cup flared, double crimped, special, square, triangle

Rose bowl, 4½"

Rose bowl, 5"

1941 additions:
Vase, 5½" crimped, flared, square, triangle

Vase, 6" double crimp, flared, square, triangle

Vase, 6¼" ftd. cupped, cup flared, double crimped, flared, fan

Vase, 8" double crimp, flared, square, triangle

Vase, 8½" double crimp, flared crimp, flip, triangle — The listed size of this vase changed to 8" after it disappeared from the line in the early 1950s and the reentered the line as the No. 3859-8" DC vase.

Vase, 8" fan

Vase, 9" flared

Vase, 10" flared

1942 additions:
Vase, 6½" swung

Vase, 6½" fan

Vase, 6½" hand

1943 additions:
Vase, 8" ftd. double crimped, fan, square, triangle

1948 additions:

Vase, 4" ftd. double crimped, fan

1949 additions:

Vase, 3" double crimped
Rose bowl, 3"

Fenton not only added new pieces to the line over the years, but the style of some of the original pieces changed over a period of time. The changes to the two candy jars are noted in the previous section. The vanity set also underwent significant modifications. In the early 1940s catalogs the cologne stoppers and the puff box lid are dome shaped. By 1948, the catalog illustrations show a pointed cologne stopper and a matching pointed finial on the puff box lid. Two different sizes of footed cake plates are listed in the catalogs. Also, early versions of the 5½" jug appear without a crimped top.

A few of the items represented as new in 1948 appear to be a reintroduction of items that were previously discontinued. Catalogs from the early 1940s list a 12" footed cake plate. When the cake plate reappeared in the line in the latter part of the decade its size had grown to 13". Also the 11" footed double crimped bowl listed in 1948 appears to be a replica of the earlier 12" footed bowl. The crescent salad plate also made a short reappearance. In the 1948 catalog its size was listed at 6½". Catalogs from the early 1940s sized this piece at 6¾".

1938

Fenton made the No. 289 Hobnail perfume bottle under a contract with Wrisley through 1940. After that time, the price advantages of machine-made bottles caused Wrisley to change suppliers. The easiest way to distinguish the difference between the two types of bottles is to look for the number of mould seams. The Fenton bottles were made from a six-part mould while the machine-made bottles used a four-part mould. The most commonly found color is French Opalescent but these bottles have also been confirmed in Cranberry Opalescent. Other colors have been reported, but there is no evidence to support that Cameo Opalescent, or Orchid colored bottles were ever supplied to Wrisley. Fenton also sold this bottle as a vase during the early 1940s This is probably a more plausible argument for the existence of the bottles in these colors. Fenton also made a No. 289 Hobnail bath salts jar and puff box base for Wrisley. The puff box was fitted with a wooden lid that matched the wooden stopper of the perfume bottle.

1939

Sales to Wrisley of the cologne bottle peaked. Sales of the No. 289 bottle approached 30 percent of the total company sales for the year. Fenton also began production of other Hobnail pattern items in Cranberry, Blue Opalescent, French Opalescent, and Green Opalescent for introduction into the regular line. The No. 389 vanity sets and eight different shapes of vases are listed in the 1939 inventory records in French Opalescent, Blue Opalescent, and Cranberry.

1940

The Hobnail pattern was extended into the regular line in Blue Opalescent, French Opalescent, Green Opalescent, and Cranberry colors. The Hobnail punch set was introduced in French Opalescent. Sets were sold two different ways. The 13-piece sets included a bowl and 12 cups. Fourteen-piece sets had a 16" underplate added. These sets are only listed through the 1942 price sheets. Footed salt and pepper shakers are listed in the January 1940 price list, but are omitted from later price lists. Sets of these are extremely difficult to find today. The 7" special rose bowl was made for the regular line, but a special version was also made for the Quoizel Lamp Company of New York. Bowls intended for use as lamp parts have an indention in the bottom to facilitate easy drilling. This same bowl was also sold to Quoizel in French Opalescent and Cranberry in the early 1950s.

1941

Fenton lost the Wrisley account to Anchor Hocking. This company could provide cheaper machine-made bottles. Also, at this time the stopper was changed to milk glass for use in the new bottles. Hobnail in the regular line was selling well and the number of pieces in the pattern continued to be expanded. Topaz Opalescent replaced Green Opalescent.

1942

Due to wartime shortages, cranberry and blue runs were sometimes made without the necessary ingredients to produce opalescent glassware. This is one explanation for the existence of the non-opalescent pieces in the cranberry and light blue colors that are sometimes found on the secondary market today. A new color, Orchid Opalescent Hobnail, was made about this time. According to Fenton records, this color was made for an importing company that could no longer obtain glassware from foreign sources during WWII.

1943

Hobnail in Topaz Opalescent was discontinued at the end of the year. Rose Overlay was added to the line, but was discontinued at the end of the year.

1946

Fenton made the No. 389 Special Vase available to Quoizel as a lamp part in French Opalescent, Blue Opalescent, and Cranberry.

1948

Hobnail survived the tribulations of the war and production continued in Blue Opalescent, French Opalescent, and Cranberry. Several discontinued pieces reappeared in the line. These included the crescent salad plate, the footed cake plate, and the large footed double crimped bowl. New items to the line were the three-piece jam set, the three-piece mayonnaise set, and the 4" footed vase.

1949

Additions to the Hobnail line late in 1949 included the No. 3 star-shaped sugar and creamer, the 5" handled basket, and flat salt and pepper shakers. Originally the star-shaped sugar and creamer were made from a blown mould and the handles were applied. By 1951, the blown mould was retired and the #3 sugar and creamer were made from a pressed mould with molded handles. The four-piece Hobnail miniature epergne was introduced in milk glass. This was the first Hobnail in milk glass to appear since a few pieces were made in the early 1940s.

1950

The presence of milk glass Hobnail in the Fenton line was reinforced with the addition of 17 more items in January. Three pieces of the Hobnail variation — No. 489 Burred Hobnail — were introduced in milk glass, French Opalescent, and Blue Opalescent. A new piece in French Opalescent and Blue Opalescent was the petite epergne set. This set was created by placing a 4" footed DC vase in a 6" DC bonbon that was made into an epergne base by adding a shallow indention to the center of the bonbon.

1951

One of the new ideas for 1951 included the addition of square shapes to the Hobnail line. Square cups and saucers, plates, and goblets were made in French Opalescent and Blue Opalescent. A square tidbit set was fashioned by drilling an 11" and 6½" plate and joining these two pieces with a metal handle. These square items did not sell well and are in short supply on the secondary market. Another item from 1951 that is scarce today is the 8" handled oval bonbon. This piece was made in Blue Opalescent and French Opalescent. However, it only remained in the line for one year. A new punch bowl was created with a handle. Fifteen-piece sets with 12 cups, a 16" underplate, and a crystal ladle were marketed in milk glass, French Opalescent, and Blue Opalescent.

1952

Fenton revived the early 1940s Peach Blow color for use with the Hobnail pattern beginning in July 1952. Peach Blow is made by casing Gold Ruby with an exterior opal layer. Twelve items were made in this color before it was discontinued at the end of 1957. Lime Opalescent Hobnail also made an appearance in the Fenton line beginning in July 1952. Twelve different items were made before the color was discontinued at the end of 1954.

1954

Fenton began production of Hobnail in three pastel milk glass colors — Blue Pastel, Green Pastel, and Rose Pastel. Blue Pastel only remained in the line for one year. Green Pastel and Rose Pastel fared slightly better. Green Pastel remained in production for two years and Rose Pastel was discontinued at the end of 1957. Blue Opalescent Hobnail, which had been in the line continuously since 1940, was discontinued in December.

1955

Turquoise milk glass replaced Blue Pastel Hobnail. Production of Hobnail in Turquoise continued through 1958.

1959

Hobnail was introduced into the regular line in transparent amber. This color was known as Antique Amber at this time. Hobnail in Antique Amber was temporarily discontinued at the end of the year. Other pieces of Amber Hobnail began to appear in 1962 and this time Amber Hobnail remained in the line through 1981.

Fenton's July catalog supplement displayed new examples of opalescent Hobnail in four different colors. A new color, Plum Opalescent, was in the line for the first time. This color is much darker than Fenton's Orchid Opalescent color of the early 1940s. The other three colors, Blue Opalescent, Topaz Opalescent, and Green Opalescent had been in the line previously, although the new green was much more blue than the earlier Green Opalescent color. Plum Hobnail continued in the line through 1962, Blue Opalescent was discontinued at the end of 1964.

1961

Hobnail made a brief appearance in Apple Green Overlay, Coral, Honey Amber, Powder Blue Overlay, and Wild Rose — cased colors with opal interiors. Only about five or six items were made in each color. Apple Green Overlay, Coral and Powder Blue Overlay were only made one year and Wild Rose Hobnail lasted two years. Hobnail in Honey Amber was discontinued at the end of 1963, with the exception of the lavabo, which continued in production through 1966.

1962

Opaque Blue Overlay Hobnail was introduced in 1962. The color was made by laying transparent Colonial Blue over an interior opal layer. Six different pieces were made in this color, but all were discontinued by the end of 1963.

1964

Fenton changed the name of transparent amber from Antique Amber to Colonial Amber. Fenton's transparent deep blue (Colonial Blue), transparent olive green (Colonial Green), and transparent orange were added to the growing list of Hobnail colors. Production of Hobnail in Colonial Blue continued through the end of 1979. Colonial Green was discontinued in 1977, when Fenton's transparent green color was changed to the brighter Springtime Green. Production of orange Hobnail ended in December, 1977.

1968

Samples of a number of items were made in the blue and yellow jade colors similar to Fenton's 1930s Chinese Yellow and Pekin Blue colors. These colors were never made successfully enough to be placed into the regular line, but enough samples were made that some pieces were sold through the Fenton gift shop. Examples of these colors in Hobnail occasionally show up on the secondary market. Hobnail in crystal enjoyed a revival. However, it made a quick exit, only lasting one year.

1970

Eleven items in Blue Marble Hobnail were introduced in January of this year and an ashtray set in this color was added the next year. Production of all pieces was discontinued by the end of 1973. Fenton's Hobnail candle bowl was packaged with assorted colored candles and a colored plastic flower ring and marketed as a decorative candle arrangement. The style and color of these arrangements was changed for the spring and fall seasons until this bundled assortment was abandoned in the middle of the decade.

1971

Fenton began decorating select items in milk glass Hobnail with hand-painted designs. The Bluebells decoration designed by Louise Piper was offered from 1971 through 1972. Special milk glass Holly decorated pieces were offered in the July catalog from 1971 through 1976 for the Christmas season. Fenton began experimenting with Hobnail in Burmese, but only one 11" vase was ever put into the line, and this piece was discontinued after only one year.

1972

Hobnail entered the line in transparent ruby. This popular color continued in the line into the 1980s.

1974

Decorated Roses on milk glass Hobnail was a hand-painted pink roses pattern available through the end of 1975.

1977

Springtime Green replaced Colonial Green as Fenton's transparent green color for Hobnail.

1978

Beginning in July, Hobnail in Blue Opalescent made a third appearance in the Fenton line with the introduction of ten different shapes. Eight of these shapes had not been made in this color previously.

1979

Eight items in Hobnail were selected to be made in Cameo Opalescent. Most pieces were discontinued by the end of 1980, but the 10" bud vase was made through mid 1982.

1980

The regular Fenton line featured assorted pieces of milk glass Hobnail. The No. 3907-26" lamp was in the line in Cranberry and numerous Ruby pieces were targeted for Valentine's Day and Christmas season appeal.

The January 1980 supplement introduced a number of Hobnail pieces to Fenton's carnival assortment. The carnival collection featured the following seven pieces:

Basket	3837-CN	Toothpick	3795-CN
Bell	3667-CN	Vase, 4½"	3854-CN
Candy and cover, oval	3786-CN	Vase, bud	3758-CN
Comport	3628-CN		

The following 14 piece assortment of Topaz Opalescent Hobnail was made for the Levay Distributing company:

Banana stand	3720-TO	Cruet	3869-TO
Basket	3837-TO	Epergne set, 4-pc.	3701-TO
Basket, 10" pie crust crimp	3830-TO	Punch set, 14 pc.	3712-TO
Bowl, 9" DC	3924-TO	Rose bowl, 4½"	3854-TO
Butter, 8½" covered	3677-TO	Rose bowl, 4½"	3861-TO
Candleholder, 4"	3974-TO	Slipper, 6" kitten	3995-TO
Creamer, sugar & lid	3606-TO	Toothpick	3795-TO

1981

The 1981–82 general catalog shows Hobnail in Cameo Opalescent, but the price lists indicate most of the items in this color were discontinued by the end of 1981.

A May 1981 flyer pictures Purple Slag that was created for Levay. A few items in Hobnail were made in this color. These included the popular No. 3667-5½" bell and the No. 3995-6" kitten slipper.

1982

In 1982, Cranberry Opalescent Hobnail was made for The Levay Distributing Company. Handled pieces had candy stripe handles. The water set consisted of an 11" pitcher and six 4½" tumblers.

Basket, 8" loop handled	3347-CR	Lamp, 36" banquet	9201-CR
Basket, 8"	3333-CR	Vase, 6½" Jack in Pulpit	3362-CR
Basket. 10" pie crust crimp	3830-CR	Water set, 7-piece	3909-CR
Cruet	3863-CR		

Fenton also made Hobnail for Levay in Blue Opalescent and Aqua Opal carnival. The champagne punch set consisted of a 12½" diameter bowl, eight 3¾" champagne goblets, and a shallow base for the bowl. The seven-piece water set was created by combining an 8¼" 54 oz. jug with six 4" 9 oz. tumblers. The 1982 listing of Aqua Opal carnival included:

Banana stand, 12" pie crust crimp	3720-IO	Epergne set, 10" Jack-in-the-Pulpit	3701-IO
Basket, 6½"	3834-IO	Punch set, champagne	3611-IO
Bell, 5½"	3645-IO	Toothpick, 2¾"	3795-IO
Cruet, mini w/stopper	3869-IO	Water set, 7-piece	3908-IO
Cruet, 6½" & stopper	3863-IO		

The same pieces listed in Aqua Opal carnival above were also made for Levay in Blue Opalescent. In addition the Blue Opalescent assortment included:

Butter, 8¼" covered	3677-BO	Punch set, 14 piece	3712-BO

The 14-piece punch set consisted of a 7-quart bowl, 12 punch cups, and a low flared stand.

The kitten slipper was made in Chocolate as a part of an assortment for Levay.

1983

Production of Hobnail for the regular line was focused on milk glass. The only other Hobnail remaining in the line was the No. 3907-26" lamp in Cranberry.

1984

Two new Cranberry offerings in the catalog included the No. 3307-15" student lamp and the No. 3308 Gone with the Wind lamp. The first pieces of Hobnail appeared in two new colors — Federal Blue and Dusty Rose. The No. 3850 vase made in Dusty Rose and Federal Blue was given free with an assortment order. An assortment of milk glass was still in the line and Fenton was again making Hobnail for Levay.

Special issue of Plum Opalescent made for Levay:

Banana stand, 12"	3720-PO	Epergne	3701-PO
Basket, 5½" DC	3735-PO	Fairy light, 3-piece	3804-PO
Basket, 8½" DC	3638-PO	Pitcher, 70-ounce ice lip	3664-PO
Basket, 12" DC	3734-PO	Relish, heart-shape	3733-PO
Bell, crimped	3645-PO	Vase, 4½" rose bowl	3323-PO
Bowl, 12" DC	3938-PO	Water set, 7-piece	3306-PO

1985

A 14-piece punch set was made in Green Opalescent as a part of Fenton's Connoisseur Collection. Production of this special set was limited to 500 sets.

1986

The three different Cranberry Hobnail lamps — No. 3307-15", No. 3907-26", and No. 3308-25" Gone with the Wind — were still in the line along with an assortment of milk glass.

1987

Fenton made the small No. 3952 DC vase in Dusty Rose (DK), Minted Cream (EO), Peaches 'n Cream (UO), and Provincial Blue Opalescent (OO). This small vase also reappeared for a brief period in Colonial Amber.

Ruby Hobnail continued to be promoted for the Christmas season with nine different pieces available for Fenton's 14-piece assortment promotion. A large assortment of milk glass was still available in the regular catalog. Fenton was proud to announce that production Hobnail was enjoying its 48th straight year.

1988

An eight-piece collection of Ruby Hobnail included the following items from the general catalog:

Basket, 6½"	3834-RU	Fairy Light, 4½"	3608-RU
Basket, 8½"	3638-RU	Slipper	3995-RU

Bonbon, 7½" handled	3706-RU	Vase, 4½"	3854-RU
Comport, footed	3628-RU		

The No. 3952-4" footed vase was made in greenish blue Teal Royale (OC), Dusty Rose (DK), Peaches 'n Cream (UO), Provincial Blue Opalescent (OO), and in cobalt Blue Royale (KK).

The 1988 limited edition Collector's Extravaganza offering featured the following items in Pink Opalescent Hobnail (UO):

Banana stand, 12"	A3720-UO	Lamp, 25" Gone with the Wind	A3308-UO
Basket, 6½"	A3834-UO	Pitcher & Bowl set	A3000-UO
Basket, loop handle	A3335-UO	Punch set, 14-piece	A3712-UO
Basket, 10" pie crust crimped	A3830-UO	Rose bowl, 4¼" crimped	A3861-UO
Bonbon, 7" handled	A3937-UO	Rose bowl, 4½" ruffled top	A3854-UO
Cruet & stopper, 6½"	A3863-UO	Toothpick, 2¾"	A3795-UO
Epergne set, miniature	A3801-UO	Vase, 6½" Jack in the Pulpit	A3362-UO
Epergne set, 10" Jack in the Pulpit	A3701-UO	Water set, 7-piece	A3908-UO

The water set was composed of an 8¼" 54 oz. pitcher and six 9 oz. tumblers. The punch set consisted of a large bowl, 12 cups, and a base for the bowl. Note the color of the Peaches 'n Cream items listed in the general catalog is the same as the Pink Opalescent color promoted for the Collector's Extravaganza offering.

Milk glass and Cranberry lamps continued to be an important part of the Hobnail line. The three Cranberry lamps from the previous years were still in the line and a milk glass No. 3808-23½" Gone with the Wind lamp was also being made.

1990 – 91

The 1990 catalog shows the production of Hobnail limited to a milk glass No. 3808-23½" GWTW lamp and two Cranberry lamps — the No. 3308-25" GWTW and No. 3907-26".

1992

The 1992 limited edition offering — Gold Pearl was an iridized topaz. From the Fenton description: "Gold Pearl begins with an opalescent formula rich in cerium and titanium. Each piece is formed from a molten glob of clear glass which is formed, cooled and returned to the flaming glory hole to develop its pearly white edges. The glass is continuously reheated in the glory hole as the metallic oxides are applied and the final shape is created." Hobnail pieces made included:

Basket, looped handle	3335-GP	Tumbler	3949-GP
Cruet and stopper	3863-GP	Vase, 6" hand	3355-GP
Lamp, 21" student	3813-GP	Water set, 5-piece	3908-GP

A few Hobnail pieces were offered in Fenton's Persian Pearl Historical Collection limited edition promotion. The green Persian Pearl color, unlike the older green colors, is green iridized. Pieces in Hobnail included:

Bowl, 12" DC	3938-XV	Candlesticks, 6"	3674-XV
Candy, ftd.	3784-XV	Epergne set, 4-piece	3701-XV

Two epergne sets, the No. 3701 and No. 3801 mini four-piece set, were included in a later 1992 Persian Pearl Historical Collection assortment. Items sold in this assortment were limited to sales with orders through May 31, 1993.

The No. 3356-8" tulip vase was made in Red Carnival for the regular line.

Lamps produced this year included the Cranberry No. 3808-25" Gone with the Wind, No. 3907-26" in Cranberry, milk glass No. 3807-21" student, milk glass No. 3907-26" pillar, and the milk glass No. 3308-23½" Gone with the Wind.

Other milk glass Hobnail items available for a limited time during 1992 included:

Basket, 6½"	3336-MI	Pitcher, 6"	3365-MI
Basket, looped handle	3335-MI	Pitcher, 11"	3360-MI
Basket, 8½"	3638-MI	Pitcher, 70 oz.	3664-MI
Basket, 12"	3734-MI	Pitcher & bowl set	3600-MI
Bell, 6"	3645-MI	Punch set, 14-piece	3712-MI
Bowl, 12"	3938-MI	Salt & Pepper	3806-MI

Cake plate, 13" ftd.	3913-MI	Slipper	3995-MI
Candle bowl, chip 'n dip	3778-MI	Tumbler, 9 oz.	3949-MI
Candleholder, 4½"	3974-MI	Vase, 6" hand	3355-MI
Candy/Butter bowl	3802-MI	Vase, 7½" JIP	3356-MI
Candy jar & cover	3886-MI	Vase, 11"	3752-MI
Cream & sugar w/cover	3606-MI		

The No. 3600 pitcher and bowl set was composed of the No. 3938-12" bowl and the No. 3360-11" pitcher. The punch set included a base, 12 cups, and the deep-style punch bowl.

1993

Fenton's 1993 Historical Collection included 12 different items in Rose Magnolia (RV) Hobnail. A punch bowl, 12 cups, and base were offered as a 14-piece set with the ware number 3712. A 5-piece water set (No. 3908-RV) was composed of the No. 3764-RV 54 oz. water pitcher and four No. 3949-RV water tumblers. Other items included:

Basket, 4½"	3834-RV	Epergne set, 10"	3701-RV
Basket, 7"	3337-RV	Lamp, 21" student w/prisms	3313-RV
Bell, 5½"	3645-RV	Vase, 4½"	3854-RV
Candy & cover	3784-RV	Vase, 7½"	3356-RV
Cruet & stopper	3863-RV		

Sales of these items were limited to orders received by May 30, 1994.

French Opalescent Baskets were shown in the Easter supplement with colored handles and crests. The FD examples had a Dusty Rose trim; F3 baskets featured light blue trim.

Basket, 9"	1156-FD	Basket, 9"	1156-F3
Basket, 6½"	3736-FD	Basket, 6½"	3736-F3

Lamps produced included the milk glass No. 3808-23½" Gone with the Wind, Cranberry No. 3308-25" Gone with the Wind, and Cranberry No. 3907-26". The Red Carnival assortment included the No. 3356-8" tulip vase.

1994

Three Hobnail baskets, No. 3638-8½", No. 1158-7", and No. 3834-4½", were shown in the Easter supplement. The colors were opal with Sea Mist Green crests and handles (FR); opal with Dusty Rose crests and handles (FD); and opal with Autumn Gold crests and handles (FT).

Fenton's new Red Carnival assortment included two Hobnail pieces this year — the No. 1167 three-piece fairy light, and the No. 3762-12 oz. pitcher.

1995

The following eight items were available in Cranberry Opalescent:

Basket, 10½"	3348-CR	Lamp, 26" Pillar	3907-CR
Fairy Light, 3-piece	3380-CR	Pitcher, 5½"	3366-CR
Lamp, 22" student w/prisms	1174-CR	Rose bowl, 4½"	3861-CR
Lamp, 25" Gone with the Wind	3308-CR	Vase, 7½" tulip	3356-CR

The Easter Basket collection of French Opalescent baskets with three different colored trims included French Opalescent with Dusty Rose trim (IH), French Opalescent with Sea Mist Green trim (IM), and French Opalescent with cobalt trim (IQ):

Basket, 6"	1159-IH	Basket, 8½"	1160-IQ
Basket, 6"	1159-IM	Basket, 10½"	3830-IH
Basket, 6"	1159-IQ	Basket, 10½"	3830-IM
Basket, 8½"	1160-IH	Basket, 10½"	3830-IQ
Basket, 8½"	1160-IM		

1996

Cranberry Opalescent items in production for the regular line included:

Basket, 8½"	3346-CR	Oil bottle & stopper	3869-CR
Basket, 10½"	3348-CR	Rose bowl, 4½"	3861-CR
Fairy light, 3 pc.	3380-CR	Vase, 7½"	1155-CR
Lamp, 22" Student w/metal base	1174-CR	Vase, 7½" tulip	3356-CR
Lamp, 25" Gone with the Wind	3308-CR		

In addition to the above items, the No. 3808-MI 23½" Gone with the Wind lamp remained in the line.

1997

A Topaz Opalescent (TS) No. 1158-8½" basket was included as part of this year's Historic Collection. Cranberry Hobnail remained in the line, but three pieces from the above selection of Cranberry were retired. Discontinued shapes were the No. 3348-10½" basket, the No. 3869 oil bottle, and the No. 1155-7½" vase.

1998

The Cranberry Hobnail No. 3308 Gone with the Wind lamp and the No. 174 student lamp with prisms were still offered to customers of the regular line. Both lamps were absent from the 1999 catalog.

2000

The following eight items in Hobnail returned to the regular line in a pink opalescent iridescent color dubbed Champagne.

Basket, 4¼"	6832-PY	Pitcher, 5½"	3366-PY
Basket, 9½"	3357-PY	Slipper	3995-PY
Fairy light, 9"	3804-PY	Vase, 5"	3350-PY
Lamp, 25" Melon	3303-PY	Vase, 11"	3752-PY

2001

Production of Champagne Hobnail was discontinued, but the Hobnail pattern remained in the line. Cranberry (CR) Hobnail returned to the line after an absence of several years. In addition, Hobnail assortments in two new colors — Willow Green Opalescent (GY) and Pink Chiffon Opalescent (YS) — were introduced.

Basket, 4¼"	6832-GY (YS)	Candy box, 7¼"	3688-GY (YS)
Basket, 7"	3346-CR	Lamp, 25" Melon	3303-GY (YS) (CR)
Basket, 9½"	3357-GY (YS)	Pitcher, 5½"	3366-GY (YS) (CR)
Bell, 5½"	3368-GY (YS)	Trinket box, 3½"	3969-GY
Boot, 4¼"	3992-YS	Vase, 4½" cupped	3669-YS (CR)
Cakeplate, 12"	3913-GY	Vase, 11"	3752-GY (YS) (CR)

The No. 6832 basket was made in violet iridescent (OQ). Also, the No. 1167-9" 3-piece fairy light was produced in violet iridescent with a milk glass crest and candle insert.

2002

Two items in Hobnail were made in a new color — Blue Topaz (SY) — an opalescent, iridescent light blue. Included in this offering were the No. 6832 small basket and the No. 3969 trinket box. In addition to all of the original pieces of Pink Chiffon Opalescent, three new items were made in this color. These included a No. 2991-18" student lamp, the No. 3969 trinket box, and the No. 3669 small vase. The trinket box in Willow Green Opalescent was deleted from the line. All of the other pieces of this color were still in production. The violet No. 6832 was still in the line. In Cranberry, the No. 3669 vase and No. 3303 Melon lamp were discontinued. Added to the Cranberry assortment were the No. 1150 student lamp, the No. 3304-25" GWTW lamp, the No. 3326-5" vase, the No. 3649-4½" vase, the No. 3856-6" vase, and the No. 3858-8" vase.

2003

Seven items in Cranberry were the only remaining Hobnail items in this year's catalog. These included the No. 3346 basket, the No. 3322-10" bowl, the No. 3304 Gone with the Wind lamp, the No. 3367-8" pitcher, the No. 3326 vase, the No. 3856 vase, and the No. 3752 vase.

Hobnail Produced for L.G. Wright

Fenton also produced opalescent Hobnail glassware for L. G. Wright. Fenton's long association with Wright began in the mid-1930s, when Fenton began producing a Hobnail barber bottle for this energetic salesman. Over a span of the next half century, Fenton produced glassware for L. G. Wright from the following Hobnail moulds:

Barber bottle   Goblet, water
Bowl, covered   Rose bowl
Bowl, finger   Salt & pepper
Comport, small ftd.   Sugar
Creamer   Tumbler

389-12 Pc. Assortment - Made in Colors -
French, Blue and Topaz Opalescent
Hand Made by Fenton

389-6½"
Ftd. Vase-Fan

389
Plate Comport

389-5½"
Triangle Vase

389
Flared Comport

389-5½"
Flared Vase

389-6½"
Ftd. Vase, D. Crpd.

389-7"
Oval Bowl

389-5½"
Tulip Vase

389-6½"
Ftd. Vase, Triangle

389-7"
Flared Bowl

389-4½"
Square Vase

389
Triangle Comport

Computer Colorized Catalog Reprint Circa 1941   Courtesy Of: The Fenton Art Glass Museum

Amber Hobnail

In addition to being produced in 1959, the three-piece No. 3810 octagonal ashtray set was also made in 1954. The items in the first listing below were made in amber in 1959. Then amber Hobnail disappeared from the line until 1962, when the slipper was made in amber. In 1963, amber survived a name change to Colonial Amber and other pieces in this color were made in Hobnail. Pieces were added and discontinued through the years and Colonial Amber Hobnail remained in the line until Fenton discontinued amber at the end of 1980. Fenton resumed production of Colonial Amber in 1987. The only item in the Hobnail pattern selected to be made at that time was the No. 3952-4" footed vase. Production continued though December 1988.

Sets and their ware numbers in amber Hobnail are as follows:	Introduced	Discontinued
Ashtray set No. 3810 (3-piece): No. 3876 small ashtray, No. 3877 medium ashtray, No. 3878 large ashtray	1959	1960
Cigarette set, No. 3603 boxed: No. 3685 cigarette box, No. 3692 lighter, 3 No. 3693 ashtrays	1967	1971
Console set No. 3704 (3-piece): No. 3724-8½" bowl, 2 No. 3774-10" candles	1959	July 1959
Juice set No. 3905 (7-piece): No. 3965 squat jug, 6 No. 3945-5 oz. tumblers	July 1959	1960

Amber Hobnail	Ware No.	Introduced	Discontinued	Value
Ashtray #1 4" octagonal	3876-AR	1959*	1960*	4.00 – 5.00
Ashtray #2 5¼" octagonal	3877-AR	1959*	1960*	5.00 – 6.00
Ashtray #3 6½" octagonal	3878-AR	1959*	1960*	6.00 – 8.00
Basket, 7" handled	3837-AR	1959	July 1959**	25.00 – 35.00
Bowl, 8½"	3724-AR	1959	July 1959	40.00 – 45.00
Butter, ¼ lb.	3977-AR	1959	1960	25.00 – 35.00
Candleholder	3974-AR	1959	July 1959	9.00 – 12.00
Candleholder, 10"	3774-AR	1959	July 1959	40.00 – 50.00
Candy jar, ftd.	3887-AR	1959	July 1959	35.00 – 40.00
Comport	3727-AR	1959	July 1959	18.00 – 20.00
Epergne set, 4-pc.	3701-AR	1959	July 1959	60.00 – 75.00
Goblet, water	3845-AR	1959	1960	9.00 – 11.00
Jug, 12 oz. syrup	3762-AR	1959	1960	20.00 – 25.00
Jug, 32 oz. squat	3965-AR	1959	1960	40.00 – 45.00
Jug, 54 oz.	3764-AR	1959	1960	85.00 – 95.00
Oil	3869-AR	1959	1960	27.00 – 30.00
Relish	3822-AR	1959	1960	10.00 – 12.00
Salt and pepper, flat	3806-AR	1959	1960	12.00 – 15.00
Sugar and cream set	3708-AR	1959	July 1959	15.00 – 25.00
Sugar and cream (star-shape)	3906-AR	1959	1960	35.00 – 45.00
Tumbler, 5 oz.	3945-AR	1959	1960	8.00 – 12.00
Tumbler, 9 oz.	3949-AR	1959	1960	15.00 – 18.00
Vase, 4½" DC	3854-AR	1959	July 1959**	7.00 – 9.00

*Initially listed in 1954 for 1 year.
**Reissued in Colonial Amber (CA). See listing below.

Colonial Amber Hobnail	Ware No.	Introduced	Discontinued	Value
Apothecary jar	3689-CA	1964	1970	50.00 – 60.00
Ashtray, ball	3648-CA	1977	1979	18.00 – 20.00
Ashtray, medium 5" round	3973-CA	1964	1968	4.00 – 6.00
Ashtray, small 3½" round	3972-CA	1964	1968	3.00 – 5.00
Ashtray, 6½" round	3776-CA	1964	1966	8.00 – 10.00
Ashtray set, 3-piece round	3610-CA	1964	1980	15.00 – 21.00
Basket, 7" handled	3837-CA	1967	1980+	25.00 – 35.00

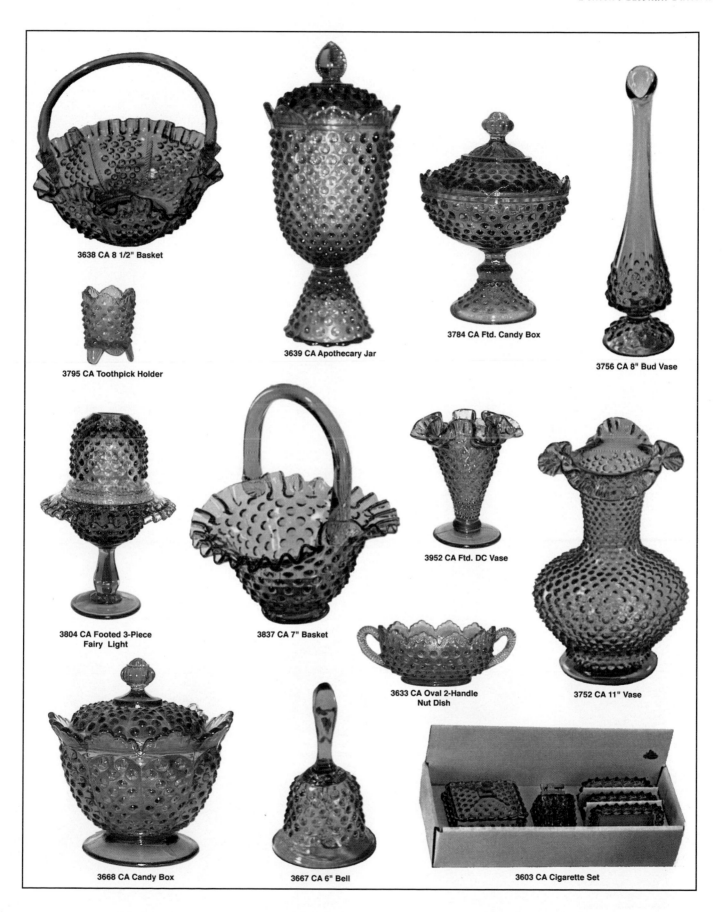

3638 CA 8 1/2" Basket

3795 CA Toothpick Holder

3639 CA Apothecary Jar

3784 CA Ftd. Candy Box

3756 CA 8" Bud Vase

3804 CA Footed 3-Piece Fairy Light

3837 CA 7" Basket

3952 CA Ftd. DC Vase

3633 CA Oval 2-Handle Nut Dish

3752 CA 11" Vase

3668 CA Candy Box

3667 CA 6" Bell

3603 CA Cigarette Set

Colonial Amber Hobnail	Ware No.	Introduced	Discontinued	Value
Basket, 8½"	3638-CA	1967	1971	30.00 – 40.00
Basket, 10"	3830-CA	1968	1978	40.00 – 50.00
Bell, 6"	3667-CA	1967	1980+	14.00 – 18.00
Bonbon, handled	3706-CA	1979	1980+	10.00 – 12.00
Bowl, 8" DC	3639-CA	1967	1969	35.00 – 40.00
Candle bowl, 4" miniature	3873-CA	1969	July 1972	12.00 – 15.00
Candle bowl, 6"	3872-CA	July 1968	1979	10.00 – 15.00
Candy/butter bowl	3802-CA	1979	1980+	35.00 – 40.00
Candy box	3668-CA	1975	1980	35.00 – 40.00
Candy box, ftd.	3784-CA	1966	1971	35.00 – 40.00
Candy box, oval covered	3786-CA	1968	July 1970	20.00 – 30.00
Cigarette box, covered	3685-CA	1967	1971	30.00 – 35.00
Cigarette set — lighter/cigarette box/3 ashtray	3603-CA	1967	1971	50.00 – 60.00
Cigarette lighter	3692-CA	1965	1971	12.00 – 15.00
Comport, 6" ftd, DC	3628-CA	1969	1980+	9.00 – 12.00
Creamer, miniature	3665-CA	1965	1969	7.00 – 9.00
Fairy light	3608-CA	1969	1980+	18.00 – 20.00
Fairy light, 3-pc. ftd.	3804-CA	1975	1980+	45.00 – 50.00
Lamp, courting, oil	3792-CA	1965	1969	55.00 – 60.00
Lamp, courting, electric	3793-CA	1965	1969	55.00 – 60.00
Nut dish	3650-CA	1967	July 1968	8.00 – 10.00
Nut dish, oval 2-H	3633-CA	1964	1969	8.00 – 10.00
Slipper	3995-CA	1962	1980	11.00 – 13.00
Toothpick holder	3795-CA	1966	1976	8.00 – 10.00
Urn, 11" covered	3986-CA	1968	1970	85.00 – 95.00
Vase, 3" DC	3853-CA	1968	1980+	6.00 – 8.00
Vase, 4" ftd. DC	3952-CA	1965	1978	6.00 – 8.00
Vase, 4½"DC	3854-CA	1969	1980+	6.00 – 8.00
Vase, 5" 3-toed	3653-CA	1965	1971	9.00 – 12.00
Vase, 8" swung bud	3756-CA	1967	1980+	14.00 – 16.00
Vase, 11"	3752-CA	1977	July 1978	20.00 – 30.00
Vase, 12" ftd. swung	3753-CA	1968	1971*	24.00 – 30.00
Vase, 24" tall swung	3652-CA	1965	1978	30.00 – 40.00

*Also made 1979 – 1980+

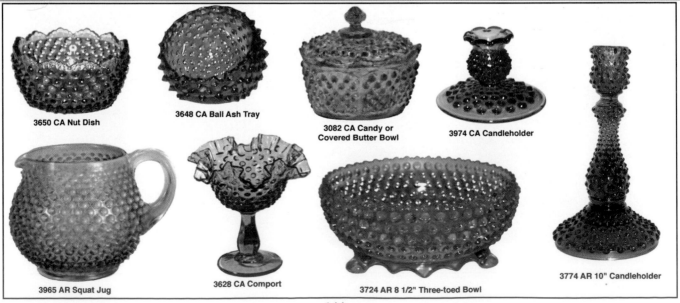

3650 CA Nut Dish

3648 CA Ball Ash Tray

3082 CA Candy or Covered Butter Bowl

3974 CA Candleholder

3965 AR Squat Jug

3628 CA Comport

3724 AR 8 1/2" Three-toed Bowl

3774 AR 10" Candleholder

Apple Green Overlay Hobnail

Apple Green Overlay pieces have a light green exterior layer of glass applied over a milk glass interior. Only five different pieces of Hobnail were made in this color and all of the production occurred during 1961.

Apple Green Overlay Hobnail	Ware No.	Introduced	Discontinued	Value
Jug, 12 oz. syrup	3762-AG	1961	1962	40.00 – 50.00
Vase, 5" DC	3850-AG	1961	1962	30.00 – 35.00
Vase, 6"	3856-AG	1961	1962	30.00 – 35.00
Vase, 8"	3858-AG	1961	1962	45.00 – 55.00
Vase, 11"	3752-AG	1961	1962	90.00 – 110.00

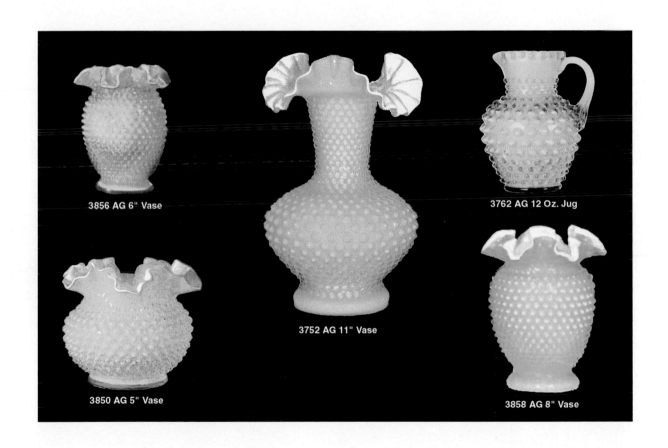

3856 AG 6" Vase

3762 AG 12 Oz. Jug

3752 AG 11" Vase

3850 AG 5" Vase

3858 AG 8" Vase

Black Hobnail

Two black Hobnail pieces in the regular line were the 6" candle bowl and the kitchen shaker. The candle bowl was also sold with a candle and floral arrangement from July through December 1970. The ware number for this arrangement was 3619-BK. The kitchen shaker was sold with a white mate using the color code BW from 1962 through 1965.

The planters were not in the regular line. They were made for floral supply wholesaler A. L. Randall of Chicago in 1970. The 8½" planter is 4¼" wide and has scallops on the top edge. The larger 10" rectangular planter is 4¼" wide and 2¾" high. It has smooth, shallow scallops on the top edge.

The toothpick, small vase, and oval 2-H bowl were sold through the Fenton Gift Shop in the mid-1970s. During the same era, the No. 3806 salt and pepper were sold as a black and white set through the Fenton Gift Shop. This set was originally produced in this color combination for the Lafayette Hotel of Marietta, Ohio.

Black Hobnail	Ware No.	Introduced	Discontinued	Value
Candle bowl, 6"	3872-BK	July 1968	1975	18.00 – 20.00
Shaker, kitchen	3602-BK	1962	1966	15.00 – 18.00

Black Hobnail items not in the regular line:

Black Hobnail	Ware No.	Introduced	Discontinued	Value
Nut dish, oval 2-H	3633-BK			18.00 – 20.00
Planter, 8½" rectangular	3697-BK			35.00 – 45.00
Planter, 10" rectangular	3799-BK			35.00 – 45.00
Toothpick	3795-BK			10.00 – 12.00
Vase, 3"	3853-BK			16.00 – 18.00
Vase, 5"	3850-BK			20.00 – 25.00

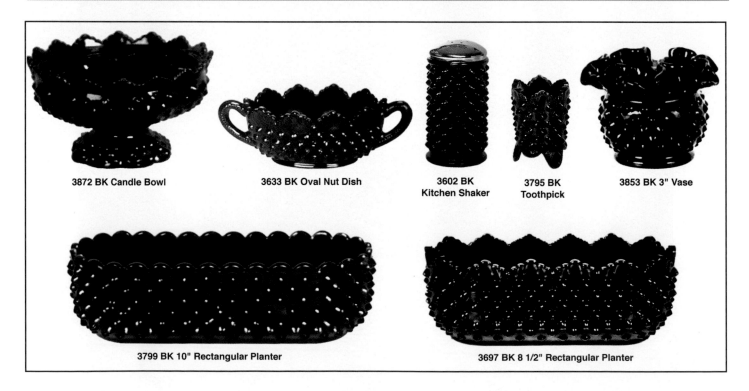

3872 BK Candle Bowl   3633 BK Oval Nut Dish   3602 BK Kitchen Shaker   3795 BK Toothpick   3853 BK 3" Vase

3799 BK 10" Rectangular Planter   3697 BK 8 1/2" Rectangular Planter

Blue Marble Hobnail

Blue Marble is a light blue opaque glass accented with opal swirls. This type of glass is sometimes referred to as slag glass by collectors. Varied effects result from swirling gathered gobs of molten blue glass with opal — thus no two pieces in this color will be exactly alike. The color was introduced into the Hobnail pattern in January 1970, when an assortment of ten shapes entered the line. Two more items were added in 1971 and the color was discontinued at the end of 1973.

Blue Marble Hobnail	Ware No.	Introduced	Discontinued	Value
Ashtray set, 3-piece round	3610-MB	1971	1973	40.00 – 45.00
Basket, 6½"	3736-MB	1970	1974	45.00 – 55.00
Bonbon, 8" handled	3706-MB	1970	1974	30.00 – 35.00
Bowl, 10" ftd.	3731-MB	1970	1974	50.00 – 60.00
Candle bowl, 6"	3872-MB	1970	1974	22.00 – 27.00
Candleholder	3974-MB	1970	July 1972	14.00 – 16.00
Candy box, covered	3886-MB	1970	1974	40.00 – 55.00
Candy box, covered slipper	3700-MB	1971	1974	40.00 – 50.00
Comport, 6" ftd., DC	3628-MB	1970	1974	27.00 – 30.00
Relish, handled, heart-shaped	3733-MB	1970	1973	30.00 – 35.00
Slipper	3995-MB	1970	1974	20.00 – 22.00
Vase, 12" ftd. swung	3753-MB	1970	1973	30.00 35.00

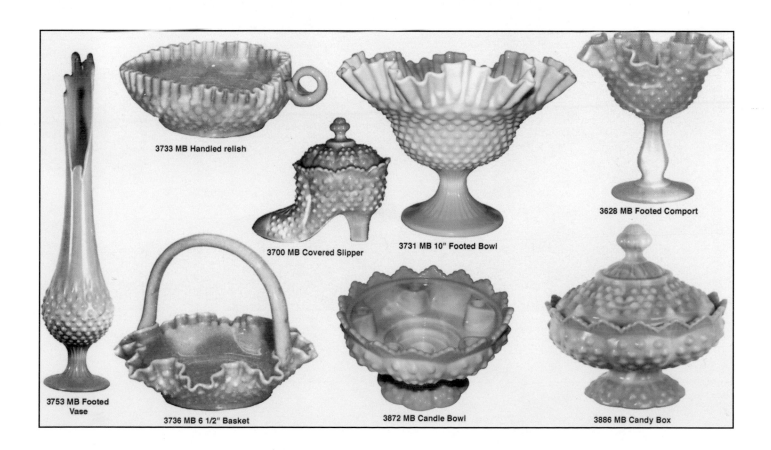

3733 MB Handled relish

3700 MB Covered Slipper

3731 MB 10" Footed Bowl

3628 MB Footed Comport

3753 MB Footed Vase

3736 MB 6 1/2" Basket

3872 MB Candle Bowl

3886 MB Candy Box

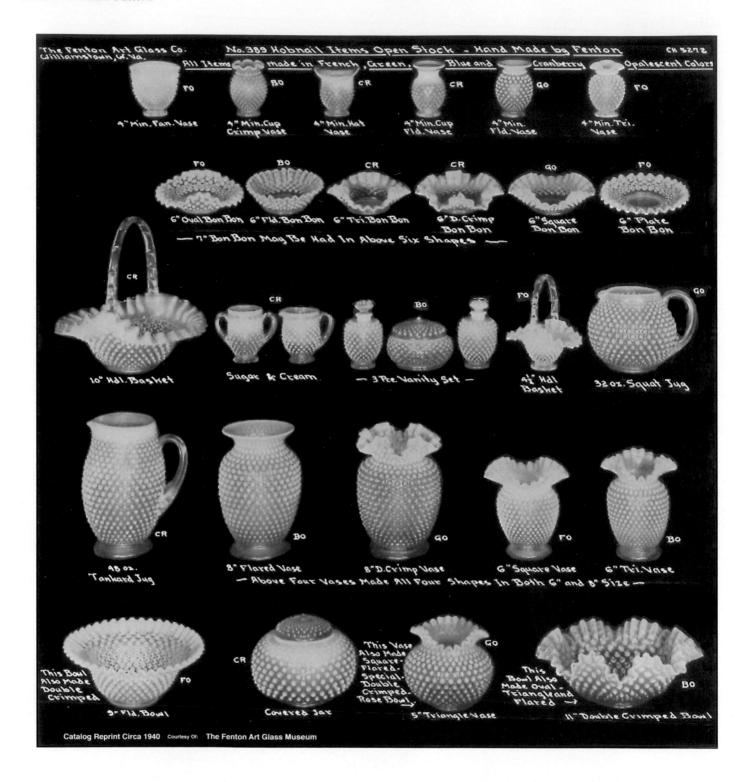

The Fenton Art Glass Co.
Williamstown, W.Va.
No. 389 Hobnail Items Open Stock – Hand Made by Fenton
CH 3272
All Items made in French, Green, Blue and Cranberry Opalescent Colors

4" Min. Fan. Vase — FO
4" Min. Cup Crimp Vase — BO
4" Min. Hat Vase — CR
4" Min. Cup Fld. Vase — CR
4" Min. Fld. Vase — GO
4" Min. Tri. Vase — FO

6" Oval Bon Bon — FO
6" Fld. Bon Bon — BO
6" Tri. Bon Bon — CR
6" D. Crimp Bon Bon — CR
6" Square Bon Bon — GO
6" Plate Bon Bon — FO

— 7" Bon Bon May Be Had In Above Six Shapes —

10" Hdl. Basket — CR
Sugar & Cream — CR
— 3 Pce. Vanity Set — BO
4½" Hdl. Basket — FO
32 oz. Squat Jug — GO

48 oz. Tankard Jug — CR
8" Flared Vase — BO
8" D. Crimp Vase — GO
6" Square Vase — FO
6" Tri. Vase — BO

— Above Four Vases Made All Four Shapes In Both 6" and 8" Size —

This Bowl Also Made Double Crimped — FO
9" Fld. Bowl
Covered Jar — CR
This Vase Also Made Square-Flared-Special-Double Crimped-Rose Bowl — 5" Triangle Vase — GO
This Bowl Also Made Oval-Triangle and Flared → 11" Double Crimped Bowl — BO

Catalog Reprint Circa 1940   Courtesy Of: The Fenton Art Glass Museum

148

Blue Opalescent Hobnail

Fenton introduced the Hobnail pattern in Blue Opalescent in 1940. This original period of production continued through December 1954. During this period, many new items were added, and other "stale" items were dropped from the line. Some items were produced for the entire period, but others, such as the vanity bottle, 6" hand vase, cookie jar, and ¼ lb. butter, were only made for a short time. Many collectors are having a difficult time finding these items and the prices below are a good indication of the demand. Other pieces which are proving hard to find include the square items made for a few years in the early 1950s. The square shapes did not sell well for Fenton. As a result, collectors are finding these square items to be in short supply.

Once an item was discontinued, it usually did not reappear during the same period of production, but there are a few exceptions. A few items that were discontinued during World War II were brought back into the line in the late 1940s or early 1950s. Catalogs from the early 1940s list a 12" footed cake plate. The footed cake plate reappeared in the line in the latter part of the decade, but its size had grown to 13". Also the 11" footed double crimped bowl listed in 1948 appears to be a replica of the earlier 12" footed bowl. The crescent salad plate also made a short reappearance. Catalogs from the early 1940s sized this piece at 6¾". When the crescent salad reappeared in the 1948 catalog, its size was listed at 6½".

During the early years, some bowls (nappies), vases, and bonbons were crimped to produce different shapes. Due to differences in terminology and slight variations in the listing of sizes, it is difficult to follow the progression of these shapes through the yearly price listings. Therefore, when an accurate period of production could not be determined, a blank space was left in the date column below. This problem was solved after July 1952 when Fenton began giving each shape a different ware number. For a more detailed comparison of the various shapes of bowls, candy jars, and vases that were in the line prior to 1952, see the introduction to this chapter.

Blue Opalescent Hobnail was reintroduced to the Fenton line in July 1959. Some items from the original era were reissued along with other pieces that had not been made before. This new production extended through December 1964. Reissued items during this period of production are marked with an asterisk in the discontinued date column below. Notice a slightly modified version of the original 5½ oz. jug reappeared with a crimped top. This new piece was called a 12 oz. syrup. A complete listing of the pieces made during this period may be found below in a separate table.

Hobnail in Blue Opalescent was revived once more in July 1978. With the exception of the No. 3837 basket and the No. 3974 cornucopia candleholder, all items in this production had not been made previously in this color. The basket and candleholder have enjoyed tremendous success in the Fenton line. They were both introduced in the early 1940s and were reissued in both of the later productions.

In addition to producing Blue Opalescent Hobnail for the regular line, Fenton also made pieces for other companies such as L. G. Wright and Levay. For a list of Hobnail made for L. G. Wright, see the Hobnail introduction at the beginning of this chapter. Fenton made the following items in blue opalescent Hobnail for Levay during 1982:

Banana stand, #3720-12"	Cruet & stopper, mini, #3869
Basket, #3834-6½"	Punch, 10-piece, #3611
Bell, #3645	Punch set, 14-piece, #3712
Butter, #3677	Toothpick holder, #3795
Cruet & stopper, #3863	Water set, 7-piece, #3908

Individual items were sometimes combined to produce sets, for added attractiveness and marketing appeal. In many cases items were also sold individually, but some of the items appear on the price lists only in the form of sets. For example, the vanity bottles and puff box did not appear on the price lists separately until 1952, when the items were assigned separate line numbers. Notice the condiment set in the listing below was marketed two different ways. The early version was sold on the large fan tray and included the footed shakers, but had no sugar and creamer. The later version included the individual sugar and creamer, used the flat shakers, and was sold with the round chrome-handled tray. Note also that the No. 3902 two-piece petite epergne set consists of the 6" bonbon with a center ring in which the No. 3952- 4" DC vase rests.

The following sets were sold in Blue Opalescent Hobnail:

	Introduced	Discontinued
Beverage set No. 3907 (7-piece): 80 oz. jug, 6-12 oz. tumblers	1947	1954
Beverage set No. 3909 (9-piece): 80 oz. jug, 8-12 oz. tumblers	1941	1954
Cigarette set (6-piece): No. 1 hat, No. 2 hat, 4 round ashtrays	1941	1944
Cigarette set (5-piece): No. 2 hat, 4 round ashtrays	1941	1943
Condiment set (5-piece): oil, mustard, ftd. salt and pepper, 10½" fan tray	1942	1950

		Introduced	Discontinued
Condiment set No. 3809 (7-piece): oil, mustard, ind. sugar & creamer, flat salt & pepper, 7¾" tray w/chrome handle		1950	1954
Console set No. 3802 (3-piece): 9" DC bowl, 2 cornucopia candle		1943	1954
Console set No. 3904 (3-piece): 9" DC bowl, 2 candleholder		1946	1955
Console set No. 3804 (3-piece): 11" DC bowl, 2 candleholder		1946	1954
Epergne set No. 3902 (2-piece)		1950	1955
Epergne set No. 3801 (4-piece)		1949	1955
Jam set No. 3903 (3-piece)*		1948	1955
Juice set No. 3905 (7-piece): squat jug, 6-5 oz. tumblers		1941	1955
Mayonnaise set No. 3803		1948	1955
Punch set No. 3807 (15 piece) w/16" torte plate		1950	1955
Vanity set No. 3805, 3-pc.		1940	1954
Wine set (7-piece): decanter, 6 wine goblets		1947	1950

*The jam set was listed as a 3-piece set, but actually was a 4-piece set. Included were the jam jar, a lid, a saucer, and a crystal ladle.

Blue Opalescent Hobnail	Ware No.	Introduced	Discontinued	Value
Ashtray, fan-shape	3872-BO	1941	1955	18.00 – 22.00
Ashtray, oval	3873-BO	1941	1955	18.00 – 22.00
Ashtray, round shallow		1941	1944	20.00 – 22.00
Basket, 4½"	3834-BO	1940	1955	45.00 – 50.00
Basket, 5½" handled	3835-BO	Oct. 1949	1955	110.00 – 135.00
Basket, 6¼" ftd. handled		July 1941	1947	65.00 – 90.00
Basket, 7" handled	3837-BO	1940	1955**	65.00 – 85.00
Basket, 8" ftd. handled		1943	1947	125.00 – 145.00
Basket, 10" handled	3830-BO	1940	1955	145.00 – 165.00
Basket, 13½"		1941	1944	350.00 – 450.00
Bonbon, 4" 2-handled		1946	1951	15.00 – 18.00
Bonbon, 5" 2-handled oval,	3935-BO	1941	1955	22.00 – 25.00
Bonbon, 5" 2-handled square		1941	1952	22.00 – 25.00
Bonbon, 5" star	3921-BO	1953	1955	30.00 – 35.00
Bonbon, 6" DC	3926-BO	1940	1955	18.00 – 20.00
Bonbon, 6" flared, oval, plate, square, triangle		1940	1952	25.00 – 30.00
Bonbon, 6½" 2-handled square, oval		July 1941	1944	25.00 – 30.00
Bonbon, 7" double crimped, flared, oval, plate, square, triangle		1940	1941	30.00 – 32.00
Bonbon, 7" handled	3937-BO	1951	1955	32.00 – 38.00
Bonbon, 8" oval, handled		1951	1952	165.00 – 185.00
Bottle, vanity	3865-BO	1940	1954	50.00 – 60.00
Bowl, finger		1942		25.00 – 30.00
Bowl, square dessert	3828-BO	1951	1954	35.00 – 45.00
Bowl, 7" DC	3927-BO	1940	1955	35.00 – 45.00
Bowl, 7 " flared, oval		1940	1944	35.00 – 45.00
Bowl, 7" special		1940		35.00 – 45.00
Bowl, 7½" flared (scalloped)		1942	1943	35.00 – 45.00
Bowl, 9" DC	3924-BO	1941	1955*	40.00 – 40.00
Bowl, 9" flared		1940		40.00 – 50.00
Bowl, 11" DC	3824-BO	1940	1954	60.00 – 65.00
Bowl, 11" flared, oval, triangle		1940	1952	125.00 – 145.00
Bowl, 11" ftd. shallow		July 1941	1944	125.00 – 145.00
Bowl, 11" ftd. DC	3923-BO	1948	1955	125.00 – 145.00
Bowl, 12" ftd. DC		July 1941	1944	125.00 – 145.00
Boxtle, vanity	3986-BO	1953	1954	400.00 – 425.00
Butter, ¼ lb.	3977-BO	July 1954	1955	300.00 – 350.00

3967 BO 80 oz. Jug

3859 BO 8 1/2" DC Vase

No. 389 8 1/2" Flared
Crimped Vase

389 BO 6 1/4" cupped
Flared Vase

No. 389 BO Covered Jar

3828 BO Square Dessert

3986 BO Vanity Boxtle

No. 389 8" Oval Handled Bonbon

3887 BO Footed Comport

No. 389 BO Elongated
Covered Jar

No. 389 11" Ftd.
Shallow Bowl

3977 BO 1/4 Lb. Butter

Blue Opalescent Hobnail	Ware No.	Introduced	Discontinued	Value
Cake plate, 12" ftd.		July 1941	1944	125.00 – 145.00
Cake plate, 13" ftd.	3913-BO	1948	1955	125.00 – 145.00
Candle, large cornucopia	3874-BO	1943	1954	45.00 – 65.00
Candle, miniature cornucopia	3971-BO	July 1941	1955	25.00 – 27.00
Candleholder	3974-BO	1941	1955**	25.00 – 27.00
Candy jar	3883-BO	1953	1955	100.00 – 125.00
Candy jar, ftd.	3980-BO	1941	1955	65.00 – 75.00
Candy jar, low	3880-BO	1951	1955	90.00 – 110.00
Candy jar, scalloped body, ftd.		1942	1944	145.00 – 165.00
Comport, ftd. covered	3887-BO	July 1953	1954*	100.00 – 125.00
Comport, 6" flared, triangular		July 1941	1943	40.00 – 50.00
Comport, 8" ftd. plate		July 1941	1943	75.00 – 85.00
Condiment set, 5-piece		1942	1944	205.00 – 250.00
Cookie jar, handled			July 1941	500.00 – 600.00
Creamer and sugar	3901-BO	1940	1955	52.00 – 60.00
Creamer and sugar, #3	3906-BO	Oct. 1949	1955	85.00 – 90.00
Creamer and sugar, individual	3900-BO	1942	1955	35.00 – 40.00
Cruet	3863-BO	July 1941	1955	100.00 – 125.00
Cup & saucer, square	3808-BO	1951	1954	85.00 – 100.00
Decanter, handled	3761-BO	July 1941	1950*	390.00 – 425.00
Epergne and block		July 1941	1943	250.00 – 300.00
Epergne set, 2-pc. petite	3902-BO	1950	1955	100.00 – 125.00
Epergne set, miniature 4-pc.	3801-BO	Oct. 1949	1955	100.00 – 125.00
Goblet, round water	3845-BO	1940	1955	20.00 – 25.00
Goblet, square water	3846-BO	1951	1954	50.00 – 60.00
Goblet, round wine	3843-BO	1940	1955*	25.00 – 30.00
Goblet, square wine	3844-BO	Dec. 1950	1954	60.00 – 70.00
Hat, No. 1		1941	1944	22.00 – 25.00
Hat, No. 2	3992-BO	1941	1954	25.00 – 30.00
Jam set, 3-pc. w/glass spoon	3903-BO	1948	1955	100.00 – 125.00
Jar, 5" covered		1940	1942	275.00 – 325.00
Jug, 4½"	3964-BO	1941	1954	40.00 – 50.00
Jug, 5½"		1941	1951*	45.00 – 55.00
Jug, 32 oz. squat	3965-BO	1940	1955	85.00 – 100.00
Jug, 48 oz. tankard		1940	1944	400.00 – 500.00
Jug, 80 oz. (NIL)	3967-BO	1941	1955	225.00 – 275.00
Mayonnaise set, 3-pc. w/glass spoon	3803-BO	1948	1955	45.00 – 55.00
Mustard and spoon	3889-BO	1942	1955	30.00 – 38.00
Oil	3869-BO	1942	1955	20.00 – 25.00
Plate, 4"		1942		12.00 – 14.00
Plate, 6½" square	3819-BO	Sept. 1950	1954	30.00 – 35.00
Plate, 6" round		1942		14.00 16.00
Plate, 8" salad	3918-BO	1940	1955	18.00 – 22.00
Plate, 11" square (diag. meas.)	3910-BO	Sept. 1950	1955	110.00 – 125.00
Plate, 16" torte	3817-BO	Sept. 1950	1955	100.00 – 120.00
Puff box	3885-BO	1940	1954	55.00 – 60.00
Punch bowl, crimped		Sept. 1950	July 1952	250.00 – 300.00
Punch bowl, flared	3827-BO	Sept. 1950	1955	250.00 – 275.00
Punch bowl, handled		1951	1952	400.00 – 600.00
Punch cup	3847-BO	Sept. 1950	1955	18.00 – 20.00
Punch set, 15-piece	3807-BO	Sept. 1950	1955	550.00 – 600.00
Relish, 3-part	3822-BO	1954	1955	85.00 – 90.00
Rose bowl, 3"		Oct. 1949	1951	80.00 – 90.00
Rose bowl, 4½"		1940	1944	40.00 – 45.00

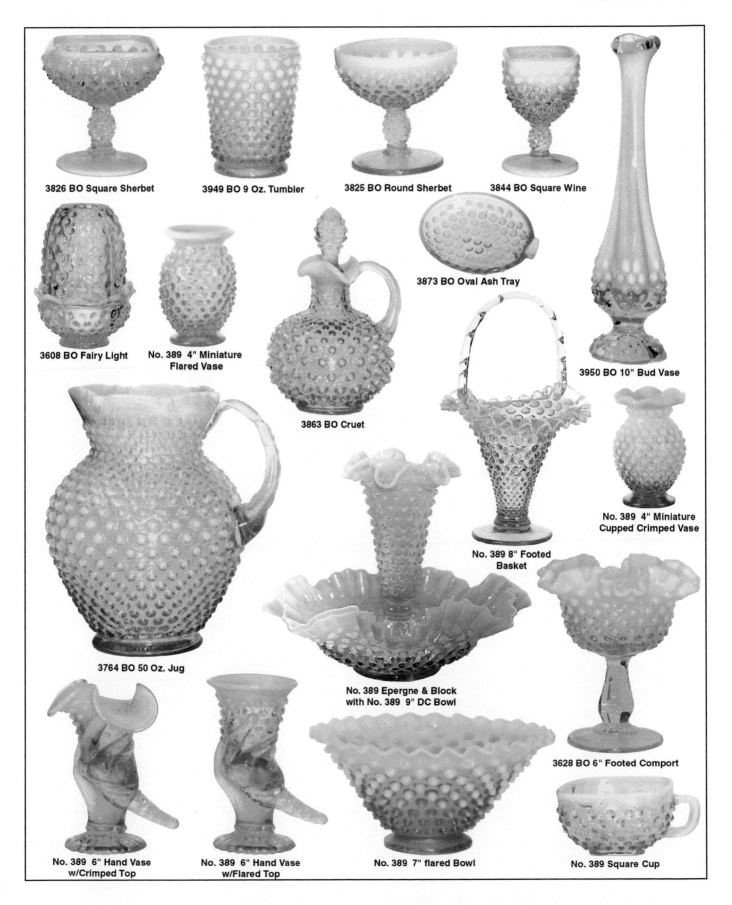

3826 BO Square Sherbet

3949 BO 9 Oz. Tumbler

3825 BO Round Sherbet

3844 BO Square Wine

3608 BO Fairy Light

No. 389 4" Miniature
Flared Vase

3873 BO Oval Ash Tray

3863 BO Cruet

3950 BO 10" Bud Vase

3764 BO 50 Oz. Jug

No. 389 8" Footed
Basket

No. 389 4" Miniature
Cupped Crimped Vase

No. 389 Epergne & Block
with No. 389 9" DC Bowl

3628 BO 6" Footed Comport

No. 389 6" Hand Vase
w/Crimped Top

No. 389 6" Hand Vase
w/Flared Top

No. 389 7" flared Bowl

No. 389 Square Cup

Blue Opalescent Hobnail	Ware No.	Introduced	Discontinued	Value
Rose bowl, 5"		1940	1944	45.00 – 50.00
Salt and pepper, flat	3806-BO	Oct. 1949	1955*	35.00 – 45.00
Salt and pepper, ftd.		1940	1944	55.00 – 75.00
Saucer, square		1951	1954	12.00 – 14.00
Sherbet	3825-BO	1940	1955	20.00 – 25.00
Sherbet, square	3826-BO	Dec. 1950	1954	40.00 – 45.00
Slipper	3995-BO	1941	1955*	18.00 – 24.00
Tidbit tray, 2-tier (square plates)		Sept. 1950		185.00 – 200.00
Tray, 6½" crescent		1948	1950	50.00 – 65.00
Tray, 6¾" crescent		1942	1943	50.00 – 65.00
Tray, 7¾" div. w/chrome handle	3879-BO	Sept. 1950	1954	85.00 – 100.00
Tray, 10½" fan		1941	1951	40.00 – 45.00
Tumbler, 5 oz.	3945-BO	1940	1955	20.00 – 25.00
Tumbler, 9 oz.	3949-BO	1940	1955	25.00 – 27.50
Tumbler, 12 oz. (barrel)	3947-BO	1941	1955	35.00 – 38.00
Tumbler, 12 oz.	3942-BO	1954	1955	38.00 – 42.00
Tumbler, 16 oz.	3946-BO	1950	1955	65.00 – 85.00
Tumbler, ftd. ice tea or highball	3842-BO	1940	1955	25.00 – 35.00
Vanity set, 3-pc.	3805-BO	1940	1954	155.00 – 185.00
Vase, 3" DC	3853-BO	Oct. 1949	1955	32.00 – 37.00
Vase, 4" ftd. DC	3952-BO	1948	1955*	20.00 – 22.00
Vase, 4" ftd. fan	3953-BO	1948	1955	22.00 – 25.00
Vase, 4" miniature fan, flared, hat		1940	1952	20.00 – 25.00
Vase, 4" miniature cup crimped		1940s	1952	15.00 – 18.00
Vase, 4" miniature cup flared, oval		1940	1952	18.00 – 20.00
Vase, 4" miniature triangle	3855-BO	1940	1955	15.00 – 18.00
Vase, 4½" DC	3854-BO	1940	1955	20.00 – 24.00
Vase, 4½" cup square, cup flared		1940	1952	20.00 – 24.00
Vase, 5" DC	3850-BO	1940	1955	25.00 – 30.00
Vase, 5" cup flared, square, triangle		1940	1952	25.00 – 30.00
Vase, 5½"crimped, flared, square, triangle, tulip		1941	1951	25.00 – 28.00
Vase, 6" DC	3856-BO	1940	1955	27.00 – 32.00
Vase, 6" flared, square, triangle		1940	1952	25.00 – 28.00
Vase, 6" hand		1942	1943	65.00 – 85.00
Vase, 6¼" ftd. cupped, cup flared, flared, triangle		1941	1949	25.00 – 30.00
Vase, 6¼" ftd. DC	3956-BO	1941	1955	27.00 – 32.00
Vase, 6¼" ftd. fan	3957-BO	1941	1955	35.00 – 38.00
Vase, 6½" fan (scalloped)		1942	1944	35.00 – 40.00
Vase, 6½" swung (scalloped)		1942	1944	40.00 – 42.00
Vase, 8" DC	3858-BO	1941	1954	65.00 – 70.00
Vase, 8" flared, square, triangle		1941		65.00 – 70.00
Vase, 8" ftd. DC	3958-BO	1943	1955	65.00 – 75.00
Vase, 8" ftd. fan	3959-BO	1943	1955	65.00 – 75.00
Vase, 8" ftd. square, triangle		1943	1949	55.00 – 60.00
Vase, 8½" DC (8" later)	3859-BO	1941		135.00 – 185.00
Vase, 8½" flip		1941		300.00 – 340.00
Vase, 8½" flared crimped, triangle		1941	1944	90.00 – 125.00
Vase, 9" flared (scalloped)		1941	1944	90.00 – 100.00
Vase, 10" flared (bottle shape)		1941	1943	150.00 – 185.00

*Reissued during the 1959 to 1964 production.
** Reissued in both the 1959 and 1978 productions.

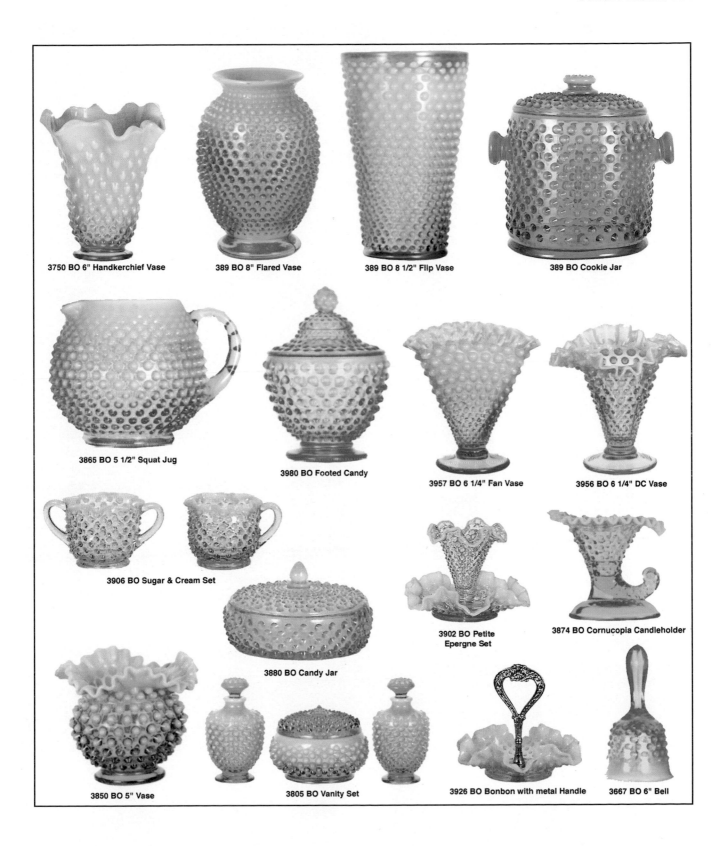

3750 BO 6" Handkerchief Vase

389 BO 8" Flared Vase

389 BO 8 1/2" Flip Vase

389 BO Cookie Jar

3865 BO 5 1/2" Squat Jug

3980 BO Footed Candy

3957 BO 6 1/4" Fan Vase

3956 BO 6 1/4" DC Vase

3906 BO Sugar & Cream Set

3902 BO Petite Epergne Set

3874 BO Cornucopia Candleholder

3880 BO Candy Jar

3850 BO 5" Vase

3805 BO Vanity Set

3926 BO Bonbon with metal Handle

3667 BO 6" Bell

Blue Opalescent Hobnail (1959)	Ware No	Introduced	Discontinued	Value
Basket, 7" handled	3837-BO	July 1959	1965	65.00 – 85.00
Bowl, 9" DC	3924-BO	July 1959	1963	40.00 – 50.00
Bowl, 10" ftd.	3731-BO	July 1959	1962	125.00 – 145.00
Candle bowl	3771-BO	July 1959	1961	45.00 – 50.00
Candleholder	3974-BO	July 1959	1963	25.00 – 27.00
Comport	3728-BO	July 1959	1965	40.00 – 45.00
Comport	3727-BO	1960	1965	40.00 – 45.00
Comport, ftd. covered	3887-BO	July 1959	1965	100.00 – 125.00
Decanter, handled	3761-BO	1960	July 1962	390.00 – 425.00
Epergne set, miniature 4-pc.	3801-BO	July 1959	1965	100.00 – 125.00
Goblet, wine	3843-BO	July 1960	1963	25.00 – 30.00
Jug, 12 oz. 5½" syrup	3762-BO	July 1959	1961	45.00 – 55.00
Relish, handled	3733-BO	1960	July 1962	70.00 – 85.00
Salt and pepper, flat	3806-BO	1960	1965	35.00 – 45.00
Slipper	3995-BO	1960	1964	20.00 – 22.00
Vase, 4" ftd. DC	3952-BO	1960	1965	20.00 – 22.00
Vase, 8" bud	3756-BO	July 1959	1965	30.00 – 35.00
Vase, 6" handkerchief	3750-BO	July 1960	1962	50.00 – 60.00
Vase, 12" medium swung	3758-BO	July 1959	July 1962	75.00 – 90.00
Vase, 18" tall swung	3759-BO	July 1959	1961	90.00 – 125.00

Blue Opalescent Hobnail (1978)	Ware No.	Introduced	Discontinued	Value
Ashtray set, 3-piece round	3610-BO	July 1978	1979	45.00 – 55.00
Basket, 7" handled	3837-BO	July 1978	1980+	65.00 – 85.00
Bell, 6"	3667-BO	July 1978	1980+	45.00 – 50.00
Candle bowl, ftd.	3971-BO	July 1978	1979	40.00 – 45.00
Candleholder	3974-BO	July 1978	1979	25.00 – 27.00
Candy/Butter bowl	3802-BO	July 1978	1980	65.00 – 75.00
Comport, 6" ftd., DC	3628-BO	July 1978	1980+	40.00 – 45.00
Fairy light	3608-BO	July 1978	1980+	40.00 – 50.00
Lamp, 26"	3907-BO	July 1978	1980+	360.00 – 400.00
Vase, 10" bud	3950-BO	July 1978	1980+	35.00 – 40.00

The following items are sometimes found, but were not a part of the regular line:

Hobnail Item	Value
1. Green Opalescent Hobnail bonbon with brass candleholder fittings	85.00 – 125.00
2. Blue Opalescent Hobnail cologne fashioned from a handleless cruet base	100.00 – 150.00
3. Cranberry Hobnail star-shaped bonbon atop a gold filigree base	150.00 – 180.00
4. Blue Opalescent Hobnail small lamp made for Edward P. Paul	85.00 – 100.00
5. Green Opalescent bonbon with a metal base	65.00 – 90.00

HAND MADE
IN AMERICA
by
Fenton

389—12'' Footed Bowl,
Double Crimped

389—12''—Footed Cake Plate

389—Min. Cornucopia
Candlestick

389—Cruet

389—Handled Decanter

389
Salt and Pepper

389
Mustard and Spoon

389
Oil Bottle

389—6½'' Vase, Swung

389—5 piece Condiment Set

389—7½'' Bowl, Flared

389—6½'' Vase, Fan

Blue Pastel Hobnail

Fenton introduced a pale blue opaque color called Blue Pastel in January 1954. The Hobnail pattern was made in this color through December 1954, when the color was discontinued. Two pieces — the 3834-4½" basket and the 3974 candle-holders — were introduced in July and were only made for six months.

Fenton combined individual pieces to produce the following set between July 1954 and January 1955:

Console set No. 3904 (3-piece): No. 3924-9" DC bowl, 2 No. 3974 candle

Blue Pastel Hobnail	Ware No.	Introduced	Discontinued	Value
Basket, 4½" handled	3834-BP	July 1954	1955	45.00 – 50.00
Basket, 7" handled	3837-BP	1954	1955	50.00 – 60.00
Berry dish	3928-BP	1954	1955	15.00 – 18.00
Bowl, 9" DC	3924-BP	1954	1955	30.00 – 35.00
Bowl, 9" square	3929-BP	1954	1955	45.00 – 55.00
Candleholder	3974-BP	July 1954	1955	20.00 – 25.00
Candy jar	3883-BP	1954	1955	60.00 – 70.00
Comport, ftd.	3920-BP	1954	1955	40.00 – 45.00
Comport, ftd. w/cover	3887-BP	1954	1955	80.00 – 90.00
Epergne set, 5-pc.	3800-BP	1954	1955	200.00 – 250.00
Epergne set, miniature 4-pc.	3801-BP	1954	1955	100.00 – 125.00
Kettle	3990-BP	1954	1955	20.00 – 25.00
Lamp, 11" hurricane	3998-BP	1954	1955	100.00 – 130.00
Slipper	3995-BP	1954	1955	25.00 – 35.00
Sugar and cream, #3	3906-BP	1954	1955	35.00 – 40.00
Vase, 4" ftd. DC	3952-BP	1954	1955	18.00 – 20.00
Vase, 4" ftd. fan	3953-BP	1954	1955	18.00 – 20.00
Vase, 4½" DC	3854-BP	1954	1955	20.00 – 27.00

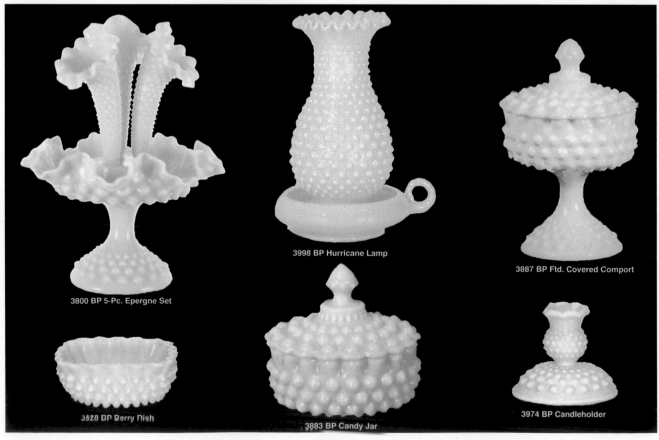

3800 BP 5-Pc. Epergne Set

3998 BP Hurricane Lamp

3887 BP Ftd. Covered Comport

3928 BP Berry Dish

3883 BP Candy Jar

3974 BP Candleholder

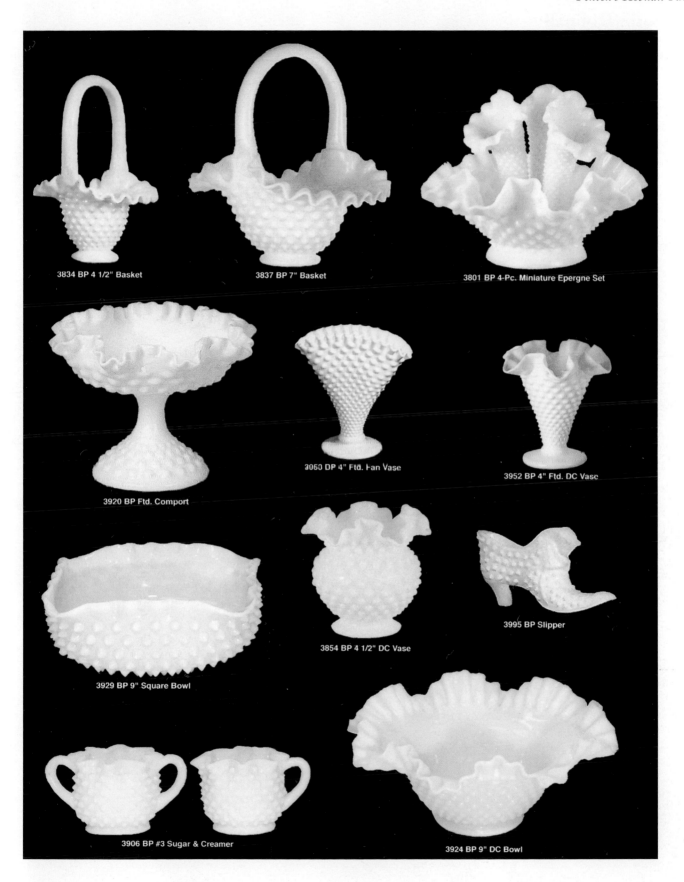

3834 BP 4 1/2" Basket

3837 BP 7" Basket

3801 BP 4-Pc. Miniature Epergne Set

3920 BP Ftd. Comport

3060 DP 4" Ftd. Fan Vase

3952 BP 4" Ftd. DC Vase

3929 BP 9" Square Bowl

3854 BP 4 1/2" DC Vase

3995 BP Slipper

3906 BP #3 Sugar & Creamer

3924 BP 9" DC Bowl

Blue Satin Hobnail

Blue Satin was a medium opaque blue satin glass that was introduced to the Fenton line in 1971. Only two pieces of the Hobnail pattern became part of the regular line in this color. The fairy light was a popular item that was made for a period of seven years. It is still a popular item with today's collectors and finding it is not very difficult. The three-footed candy box was only made for two years and this piece is elusive today.

Blue Satin Hobnail	Ware No.	Introduced	Discontinued	Value
Candy box	3984-BA	1974	1976	60.00 – 80.00
Fairy light	3608-BA	1974	1981	30.00 – 35.00

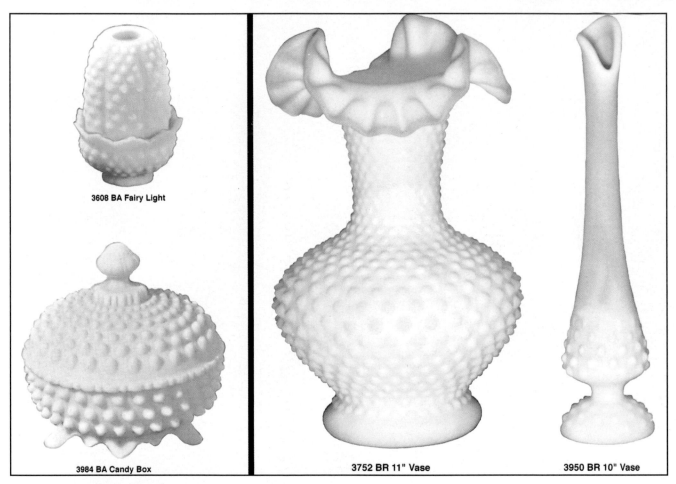

3608 BA Fairy Light

3984 BA Candy Box

3752 BR 11" Vase

3950 BR 10" Vase

Burmese Hobnail

Fenton's new Burmese color appeared in the line in 1970. The next year, Fenton made a tall vase in Burmese. The experiment with the Hobnail pattern in this color must not have been successful, since the vase was only made for one year and no other pieces were put into the line. The No. 3950 bud vase was introduced into the Fenton line in milk in 1952. There are no records of it having been in the regular line in Burmese.

Burmese Hobnail	Ware No.	Introduced	Discontinued	Value
Vase, 11"	3752-BR	1971	1972	150.00 – 180.00
Vase, 10" bud	3950-BR			N.D.

Cameo Opalescent Hobnail

Fenton's Cameo Opalescent color was first produced in 1926 and 1927. Amber Opalescent, or more correctly, Cameo Opalescent, returned to the regular Fenton line in 1978. The next year a few of the more popular pieces of Hobnail began to appear in Cameo Opalescent. Cameo Opalescent remained in the Fenton line through 1982, but most of the Hobnail in this color was discontinued before then.

Cameo Opalescent Hobnail	Ware No.	Introduced	Discontinued	Value
Basket, 7" handled	3837-CO	1979	1982	60.00 – 65.00
Bell, 6"	3667-CO	1979	1981	28.00 – 30.00
Candy/Butter bowl	3802-CO	1979	1981	35.00 – 40.00
Comport, 6" ftd., DC	3628-CO	1979	1982	20.00 – 25.00
Fairy light	3608-CO	1979	1981	35.00 – 38.00
Lamp, 26"	3907-CO	1979	1982	250.00 – 300.00
Vase, 4½" ftd. DC	3854-CO	1979	1982	12.00 – 15.00
Vase, 10" bud	3950-CO	1979	July 1982	24.00 – 30.00

3628 CO 6"
Ftd. DC Comport

3667 CO 6" Bell

3950 CO 10"
Bud Vase

3802 CO Candy
or Butter Bowl

3907 CO 26" Lamp

3854 CO 4 1/2"
Ftd. DC Vase

3837 CO 7"
Basket

Colonial Blue Hobnail

Fenton added the transparent deep blue color called Colonial Blue to the line in 1962. The Hobnail pattern was introduced to the line in this color in 1964. Production of the final 11 shapes in the Colonial Blue color ended in December 1979. With the exception of one piece, all of the transparent blue Hobnail was produced in the Colonial Blue color. The color code "BG" was used for the opaque blue candle bowl that was made in 1975.

Blue Hobnail	Ware No.	Introduced	Discontinued	Value
Candle bowl, 6"	3872-BG	1975	1976	14.00 – 18.00

Colonial Blue Hobnail	Ware No.	Introduced	Discontinued	Value
Apothecary jar	3689-CB	1964	July 1968	110.00 – 135.00
Ashtray, ball	3648-CB	1977	1979	22.00 – 25.00
Ashtray, medium round	3973-CB	1964	1966	8.00 – 10.00
Ashtray, small round	3972-CB	1964	1966	5.00 – 8.00
Ashtray, large round	3776-CB	1964	1966	12.00 – 14.00
Ashtray set, 3-piece round	3610-CB	1964	1978	25.00 – 32.00
Basket, 7" handled	3837-CB	1967	1980	35.00 – 40.00
Basket, 8½"	3638-CB	1967	July 1970	40.00 – 45.00
Basket, 10"	3830-CB	1968	1978	55.00 – 65.00
Bell, 6"	3667-CB	1967	1980	22.00 – 25.00
Bonbon, handled	3706-CB	1979	1980	14.00 – 18.00
Candle bowl, 4" miniature	3873-CB	1969	July 1972	18.00 – 20.00
Candle bowl, 6"	3872-CB	1969	1980	14.00 – 18.00
Candy box	3668-CB	1975	1978	32.00 – 38.00
Candy box, ftd.	3784-CB	1966	1970	35.00 – 45.00
Candy box, oval covered	3786-CB	1968	1970	30.00 – 35.00
Candy/butter bowl	3802-CB	1979	1980	25.00 – 30.00
Cigarette lighter	3692-CB	1965	1969	18.00 – 20.00
Comport, 6" ftd., DC	3628-CB	1975	1980	14.00 – 16.00
Creamer, miniature	3665-CB	1965	1969	7.00 – 9.00
Fairy light	3608-CB	1969	1980	25.00 – 30.00
Fairy light, 3-pc. ftd.	3804-CB	1975	1980	50.00 – 60.00
Lamp, courting, oil	3792-CB	1965	1968	75.00 – 85.00
Lamp, courting, electric	3793-CB	1965	1968	75.00 – 85.00
Nut dish, oval 2-H	3633-CB	1964	July 1968	10.00 – 12.00
Toothpick holder	3795-CB	1966	1976	12.00 – 14.00
Slipper	3995-CB	1964	July 1979	18.00 – 20.00
Vase, 3" DC	3853-CB	1968	1978	8.00 – 10.00
Vase, 4" ftd. DC	3952-CB	1965	1979	10.00 – 12.00
Vase, 4½" DC	3854-CB	1975	1980	10.00 – 12.00
Vase, 5" 3-toed	3653-CB	1965	1970	14.00 – 16.00
Vase, 8" swung bud	3756-CB	1967	1980	10.00 – 14.00
Vase, 11"	3752-CB	1977	1978	25.00 – 35.00
Vase, 12" ftd. swung	3753-CB	1968	1971**	35.00 – 40.00
Vase, 24" tall swung	3652-CB	1965	1978	50.00 – 60.00

**Also made in 1979.

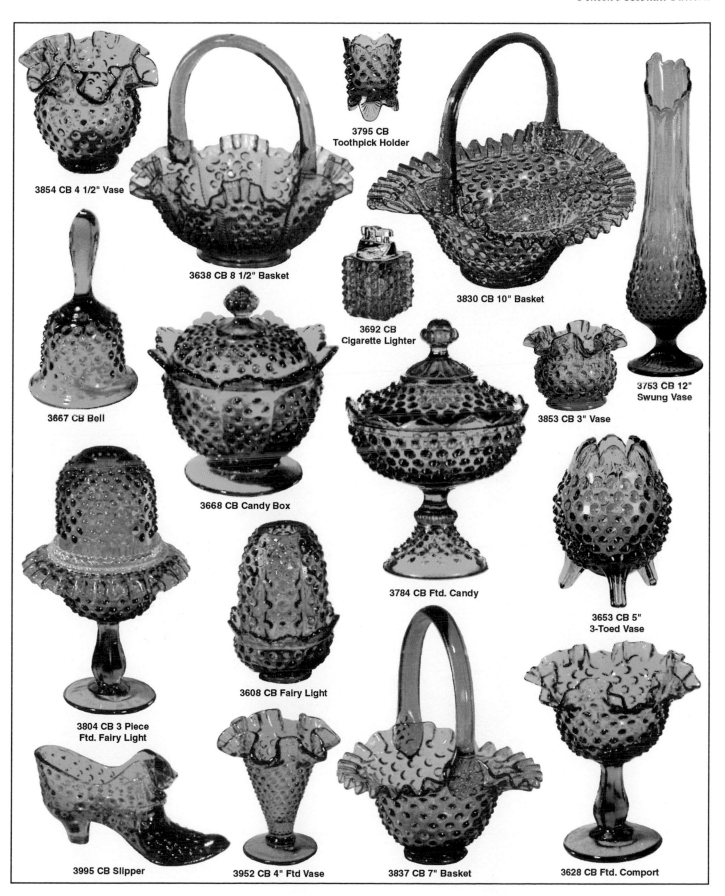

3854 CB 4 1/2" Vase

3638 CB 8 1/2" Basket

3795 CB
Toothpick Holder

3830 CB 10" Basket

3692 CB
Cigarette Lighter

3667 CB Bell

3668 CB Candy Box

3784 CB Ftd. Candy

3853 CB 3" Vase

3753 CB 12"
Swung Vase

3653 CB 5"
3-Toed Vase

3804 CB 3 Piece
Ftd. Fairy Light

3608 CB Fairy Light

3995 CB Slipper

3952 CB 4" Ftd Vase

3837 CB 7" Basket

3628 CB Ftd. Comport

Coral Hobnail

Five different Hobnail pieces were produced in a pastel peach color overlay called Coral in 1961. The Coral color was produced by casing a light pink outer layer over an opal interior layer. Coral is sometimes confused with the Wild Rose color. Wild Rose is an opaque cranberry color; coral is lighter — more of a peach-colored pink. Other items in Coral were made in the Bubble Optic, Jacqueline, and Wild Rose with Bowknot patterns.

Coral Hobnail	Ware No.	Introduced	Discontinued	Value
Jug, 12 oz. syrup	3762-CL	1961	1962	35.00 – 45.00
Vase, 5" DC	3850-CL	1961	1962	35.00 – 45.00
Vase, 6"	3856-CL	1961	1962	40.00 – 50.00
Vase, 8"	3858-CL	1961	1962	55.00 – 65.00
Vase, 11"	3752-CL	1961	1962	125.00 – 150.00

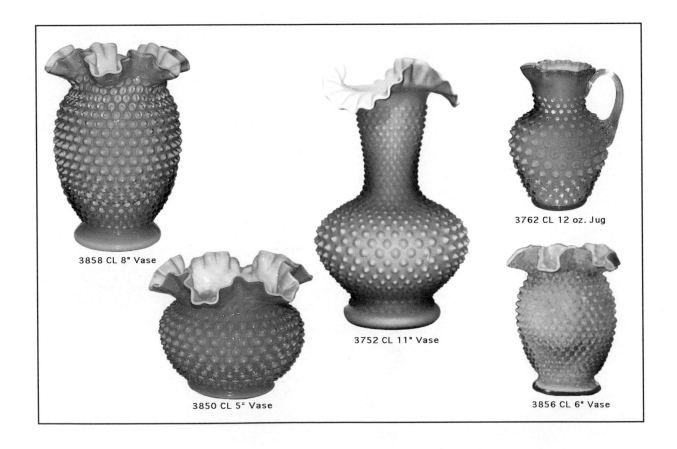

3858 CL 8" Vase

3762 CL 12 oz. Jug

3850 CL 5" Vase

3752 CL 11" Vase

3856 CL 6" Vase

Cranberry Hobnail

The only way to make this long-favored Early American glass and achieve the true Cranberry color is to encase a layer of gold ruby inside a layer of opalescent glass. Truly a luxury glass, this costly and time consuming process has been uniquely developed by Fenton.

3830 CR
10" BASKET

3752 CR
11" VASE

3927 CR
7" BOWL

3870 CR
CANDLEHOLDER

3837 CR
7" BASKET

3924 CR
9" BOWL

3863 CR
CRUET

3850 CR
5" VASE

3762 CR
12 OZ. PITCHER

3854 CR
4½" VASE

Catalog Reprint Courtesy Of: The Fenton Art Glass Museum

Cranberry Hobnail	Ware No.	Introduced	Discontinued	Value
Bowl, 7" special		1940		55.00 – 65.00
Bowl, 9" DC	3924-CR	1940	1978	70.00 – 90.00
Bowl, 9" flared		1940	1944	80.00 – 95.00
Bowl, 11" DC	3824-CR	1940	1955	80.00 – 90.00
Bowl, 11" flared, oval, triangular		1940	1944	90.00 – 100.00
Candleholder	3870-CR	1953	1978	55.00 – 65.00
Candy jar	3883-CR	July 1954	1959	180.00 – 200.00
Creamer and sugar	3901-CR	1940	1944	80.00 – 90.00
Creamer and sugar, #3		Oct. 1949	1951	200.00 – 250.00
Cruet	3863-CR	July 1941	1978	135.00 – 150.00
Decanter, handled		July 1941	1950	500.00 – 600.00
Jam set, 3-pc. w/glass spoon	3903-CR	1948	1957	165.00 – 180.00
Jar, 5" covered		1940	1943	400.00 – 450.00
Jug, 32 oz. squat		1940	1950	125.00 – 150.00
Jug, 4½"	3964-CR	1941	1955	50.00 – 60.00
Jug, 5½"		1941	1950	50.00 – 60.00
Jug, 12 oz. 5½" syrup	3762-CR	1969	1978	50.00 – 60.00
Jug, 48 oz. tankard		1940	1944	500.00 – 600.00
Jug, 70 oz. ice lip	3664-CR	1965	1969	300.00 – 325.00
Jug, 80 oz. (NIL)	3967-CR	1941	1967	300.00 – 325.00
Lamp, 19" student	3707-CR	1968	1975	250.00 – 300.00
Lamp, 26"	3907-CR	1977	1980+	225.00 – 250.00
Mayonnaise set, 3-pc. w/glass spoon	3803-CR	1948	1957	90.00 – 110.00
Oil	3869-CR	Oct. 1949	1965	90.00 – 110.00
Puff box	3885-CR	1940	1957	75.00 – 80.00
Rose bowl, 3"		Oct. 1949	1951	90.00 – 125.00
Rose bowl, 4½"		1940	1944	50.00 – 60.00
Rose bowl, 5"		1940	1944	90.00 – 110.00
Salt and pepper	3806-CR	July 1954	1968	85.00 – 100.00
Tumbler, 12 oz.	3947-CR	1941	1968	48.00 – 57.00
Vanity set, 3-pc.	3805-CR	1940	1957	245.00 – 260.00
Vase, 3" DC	3853-CR	Oct. 1949	July 1956	78.00 – 80.00
Vase, 4" miniature fan, flared, hat		1940	1951	30.00 – 35.00
Vase, 4" miniature cup crimped		1940	1951	30.00 – 35.00
Vase, 4" miniature cup flared, oval		1940	1951	30.00 – 35.00
Vase, 4" miniature triangle	3855-CR	1940	1957	30.00 – 35.00
Vase, 4½" double crimped	3854-CR	1940	1978	40.00 – 50.00
Vase, 4½" cup square, cup flared		1940	1949	45.00 – 55.00
Vase, 5" DC	3850-CR	1940	1978	60.00 – 70.00
Vase, 5" cup flared, square, triangle		1940	1944	60.00 – 75.00
Vase, 5½" crimped, flared, square, triangle, tulip		1941	1951	45.00 – 55.00
Vase, 6" DC	3856-CR	1940	1957	65.00 – 75.00
Vase, 6" flared, square, triangle		1940	1944	75.00 – 85.00
Vase, 8" DC	3858-CR	1941	1973	95.00 – 125.00
Vase, 8" flared, square, triangle		1941		N.D.
Vase, 8½" DC (8" later)	3859-CR	1953	July 1961	200.00 – 225.00*
Vase, 8½" flared crimped, flip triangle		1941	1944	200.00 – 250.00
Vase, 10" flared (bottle shape)		1941	1944	200.00 – 225.00

*Flip vase 250.00 – 350.00

3637 CR 7" Basket

3835 CR 5 1/2" Basket

3870 CR Candleholder

No. 389 Handled Decanter

No. 389 13 1/2" Basket

3837 CR 7" Basket

3834 CR 4 1/2" Basket

No 389 5 1/2" Vase

3863 CR Cruet

3830 CR 10" Basket

3883 CR Candy

No. 389 9" Flared Bowl

3853 CR 3" DC Vase

3924 CR 9" DC Bowl

No. 389 10" Vase

No. 389 48 Oz. Tankard Jug

3824 CR 11" DC Bowl

3803 CR Mayonnaise Set

3927 CR 7" Bowl

3926 CR 6" DC Bonbon

No 389 7" Special Rose Bowl

No 389 5" Rose Bowl

3762 CR 12 Oz. Pitcher

Crystal Hobnail

Initially, Fenton made crystal Hobnail in the early 1940s. The pieces below appeared in the price lists and inventory records for 1940 and 1941.

Crystal Hobnail (1940s)	Value
Creamer	4.00 – 5.00
Goblet, water	5.00 – 6.00
Goblet, wine	6.00 – 7.00
Jug, 48 oz. tankard	30.00 – 35.00
Plate, 8" salad	2.00 – 4.00
Sherbet	4.00 – 5.00
Sugar	4.00 – 5.00
Tumbler, 5 oz. flat	5.00 – 6.00
Tumbler, 9 oz. flat	6.00 – 7.00
Tumbler, 12 oz. flat	8.00 – 10.00
Tumbler, 12 oz. ftd.	12.00 – 14.00

The No. 3869 oil bottle may be found in crystal. Although this bottle was never in the regular Fenton line, it may be found on occasion. One turn of this oil bottle was made for a company in Philadelphia during the early 1950s.

After a long dormant period, crystal Hobnail was brought out of retirement, reappearing in a 1968 catalog supplement. The pieces were listed on the price lists for 1968, but were gone from the 1969 price listings. Whereas most of the early crystal Hobnail consisted of basic tableware pieces, this later version was composed primarily of accessory items.

The jam & jelly set was composed of two marmalades with lids and spoons on a tray with a metal handle. Three different sizes of round ashtrays were combined to form the No. 3610 ashtray set. The No. 3794 tidbit was made by using a metal center handle to combine an 8½" top plate with a 13½" bottom plate.

Crystal Hobnail (1960s)	Ware No.	Value
Ashtray set, 3-piece	3610-CY	10.00 – 12.00
Basket, 10" handled	3830-CY	20.00 – 25.00
Basket, 7" handled	3837-CY	12.00 – 15.00
Bowl, 9"	3924-CY	8.00 – 10.00
Butter, ¼ lb. oval	3777-CY	10.00 – 12.00
Cake plate, ftd.	3913-CY	12.00 – 15.00
Candleholder, 6"	3674-CY	6.00 – 8.00
Candy box, oval 4-ftd.	3786-CY	10.00 – 12.00
Creamer, sugar and cover	3606-CY	8.00 – 12.00
Jam and jelly set	3915-CY	18.00 – 20.00
Relish, 3-part	3822-CY	8.00 – 10.00
Shaker	3609-CY	4.00 – 5.00
Slipper	3995-CY	6.00 – 8.00
Tidbit	3794-CY	15.00 – 20.00
Toothpick holder	3795-CY	4.00 – 6.00
Urn, 11" covered	3986-CY	30.00 – 35.00
Vase, ftd.	3753-CY	6.00 – 8.00
Vase, 8" bud	3756-CY	6.00 – 8.00

171

Custard/Glossy Custard Hobnail

Only two pieces of the popular Hobnail pattern were listed in Custard. The three-footed candy box was only made for two years and is not easily found. The fairy light was made for a longer period and is fairly common today.

The No. 3958-6¼" crimped vase and the 6" candle bowl in the photo below were made in glossy custard. They were primarily packaged as part of floral and candle arrangement assortments. Several different seasonal arrangements were usually offered over the course of a year. For more information on candle and floral arrangements, see page 246.

Custard Hobnail	Ware No.	Introduced	Discontinued	Value
Candy box	3984-CU	1974	1976	35.00 – 40.00
Fairy light	3608-CU	1972	1978	25.00 – 35.00
Glossy Custard Hobnail	**Ware No.**	**Introduced**	**Discontinued**	**Value**
Candle bowl, 6"	3872-CT	July 1973	1977	15.00 – 18.00
Comport, ftd.	3628-CT			16.00 – 18.00
Vase, 6¼"	3956-CT			15.00 – 18.00
Vase, 4" ftd.	3952-CT			10.00 – 12.00

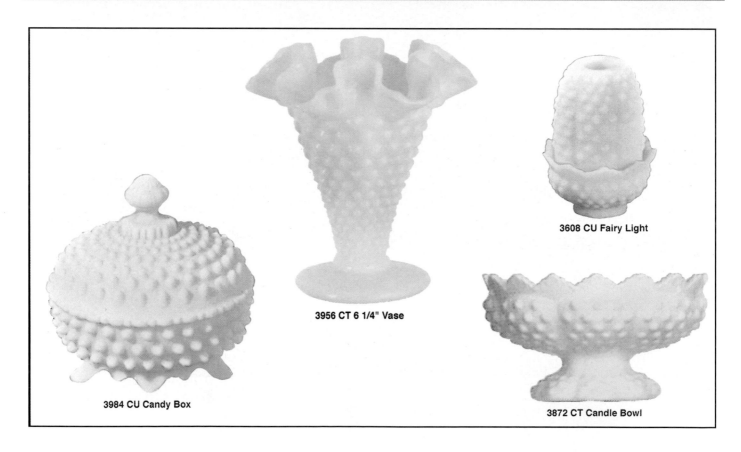

3608 CU Fairy Light

3956 CT 6 1/4" Vase

3984 CU Candy Box

3872 CT Candle Bowl

Decorated Hobnail (Blue Bell)

Beginning in 1971, Fenton began offering various Hobnail pattern pieces with hand-painted decorations. The first decoration, introduced in January 1971, was Blue Bell — a decoration created by Louise Piper. The pattern consisted of small blue flowers hand painted on milk glass Hobnail. Small hand-painted sprigs of holly on satin milk glass in a pattern called Decorated Holly came along in July 1971 for the Christmas season. Decorated Roses was only made for a short time. This pink rose decoration was introduced in 1974, and was discontinued at the end of 1975.

Decorated Blue Bell	Ware No.	Introduced	Discontinued	Value
Basket, 6½"	3736-BB	1971	1973	90.00 – 100.00
Basket, 12" oval	3839-BB	1971	July 1972	110.00 – 135.00
Bell, 6"	3667-BB	1971	1973	30.00 – 35.00
Bonbon, 6"	3926-BB	1971	1973	18.00 – 25.00
Bonbon, 8" handled	3706-BB	1971	1972	30.00 – 40.00
Candy box, covered	3886-BB	1971	1973	60.00 – 80.00
Candy or jam box, covered	3600-BB	1972	1973	75.00 – 85.00
Comport, ftd.	3920-BB	1971	July 1972	32.00 – 37.00
Fairy light	3608-BB	1971	1973	45.00 – 55.00
Toothpick holder	3795-BB	1972	July 1972	22.00 – 27.00
Vase, 8" swung bud	3756-BB	1971	July 1972	25.00 – 30.00
Vase, 8½" fan	3852-BB	1972	1973	85.00 – 90.00
Vase, 12" ftd. swung	3753-BB	1971	1972	65.00 – 75.00

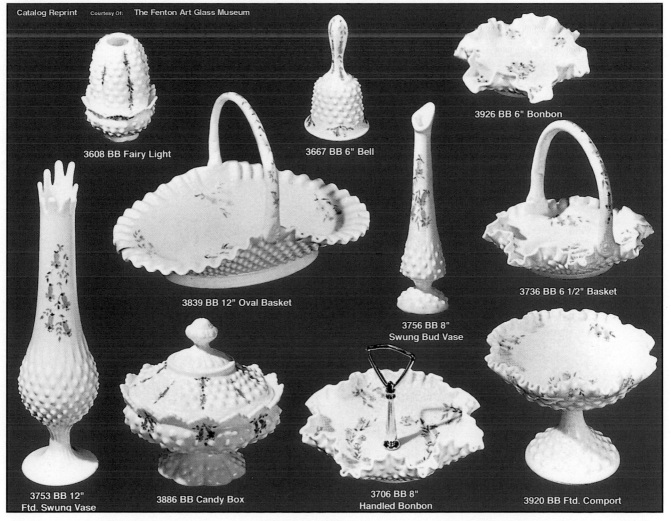

Catalog Reprint   Courtesy Of: The Fenton Art Glass Museum

3608 BB Fairy Light

3667 BB 6" Bell

3926 BB 6" Bonbon

3839 BB 12" Oval Basket

3756 BB 8" Swung Bud Vase

3736 BB 6 1/2" Basket

3753 BB 12" Ftd. Swung Vase

3886 BB Candy Box

3706 BB 8" Handled Bonbon

3920 BB Ftd. Comport

Decorated Hobnail (Holly)

Decorated Holly was only offered from July to December, in the years indicated.

Decorated Holly	Ware No.	Introduced	Discontinued	Value
Basket, 7" handled	3837-DH	July 1973	1975	55.00 – 65.00
Basket, 8½" handled	3638-DH	July 1972	1973	80.00 – 90.00
Bell, 6"	3667-DH	July 1971	1976	35.00 – 40.00
Candleholder	3974-DH	July 1971	1972	15.00 – 20.00
Candleholder, 6"	3674-DH	July 1971	1972	30.00 – 35.00
Candy box, covered	3886-DH	July 1973	1974	50.00 – 60.00
Comport, 6" ftd., DC	3628-DH	July 1973	1974	35.00 – 38.00
Fairy light	3608-DH	July 1971	1976	45.00 – 50.00
Vase, 6" handkerchief	3951-DH	July 1973	1974	45.00 – 50.00
Vase, 10" bud	3950-DH	July 1974	1975	30.00 – 35.00

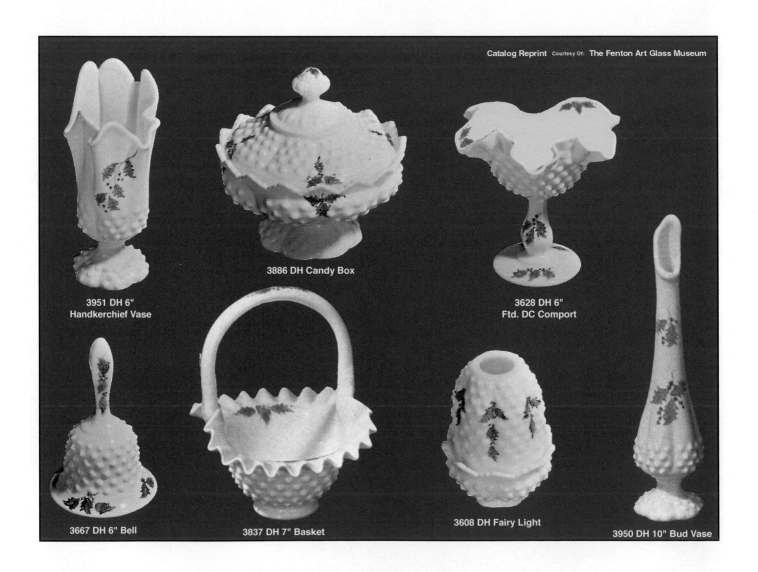

Catalog Reprint Courtesy Of: The Fenton Art Glass Museum

3951 DH 6" Handkerchief Vase

3886 DH Candy Box

3628 DH 6" Ftd. DC Comport

3667 DH 6" Bell

3837 DH 7" Basket

3608 DH Fairy Light

3950 DH 10" Bud Vase

Decorated Hobnail (Roses)

Dainty pink roses were the feature of this hand-painted decoration that was set against a white Hobnail background. Nine different items in milk glass Hobnail with this decoration were introduced in the January 1974 supplement. New pieces were not added and the decoration was discontinued at the end of 1975.

Decorated Roses	Ware No.	Introduced	Discontinued	Value
Ashtray, medium	3973-RW	1974	July 1975	20.00 – 22.00
Basket, 7" handled	3837-RW	1974	1976	55.00 – 70.00
Bell, 6"	3667-RW	1974	1976	35.00 – 38.00
Candy box, covered	3886-RW	1974	1976	60.00 – 75.00
Comport, 6" ftd., DC	3628-RW	1974	July 1975	35.00 – 38.00
Fairy light	3608-RW	1974	1976	45.00 – 50.00
Lamp, 21" student	3807-RW	1974	1976	200.00 – 250.00
Nut dish, oval 2-H	3633-RW	1974	1976	22.00 – 28.00
Vase, 10" bud	3950-RW	1974	1976	32.00 – 35.00

3633 RW Oval Nut Dish

3886 RW Candy Box

3950 RW 10" Bud Vase

3837 RW 7" Basket

3628 RW Ftd. Comport

3667 RW Bell

3973 RW Medium Ash Tray

3608 RW Fairy Light

3807 RW 21" Student Lamp

French Opalescent Hobnail

Hobnail in French Opalescent entered the Fenton line in 1940. This crystal glass with opalescent hobs proved to be popular through the 1940s and early 1950s. Therefore, numerous additions to the pattern were made in this color through the years. Most of the Hobnail items in this color were discontinued by the mid-1950s. However, a few of the more popular items such as the bell, salt and pepper shakers, goblet, ashtray set, and the juice set were made for many more years.

Included among the hard-to-find pieces are the 8" oval handled bonbon, the petite epergne set, the vanity boxtle, and the 5" covered jar. The tray for the No. 3917 creamer and sugar set and No. 3916 oil and vinegar set was only made one year — 1955. The jam and jelly set which used this same tray was also only made this year. Although it was made relatively late — in 1964 — the No. 3664-70 oz. jug was only produced for one year. Therefore, it has become one of the more elusive pieces in this color.

Examples of sets marketed by Fenton with their accompanying ware numbers are as follows:

Sets	Introduced	Discontinued
Ashtray set No. 3810: No. 3876, No. 3877, No. 3878 octagonal ashtrays	1954	1956
Beverage set No. 3907 (7-piece): 80 oz. jug, 6-12 oz. tumblers	1947	1954
Beverage set No. 3909 (9-piece): 80 oz. jug, 8-12 oz. tumblers	1941	1954
Cigarette set (6-piece): No. 1 hat, No. 2 hat, 4 round ashtrays	1941	1944
Cigarette set (5-piece): No. 2 hat, 4 round ashtrays	1941	1943
Condiment set (5-piece): oil, mustard, ftd. salt and pepper, 10½" fan tray	1942	1950
Condiment set No. 3809 (7-piece): oil, mustard, ind. sugar & creamer, flat salt & pepper, 7¾" tray with chrome handle	1950	1954
Console set No. 3802 (3-piece): 9" DC bowl, 2 cornucopia candle	1943	1954
Console set No. 3904 (3-piece): 9" DC bowl, 2 candle holders	1946	1956
Console set No. 3804 (3-piece): 11" DC bowl, 2 candle holders	1946	1954
Creamer and sugar set No. 3906: star-shaped	1949	1956
Creamer and sugar set No. 3917: Ware No. 3906 on an oval scalloped edge tray with a chrome handle	1955	1956
Epergne set No. 3902 (2-piece) petite	1950	1955
Jam set (3-piece) with crystal spoon No. 3903	1948	1956
Juice set No. 3905 (7-piece): Squat jug, 6-5 oz. tumblers.	1941	1961
Mayonnaise set (3-piece) No. 3803 with 5" crystal ladle	1948	1957
Oil and vinegar set No. 3916: 2 No. 3869 oil bottles on an oval scalloped tray with a chrome handle	1955	1956
Vanity set No. 3805 (3-piece); puff box, 2 colognes	1940	1954
Wine set (7-piece): decanter, 6 wine goblets	1947	1950

The No. 3902 two-piece petite epergne set consists of the 6" bonbon with a center ring in which the No. 3952-4" DC vase rests. Although the vanity sets were first made in 1940, vanity bottles and puff boxes did not appear on the price lists separately before the introduction of ware numbers in July 1952.

Several early pieces disappeared from the Fenton price lists during the mid-1940s, but were made again later in the decade. The 12" footed DC bowl listed in the early 1940s disappeared from the price listings in 1944. When the bowl returned to the line in 1948, it was listed as an 11" footed bowl. The footed cake plate which is made from the same mould also was listed as an inch smaller when it returned in 1948. The crescent tray was introduced in 1942. It was also made in 1943, but is not listed again until 1948.

The boxtle is a three-piece combination vanity set. It consists of a powder box base, a powder box lid which also contains the base for the perfume, and a stopper with a long dauber which fits into the perfume base. The original boxtle was made in French Opalescent during 1953. In 1982 a limited edition of 800 French Opalescent boxtles was made for Cosmetics 'N Glass. These later issues are marked with the Fenton logo on the base.

A few sizes of Easter baskets in French Opalescent with colored edges and handles have been produced in recent years. For more information on these items see the introduction to this chapter.

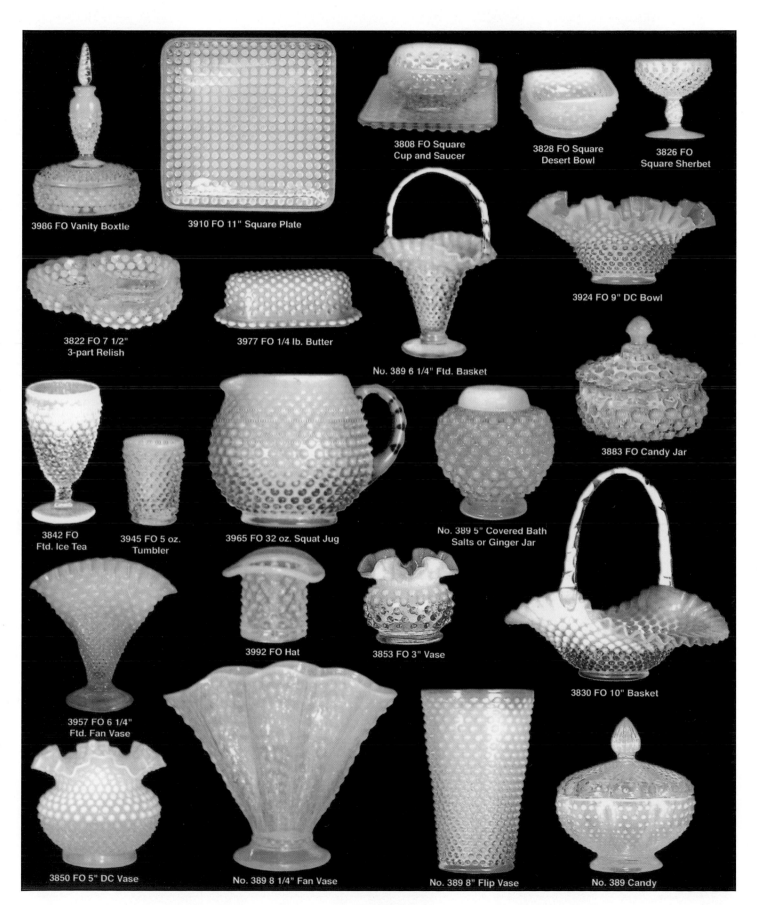

3986 FO Vanity Boxtle

3910 FO 11" Square Plate

3808 FO Square
Cup and Saucer

3828 FO Square
Desert Bowl

3826 FO
Square Sherbet

3822 FO 7 1/2"
3-part Relish

3977 FO 1/4 lb. Butter

No. 389 6 1/4" Ftd. Basket

3924 FO 9" DC Bowl

3883 FO Candy Jar

3842 FO
Ftd. Ice Tea

3945 FO 5 oz.
Tumbler

3965 FO 32 oz. Squat Jug

No. 389 5" Covered Bath
Salts or Ginger Jar

3957 FO 6 1/4"
Ftd. Fan Vase

3992 FO Hat

3853 FO 3" Vase

3830 FO 10" Basket

3850 FO 5" DC Vase

No. 389 8 1/4" Fan Vase

No. 389 8" Flip Vase

No. 389 Candy

French Opalescent Hobnail	Ware No.	Introduced	Discontinued	Value
Ashtray, fan-shape	3872-FO	1941	1955	18.00 – 20.00
Ashtray, oval	3873-FO	1941	1957	15.00 – 18.00
Ashtray, round shallow		1941	1944	18.00 – 20.00
Ashtray #1 4" octagonal	3876-FO	1954	1956	18.00 – 20.00
Ashtray #2 5¼" octagonal	3877-FO	1954	1956	20.00 – 22.00
Ashtray #3 6½" octagonal	3878-FO	1954	1956	22.00 – 25.00
Ashtray set, octagonal	3810-FO	1954	1956	60.00 – 67.00
Ashtray set, round	3610-FO	1978	1979	60.00 – 67.00
Basket, 4½"	3834-FO	1940	1956	30.00 – 35.00
Basket, 5½" handled	3835-FO	Oct. 1949	1955	65.00 – 75.00
Basket, 6¼" ftd. handled		July 1941	1947	45.00 – 55.00
Basket, 7" handled	3837-FO	1940	July 1956	40.00 – 50.00
Basket, 8" ftd. handled		1943	1947	70.00 – 80.00
Basket, 10" handled	3830-FO	1940	July 1954	90.00 – 110.00
Basket, 13½"		1941	1944	250.00 – 300.00
Bell, 6"	3667-FO	1978	1981	35.00 – 45.00
Bonbon, 4" 2-handled		1946	1951	12.00 – 14.00
Bonbon, 5" 2-handled oval,	3935-FO	1941	1956	14.00 – 18.00
Bonbon, 5" 2-handled square		1941	1952	14.00 – 18.00
Bonbon, 5" star	3921-FO	1953	1957	30.00 – 35.00
Bonbon, 6" DC	3926-FO	1940	1956	10.00 – 12.00
Bonbon, 6" flared, oval, plate, square, triangle		1940	1952	12.00 – 15.00
Bonbon, 6½" 2-handled square, oval		July 1941	1944	18.00 – 22.00
Bonbon, 7" handled	3937-FO	1951	1956	18.00 – 22.00
Bonbon, 8" oval, handled		1951	1952	100.00 – 125.00
Bottle, vanity	3865-FO	1940	1954	35.00 – 45.00
Bowl, finger		1942		14.00 – 18.00
Bowl, square dessert	3828-FO	1951	1955	25.00 – 28.00
Bowl, 7" DC	3927-FO	1940	1957	20.00 – 25.00
Bowl, 7 " flared, oval		1940	1944	22.00 – 27.00
Bowl, 7" special		1940		25.00 – 32.00
Bowl, 7½" flared (scalloped)		1942	1943	22.00 – 27.00
Bowl, 9" DC	3924-FO	1941	1956	35.00 – 40.00
Bowl, 9" flared		1940		35.00 – 40.00
Bowl, 11" DC	3824-FO	1940	1955	45.00 – 50.00
Bowl, 11" flared, oval, triangle		1940	1952	50.00 – 55.00
Bowl, 11" ftd. shallow		July 1941	1944	80.00 – 95.00
Bowl, 11" ftd. DC	3923-FO	1948	1955	80.00 – 95.00
Bowl, 12" ftd. DC		July 1941	1944	80.00 – 95.00
Boxtle, vanity	3986-FO	1953	1954	250.00 – 275.00
Butter, ¼ lb.	3977-FO	July 1954	1956	140.00 – 160.00
Cake plate, 13" ftd.	3913-FO	1948	1956	80.00 – 95.00
Cake plate, 12" ftd.		July 1941	1944	80.00 – 95.00
Candle, large cornucopia	3874-FO	1943	1954	40.00 – 45.00
Candle, miniature cornucopia	3971-FO	July 1941	1956	15.00 – 20.00
Candleholder	3974-FO	1941	1955	18.00 – 20.00
Candy jar	3883-FO	1953	1955	55.00 – 60.00
Candy jar, ftd.	3980-FO	1941	1954	55.00 – 60.00
Candy jar, low	3880-FO	1951	1955	55.00 – 60.00
Candy jar, scalloped body, ftd.		1942	1944	80.00 – 100.00
Comport, ftd. covered	3887-FO	July 1953	1954	65.00 – 80.00
Comport, 6" flared, triangular		July 1941	1943	25.00 – 30.00
Comport, 8" ftd. plate		July 1941	1943	55.00 – 60.00

Catalog Reprint Composite Circa 1948   Courtesy Of: The Fenton Art Glass Museum

No. 389 Mustard
and Spoon

No. 389 5"
Handled Bonbon

No. 389 6"
Nappy

No. 389 Fan Ash Tray

No. 389 4"
Handled Bonbon

No. 389 Individual
Sugar and Cream

No. 389 Oil

No. 389
Sugar and Cream

No. 389 Candleholder

No. 389 Slipper

No. 389
Oval Ash Tray

No. 389 3-Piece Vanity Set

No. 389 Handled Decanter

No. 389 Cruet

French Opalescent Hobnail	Ware No.	Introduced	Discontinued	Value
Condiment set, 5-piece		1942	1944	98.00 – 122.00
Cookie jar, handled		July 1941		250.00 – 300.00
Creamer and sugar	3901-FO	1940	1957	35.00 – 45.00
Creamer and sugar, #3	3906-FO	Oct. 1949	1956	55.00 – 65.00
Creamer and sugar set on tray	3917-FO	1955	1956	70.00 – 100.00
Creamer and sugar, individual	3900-FO	1942	1956	25.00 – 30.00
Cruet	3863-FO	July 1941	1957	65.00 – 75.00
Cup and saucer, square	3808-FO	1951	1955	35.00 – 40.00
Decanter, handled		July 1941	1950	200.00 – 225.00
Epergne and block		July 1941	1943	165.00 – 195.00
Epergne set, 2-pc. petite	3902-FO	1950	1955	65.00 – 85.00
Epergne set, miniature 4-pc.	3801-FO	Oct. 1949	1957	80.00 – 85.00
Goblet, round water	3845-FO	1940	1965	18.00 – 20.00
Goblet, square water	3846-FO	Dec. 1950	1955	30.00 – 35.00
Goblet, wine	3843-FO	1940	1957	20.00 – 25.00
Goblet, square wine	3844-FO	Dec. 1950	1955	35.00 – 45.00
Hat, No. 1		1941	1944	14.00 – 18.00
Hat, No. 2	3992-FO	1941	1954	22.00 – 27.00
Jam & jelly	3915-FO	1955	1956	100.00 – 115.00
Jam set, 3-pc. w/glass spoon	3903-FO	1948	1956	65.00 – 85.00
Jar, 5" bath salts or ginger				30.00 – 35.00
Jar, 5" covered (Hobnail lid)		1940	1942	185.00 – 225.00
Jug, 4½"	3964-FO	1941	1954	20.00 – 25.00
Jug, 5½"		1941	1951	25.00 – 30.00
Jug, 32 oz. squat	3965-FO	1940	July 1962	55.00 – 65.00
Jug, 48 oz. tankard		1940	1944	250.00 – 275.00
Jug, 70 oz. (IL)	3664-FO	1964	1965	150.00 – 175.00
Jug, 80 oz. (NIL)	3967-FO	1941	1956	150.00 – 180.00
Mayonnaise set, 3-pc. w/glass ladle	3803-FO	1948	1957	25.00 – 28.00
Mustard and spoon	3889-FO	1942	1957	25.00 – 28.00
Oil	3869-FO	1942	1963	25.00 – 30.00
Oil & vinegar set on tray	3916-FO	1955	1956	85.00 – 93.00
Plate, 4"		1942		8.00 – 10.00
Plate, 6½" square	3819-FO	Sept. 1950	1955	20.00 – 25.00
Plate, 6" round		1942		8.00 – 10.00
Plate, 8" salad	3918-FO	1940	1957	12.00 – 15.00
Plate, 11" square (diag. meas.)	3910-FO	Sept. 1950	1955	40.00 – 45.00
Plate, 16" torte	3817-FO	Sept. 1950	1955	45.00 – 50.00
Puff box	3885-FO	1940	1954	35.00 – 45.00
Punch bowl, crimped		Sept. 1950	July 1952	200.00 – 250.00
Punch bowl, flared	3827-FO	Sept. 1950	1955	200.00 – 250.00
Punch bowl, handled		Dec. 1950	1952	300.00 – 400.00
Punch cup	3847-FO	Sept. 1950	1955	10.00 – 14.00
Punch set, 15-piece	3807-FO	Sept. 1950	1955	325.00 – 425.00
Relish, 12" divided	3740-FO			100.00 – 150.00
Relish, 3-part	3822-FO	1954	1957	35.00 – 45.00
Rose bowl, 3"		Oct. 1949	1951	25.00 – 28.00
Rose bowl, 4½"		1940	1944	25.00 – 30.00
Rose bowl, 5"		1940	1955	30.00 – 40.00
Salt and pepper, flat	3806-FO	Oct. 1949	1965	35.00 – 40.00
Salt and pepper, ftd.		1940	1944	45.00 – 60.00
Saucer, square		1951	1955	8.00 – 10.00
Sherbet	3825-FO	1940	1965	10.00 – 12.00
Sherbet, square	3826-FO	1951	1955	25.00 – 30.00
Slipper	3995-FO	1941	1956	14.00 – 18.00
Tidbit tray, 2-tier (square plates)		Sept. 1950		100.00 – 125.00

No. 389 3-Piece Mayonnaise Set

No. 389 3" Rose Bowl

No. 389 No. 3 Sugar & Cream Set

No. 389 3-Piece Jam Set

No. 389 Cornucopia

No. 389 5 1/2" Handled Basket

No. 389 Salt & Pepper

No. 389 6 1/2" Crescent Tray

No. 389 13" Ftd. Cake Plate

Catalog Reprint
Circa 1949-1950

Courtesy Of:

The Fenton
Art Glass Museum

No. 389 11" Ftd. Bowl

No. 389 4 1/2" Handled Jug

No. 389 5 1/2" Handled Jug

French Opalescent Hobnail	Ware No.	Introduced	Discontinued	Value
Tray, 6½" crescent		1948	1950	35.00 – 40.00
Tray, 6¾" crescent		1942	1943	35.00 – 40.00
Tray, 7¾" div. w/chrome handle	3879-FO	Sept. 1950	1954	55.00 – 65.00
Tray, 10½" fan		1941	1951	30.00 – 35.00
Tumbler, 5 oz.	3945-FO	1940	1965	14.00 – 18.00
Tumbler, 9 oz.	3949-FO	1940	1965	18.00 – 20.00
Tumbler, 12 oz.	3942-FO	1954	1957	25.00 – 30.00
Tumbler, 12 oz. (barrel)	3947-FO	1941	1954	25.00 – 30.00
Tumbler, 16 oz.	3946-FO	1950	1965	45.00 – 50.00
Tumbler, ftd. ice tea or highball	3842-FO	1940	1965	25.00 – 28.00
Vanity set, 3-pc.	3805-FO	1940	1955	105.00 – 135.00
Vase, 3" DC	3853-FO	Oct. 1949	1956	10.00 – 12.00
Vase, 4" ftd. DC	3952-FO	1948	1956	12.00 – 15.00
Vase, 4" ftd. fan	3953-FO	1948	1956	18.00 – 20.00
Vase, 4" miniature fan, flared, hat		1940	1952	14.00 – 16.00
Vase, 4" miniature cup crimped		1940	1952	14.00 – 16.00
Vase, 4" miniature cup flared, oval		1940	1952	14.00 – 16.00
Vase, 4" miniature triangle	3855-FO	1940	July 1956	14.00 – 16.00
Vase, 4½" DC	3854-FO	1940	1956	18.00 – 20.00
Vase, 4½" cup square, cup flared		1940	1952	18.00 – 20.00
Vase, 5" DC	3850-FO	1940	1955	20.00 – 28.00
Vase, 5" cup flared, square, triangle		1940	1952	20.00 – 25.00
Vase, 5½" crimped, flared, square, triangle, tulip		1941	1951	25.00 – 30.00
Vase, 6" DC	3856-FO	1940	1954	25.00 – 30.00
Vase, 6" flared, square, triangle		1940	1952	25.00 – 30.00
Vase, 6" hand		1942	1943	30.00 – 35.00
Vase, 6¼" ftd. cupped, cup flared, flared, triangle		1941	1949	30.00 – 35.00
Vase, 6¼" ftd. DC	3956-FO	1941	1956	30.00 – 35.00
Vase, 6¼" ftd. fan	3957-FO	1941	1956	30.00 – 35.00
Vase, 6½" fan (scalloped)		1942	1944	30.00 – 35.00
Vase, 6½" swung (scalloped)		1942	1944	30.00 – 35.00
Vase, 8" DC	3858-FO	1941	1954	45.00 – 50.00
Vase, 8" flared, square, triangle		1941	1949	45.00 – 50.00
Vase, 8" ftd. DC	3958-FO	1940	1956	40.00 – 45.00
Vase, 8" ftd. fan	3959-FO	1941	1956	40.00 – 45.00
Vase, 8" ftd. square, triangle		1943	1949	40.00 – 45.00
Vase, 8½" DC, flared crimped, triangle		1941	1951	40.00 – 45.00
Vase, 8½" flip		1941		150.00 – 200.00
Vase, 9" flared (scalloped)		1941	1944	55.00 – 65.00
Vase, 10" flared (bottle shape)		1941	1943	100.00 – 125.00

TOOLS OF THE TRADE

If you were to accept our invitation on the opposite page, you would see our skilled glassworkers working with these same ancient tools of the trade just as they were used many centuries ago.

The Buffer, a flat piece of cherry wood, is held against the hot glass as it is spun by the gaffer or finisher. With the buffer the finisher shapes the molten glass into its final form. His reliance on hand and eye skills cause the slight but delightful variations in each Fenton plate.

The Pucellas, often called the "Tool" (with a capital "T") becomes a set of additional fingers for the skilled glass craftsman. Its rounded ends leave no mark on the rapidly hardening glass, yet it is used to perfect the shape of many pieces. With it, the finisher and the handler deepen crimps, pull lips, notch handles. The steels used to make these tools are better now, but the tool itself is a duplicate of one used centuries ago.

The Finisher's Bench is another age old piece of equipment in a handmade glass plant. Up and down its long arms the finisher spins the pontil, snap or blowpipe with molten glass at its end, shaping the piece as he spins it. Let him stop for a moment and the almost liquid glass sags out of shape. Fenton Hobnail Milk Glass, to be seen on the next four pages, has been shaped by these same age old tools.

Green Opalescent Hobnail

Fenton's Green Opalescent color, introduced in 1940, was produced by adding uranium or chromium to the basic French Opalescent batch. The original Green Opalescent color was a light to medium green and often had a yellow tint. This color was discontinued in 1941. Topaz Opalescent replaced Green Opalescent in the 1941 catalog. Hobnail in a green opalescent color called Lime Green Opalescent returned to the Fenton regular line in July 1952. This new color was dark green cased with French Opalescent. The resulting color was lighter and more yellow than the earlier Green Opalescent production. Production of Lime Green Opalescent Hobnail was discontinued in 1955. For information about Lime Green Opalescent Hobnail, see page 194. Production of Hobnail in Green Opalescent (GO) Hobnail began again in July 1959. However, this version was a deep blue-green opalescent color.

Due to the vast color differences in the two eras of production, the Green Opalescent Hobnail listing is divided into two sections. The first list includes Hobnail items made in the early 1940s. Note the 7" handled basket and the 4½" footed DC vase were also made in the darker color during the 1959 issue. The second listing details pieces made in the deep blue-green color of the 1959 issue.

In 1985, a Green Opalescent punch set was made as a part of the Connoisseur Collection. The set consisted of a punch bowl, base, and 12 cups. This set will be marked with the Fenton logo. This punch set was not made during any of the earlier productions and none of the earlier issues are marked with the Fenton logo.

Green Opalescent Hobnail (1940)	Introduced	Discontinued	Value
Basket, 4½" handled	1940	1941	95.00 – 120.00
Basket, 7" handled	1940	1941	145.00 – 175.00
Basket, 10" handled	1940	1941	200.00 – 250.00
Bonbon, 6" double crimp, flared, oval, plate, square, triangle	1940	1941	22.00 – 27.00
Bottle, cologne	1940	1941	100.00 – 125.00
Bowl, 7" flared, oval	1940	1941	45.00 – 55.00
Bowl, 7" special	1940	1941	50.00 – 60.00
Bowl, 9" crimped, flared,	1940	1941	70.00 – 80.00
Bowl, 11" double crimp, flared, oval, triangle	1940	1941	95.00 – 110.00
Creamer	1940	1941	30.00 – 40.00
Jar, 5" covered	1940	1941	400.00 – 500.00
Jug, 32 oz. squat	1940	1941	190.00 – 225.00
Jug, 48 oz. tankard	1940	1941	450.00 – 500.00
Nappy, 6" double crimp, flared, oval, plate, square, triangle	1940	1941	22.00 – 27.00
Nappy, 7 " double crimp, flared, oval, plate, square, triangle	1940	1941	35.00 – 45.00
Puff box	1940	1941	140.00 – 165.00
Rose bowl, 4½"	1940	1941	65.00 – 85.00
Rose bowl, 5"	1940	1941	70.00 – 90.00
Salt and pepper, ftd.	1940	1941	200.00 – 250.00
Sugar	1940	1941	35.00 – 45.00
Tumbler, 9 oz.	1940	1941	40.00 – 45.00
Vanity Set, 3-pc.	1940	1941	340.00 – 415.00
Vase, 4" miniature cup crimp, cup flared, fan, flared, hat, triangle	1940	1941	30.00 – 35.00
Vase, 4½" double crimp, cup flared, cup square	1940	1941	40.00 – 45.00
Vase, 5" double crimp, cup flared, square, triangle	1940	1941	50.00 – 60.00
Vase, 6" double crimp, flared, square, triangle	1940	1941	75.00 – 85.00
Vase, 8" double crimp, flared, square, triangle	1940	1941	120.00 – 140.00

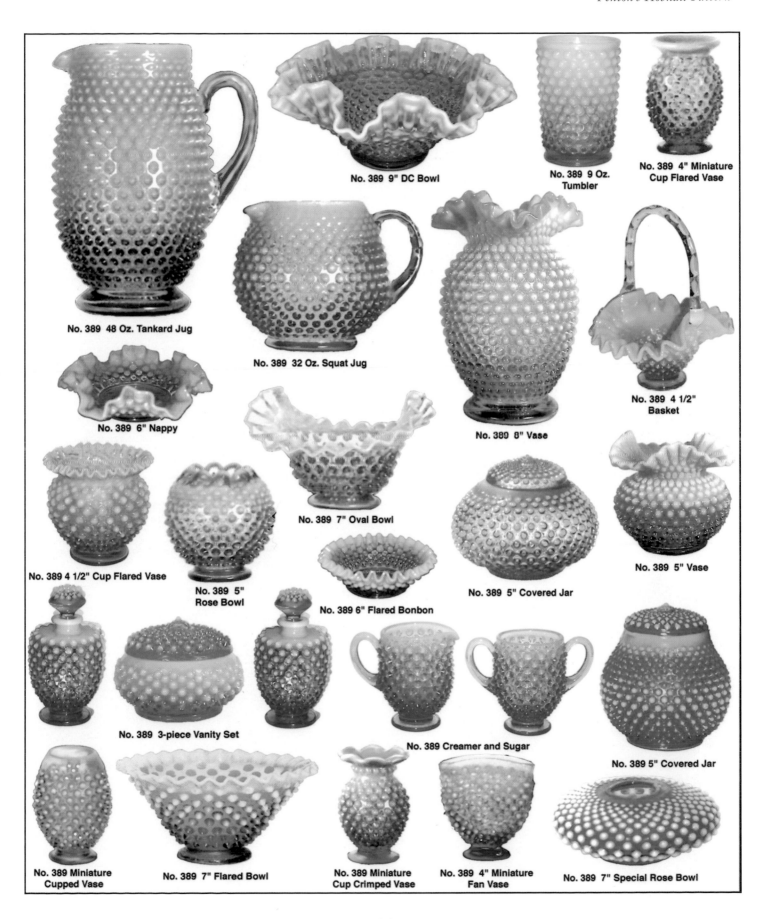

No. 389 9" DC Bowl

No. 389 9 Oz. Tumbler

No. 389 4" Miniature Cup Flared Vase

No. 389 48 Oz. Tankard Jug

No. 389 32 Oz. Squat Jug

No. 389 8" Vase

No. 389 4 1/2" Basket

No. 389 6" Nappy

No. 389 4 1/2" Cup Flared Vase

No. 389 5" Rose Bowl

No. 389 7" Oval Bowl

No. 389 6" Flared Bonbon

No. 389 5" Covered Jar

No. 389 5" Vase

No. 389 3-piece Vanity Set

No. 389 Creamer and Sugar

No. 389 5" Covered Jar

No. 389 Miniature Cupped Vase

No. 389 7" Flared Bowl

No. 389 Miniature Cup Crimped Vase

No. 389 4" Miniature Fan Vase

No. 389 7" Special Rose Bowl

Green Opalescent Hobnail (1959)	Ware No.	Introduced	Discontinued	Value
*Basket, 7" handled	3837-GO	July 1959	July 1961	90.00 – 125.00
Bowl, 10" ftd.	3731-GO	July 1959	July 1961	90.00 – 100.00
Bowl, 9 " DC	3924-GO	July 1959	July 1961	65.00 – 75.00
Bowl, violet	3754-GO	1960	July 1961	30.00 – 40.00
Candle bowl	3771-GO	July 1959	1960	55.00 – 65.00
Candleholder	3974-GO	July 1959	July 1961	30.00 – 40.00
Comport	3728-GO	July 1959	July 1961	38.00 – 42.00
Comport	3727-GO	1960	July 1961	40.00 – 45.00
Comport, ftd. covered	3887-GO	July 1959	July 1961	125.00 – 145.00
Epergne set, miniature	3801-GO	July 1959	July 1961	145.00 – 185.00
Jug, 12 oz. syrup	3762-GO	July 1959	1960	65.00 – 85.00
Relish, handled	3733-GO	1960	July 1961	75.00 – 125.00
Slipper	3995-GO	1960	July 1961	20.00 – 25.00
*Vase, 4 ftd. DC	3952-GO	1960	July 1961	20.00 – 22.00
Vase, 6" handkerchief	3750-GO	July 1960	July 1961	35.00 – 50.00
Vase, 8" bud	3756-GO	July 1959	July 1961	30.00 – 40.00
Vase, 12" medium swung	3758-GO	July 1959	July 1961	100.00 – 125.00
Vase, 18" tall swung	3759-GO	July 1959	1960	150.00 – 185.00

*Also produced in the early 1940s

3754 GO
Violet Bowl

3952 GO
4" Ftd. DC Vase

3731 GO 10" Ftd. Bowl

3727 GO Comport

3801 GO Miniature Epergne

3887 GO
Ftd. Covered Comport

3771 GO Candle Bowl

3756 GO
8" Bud Vase

3728 GO Comport

3759 GO 18" Swung Vase

The Fenton Art Glass Co. Williamstown, W. Va.
No. 389 Hobnail Items Open Stock - Hand made by Fenton   CH 5272

All Items made in French, Green, Blue and Cranberry Opalescent Color

4" Min. Fan Vase — 4" Min. Cup Crimp Vase — 4" Min. Hat Vase — 4" Min. Cup Fld. Vase — 4" Min. Fld. Vase — 4" Min. Tri. Vase

6" Oval Bon Bon — 6" Fld. Bon Bon — 6" Tri. Bon Bon — 6" D. Crimp Bon Bon — 6" Square Bon Bon — 6" Plate Bon Bon

— 7" Bon Bon May Be Had In Above Six Shapes —

10" Hdl. Basket — Sugar & Cream — 3 Pce. Vanity Set — 4½" Hdl. Basket — 32 oz. Squat Jug

48 oz. Tankard Jug — 8" Flared Vase — 8" D. Crimp Vase — 6" Square Vase — 6" Tri. Vase

— Above Four Vases Made All Four Shapes In Both 6" and 8" Size —

9" Fld. Bowl — Covered Jar — 5" Triangle Vase — 11" Double Crimped Bowl

187

Green Pastel Hobnail

Hobnail was made in a light opaque green color that Fenton called Green Pastel from January 1954 through December 1955. The short period of production has resulted in a low supply of this color on the secondary market.

		Introduced	**Discontinued**
Fenton combined items to produce the following set: Console set No. 3904 (3-piece): No. 3924-9" DC bowl, two No. 3974 candles		July 1954	1956

Green Pastel Hobnail	Ware No.	Introduced	Discontinued	Value
Basket, 4½"	3834-GP	1955	1956	35.00 – 40.00
Basket, 7" handled	3837-GP	1954	1956	55.00 – 60.00
Berry dish	3928-GP	1954	1956	11.00 – 15.00
Bonbon, 6" DC	3926-GP	1955	1956	12.00 – 14.00
Bowl, 9" DC	3924-GP	1954	1956	30.00 – 35.00
Bowl, 9" square	3929-GP	1954	1956	45.00 – 50.00
Candleholder	3974-GP	1955	1956	20.00 – 25.00
Candy jar	3883-GP	1954	1956	55.00 – 60.00
Comport, ftd.	3920-GP	1954	1956	30.00 – 35.00
Comport, ftd. w/cover	3887-GP	1954	1956	65.00 – 70.00
Creamer and sugar, #3	3906-GP	1954	1956	25.00 – 30.00
Epergne set, 5-pc.	3800-GP	1954	1955	200.00 – 250.00
Epergne set, miniature 4-pc.	3801-GP	1954	1956	100.00 – 125.00
Jardiniere, 4½"	3994-GP	July 1955	1956	30.00 – 35.00
Kettle	3990-GP	1954	1956	20.00 – 25.00
Lamp, 11" hurricane	3998-GP	1954	1956	90.00 – 110.00
Slipper	3995-GP	1954	1956	25.00 – 35.00
Vase, 4" ftd. DC	3952-GP	1954	1956	10.00 – 12.00
Vase, 4" ftd. fan	3953-GP	1954	1956	12.00 – 15.00
Vase, 4½" DC	3854-GP	1954	1956	20.00 – 22.00

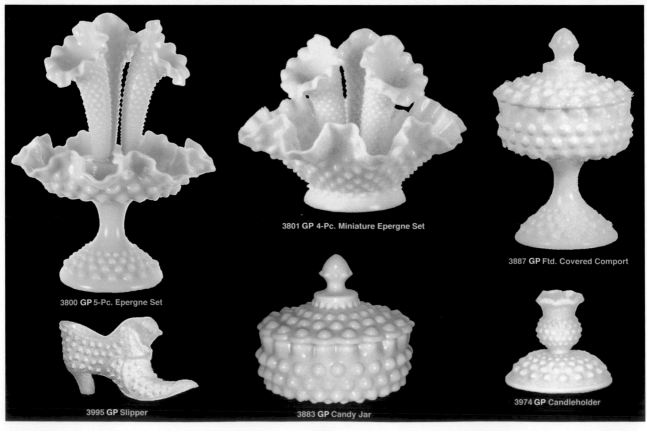

3800 **GP** 5-Pc. Epergne Set

3801 GP 4-Pc. Miniature Epergne Set

3887 **GP** Ftd. Covered Comport

3995 **GP** Slipper

3883 **GP** Candy Jar

3974 **GP** Candleholder

3834 GP 4 1/2" Basket

3837 GP 7" Basket

3998 GP Hurricane Lamp

3920 GP Ftd. Comport

3953 GP 4" Ftd. Fan Vase

3952 GP 4" Ftd. DC Vase

3929 GP 9" Square Bowl

3928 GP Berry Dish

3854 GP 4 1/2" DC Vase

3906 GP #3 Sugar & Creamer

3924 GP 9" DC Bowl

Green Transparent Hobnail

Fenton's Colonial Green is a transparent olive green color. This color made its debut in July 1963 and was replaced by a lighter and more vivid green, called Springtime Green, in 1977. For more information on candle bowl arrangements and lamps, see the chapters on these respective subjects. Today, there are not very many collectors seeking this color of Hobnail and most of the pieces are fairly easy to find by anyone who desires them.

Colonial Green Hobnail	Ware No.	Introduced	Discontinued	Value
Apothecary jar	3689-CG	1964	1970	55.00 – 65.00
Ashtray, medium round	3973-CG	1964	1968	4.00 – 6.00
Ashtray, small round	3972-CG	1964	1968	3.00 – 5.00
Ashtray, large round	3776-CG	1964	1966	8.00 – 10.00
Ashtray set, 3-piece round	3610-CG	1964	1977	15.00 – 21.00
Basket, 7" handled	3837-CG	1967	1977	25.00 – 30.00
Basket, 8½"	3638-CG	1967	1971	25.00 – 35.00
Basket, 10"	3830-CG	1968	1977	40.00 – 45.00
Bell, 6"	3667-CG	1967	1977	18.00 – 20.00
Candle bowl, 4" miniature	3873-CG	1969	July 1972	12.00 – 14.00
Candle bowl, 6"	3872-CG	July 1968	1977	10.00 – 15.00
Candy box	3668-CG	1975	1977	25.00 – 30.00
Candy box, ftd.	3784-CG	1966	1971	30.00 – 35.00
Candy box, oval covered	3786-CG	1968	July 1970	18.00 – 20.00
Cigarette lighter	3692-CG	1965	1969	25.00 – 30.00
Comport, 6" ftd., DC	3628-CG	1969	1977	10.00 – 12.00
Creamer, miniature	3665-CG	1965	1969	7.00 – 9.00
Fairy light	3608-CG	1969	1977	20.00 – 22.00
Fairy light, 3-pc. ftd.	3804-CG	1975	1977	45.00 – 50.00
Lamp, courting, oil	3792-CG	1965	1968	55.00 – 60.00
Lamp, courting, electric	3793-CG	1965	1968	55.00 – 60.00
Nut dish, oval 2-H	3633-CG	1964	1969	8.00 – 10.00
Slipper	3995-CG	1964	1977	10.00 – 14.00
Toothpick holder	3795-CG	1966	1976	8.00 – 10.00
Urn, 11" covered	3986-CG	1968	1969	85.00 – 100.00
Vase, 3" DC	3853-CG	1968	1977	6.00 – 8.00
Vase, 4" ftd. DC	3952-CG	1965	1977	6.00 – 8.00
Vase, 4½" DC	3854-CG	1969	1977	6.00 – 8.00
Vase, 5" 3-toed	3653-CG	1965	1971	10.00 – 14.00
Vase, 8" swung bud	3756-CG	1967	1977	14.00 – 16.00
Vase, 12" ftd. swung	3753-CG	1968	1971	22.00 – 25.00
Vase, 24" tall swung	3652-CG	1965	1977	30.00 – 40.00

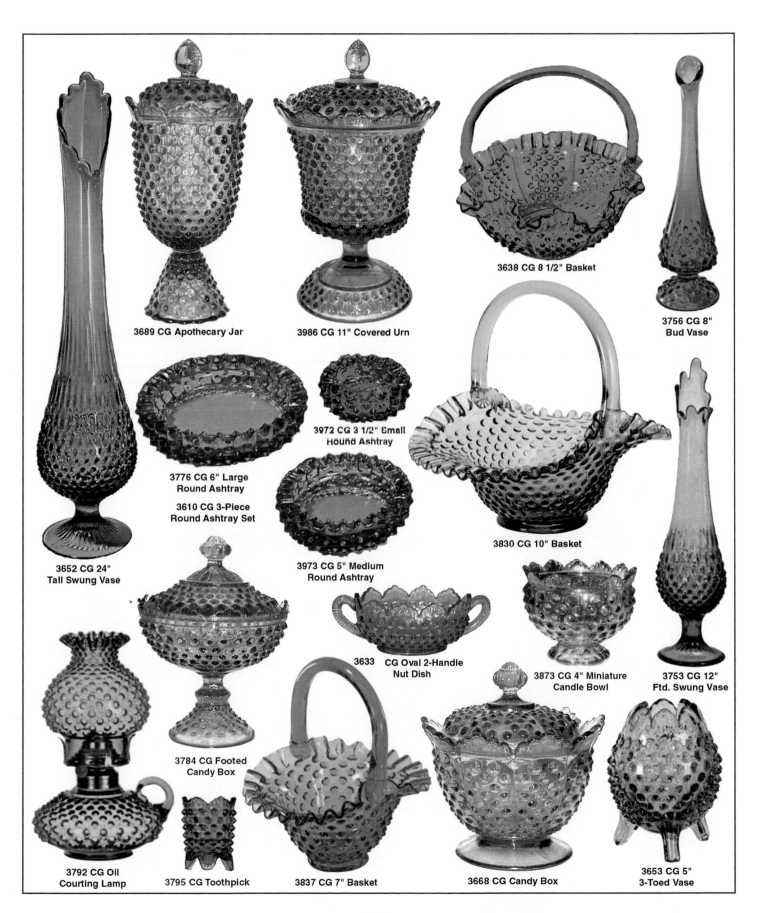

3689 CG Apothecary Jar

3986 CG 11" Covered Urn

3638 CG 8 1/2" Basket

3756 CG 8"
Bud Vase

3972 CG 3 1/2" Small
Round Ashtray

3776 CG 6" Large
Round Ashtray

3610 CG 3-Piece
Round Ashtray Set

3973 CG 5" Medium
Round Ashtray

3830 CG 10" Basket

3652 CG 24"
Tall Swung Vase

3633 CG Oval 2-Handle
Nut Dish

3873 CG 4" Miniature
Candle Bowl

3753 CG 12"
Ftd. Swung Vase

3784 CG Footed
Candy Box

3792 CG Oil
Courting Lamp

3795 CG Toothpick

3837 CG 7" Basket

3668 CG Candy Box

3653 CG 5"
3-Toed Vase

Green Transparent Hobnail (Springtime Green)

Transparent emerald Springtime Green replaced Colonial Green in the Fenton line in 1977. Springtime Green was discontinued after December 1978.

Springtime Green Hobnail	Ware No.	Introduced	Discontinued	Value
Ashtray, ball	3648-GT	1977	1979	22.00 – 27.00
Ashtray set, 3-piece	3610-GT	1977	1978	25.00 – 30.00
Basket, 7" handled	3837-GT	1977	1979	35.00 – 45.00
Bell, 6"	3667-GT	1977	1979	20.00 – 25.00
Candy box	3668-GT	1977	1979	45.00 – 55.00
Comport, 6" ftd, DC	3628-GT	1977	1979	22.00 – 27.00
Fairy light	3608-GT	1977	1979	30.00 – 32.00
Slipper	3995-GT	1977	1979	18.00 – 22.00
Vase, 4½" DC	3854-GT	1977	1979	10.00 – 12.00
Vase, 8" swung bud	3756-GT	1977	1979	14.00 – 18.00
Vase, 11"	3752-GT	1977	1978	35.00 – 45.00

Catalog Reprint Circa 1978
Courtesy Of:
The Fenton Art Glass Museum

3837 GT
7" BASKET

3752 GT
11" VASE

3995 GT
SLIPPER

3608 GT
FAIRY LIGHT

3854 GT
4½" VASE

3667 GT
BELL

3668 GT
CANDY BOX

Honey Amber Hobnail

In the early 1960s seven shapes of Hobnail were made in an amber color cased with opal glass. The new color was called Honey Amber. With the exception of the lavabo, the rest of the Hobnail pieces were only made for a few years.

Honey Amber Hobnail	Ware No.	Introduced	Discontinued	Value
Jug, 12 oz. syrup	3762-HA	1961	1964	30.00 – 35.00
Lavabo	3867-HA	1962	1967	180.00 – 200.00
Vase, 5" DC	3850-HA	1961	1963	25.00 – 27.00
Vase, 5½" DC	3656-HA	1962	1964	27.00 – 32.00
Vase, 6"	3856-HA	1961	1963	30.00 – 40.00
Vase, 8"	3858-HA	1961	1963	40.00 – 50.00
Vase, 11"	3752-HA	1961	1963	85.00 – 95.00

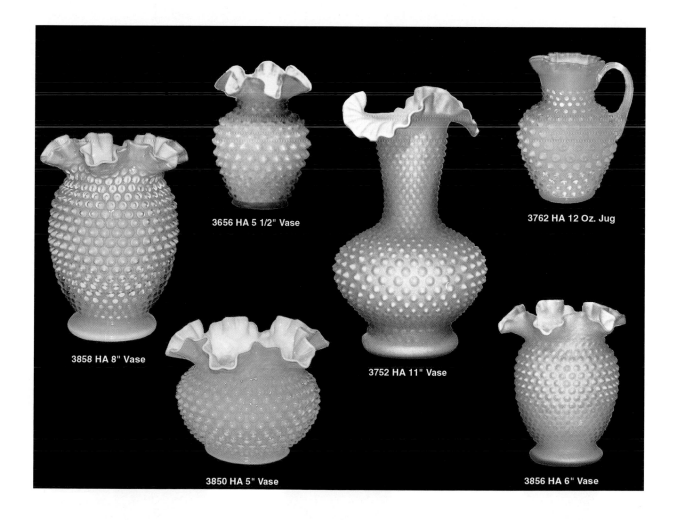

3656 HA 5 1/2" Vase

3762 HA 12 Oz. Jug

3858 HA 8" Vase

3752 HA 11" Vase

3850 HA 5" Vase

3856 HA 6" Vase

Milk Glass Hobnail

The following seven items were listed in milk glass in a 1940 price list:

Goblet, water	Tumbler, 9 oz.
Goblet, wine or cocktail	Tumbler, 5 oz.
Plate, 8"	Tumbler, ice tea or highball
Sherbet	

These items disappeared from the 1941 price listing and milk glass Hobnail did not reappear in the Fenton line again until January 1950. Most collectors refer to this date as the formal introduction of Hobnail in milk glass. Over the next four decades Fenton produced one of its most successful patterns. Pieces were made in just about every imaginable shape. Some pieces remained in the line for decades, but a few only lasted for six months or a year.

Fenton often combined several individual pieces to produce sets. Many times the individual pieces were listed and sold separately, but certain items such as creamers and sugars or salt and peppers might only have been available as sets.

Ashtray set, 3-piece (No. 3610) — a No. 3972 ashtray, a No. 3973 ashtray, and a No, 3776 ashtray

Ashtray set, 3-piece (No. 3810) — a No. 3876 ashtray, a No. 3877 ash tray, and a No. 3878 ashtray

Centerpiece set, 3-piece (No. 3742) — a No. 3748 chip 'n dip candle bowl, a No. 3745-7" candleholder, and a No. 3746 candle epergne

Cigarette set (No. 3603) — 3 rectangular No. 3693 ashtrays, a No. 3685 covered cigarette box, and a No. 3692 cigarette lighter

Condiment set, 7-piece (No. 3809) — No. 3900 sugar and creamer, No. 3869 oil, No 3889 mustard and spoon, No. 3806 salt and pepper, and No. 3879 tray with chrome handle

Console set (No. 3704) — a No. 3724-8½" bowl and 2 No. 3774-10" candleholders

Console set (No. 3802) — a No. 3924-9" bowl and 2 No. 3874 cornucopia candleholders

Console set No. 3904) — a No. 3924-9" bowl and 2 No. 3974 candleholders

Epergne set (No. 3800) — the No. 3920-footed comport was used with a flower frog and 3-5" long epergne horns

Jam and jelly set (No 3915) — 2 marmalade jars with a crystal ladle from the No. 3903 jam set on a 7½" x 3¾" chrome handled tray

Juice set (No. 3905) — a No. 3965 squat jug and 6 No. 3945-5 oz. juice tumblers

Napkin ring set (No. 3904) — four napkin rings were sold in a gift box

Oil and mustard set (No. 3715) — consists of a No. 3869 oil bottle, a No. 3889 mustard, and a 7½" x 3¾" chrome handled tray

Oil and vinegar set (No. 3916) — consists of 2 No. 3869 oil bottles and a 7½" x 3¾" chrome handled tray

Punch set, 10-piece (No. 3908) — a No. 3820 octagonal punch bowl and 8 No. 3840 punch cups with a No. 9520 milk glass punch ladle. This set was also sold with 12 cups as ware number 3911.

Punch set, 15-piece (No. 389) — was offered with a handled, flared or crimped bowl in September 1950. The set included a bowl, 12 cups, a 16" torte plate as the liner, and a ladle. The handled bowl was discontinued by January 1952.

Punch set, 15-piece (No. 3712) — has a 7 quart bowl and 12 cups; No. 3718-21 piece set uses the same No. 3722 bowl, but has 18 cups

Sugar, creamer and tray (No, 3917) — star-shaped No. 3906 sugar and creamer with a 7 ½" x 3¾" tray

Vanity set, 3-piece (No. 3805) — a No. 3885 puff box and 2 No. 3865 vanity bottles. This set was also offered with an optional vanity tray from January 1960 through December 1964.

Items with identical ware numbers:

The Ware Number 3704 was used for a console set from January 1958 through June 1961. From January 1975 through December 1977 it represented a two-piece epergne set. No. 3778 was a punch bowl base in 1958. It represented an ashtray/chip 'n dip/candle bowl utility piece in the 1970s and 1980s. A 15-piece punch set was sold using ware number 3807 from January 1959 through June 1959. Starting in 1971, this ware number was used for a 21" student lamp. Ware number 3885 was originally used with the small puff box. Starting in 1968, this code became the ware number for the footed candy jar. Ware Number 3886 was used for a honey jar from 1953 through 1959. After 1969, this number was used for a covered candy box. The petite epergne set made between 1961 and 1965 used the Ware Number 3902. The 3902 number was also used for a sugar and creamer set sold from 1969 through June 1983. Ware Number 3904 was shared by a console set and a napkin ring set. The set of napkin rings was made from 1976 through 1977 and the console set was marketed from 1952 through 1958.

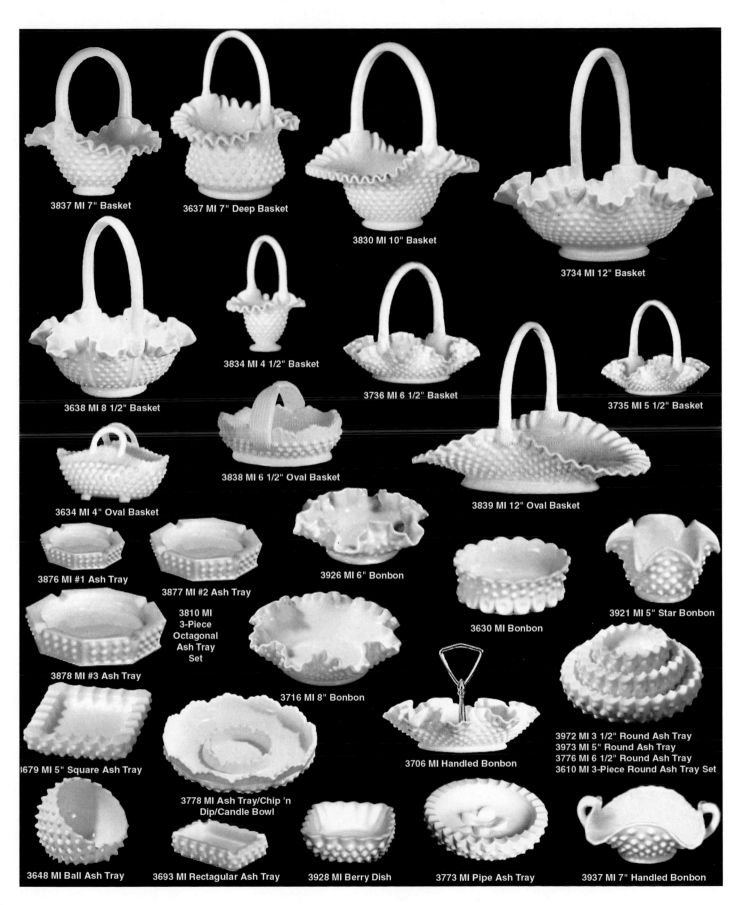

3837 MI 7" Basket

3637 MI 7" Deep Basket

3830 MI 10" Basket

3734 MI 12" Basket

3638 MI 8 1/2" Basket

3834 MI 4 1/2" Basket

3736 MI 6 1/2" Basket

3735 MI 5 1/2" Basket

3634 MI 4" Oval Basket

3838 MI 6 1/2" Oval Basket

3839 MI 12" Oval Basket

3876 MI #1 Ash Tray

3877 MI #2 Ash Tray

3926 MI 6" Bonbon

3921 MI 5" Star Bonbon

3810 MI 3-Piece Octagonal Ash Tray Set

3630 MI Bonbon

3878 MI #3 Ash Tray

3716 MI 8" Bonbon

3679 MI 5" Square Ash Tray

3778 MI Ash Tray/Chip 'n Dip/Candle Bowl

3706 MI Handled Bonbon

3972 MI 3 1/2" Round Ash Tray
3973 MI 5" Round Ash Tray
3776 MI 6 1/2" Round Ash Tray
3610 MI 3-Piece Round Ash Tray Set

3648 MI Ball Ash Tray

3693 MI Rectagular Ash Tray

3928 MI Berry Dish

3773 MI Pipe Ash Tray

3937 MI 7" Handled Bonbon

Two different pieces that used Ware Number 3971 were the miniature cornucopia candleholder and a footed candle bowl. The cornucopia candleholder was made from 1950 through June 1956, and the candle bowl was made in 1978 and 1979. Two other items that were both only made for short periods also shared the same ware number. No. 3986 was used for the vanity boxtle in 1953 and 1954 and for the 11" covered urn in 1968 and 1969.

Short periods of production is one contributing factor that causes some Hobnail items to be elusive. Items made for two years or less are noted in the following lists.

Items made for two years: No. 3612 spoon holder, No. 3646 14 oz. stein, No, 3647 egg cup, No. 3648 ball ashtray, No. 3650 nut or ice cream dish, No. 3658-12" three-toed vase, No. 3713-11" hurricane lamp, No. 3852-8½" fan vase, No. 3855-10" handkerchief vase, No. 3904 napkin ring set (4), No. 3912, 8½" plate, No. 3951 handkerchief vase, No. 3986 vanity boxtle, No. 3986-11" covered urn.

Items made for one year: No. 3678 crescent candleholder, No. 3778 punch bowl base, No. 3797 cinnamon sugar shaker, No. 3800 five-piece footed epergne set, No. 3922 chip 'n dip.

Items made for six months: No. 3730 ribbon candy bowl, No. 3836 wall planter, No. 3947-12 oz. tumbler (barrel-shaped).

Two styles of salt and pepper sets were sold in mixed colors — one white and one black. The No. 3602-BW salt and pepper set was sold in this color combination from 1962 through 1966. Another shaker set, No. 3806-BW, was also sold in this color combination. This set was available from 1962 through June 1977. The heart-shaped relish was made with and without a handle. The handled version (No. 3733) was available from January 1958 through December 1987. Two different versions of the same style courting lamp were sold. No. 3792 represented the oil lamp variety and No. 3793 was available for those who preferred an electric lamp. Ware Number 3895 was a dual function item. It was listed in some catalogs as a toothpick/candleholder.

Over the years, Fenton sometimes changed the names of items in the catalogs. For example, the No. 3887 covered comport was called a candy after 1958. The No. 3630 bonbon was also sometimes referred to as an ice cream or nut dish.

Design variations in some pieces with the same ware number will be seen. The No. 3702 sugar and creamer may be found with or without a beaded edge around the top. In the photo the creamer has a plain top and the sugar has a beaded top. There are two different styles of No. 3974 candleholders. One has a rounded base and the other style is more flat. The flat style is about 3" high and the one with the rounded base is 3½" tall. Several variations of the No. 3822 cloverleaf-shaped relish may be found. It first appeared in the line in January 1954 as an undivided relish. It was made in this fashion through December 1956. In January 1956 another style of this relish with the same ware number was offered. This new version was divided into three sections with a smooth top on the divisions. It was made in this style through December 1972. Starting in January 1973, scallops were added to the three partitioning panels. Two different sizes of No. 3843 wine goblet were made. The original goblet was 3¾" high and held 3 ounces. Later, a larger wine goblet was substituted. The later goblet was 4½" high and held 4 ounces. The No. 3991 hat made several appearances in the Fenton line. From 1950 through 1956 it was made with burred hobs. Fenton produced it from 1961 through 1969 with plain hobs. It reappeared again in 1987 and remained in the line through 1988 with burred hobs.

A few items were discontinued and then brought back into the line at a later time. The No. 3634 oval basket was initially made from January 1963 through December 1968. Later, it was made again in 1979 and 1987. The No. 3680 covered cookie jar was originally in the line from January 1962 through December 1973. Later, it was made again in 1987. The No. 3920 footed comport was originally produced from 1954 through 1979. It was reissued in 1987. The No. 3937-7" bonbon — introduced in 1950 — was discontinued in 1976. It also reappeared in 1987 and remained in the line through 1988. These later productions will be marked with the Fenton logo. Several other pieces were reissued when milk glass Hobnail was made in 1991 and 1992. For a list of the items made during this period see the introduction to the Hobnail section.

A modified milk glass Hobnail design called Burred Hobnail with a No. 489 line number was made during the early 1950s. Pieces of this pattern have small burr marks around the base of each hob. For more information on this pattern see page 273.

Several pieces in the late 1980s were made with hobnails in a waved design. Included in this issue were a basket (No. 3032-8"), bell (No, 3067-6¾"), and a rose bowl (No. 3022-3¾"). Another later piece was made by adapting an earlier mould. The No. 3305 mini lamp was made from the base of the No. 3600 candy box. A hole was drilled into the bottom; the base was then inverted and a lamp fixture was attached. The finished lamp was outfitted with a parchment shade with a stenciled design.

Fenton Candy Boxes

Each year, Fenton Candy Boxes are on our "best sellers" list. "How sweet they are" — for gifts, for decorative accents, and of course, for sales.

3784 MI

3885 MI

3886 MI

3668 MI

3600 MI

3984 MI

3786 MI

3700 MI

3802 MI

Catalog Reprint Circa 1977 Courtesy Of: The Fenton Art Glass Museum

Dates in parenthesis in the discontinued column indicate the last date an item was listed in the Fenton catalog for sale as a separate piece. After that time, it was still in production until the final date but only available as part of a set.

Milk Glass Hobnail	Ware No.	Introduced	Discontinued	Value
Apothecary jar	3689-MI	1964	1973	85.00 – 100.00
Ashtray/chip n' dip/candle bowl	3778-MI	1971	1980+	20.00 – 25.00
Ashtray, pipe	3773-MI	1963	1968	60.00 – 70.00
Ashtray, rectangular	3693-MI	July 1962	1976	10.00 – 12.00
Ashtray #1, sm. octagonal	3876-MI	July 1954	1977 (1966)	6.00 – 8.00
Ashtray #2, med. octagonal	3877-MI	July 1954	1977 (1968)	8.00 – 10.00
Ashtray #3, lg. octagonal	3878-MI	July 1954	1977 (1966)	10.00 – 12.00
Ashtray, 3-pc. set octagonal	3810-MI	July 1954	1977	25.00 – 30.00
Ashtray, 4¾" ball	3648-MI	1977	1979	28.00 – 35.00
Ashtray, 5" square	3679-MI	1961	1978	18.00 – 20.00
Ashtray, 6½" round	3776-MI	1963	1968	8.00 – 10.00
Ashtray, round, medium	3973-MI	1964	1968	6.00 – 8.00
Ashtray, round, small	3972-MI	1964	1968	4.00 – 6.00
Ashtray set, 3-pc. round	3610-MI	1964	1980+	18.00 – 25.00
Banana bowl	3720-MI	July 1959	1980+	35.00 – 45.00
Banana bowl, low	3620-MI	1961	1979	35.00 – 45.00
Basket, 4" oval	3634-MI	1963	1968*	25.00 – 30.00
Basket, 4½"	3834-MI	1950	1980+	20.00 – 25.00
Basket, 5½"	3735-MI	1971	1980+	25.00 – 30.00
Basket, 6½"	3736-MI	1958	1980+	30.00 – 35.00
Basket, 6½" oval	3838-MI	1960	1969	25.00 – 30.00
Basket, 7" deep	3637-MI	1963	1978	50.00 – 60.00
Basket, 7" handled	3837-MI	1951	1980+	30.00 – 35.00
Basket, 8½"	3638-MI	1967	1980+	30.00 – 38.00
Basket, 10"	3830-MI	July 1953	1980+	45.00 – 60.00
Basket, 12"	3734-MI	July 1959	1980+	60.00 – 65.00
Basket, 12" oval	3839-MI	1960	1975	55.00 – 65.00
Bell, 6"	3667-MI	1967	1980+	20.00 – 22.00
Berry dish	3928-MI	July 1954	1968	11.00 – 13.00
Bonbon (ice cream & nut dish)	3630-MI	1961	1978	14.00 – 16.00
Bonbon, 5" handled	3935-MI	1950	July 1956	14.00 – 16.00
Bonbon, 5" star	3921-MI	1953	1970	18.00 – 20.00
Bonbon, 6"	3926-MI	1950	1980+	7.00 – 9.00
Bonbon, 7" handled	3937-MI	1951	1980+	14.00 – 16.00
Bonbon, 8"	3716-MI	July 1960	1981	18.00 – 20.00
Bonbon, 8" handled	3706-MI	1969	1980+	20.00 – 22.00
Boot, 4"	3992-MI	1971	1980+	16.00 – 18.00
Bottle, vanity	3865-MI	1955	1960 (1957)	45.00 – 55.00
Bowl, 3-toed	3635-MI	1963	1980+	22.00 – 27.00
Bowl, 7"	3927-MI	1950	1981	35.00 – 40.00
Bowl, 8"	3626-MI	1961	1969	35.00 – 42.00
Bowl, 8" DC	3639-MI	1967	1979	27.00 – 30.00
Bowl, 8½"	3724-MI	1958	1978	35.00 – 45.00
Bowl, 8" oval	3625-MI	1961	July 1978	25.00 – 30.00
Bowl, 9"	3924-MI	1951	1980+	30.00 – 35.00
Bowl, 9" cupped	3735-MI	July 1959	1965	85.00 – 100.00
Bowl, 9" ftd. oval	3621-MI	1965	1977	45.00 – 55.00
Bowl, 9" square	3929-MI	July 1954	July 1961	50.00 – 60.00
Bowl, cereal	3719-MI	1960	1964	40.00 – 45.00

3725 MI Jelly Dish

3688 MI Covered
Candy Jar

3680 MI Covered
Cookie Jar

3986 MI 11" Covered Urn

3628 MI Footed Comport

3777 MI 1/4 lb.
Oval Covered Butter

3804 MI 3-Piece Fairy Light

3701 MI 4-Piece
Epergne Set

3797 MI Cinnamon
Sugar Shaker

3780 MI Wedding Jar

3742 MI 3-Piece
Centerpiece Set

3924 MI 9" Bowl

3670 MI
Low Candleholder

3635 MI 8" 3-Toed Bowl

3872 MI Footed
Candle Bowl

3977 MI 1/4 lb.
Covered Butter

3623 MI 10 1/2" Bowl

3620 Low Banana Bowl

3621 MI 9" Footed
Oval Bowl

3677 MI Covered Butter & Cheese

3720 MI Banana Bowl

3724 MI 8 1/2" Bowl

Milk Glass Hobnail	Ware No.	Introduced	Discontinued	Value
Bowl, 9½" shallow	3622-MI	1961	1969	50.00 – 55.00
Bowl, 10½" low ftd.	3623-MI	1961	1965	80.00 – 90.00
Bowl, 10½" ftd.	3723-MI	1957	1978	35.00 – 45.00
Bowl, 10½" ftd. DC	3624-MI	1961	1980+	30.00 – 32.00
Bowl, 10" ftd.	3731-MI	July 1959	1980	25.00 – 30.00
Bowl, 12"	3938-MI	July 1960	1980+	35.00 – 40.00
Bowl, 12" celery	3739-MI	July 1959	1963	60.00 – 70.00
Bowl, hanging	3705-MI	July 1959	1968	140.00 – 160.00
Bowl, Ribbon Candy	3730-MI	July 1959	July 1961	50.00 – 60.00
Bowl, violet	3754-MI	1960	1969	16.00 – 20.00
Boxtle, 3-pc. vanity	3986-MI	1953	1955	185.00 – 200.00
Butter, ¼ #	3977-MI	July 1954	1978	25.00 – 30.00
Butter, ¼ # oval	3777-MI	1963	1980+	20.00 – 28.00
Butter and cheese, covered	3677-MI	1961	1968	150.00 – 175.00
Cake plate, ftd.	3913-MI	1956	1980+	35.00 – 40.00
Candle bowl	3771-MI	July 1959	1969	20.00 – 25.00
Candle bowl, ftd.	3971-MI	1978	1980	45.00 – 48.00
Candle bowl, 4" miniature	3873-MI	1969	1977	20.00 – 25.00
Candle bowl, 6"	3872-MI	July 1968	1980+	14.00 – 18.00
Candle epergne	3746-MI	1973	1976	25.00 – 30.00
Candleholder, crescent	3678-MI	1962	1963	65.00 – 75.00
Candleholder	3770-MI	July 1959	1965	40.00 – 50.00
Candleholder	3974-MI	1951	1980+	10.00 – 12.00
Candleholder, 2-lite	3672-MI	1961	1971	25.00 – 38.00
Candleholder, 2" low	3670-MI	1961	1969	15.00 – 18.00
Candleholder, 4"	3775-MI	1972	1977	25.00 – 28.00
Candleholder, 6"	3674-MI	1961	1980+	18.00 – 22.00
Candleholder, 7"	3745-MI	1973	1976	28.00 – 32.00
Candleholder, 10"	3774-MI	1958	1971	22.00 – 27.00
Candleholder, ftd.	3673-MI	1962	1976	18.00 – 22.00
Candleholder, handled	3870-MI	1953	1974	22.00 – 25.00
Candleholder, lg. cornucopia	3874-MI	July 1953	1965	25.00 – 30.00
Candleholder, miniature cornucopia	3971-MI	1950	1957	35.00 – 45.00
Candy or jam box, covered	3600-MI	1971	1980+	45.00 – 50.00
Candy box, covered	3886-MI	1969	1980+	30.00 – 35.00
Candy box, 6" covered	3984-MI	1974	1978	55.00 – 58.00
Candy box, covered slipper	3700-MI	1971	1980+	35.00 – 40.00
Candy box, ftd.	3784-MI	1966	1982	35.00 – 40.00
Candy box, oval covered	3786-MI	1960	1980+	22.00 – 25.00
Candy dish, covered	3668-MI	1975	1980	45.00 – 55.00
Candy/butter bowl	3802-MI	1974	1980+	25.00 – 35.00
Candy jar, ftd.	3885-MI	1968	1978	50.00 – 60.00
Candy jar, ftd.	3887-MI	July 1953	1969	40.00 – 45.00
Candy jar, ftd.	3980-MI	1951	1976	25.00 – 30.00
Candy jar (powder box)	3880-MI	1953	1976	40.00 – 45.00
Candy jar	3883-MI	1953	1969	27.00 – 32.00
Candy jar and cover	3688-MI	1963	1977	70.00 – 85.00
Centerpiece set (3745, 3746, 3748)	3742-MI	1973	1976	125.00 – 145.00
Chip 'n Dip	3703-MI	1958	1980	55.00 – 65.00
Chip 'n Dip	3922-MI	1970	1971	600.00 – 700.00
Chip 'n Dip candle bowl	3748-MI	1973	1976	20.00 – 25.00
Cigarette box	3685-MI	1961	1972	25.00 – 35.00

3704 MI 2-Piece Epergne Set

3689 MI Apothecary Jar

3761 MI Handled Decanter

3998 MI Hurricane Lamp

3886 MI Honey Jar

3640 MI Oval Pickle Dish

3917 MI Sugar & Creamer Set

3906 MI Sugar & Creamer

3633 MI Oval Nut Dish

3647 MI Egg Cup

3672 MI 2-Lite Candleholder

3607 MI Handled Relish

3740 MI 12" Divided Relish

3702 MI Sugar & Creamer

3612 MI Spoon Holder

3667 MI Bell

3916 MI Oil & Vinegar Set

3869 MI Oil

3922 MI Chip 'n Dip

3674 MI 6" Candleholder

3775 MI Candleholder

3608 MI Fairy Light

3974 MI Candleholder

Milk Glass Hobnail	Ware No.	Introduced	Discontinued	Value
Cigarette lighter	3692-MI	July 1962	1978	18.00 – 22.00
Cigarette set — lighter/cigarette box/3 ashtrays	3603-MI	July 1962	1978	63.00 – 105.00
Comport	3728-MI	1956	1980+	18.00 – 20.00
Comport	3727-MI	1958	1980	14.00 – 18.00
Comport, ftd.	3920-MI	1954	1980+	18.00 – 22.00
Comport, 6" ftd., DC	3628-MI	1962	1980+	14.00 – 16.00
Condiment set, 7-pc.	3809-MI	Sept. 1950	1974	88.00 – 108.00
Console set (1-3924 & 2-3974)	3904-MI	1951	1959	50.00 – 60.00
Console set (1-3724 & 2-3774)	3704-MI	1958	July 1961	85.00 – 95.00
Console set (1-3924 & 2-3874)	3802-MI	1954	1958	80.00 – 95.00
Cookie jar and cover	3680-MI	1962	1974**	100.00 – 125.00
Creamer and sugar	3901-MI	1950	1968	18.00 – 22.00
Creamer and sugar	3702-MI	1970	1974	25.00 – 29.00
Creamer, miniature	3665-MI	July 1965	1969	8.00 – 10.00
Creamer, sugar and lid	3606-MI	1961	1980+	20.00 – 25.00
Creamer, sugar and lid	3902-MI	1969	1980+	30.00 – 35.00
Creamer and sugar, #3 (crimped)	3906-MI	1951	1981	24.00 – 28.00
Creamer and sugar, individual	3900-MI	1950	1973	15.00 – 18.00
Creamer and sugar, flat	3708-MI	1956	1969	25.00 – 30.00
Creamer, sugar and tray	3917-MI	1955	1980+	40.00 – 45.00
Cruet	3863-MI	1952	1975	20.00 – 25.00
Decanter, handled	3761-MI	1960	1968	200.00 – 225.00
Dish, peanut	3627-MI	1962	1978	15.00 – 18.00
Dish, 8" oval pickle	3640-MI	1964	1980+	18.00 – 20.00
Egg cup	3647-MI	1970	1972	95.00 – 110.00
Epergne, petite for #3674 candle	3671-MI	1961	1966	20.00 – 25.00
Epergne set	3701-MI	July 1956	1980+	45.00 – 50.00
Epergne set, 2-piece	3704-MI	1975	1978	80.00 – 100.00
Epergne set, 2-pc.	3902-MI	1961	1966	50.00 – 55.00
Epergne set, 5-pc. ftd.	3800-MI	1954	1955	185.00 – 200.00
Epergne set, 4-pc. miniature	3801-MI	1950	1978	35.00 – 45.00
Fairy light	3608-MI	1970	1980+	20.00 – 25.00
Fairy light, 3-pc.	3804-MI	1975	1982	65.00 – 75.00
Goblet, water	3845-MI	1954	1975	18.00 – 20.00
Goblet, wine	3843-MI	July 1960	1968	15.00 – 18.00
Hat	3991-MI	July 1952	1969**	14.00 – 16.00
Honey jar	3886-MI	1953	1960	85.00 – 95.00
Ivy ball	3726-MI	July 1959	1969	15.00 – 18.00
Ivy ball	3757-MI	1957	1969	15.00 – 18.00
Jam, jelly and tray	3915-MI	1955	1975	50.00 – 55.00
Jam jar w/clear ladle	3601-MI	1970	1980+	25.00 – 35.00
Jam set, 3-pc.	3903-MI	1950	1974	25.00 – 30.00
Jardiniere, 4½"	3994-MI	1952	1969	14.00 – 18.00
Jardiniere, 5½"	3898-MI	1975	1979	25.00 – 30.00
Jardiniere, 6"	3996-MI	1952	1969	18.00 – 25.00
Jelly dish	3725-MI	1958	1968	32.00 – 42.00
Jug, 12 oz. syrup	3762-MI	1958	1979	20.00 – 22.00
Jug, 32 oz. squat	3965-MI	July 1952	1968	32.00 – 42.00
Jug, 54 oz.	3764-MI	1958	1981	60.00 – 70.00
Jug, 70 oz. 9½", ice lip	3664-MI	1964	1980+	60.00 – 75.00
Jug, 80 oz.	3967-MI	July 1953	1969	85.00 – 110.00

3908 MI 10-Piece
Punch Set

3911 MI 14-Piece
Punch Set

3847 MI
Punch Cup

3712 MI 15-Piece
Punch Set

3718 MI 21-Piece
Punch Set

3840 MI
Punch Cup

3820 MI Punch Bowl

3722 MI 15" Punch Bowl
3778 MI Punch Base

3870 MI Candleholder

3605 MI Covered Mustard
with Spoon

3700 MI Covered Shoe Candy Box

3609 Salt & Pepper

3631 MI Footed
Nut Dish

3764 MI 54 Oz. Jug

3949 MI
9 Oz. Tumbler

3945 MI
5 Oz. Tumbler

3664 MI 70 Oz.
Ice Lip Jug

3767 MI
7 Oz. Oil

3845 MI
Goblet

3843 MI
Wine Goblet
(4 Oz.)

3843 MI
Wine Goblet
(3 Oz.)

3965 Squat Jug

3880 MI Candy Jar

3863 MI Cruet

3805 MI 3-Piece Vanity Set on No. 3775 MI 12" Tray

3646 MI 14 Oz. Stein

3709 MI 2-Tier Server

205

Milk Glass Hobnail	Ware No.	Introduced	Discontinued	Value
Kettle	3990-MI	1950	1969	12.00 – 14.00
Ladle, punch	9527-MI	1950		25.00 – 35.00
Lamp, courting, oil	3792-MI	1965	1972	90.00 – 125.00
Lamp, courting, electric	3793-MI	1965	1972	90.00 – 125.00
Lamp, 11" hurricane	3713-MI	1979	1981	150.00 – 190.00
Lamp, 19" student	3707-MI	1966	1977	200.00 – 225.00
Lamp, 21" student	3807-MI	1971	1980+	200.00 – 225.00
Lamp, 22" GWTW	3808-MI	1976	1980+	200.00 – 250.00
Lamp, hurricane w/handled base	3998-MI	1952	1970	40.00 – 45.00
Lavabo	3867-MI	July 1955	1977	100.00 – 125.00
Mayonnaise set	3803-MI	1950	1980+	18.00 – 20.00
Mustard and spoon	3605-MI	1970	July 1976	25.00 – 30.00
Mustard and spoon	3889-MI	1950	1969	14.00 – 16.00
Mustard kettle	3979-MI	1954	1967	14.00 – 16.00
Napkin rings, set of 4	3904-MI	1976	1978	100.00 – 140.00
Nut dish	3650-MI	1967	1969	35.00 – 40.00
Nut dish	3729-MI	July 1956	1965	15.00 – 18.00
Nut dish, 2¾" ftd.	3631-MI	1962	1968	15.00 – 18.00
Nut dish, 5" ftd.	3629-MI	1962	1978	14.00 – 16.00
Nut dish, oval	3732-MI	1958	1966	14.00 – 16.00
Nut dish, oval 2-H	3633-MI	1964	1980+	15.00 – 18.00
Oil, vinegar	3869-MI	1950	1973	12.00 – 14.00
Oil, 7 oz.	3767-MI	1956	1965	70.00 – 80.00
Oil, mustard and tray	3715-MI	1956	July 1961	30.00 – 46.00
Oil, vinegar and tray	3916-MI	1955	1978	45.00 – 55.00
Pitcher vase	3760-MI	1960	1977	65.00 – 75.00
Planter, 4½" square	3699-MI	1961	1980+	14.00 – 16.00
Planter, 8" crescent	3798-MI	July 1960	1966	30.00 – 35.00
Planter, 8½"	3697-MI	1966	1980	18.00 – 22.00
Planter, 9"	3690-MI	1962	1977	25.00 – 28.00
Planter, 10"	3799-MI	1960	1979	25.00 – 28.00
Planter, 10" crescent	3698-MI	1961	1966	45.00 – 55.00
Planter, 9" wall	3836-MI	1956	July 1956	45.00 – 55.00
Plate, 8" crimped	3816-MI	1956	1968	16.00 – 19.00
Plate, 8½"	3912-MI	1955	1957	25.00 – 28.00
Plate, 13½"	3714-MI	July 1959	1967	45.00 – 55.00
Plate, 16" torte	3817-MI	Sept. 1950	July 1969	55.00 – 60.00
Puff box	3885-MI	1955	1960 (1957)	55.00 – 65.00
Punch bowl base	3778-MI	1958	1959	30.00 – 45.00
Punch bowl, 7 quart	3722-MI	1958	1959	275.00 – 325.00
Punch bowl, flared	3827-MI	Sept. 1950	July 1959	225.00 – 250.00
Punch bowl, handled		Sept. 1950	1952	800.00 – 900.00
Punch bowl, octagonal	3820-MI	July 1953	1958	300.00 – 350.00
Punch cup	3847-MI	Sept. 1950	1966	18.00 – 20.00
Punch cup, octagonal	3840-MI	July 1953	1958	22.00 – 24.00
Punch set, 10-pc. (octagonal)	3908-MI	1953	1954	500.00 – 560.00
Punch set, 14-pc. (octagonal)	3911-MI	1953	1958	550.00 – 630.00
Punch set, 15-pc. (7 quart)	3712-MI	1958	1966***	500.00 – 550.00
Punch set, 15-pc. crimped bowl		Sept. 1950	July 1952	500.00 – 550.00
Punch set, 15-pc. (4 quart)	3807-MI	Sept. 1950	July 1959	500.00 – 550.00
Punch set, 21-pc. (7 quart)	3718-MI	1958	1960	700.00 – 800.00

3904 MI Napkin Ring
(Set of Four)

3938 MI 12" Bowl

3920 MI 8" Footed Comport

3732 MI Oval Nut Dish

3627 Footed Peanut Dish

3956 MI 6 1/4" Footed Vase

3629 MI Footed Nut Dish

3755 MI Tall
Handkerchief Vase

3727 MI 8" Comport

3895 MI
Toothpick

3795 MI
Toothpick

3728 MI Comport

3903 MI Jam Set

3774 MI 10" Candleholder

3650 MI Nut or
Ice Cream Dish

3033 MI Heart Candy Dish
(No Handle)

3639 MI 8" DC Bowl

3803 MI Mayonnaise Set

3809 MI 7-Piece Condiment Set

3958 8" Footed Vase

3792 MI Courting Lamp

3959 MI 8" Footed Fan Vase

3992 MI Boot

3731 MI 10" Footed Bowl

Milk Glass Hobnail	Ware No.	Introduced	Discontinued	Value
Vase, 8" ftd. DC	3958-MI	1956	1972	14.00 – 20.00
Vase, 8" swung bud	3756-MI	1957	1980+	12.00 – 14.00
Vase, 8½" fan	3852-MI	1971	1973	140.00 – 160.00
Vase, 9"	3755-MI	1960	1963	25.00 – 30.00
Vase, 9"	3659-MI	1963	1974	25.00 – 35.00
Vase, 10" bud	3950-MI	1972	1980+	20.00 – 22.00
Vase, 10" handkerchief	3855-MI	1977	July 1978	35.00 – 45.00
Vase, 11"	3752-MI	1958	1980+	28.00 – 32.00
Vase, 12" 3-toed	3658-MI	1967	1969	140.00 – 165.00
Vase, 12" ftd. swung	3753-MI	July 1959	1980+	20.00 – 22.00
Vase, (14" – 16") tall swung	3755-MI	1971	1980+	25.00 – 30.00
Vase, 12" medium swung	3758-MI	July 1959	1981	15.00 – 20.00
Vase, 18" tall swung	3759-MI	July 1959	1977	35.00 – 40.00
Vase, 24" swung	3652-MI	1965	1981	40.00 – 50.00
Wedding jar	3780-MI	1957	1977	28.00 – 32.00

*Reissued in 1979 and again in 1987.
**Reissued in 1987.
***Reissued 1991-1993.

In the July 1964 supplement, Fenton introduced wrought iron hangers for existing milk glass shapes. These hangers were designed by Dave Ellies of Columbus, Ohio. The hangers were discontinued at the end of the year. Examples of the offering are pictured in a catalog reprint on page 252.

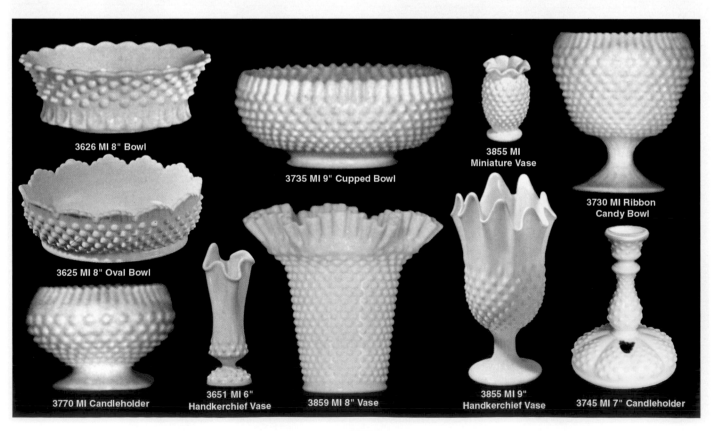

3626 MI 8" Bowl

3735 MI 9" Cupped Bowl

3855 MI Miniature Vase

3730 MI Ribbon Candy Bowl

3625 MI 8" Oval Bowl

3770 MI Candleholder

3651 MI 6" Handkerchief Vase

3859 MI 8" Vase

3855 MI 9" Handkerchief Vase

3745 MI 7" Candleholder

3800 MI 4-Piece Epergne Set

3723 MI Footed Bowl

3699 Square Planter

3867 MI Lavabo

3902 MI Covered Sugar & Creamer

3697 MI 8 1/2" Planter

3690 MI 9 1/2" Planter

3996 MI 6" Jardiniere

3703 MI Chip 'n Dip

3606 MI Covered Sugar & Creamer

3685 Cigarette Box

3708 MI Sugar & Creamer

3898 MI Jardiniere

3799 MI 10" Planter

3692 Cigarette Lighter

3900 MI Individual Sugar & Creamer

3822 MI 7 1/2" Relish

3798 MI 8" Crescent Planter

3698 MI 10" Crescent Planter

Opal Hobnail

Opal Hobnail is similar in appearance to milk glass Hobnail, but Opal is a more translucent glass than milk glass. The two lamps listed below were made with this type of glass in 1969. This formula of glass had better heat resistance than milk glass and the more translucent properties of this glass allowed more light to penetrate through the glass.

Opal Hobnail	Ware No.	Introduced	Discontinued	Value
Boudoir lamp	3604-OP	1969	1970	100.00 – 125.00
Fairy light, 2-piece	3608-OP	1969	1970	25.00 – 30.00

3608 OP Fairy Light

Opaque Blue Overlay Hobnail

Opaque Blue Overlay is a Fenton color that was introduced in 1962. This color was made by casing an exterior layer of Colonial Blue with an interior layer of opal. Pieces of Bubble Optic, Hobnail, Wild Rose with Bowknot, and a few lamps were made in this color. All items in Opaque Blue except the 11½" Bubble Optic vase and the lamps were discontinued by 1964.

Opaque Blue Overlay Hobnail	Ware No.	Introduced	Discontinued	Value
Jug, 12 oz. syrup	3762-OB	1962	1964	40.00 – 45.00
Lavabo	3867-OB	1962	1964	200.00 – 225.00
Vase, 5" DC	3850-OB	1962	1963	35.00 – 50.00
Vase, 5½" DC	3656-OB	1962	1964	35.00 – 50.00
Vase, 6"	3856-OB	1962	1963	45.00 – 55.00
Vasc, 11"	3752-OB	1962	1964	125.00 – 175.00

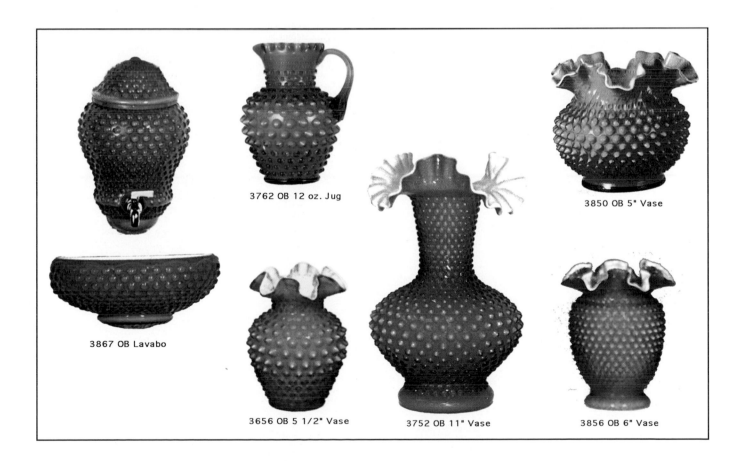

3762 OB 12 oz. Jug

3850 OB 5" Vase

3867 OB Lavabo

3656 OB 5 1/2" Vase

3752 OB 11" Vase

3856 OB 6" Vase

Orange Hobnail

Due to the heat sensitivity of the chemicals used to produce the color, Fenton's transparent Orange is often more amberina than orange. Introduction of Hobnail in Orange began in 1964 when the slipper made its appearance in this color. The slipper is the only item that was made for the entire length of time Orange was in the line. Other items were gradually introduced and the number of different pieces being produced peaked in about 1969. Production of Orange Hobnail continued until Fenton discontinued using the color at the end of 1977.

Orange Hobnail	Ware No.	Introduced	Discontinued	Value
Ashtray, ball	3648-OR	1977	1978	14.00 – 18.00
Ashtray, medium 5¼" round	3973-OR	1965	1966	7.00 – 9.00
Ashtray, small 3" round	3972-OR	1965	1966	4.00 – 6.00
Ashtray, 6½" round	3776-OR	1965	1966	10.00 – 12.00
Ashtray set, 3-piece round	3610-OR	1965	1970	22.00 – 27.00
Basket, 7" handled	3837-OR	1967	1978	27.00 – 37.00
Basket, 8½"	3638-OR	1967	1971	35.00 – 45.00
Basket, 10"	3830-OR	1968	July 1970	65.00 – 75.00
Bell, 6"	3667-OR	1977	1978	20.00 – 25.00
Candy box, ftd.	3784-OR	1966	July 1970	30.00 – 35.00
Candy box, oval covered	3786-OR	1968	1970	22.00 – 25.00
Cigarette lighter	3692-OR	1965	1969	14.00 – 20.00
Comport, 6" ftd., DC	3628-OR	1969	1978	12.00 – 14.00
Creamer, miniature	3665-OR	1965	1969	5.00 – 6.00
Fairy light	3608-OR	1969	1978	28.00 – 30.00
Slipper	3995-OR	1964	1978	18.00 – 20.00
Toothpick holder	3795-OR	1966	1976	8.00 – 10.00
Vase, 3" DC	3853-OR	1968	1978	10.00 – 12.00
Vase, 4" ftd. DC	3952-OR	1965	1978	8.00 – 10.00
Vase, 4½" DC	3854-OR	1969	1978	12.00 – 14.00
Vase, 5" 3-toed	3653-OR	1965	1970	12.00 – 14.00
Vase, 8" swung bud	3756-OR	1967	1978	14.00 – 16.00
Vase, 11"	3752-OR	1977	1978	35.00 – 45.00
Vase, 12" ftd. swung	3753-OR	1968	1971	35.00 – 45.00
Vase, 24" tall swung	3652-OR	1965	July 1975	55.00 – 65.00

Orange Hobnail

The many shades of orange and gold, the colors of Autumn, make these pieces delightfully warm accents.

3628 OR
FTD. COMPORT

3837 OR
7" BASKET

3667 OR
BELL

3752 OR
11" VASE

3756 OR
BUD VASE

3854 OR
4½" VASE

3608 OR
FAIRY LIGHT

3952 OR
4" VASE

3853 OR
3" VASE

3995 OR
SLIPPER

Catalog Reprint Circa 1978   Courtesy Of: The Fenton Art Glass Museum

Orchid Opalescent Hobnail

Orchid Opalescent Hobnail was made sometime during the mid-1940s. There is not a catalog or price sheet listing items available for this color. Instead, pieces that have been found and are known to exist in collections are included in the listing below. Current indications are that this color was not a part of the regular Fenton line. Instead it appears as if this may have been a special color that was developed to satisfy the needs of an importer whose regular supply of foreign glassware was interrupted due to the travails of WWII.

Collectors should be aware that some lavender pieces of French Opalescent Hobnail may sometimes be seen. These pieces may appear to be similar in color to Orchid Opalescent and may be confusing. The change in color of French Opalescent Hobnail may be achieved by exposing the pieces to either sunlight or the rays of some other UV light source.

Orchid Opalescent Hobnail	Value
Basket, 4½" handled	90.00 – 125.00
Basket, 6¼" ftd. handled	150.00 – 175.00
Basket, 7½" handled	100.00 – 145.00
Basket, 8" ftd. handled	190.00 – 225.00
Vase, 4" miniature	30.00 – 35.00
Vase, 6¼" fan	60.00 – 80.00
Vase, 5"	60.00 – 80.00
Vase, 6¼" ftd. DC	55.00 – 65.00
Vase, 5½"	60.00 – 70.00
Vase, 6"	60.00 – 85.00

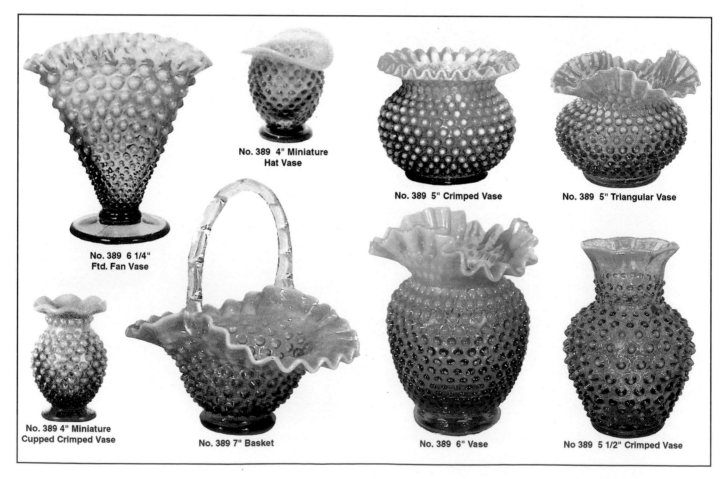

No. 389 4" Miniature Hat Vase

No. 389 5" Crimped Vase

No. 389 5" Triangular Vase

No. 389 6 1/4" Ftd. Fan Vase

No. 389 4" Miniature Cupped Crimped Vase

No. 389 7" Basket

No. 389 6" Vase

No 389 5 1/2" Crimped Vase

Peach Blow Hobnail

Peach Blow is a cased glass with a milk glass exterior layer and a gold ruby interior layer. Pieces of Hobnail were made in this color from July 1952 through December 1957.

Twelve items in Hobnail were introduced in the original presentation and one additional item came into the line six months later. The hurricane lamp was the first piece to be discontinued and the other items were gradually phased out. The 7" DC bowl was the only piece still being made in 1957.

Peach Blow Hobnail	Ware No.	Introduced	Discontinued	Value
Basket, 5½" handled	3835-PB	July 1952	1956	75.00 – 85.00
Basket, 7" handled	3837-PB	July 1952	1957	90.00 – 110.00
Basket, 10" handled	3830-PB	July 1952	1957	160.00 – 180.00
Bonbon, 5" star	3921-PB	1953	1957	45.00 – 55.00
Bonbon, 6" DC	3926-PB	July 1952	1957	20.00 – 25.00
Bowl, 7" DC	3927-PB	July 1952	1958	35.00 – 45.00
Bowl, 9" DC	3924-PB	July 1952	1957	65.00 – 75.00
Lamp, 11" hurricane	3998-PB	July 1952	1954	110.00 – 135.00
Vase, 3" DC	3853-PB	July 1952	1956	25.00 – 32.00
Vase, 4" miniature	3855-PB	July 1952	1956	20.00 – 25.00
Vase, 4½" DC	3854-PB	July 1952	1957	30.00 – 35.00
Vase, 5" DC	3850-PB	July 1952	1956	40.00 – 50.00
Vase, 6" DC	3856-PB	July 1952	1956	45.00 – 55.00

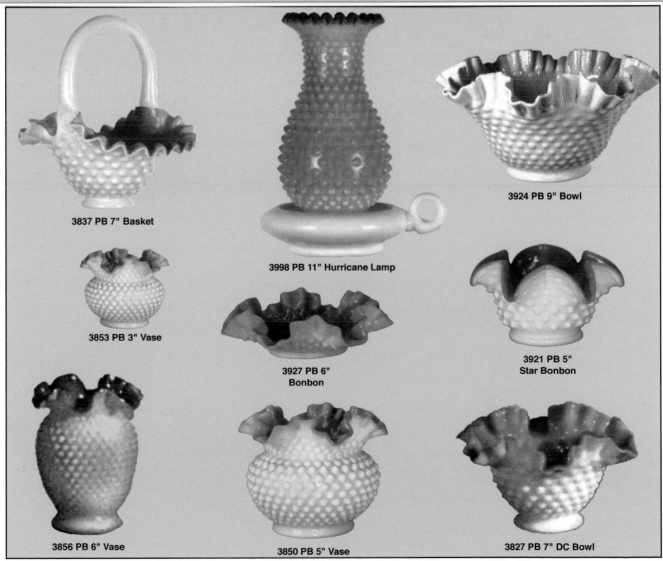

3837 PB 7" Basket

3853 PB 3" Vase

3998 PB 11" Hurricane Lamp

3927 PB 6" Bonbon

3924 PB 9" Bowl

3921 PB 5" Star Bonbon

3856 PB 6" Vase

3850 PB 5" Vase

3827 PB 7" DC Bowl

Plum Opalescent Hobnail

Plum Opalescent is a deep purple color that is accented with white hobs and trim. This is a heat sensitive color that was obtained by pressing items made with the Cranberry Gold Ruby formula. Production difficulties are the cause of color variations, and purists who are trying to find pieces that match perfectly are going to find this task challenging. A total of 19 different items were made during the initial period of production, which ranged from July 1959 until January 1963.

When Fenton introduced the Plum Opalescent color into the Hobnail line in 1959, the original offering included the following 12 items:

Item	Ware No.	Value
Basket, 7"	3837-PO	160.00 – 180.00
Bowl, 9"	3924-PO	95.00 – 120.00
Bowl, 10" footed	3731-PO	185.00 – 210.00
Candle bowl	3771-PO	110.00 – 125.00
Candle holder	3974-PO	45.00 – 55.00
Candy jar, footed	3887-PO	185.00 – 200.00
Comport	3728-PO	65.00 – 85.00
Epergne set, miniature	3801-PO	245.00 – 290.00
Jug, 12 ounce syrup	3762-PO	100.00 – 110.00
Vase, 8" bud	3756-PO	65.00 – 70.00
Vase, 12" medium swung	3758-PO	120.00 – 140.00
Vase, 18" tall swung	3759-PO	225.00 – 250.00

In 1960, the following five items were added to the line in the Plum Opalescent color:

Item	Ware No.	Value
Basket, 12" oval	3839-PO	400.00 – 500.00
Comport	3727-PO	100.00 – 125.00
Decanter, handled	3761-PO	500.00 – 550.00
Pitcher vase	3760-PO	275.00 – 325.00
Vase, 9"	3755-PO	165.00 – 175.00

The 9" bowl, candy jar, candle holders, 12 ounce syrup jug, and the 9" vase were discontinued in 1961. At this time, two additional items were introduced:

Item	Ware No.	Value
Goblet, wine	3843-PO	90.00 – 120.00
Vase, 6" handkerchief	3750-PO	75.00 – 85.00

The tall vase and the 6" vase were dropped from the line in 1962. The remaining pieces were made until January 1963. The entire production was then discontinued.

Today, none of these items are easily found, but the pieces which collectors are finding most difficult to obtain are the 6" vase, decanter, pitcher, 12" basket, and wine goblets. Look for the values of these items to continue to escalate.

In 1984, Fenton produced a very limited run of Plum Opalescent Hobnail for the LeVay Distributing Company of Illinois. These later items bear the Fenton logo on the bottom and do not duplicate the items originally made in this color. Thirteen pieces of Hobnail were made. The No. 3664 pitcher and No. 3938 bowl were combined to produce a No. 3303 pitcher and bowl set. The seven-piece No. 3306 water set was only marketed as a set. However, some tumblers sold through the gift shop may have been combined by individuals with the No. 3664 pitcher to produce water sets which were not like the sets sold by LeVay.

Items made for LeVay include:

Item	Ware No.	Item	Ware No.
Banana stand, 12"	3720-PO	Epergne	3701-PO
Basket, 5½" DC	3735-PO	Fairy light, 3-piece	3804-PO
Basket, 8½" DC	3638-PO	Pitcher, 70 ounce ice lip	3664-PO
Basket, 12" DC	3734-PO	Relish, heart-shape	3733-PO
Bell, crimped	3645-PO	Vase, 4½" rose bowl	3323-PO
Bowl, 12" DC	3938-PO	Water set, 7-piece	3306-PO

Collectors are also finding these later items hard to find, and the lack of availability of many of these items on today's secondary market is a result of the short production period.

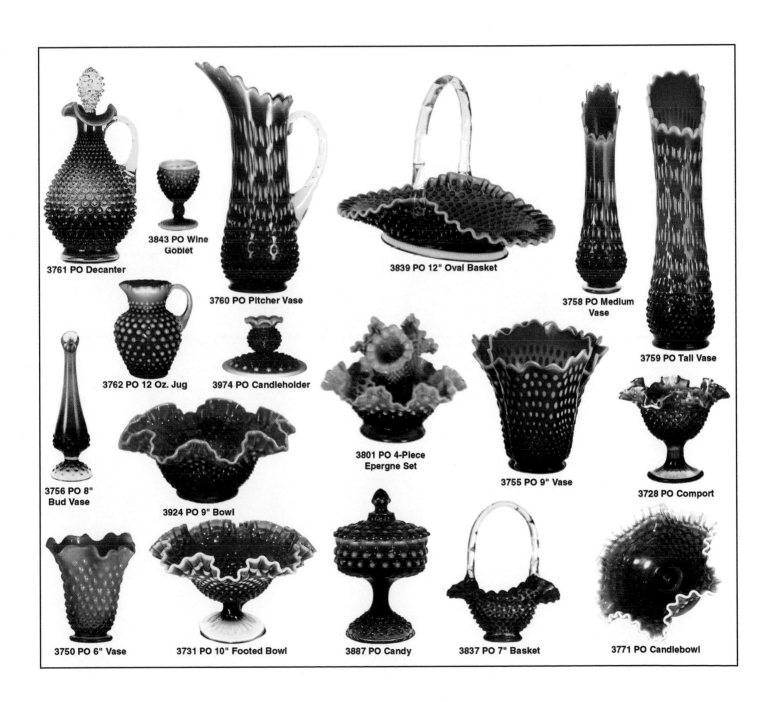

3761 PO Decanter

3843 PO Wine Goblet

3760 PO Pitcher Vase

3839 PO 12" Oval Basket

3758 PO Medium Vase

3759 PO Tall Vase

3762 PO 12 Oz. Jug

3974 PO Candleholder

3801 PO 4-Piece Epergne Set

3755 PO 9" Vase

3728 PO Comport

3756 PO 8" Bud Vase

3924 PO 9" Bowl

3750 PO 6" Vase

3731 PO 10" Footed Bowl

3887 PO Candy

3837 PO 7" Basket

3771 PO Candlebowl

Powder Blue Overlay Hobnail

Powder Blue Overlay was produced by casing a very light blue layer of colored glass over an opal interior layer. This color was introduced in the January 1961 supplement and was discontinued at the end of December 1961. Only five different shapes of Hobnail were made in this pale blue color.

Powder Blue Overlay Hobnail	Ware No.	Introduced	Discontinued	Value
Jug, 12 oz. syrup	3762-BV	1961	1962	35.00 – 45.00
Vase, 5" DC	3850-BV	1961	1962	30.00 – 35.00
Vase, 6"	3856-BV	1961	1962	30.00 – 35.00
Vase, 8"	3858-BV	1961	1962	50.00 – 60.00
Vase, 11"	3752-BV	1961	1962	90.00 – 110.00

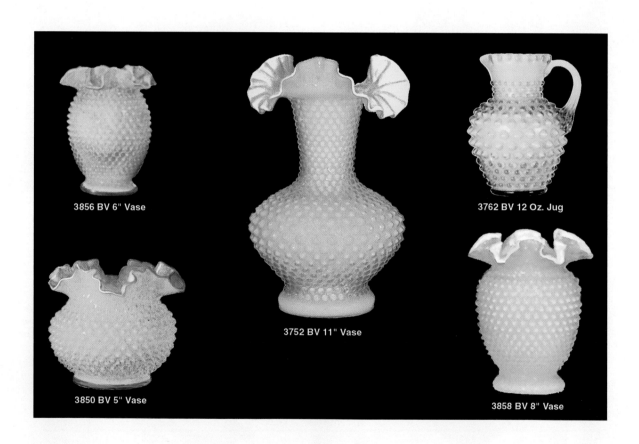

3856 BV 6" Vase

3762 BV 12 Oz. Jug

3752 BV 11" Vase

3850 BV 5" Vase

3858 BV 8" Vase

Rose Overlay Hobnail

Rose Overlay Hobnail is a cased glass introduced into the Fenton line in 1943. The color was made by combining an interior layer of opal glass with an exterior layer of transparent rose colored glass. The resulting combination produced a very sparkling pink glassware. Since only blown pieces could be produced in this color, the pattern proved to be more expensive to make than the public was willing to accept. Thus, the color was discontinued at the end of 1943. This short period of production has made examples of this color very hard to find.

Rose Overlay Hobnail	Value
Basket, 4½" handled	75.00 – 100.00
Basket, 7" handled	100.00 – 125.00
Basket, 10" handled	275.00 – 375.00
Bonbon, 6" oval, flared, triangle, DC, square, plate	27.00 – 30.00
Bottle, cologne	100.00 – 125.00
Bowl, 7" flared, oval	50.00 – 60.00
Bowl, 10" DC	95.00 – 110.00
Creamer	25.00 – 30.00
Cruet	120.00 – 140.00
Decanter	350.00 – 450.00
Jug, 4½"	40.00 – 50.00
Jug, 5½"	50.00 – 60.00
Jug, squat	100.00 – 125.00
Puff box	90.00 – 100.00

Rose Overlay Hobnail	Value
Rose bowl, 4½"	60.00 – 70.00
Rose bowl, 5"	70.00 – 80.00
Sugar	25.00 – 30.00
Vanity set, 3-pc.	290.00 –350.00
Vase, miniature, fan, hat, flared, cup crimped, cup flared, triangle	20.00 – 25.00
Vase, 4½" cup flared, cup square, DC	20.00 – 30.00
Vase, 5" flared, DC, square, triangle	25.00 – 35.00
Vase, 5½" crimped, square, flared, triangle	25.00 – 35.00
Vase, 6" flared, DC, square, triangle	40.00 – 60.00
Vase, 8" flared, DC, square, triangle	80.00 – 100.00
Vase, 9" flared, DC,	90.00 – 120.00
Vase, 11" flared, DC, oval, triangle	150.00 – 170.00

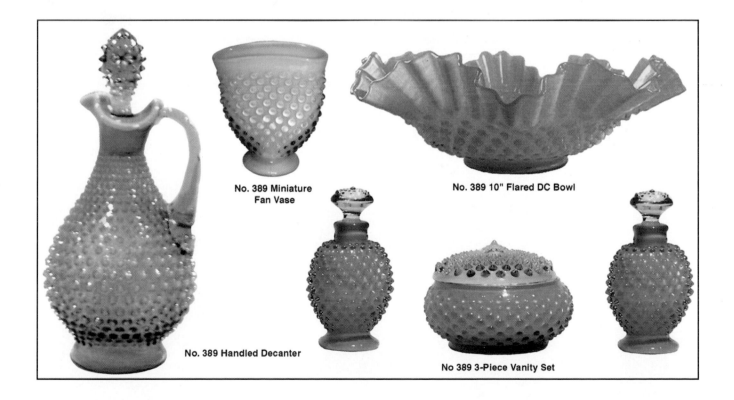

No. 389 Miniature Fan Vase

No. 389 10" Flared DC Bowl

No. 389 Handled Decanter

No 389 3-Piece Vanity Set

Rose Pastel Hobnail

Rose Pastel is a light opaque pink color. Hobnail was introduced in this color in 1954. During the next three years 20 different pieces of Hobnail were produced in Rose Pastel. Several pieces — the candy jar, the covered comport, the five-piece epergne set, and the hurricane lamp — were only made in 1954. Therefore, due to the short period of production, collectors should expect finding these items will be a difficult task.

Fenton combined individual pieces to produce the following set:

Console set No. 3904 (3-piece): 9" DC bowl, 2 candleholders

Rose Pastel Hobnail	Ware No.	Introduced	Discontinued	Value
Basket, 4½"	3834-RP	July 1954	1957	30.00 – 40.00
Basket, 7" handled	3837-RP	1954	1958	45.00 – 55.00
Berry dish (square)	3928-RP	1954	1957	11.00 – 15.00
Bonbon, 6" DC	3926-RP	1955	1957	12.00 – 14.00
Bowl, 9" DC	3924-RP	1954	1957	30.00 – 35.00
Bowl, 9" square	3929-RP	1954	1957	45.00 – 55.00
Candleholder	3974-RP	1955	1957	20.00 – 22.00
Candy jar	3883-RP	1954	1955	50.00 – 60.00
Comport, ftd.	3920-RP	1954	1958	30.00 – 35.00
Comport, ftd. w/cover	3887-RP	1954	1955	55.00 – 65.00
Creamer and sugar, #3	3906-RP	1954	1957	35.00 – 45.00
Epergne set, 5-pc.	3800-RP	1954	1955	150.00 – 200.00
Epergne set, miniature 4-pc.	3801-RP	1954	1958	80.00 – 90.00
Kettle	3990-RP	1954	1957	18.00 – 20.00
Lamp, 11" hurricane	3998-RP	1954	1955	90.00 – 100.00
Slipper	3995-RP	1954	1957	20.00 – 25.00
Vase, 4" ftd. DC	3952-RP	1954	1957	12.00 – 14.00
Vase, 4" ftd. fan	3953-RP	1954	1957	14.00 – 15.00
Vase, 4½" DC	3854-RP	1954	1957	20.00 – 22.00

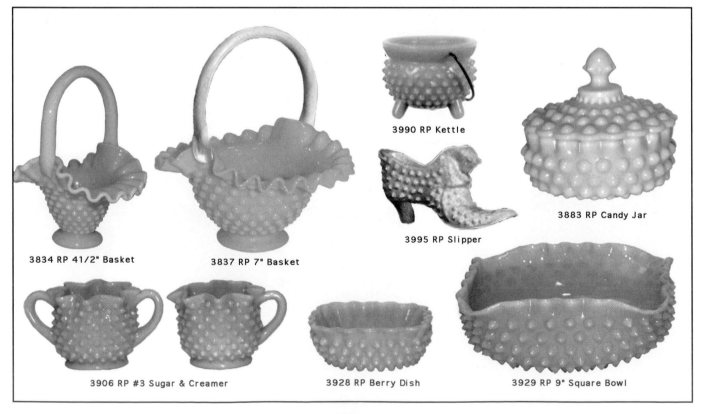

3834 RP 41/2" Basket

3837 RP 7" Basket

3990 RP Kettle

3995 RP Slipper

3883 RP Candy Jar

3906 RP #3 Sugar & Creamer

3928 RP Berry Dish

3929 RP 9" Square Bowl

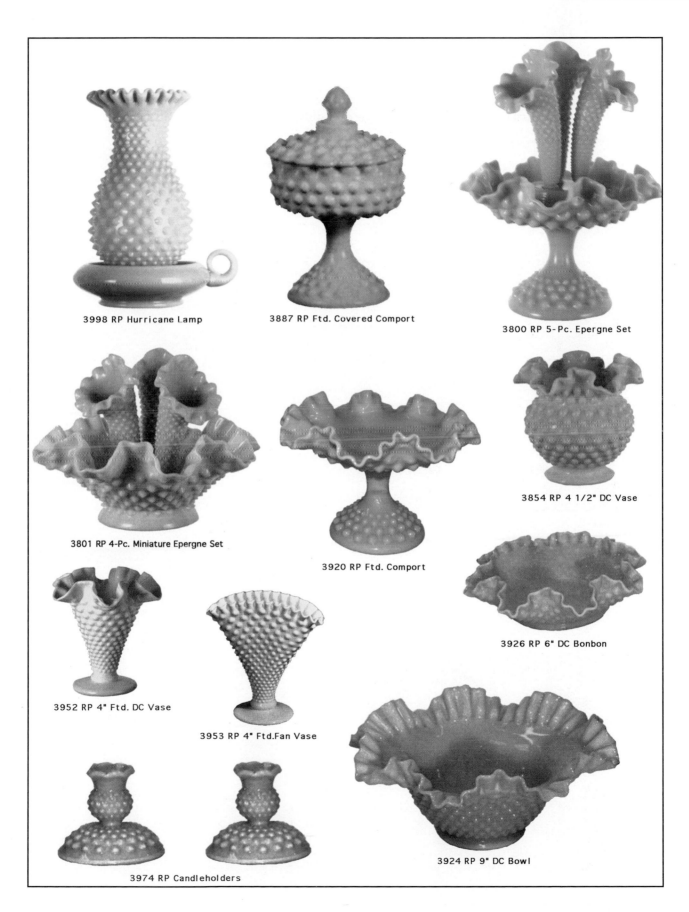

3998 RP Hurricane Lamp

3887 RP Ftd. Covered Comport

3800 RP 5-Pc. Epergne Set

3801 RP 4-Pc. Miniature Epergne Set

3920 RP Ftd. Comport

3854 RP 4 1/2" DC Vase

3926 RP 6" DC Bonbon

3952 RP 4" Ftd. DC Vase

3953 RP 4" Ftd.Fan Vase

3924 RP 9" DC Bowl

3974 RP Candleholders

Ruby Hobnail

Fenton began making Ruby Hobnail in 1972, and production of many pieces continued into the 1980s. Several items such as the student lamp, decanter, wine goblets, and the ball-shape ashtray were not made for very long and are not easily found today.

Fenton continued its tradition of offering colorful items for the Christmas season by producing a special 14-piece holiday assortment of Ruby Hobnail in the last half of 1987. The nine different pieces included in this production are as follows:

Item	Ware No.	Item	Ware No.
Basket, 4½"	3834-RU	Comport, ftd.	3628-RU
Basket, 8½"	3638-RU	Fairy light	3608-RU
Bell	3369-RU	Slipper	3995-RU
Bonbon (metal handle)	3706-RU	Vase, 4½"	3854-RU
Candle bowl	3778-RU		

Ruby Hobnail	Ware No.	Introduced	Discontinued	Value
Ashtray, ball	3648-RU	1977	1979	20.00 – 25.00
Ashtray set, 3-piece round	3610-RU	1976	1979	30.00 – 35.00
Basket, 7" handled	3837-RU	1972	1980+	25.00 – 35.00
Basket, 12" handled	3734-RU	1972	1980+	50.00 – 65.00
Bell, 6"	3667-RU	1972	1980+	20.00 – 30.00
Bonbon, 8"	3716-RU	1972	1980+	18.00 – 20.00
Bonbon, 8" handled	3706-RU	1972	1980+	22.00 – 25.00
Candleholder	3974-RU	1972	1980+	14.00 – 16.00
Candy box, covered	3886-RU	1972	1980	35.00 – 45.00
Comport, 6" ftd., DC	3628-RU	1972	1980+	20.00 – 25.00
Decanter, handled	3761-RU	1977	1979	200.00 – 225.00
Fairy light	3608-RU	1972	1980+	25.00 – 35.00
Goblet, wine	3843-RU	1977	1979	18.00 – 22.00
Lamp, 21" student	3807-RU	1972	1975	125.00 – 150.00
Slipper	3995-RU	1966	1980	15.00 – 17.00
Vase, 3" DC	3853-RU	1972	1980+	14.00 – 16.00
Vase, 4½"DC	3854-RU	1976	1980+	18.00 – 20.00
Vase, 8" swung bud	3756-RU	1976	1980+	14.00 – 18.00
Vase, 11"	3752-RU	1977	1980	35.00 – 45.00
Vase, 12" ftd. swung	3753-RU	1972	1980	45.00 – 55.00

Catalog Reprint Composite Circa 1977 Courtesy Of: The Fenton Art Glass museum

3756 RU
Bud Vase

3843 RU
Wine Goblet

3761 RU Wine Decanter

3734 RU
12" Basket

3752 RU 11" Vase

3837 RU
7" Basket

3628 RU
Footed Comport

3886 RU Candy Box

3706 RU
Handled Bonbon

3995 RU Slipper

3608 RU
Fairy Light

3667 RU Bell

3853 RU 3" Vase

3974 RU
Candleholder

3610 RU 3-Pc. Ash Tray Set

3648 RU Ball Ash Tray

3716 RU 8" Bonbon

3753 RU Footed Vase

Ruby Overlay Hobnail

3923 RO 10" Flared Bowl

3965 RO Squat Jug

3830 RO 10" Basket

3863 RO Cruet

3805 RO 3-piece Vanity Set

A number of Ruby Overlay Hobnail pieces were made for Sears, Roebuck and Company in the late 1960s. This color was produced by casing an interior layer of Gold Ruby with an exterior layer of crystal. The pieces below that are listed in the Sears catalog are marked with an asterisk. Other items in this color have appeared, and at the present time ,there is not a complete listing of this color.

Ruby Overlay Hobnail	Ware No.	Value
Basket, 4½" handled	3834-RO	45.00 – 55.00
*Basket, 7" handled	3837-RO	85.00 – 95.00
*Basket, 10" handled	3830-RO	150.00 – 175.00
Bottle, cologne	3865-RO	100.00 – 125.00
*Bowl, 7" DC	3927-RO	40.00 – 50.00
*Bowl, 9" DC	3924-RO	55.00 – 65.00
Bowl, 11" DC	3923-RO	65.00 – 75.00
*Candleholder	3870-RO	45.00 – 55.00
*Cruet	3863-RO	120.00 – 140.00
Jug, squat	3965-RO	100.00 – 125.00
*Pitcher, syrup	3762-RO	50.00 – 60.00
Puff box	3885-RO	75.00 – 85.00
*Vase, 4½" DC	3854-RO	30.00 – 40.00
Vase, 5"	3850-RO	35.00 – 45.00
*Vase, 8" DC	3858-RO	80.00 – 90.00
*Vase, 11"	3752-RO	125.00 – 150.00

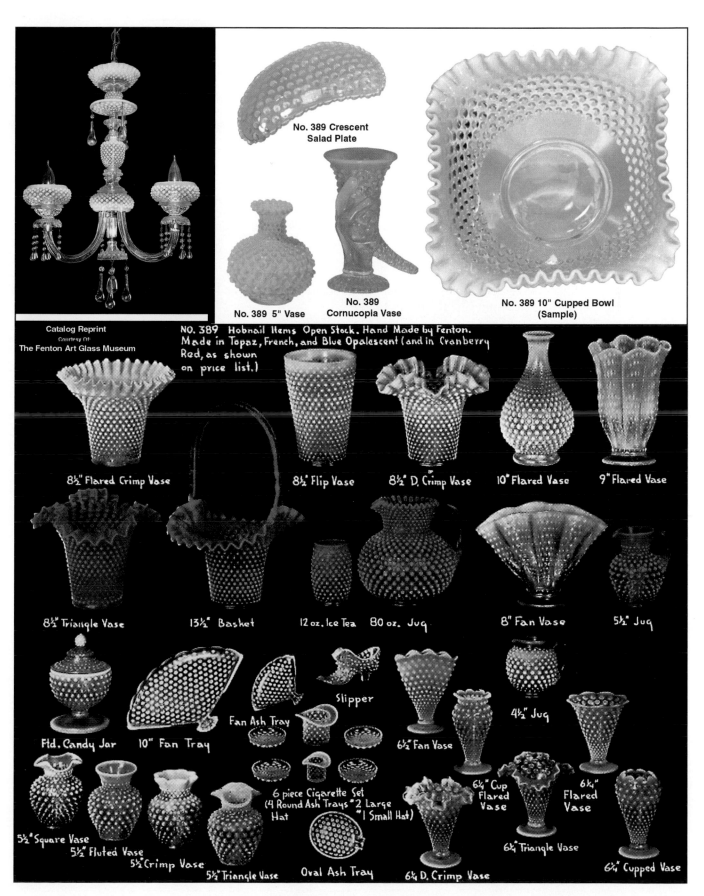

No. 389 Crescent Salad Plate

No. 389 5" Vase

No. 389 Cornucopia Vase

No. 389 10" Cupped Bowl (Sample)

Catalog Reprint
Courtesy Of
The Fenton Art Glass Museum

NO. 389 Hobnail Items Open Stock. Hand Made by Fenton. Made in Topaz, French, and Blue Opalescent (and in Cranberry Red, as shown on price list.)

8½" Flared Crimp Vase

8½" Flip Vase

8½" D. Crimp Vase

10" Flared Vase

9" Flared Vase

8½" Triangle Vase

13½" Basket

12 oz. Ice Tea

80 oz. Jug

8" Fan Vase

5½" Jug

Ftd. Candy Jar

10" Fan Tray

Fan Ash Tray

Slipper

6½" Fan Vase

4½" Jug

5½" Square Vase

5½" Fluted Vase

5½" Crimp Vase

5½" Triangle Vase

6 piece Cigarette Set (4 Round Ash Trays "2 Large Hat "1 Small Hat)

Oval Ash Tray

6¼" D. Crimp Vase

6¼" Cup Flared Vase

6¼" Triangle Vase

6¼" Flared Vase

6¼" Cupped Vase

Topaz Opalescent Hobnail

Topaz Opalescent Hobnail was introduced in 1941. Production of this color of Hobnail appears to have ended by 1944, but company records from this era are incomplete. However, inventory records from 1944 do not list any Hobnail in Topaz. Later, in 1959, the Topaz Opalescent color was released again. Items in the listing below that were also produced in the 1959 reissue are indicated with their respective ware numbers. The complete list of pieces produced in 1959 follows the 1940s listing below.

The No. 3794 tidbit tray has a chrome handle. The bottom plate is 13" in diameter and the top plate was made from an 8" salad plate. Two styles of candy jars are shown in the early reprints. The earlier jar, made in 1941, is footed with a round smooth bowl. The candy jar that was introduced in 1942 is round with a scalloped bowl.

Items Combined and Sold as Sets:	Introduced	Discontinued
Beverage set (9-piece): 80 oz. jug, 8-12 oz. tumblers	1941	1944
Cigarette set (6-piece): No. 1 hat, No. 2 hat, 4 round ashtrays	1941	1944
Cigarette set (5-piece): No. 2 hat, 4 round ashtrays	1941	1944
Juice set (7-piece): Squat jug, 6-5 oz. tumblers	1941	1944
Condiment set (5-piece): 10½" fan tray, salt, pepper, oil bottle, mustard & spoon	1942	1944
Console set (3-piece): 9" DC bowl, 2 cornucopia candleholders	1943	1944
Vanity set, (3-piece): puff box, 2 colognes	1940	1944

Later issues of Topaz Opalescent Hobnail include pieces made for LeVay in 1980. LeVay called this color Vaseline Opalescent and offered their customers the following 14 items:

Banana stand, 12"	3720-TO	Cruet	3869-TO
Basket, 7"	3837-TO	Epergne, 4-piece	3701-TO
Basket, 10" crimped	3750-TO	*Punch set, 14-piece	3712-TO
Bowl, 9" DC	3924-TO	Rose bowl, 4½"	3854-TO
Butter and cover	3677-TO	Rose bowl, 4¼"	3861-TO
Candleholder, 4"	3974-TO	Slipper	3995-TO
Cream and covered sugar	3606-TO	Toothpick	3795-TO

*The punch set was a special limited edition of 150 sets.

Another issue of Topaz Opalescent Hobnail for LeVay in 1983 included:

Basket, 7" DC	3337-TO	Epergne set, 4-pc.	3801-TO
Basket, small DC	3335-TO	Rose bowl, 4½" cupped	3323-TO
Bowl, 9" single crimped	3324-TO	Salt & pepper	3609-TO
Bowl, 11" ftd. DC	3325-TO	Toothpick	3392-TO
Candleholder, cornucopia	3874-TO	Water set, 7-piece	3306-TO
Cream & sugar set	3901-TO		

The water set included an 11" 46 oz. pitcher and six 4½" 9 oz. tumblers.

Six items in Topaz Iridescent Hobnail were part of the Historic Collection limited edition offering called Gold Pearl in 1993. Pieces of Gold Pearl Hobnail included in the assortment were:

Basket w/looped handle	3335-GP	Tumbler	3949-GP
Cruet and stopper	3863-GP	Water set, 5-pc	3908-GP
Lamp, 21" student w/prisms	3313-GP	Vase, 6" hand	3355-GP

Topaz Opalescent Hobnail (1941)	Ware No.	Introduced	Discontinued	Value
Ashtray, fan-shape		1941	1944	25.00 – 28.00
Ashtray, oval	3873-TO	1941	1944	25.00 – 28.00
Ashtray, round shallow		1941	1944	30.00 – 32.00
Basket, 4½" handled	3834-TO	1941	1944	125.00 – 145.00
Basket, 6¼" ftd. handled		July 1941	1944	110.00 – 125.00
Basket, 7" handled	3837-TO	1941	1944	125.00 – 140.00
Basket, 8" ftd. handled		1943	1944	150.00 – 180.00
Basket, 10" handled		1941	1944	200.00 – 225.00
Basket, 13½" handled		1941	1944	400.00 – 500.00
Bonbon, 5" 2-handled square, oval		1941	1944	30.00 – 35.00
Bonbon, 6½" handled square, oval		July 1941	1944	40.00 – 45.00
Bottle, cologne		1941	1944	140.00 – 150.00

No. 389 9oz. Tumbler

No. 389 12 Oz. Barrel Tumbler

No. 389 80 Oz, Jug

No. 389 48 Oz. Tankard Jug

#389 4 1/2" Handled Jug

No. 3869 TO Oil

No. 389 16 Oz. Tumbler

No. 389 32 Oz. Squat Jug

No. 3762 TO 12 Oz. Syrup

No. 309 Mustard

No. 389 5 Oz. Tumbler

No. 389 5 1/2" Handled Jug

No. 3901 TO Creamer

3806 TO Flat Salt and Pepper

No. 389 Footed Salt

No. 389 Footed Pepper

3995 TO Slipper

No. 389 Ftd. Hndled Basket

No. 3901 TO Sugar

No. 389 10" Handled Basket

No. 389 4 1/2" Handled Basket

No. 3837 7" Handled Basket

229

Topaz Opalescent Hobnail (1941)	Ware No.	Introduced	Discontinued	Value
Bowl, 7" flared, oval		1941	1944	45.00 – 55.00
Bowl, 7" special		1941	1943	55.00 – 65.00
Bowl, 7½" flared		1942	1943	50.00 – 60.00
Bowl, 9" double crimped, flared		1941	1944	80.00 – 90.00
Bowl, 11" double crimped, flared, oval, triangle		1941	1944	95.00 – 120.00
Bowl, 11" ftd. shallow		July 1941	1943	100.00 – 145.00
Bowl, 12" ftd., DC		July 1941	1944	100.00 – 145.00
Cake plate, 12" ftd.		July 1941	1944	145.00 – 185.00
Candle, cornucopia		1943	1944	80.00 – 95.00
Candle, miniature cornucopia	3971-TO	July 1941	1944	35.00 – 40.00
Candleholder		1941	1944	35.00 – 45.00
Candy jar, ftd.		1941	1944	150.00 – 185.00
Candy jar, scalloped body, ftd.		1942	1944	200.00 – 225.00
Comport, 6" flared, triangular		July 1941	1943	55.00 – 75.00
Comport, 8" ftd. plate		July 1941	1943	100.00 – 125.00
Condiment set, 5-piece		1942	1944	260.00 – 330.00
Cookie jar, handled		July 1941	1943	600.00 – 700.00
Creamer	3901-TO	1941	1944	35.00 – 40.00
Creamer, individual		1942	1944	30.00 – 32.00
Cruet		July 1941	1944	200.00 – 225.00
Decanter, handled		July 1941	1944	600.00 – 650.00
Epergne and block		July 1941	1943	250.00 – 350.00
Goblet, water		1942	1944	35.00 – 40.00
Goblet, wine or cocktail		1942	1944	35.00 – 40.00
Hat, No. 1		1941	1944	60.00 – 70.00
Hat, No. 2		1941	1944	40.00 – 50.00
Jar, 5" covered		1941		500.00 – 600.00
Jug, 4½"		1941	1944	90.00 – 110.00
Jug, 5½"		1941	1944	90.00 – 110.00
Jug, 32 oz. squat		1941	1944	150.00 – 185.00
Jug, 48 oz. tankard		1941	1944	400.00 – 450.00
Jug, 80 oz. (NIL)		1941	1944	300.00 – 350.00
Mustard and spoon		1942	1944	60.00 – 85.00
Nappy, 6" double crimped, flared, oval, plate, square, triangle		1941	1944	45.00 – 55.00
Oil	3869-TO	1942	1944	95.00 – 110.00
Plate, 8"		1942	1944	40.00 – 45.00
Puff box and cover		1941	1944	125.00 – 150.00
Rose bowl, 4½"		1941	1944	70.00 – 80.00
Rose bowl, 5"		1941	1944	80.00 – 90.00
Salt and pepper, ftd.		1941	1944	100.00 – 125.00
Sherbet		1942	1944	25.00 – 35.00
Slipper	3995-TO	1941	1944	30.00 – 35.00
Sugar	3901-TO	1941	1944	35.00 – 40.00
Sugar, individual		1942	1944	30.00 – 32.00
Tray, 6¾" crescent		1942	1943	90.00 – 125.00
Tray, 10½" fan		1941	1944	55.00 – 60.00
Tumbler, 5 oz. flat		1941	1944	25.00 – 30.00
Tumbler, 9 oz. flat		1941	1944	35.00 – 40.00
Tumbler, 12 oz. flat (barrel-shape)		1941	1944	50.00 – 55.00
Tumbler, ftd. 12 oz. highball or ice tea		1942	1944	60.00 – 80.00
Vanity set, 3-pc.		1941	1944	405.00 – 450.00
Vase, 4" miniature DC	3855-TO	1941		25.00 – 35.00
Vase, 4" miniature cup flared, fan, flared, hat, triangle		1941	1944	32.00 – 38.00
Vase, 4" miniature oval		1941	1944	32.00 – 39.00
Vase, 4½" double crimped, cup flared, cup square		1941	1944	40.00 – 50.00
Vase, 5" double crimped, cup flared, square, triangle		1941	1944	50.00 – 60.00
Vase, 5½" flat crimped, flared, square, triangle		1941	1944	50.00 – 60.00

3913 TO Ftd. Cake Plate

3974 TO Candleholder

No. 389 Vanity Set

3740 TO 12" Divided Relish

3728 TO Ftd. Comport

No. 389 6" DC Bonbon

3761 TO Decanter

3727 TO 8" Comport

3971 Miniature Cornucopia Candleholder

No. 389 2" Hat

3883 TO Candy Jar

3887 TO Ftd. Covered Comport

No. 389 Ash Tray

No. 389 5" Sq. Handled Bonbon

No. 389 Ftd. Candy Jar

3801 TO Miniature Epergne Set

3733 TO 12" Handled Relish (Celery)

3730 TO 8" Ribbon Candy Bowl

3705 TO 11" Hanging Bowl

No. 389 Cookie Jar

Topaz Opalescent Hobnail (1941)	Ware No.	Introduced	Discontinued	Value
Vase, 6" flat DC		1941	1944	70.00 – 75.00
Vase, 6" flat flared, square, triangle	3856-TO	1941	1944	70.00 – 75.00
Vase, 6" hand, flared, DC		1942	1943	160.00 – 190.00
Vase, 6½" fan (scalloped)		1942	1944	65.00 – 75.00
Vase, 6½" swung		1942	1944	45.00 – 60.00
Vase, 6¼" ftd. DC	3956-TO	1941	1944	50.00 – 65.00
Vase, 6¼" ftd. cupped, cup flared, flared, triangle, fan		1941	1944	70.00 – 80.00
Vase, 8" DC	3858-TO	1941	1944	200.00 – 225.00
Vase, 8" flared, square, triangle		1941	1944	220.00 – 240.00
Vase, 8" ftd. double crimped, fan, square, triangle		1943	1944	200.00 – 275.00
Vase, 8½" flip		1941		250.00 – 350.00
Vase, 9" flared		1941	1944	150.00 – 185.00
Vase, 10" flared		1941	1943	200.00 – 225.00

Topaz Opalescent Hobnail (1959)	Ware No.	Introduced	Discontinued	Value
Banana bowl	3720-TO	July 1959	July 1960	195.00 – 225.00
Basket, 7" handled	3837-TO	1959	1961	125.00 – 140.00
Basket, 10"	3830-TO	1959	1960	200.00 – 225.00
Basket, 12"	3734-TO	July 1959	July 1960	250.00 – 275.00
Bowl, 7"	3927-TO	1959	1960	45.00 – 55.00
Bowl, 8½" 3-ftd.	3724-TO	1959	July 1959	225.00 – 250.00
Bowl, 10" ftd.	3731-TO	July 1959	July 1960	125.00 – 150.00
Bowl, 10½" ftd.	3723-TO	1959	1960	150.00 – 185.00
Bowl, 12" celery	3739-TO	July 1959	1960	200.00 – 225.00
Bowl, 9" DC	3924-TO	1959	1961	80.00 – 90.00
Bowl, 9" cupped	3735-TO	July 1959	July 1960	200.00 – 250.00
Bowl, hanging	3705-TO	July 1959	1960	300.00 – 325.00
Bowl, 8" Ribbon Candy	3730-TO	July 1959	July 1960	175.00 – 225.00
Cake plate, 13" ftd.	3913-TO	1959	1960	145.00 – 185.00
Candle bowl	3771-TO	July 1959	July 1960	75.00 – 90.00
Candleholder	3974-TO	1959	1961	35.00 – 45.00
Candleholder	3770-TO	July 1959	July 1960	65.00 – 75.00
Candy jar	3883-TO	1959	July 1960	125.00 – 150.00
Comport, 7"	3727-TO	1959	July 1960	65.00 – 75.00
Comport	3728-TO	1959	1961	65.00 – 75.00
Comport, ftd.	3920-TO	July 1959	1961	75.00 – 90.00
Comport, ftd. covered	3887-TO	1959	1961	150.00 – 185.00
Decanter, handled	3761-TO	1960	1961	600.00 – 650.00
Epergne set, miniature	3801-TO	1959	July 1961	200.00 – 225.00
Ivy ball, 4¾"	3726-TO	July 1959	1961	65.00 – 85.00
Jug, 12 oz. syrup	3762-TO	1959	1961	90.00 – 110.00
Plate, 8"	3816-TO	July 1959	1960	40.00 – 45.00
Plate, 13½"	3714-TO	July 1959	1960	80.00 – 95.00
Relish, handled	3733-TO	1959	July 1960	85.00 – 95.00
Relish, 12" divided	3740-TO	July 1959	1960	225.00 – 250.00
Salt and pepper, flat	3806-TO	1960	1961	85.00 – 95.00
Sandwich tray, 13" w/chrome handle	3791-TO	July 1959	1960	85.00 – 90.00
Slipper	3995-TO	1960	1962	30.00 – 35.00
Tidbit, 2-tier, chrome handle	3794-TO	July 1959	1960	120.00 – 140.00
Vase, 4½" DC	3854-TO	1959	1961	40.00 – 50.00
Vase, 5"	3850-TO	1959	1961	50.00 – 60.00
Vase, 8"	3859-TO	1959	July 1960	225.00 – 250.00
Vase, 6¼" ftd. DC	3956-TO	1959	1960	50.00 – 65.00
Vase, 8" bud	3756-TO	1959	July 1961	45.00 – 60.00
Vase, 12" ftd. swung	3753-TO	July 1959	July 1960	125.00 – 150.00
Vase, 14" medium swung	3758-TO	July 1959	July 1960	140.00 – 160.00
Vase, 18" tall swung	3759-TO	July 1959	July 1960	150.00 – 185.00

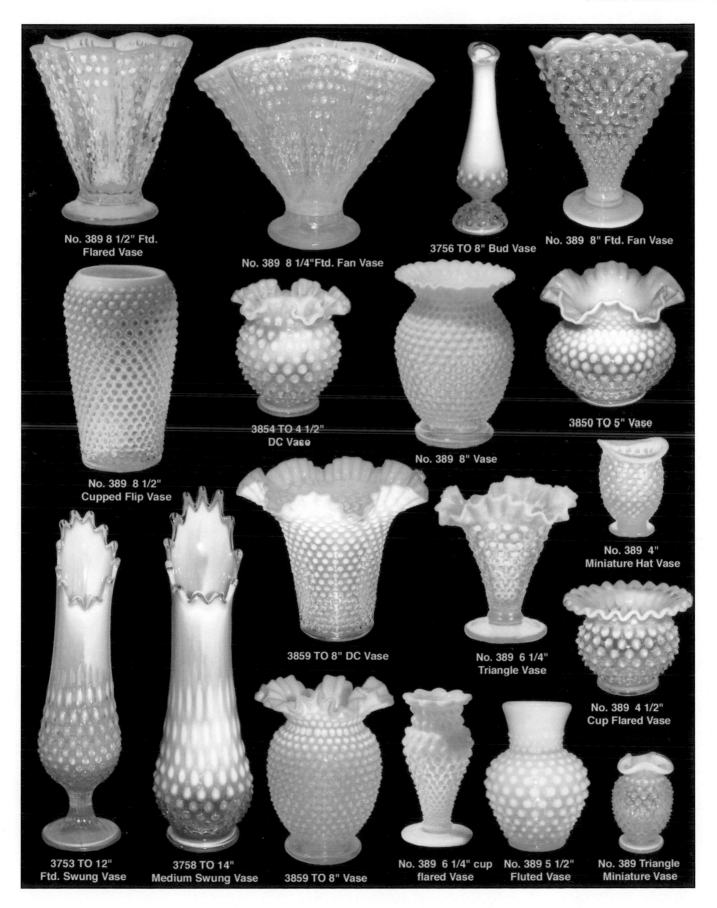

No. 389 8 1/2" Ftd.
Flared Vase

No. 389 8 1/4"Ftd. Fan Vase

3756 TO 8" Bud Vase

No. 389 8" Ftd. Fan Vase

No. 389 8 1/2"
Cupped Flip Vase

3854 TO 4 1/2"
DC Vase

No. 389 8" Vase

3850 TO 5" Vase

No. 389 4"
Miniature Hat Vase

3859 TO 8" DC Vase

No. 389 6 1/4"
Triangle Vase

No. 389 4 1/2"
Cup Flared Vase

3753 TO 12"
Ftd. Swung Vase

3758 TO 14"
Medium Swung Vase

3859 TO 8" Vase

No. 389 6 1/4" cup
flared Vase

No. 389 5 1/2"
Fluted Vase

No. 389 Triangle
Miniature Vase

Turquoise Hobnail

Fenton's opaque Turquoise is sometimes confused with Blue Pastel that was made in the mid-1950s. Turquoise appears darker and is more blue-green than Blue Pastel. Turquoise Hobnail was first produced in 1955 and the line was discontinued at the end of 1958.

	Introduced	Discontinued
The following items were sold as sets:		
Console set No. 3904 (3-piece): 9" DC bowl, 2 candles	1955	1959
Juice set No. 3905 (7-piece): Squat jug, 6-5 oz. tumblers	1955	1957
Vanity set No. 3805, (3-piece) puff box, 2 colognes	1955	1957

The base to the No. 3867 Lavabo was also sold as a separate item for six months between January and July 1956. During this period this base was advertised as the No. 3836 wall planter.

Turquoise Hobnail	Ware No.	Introduced	Discontinued	Value
Basket, 4½" handled	3834-TU	1955	1959	30.00 – 35.00
Basket, 7" handled	3837-TU	1955	1959	40.00 – 50.00
Berry dish	3928-TU	1955	1957	12.00 – 14.00
Bonbon, 6" DC	3926-TU	1955	1958	10.00 – 12.00
Bottle, vanity	3865-TU	1956	1957	55.00 – 65.00
Bowl, 9" DC	3924-TU	1955	1959	35.00 – 45.00
Bowl, 9" square	3929-TU	1955	1957	50.00 – 55.00
Cake plate, 13" ftd.	3913-TU	1955	1958	75.00 – 85.00
Candleholder	3974-TU	1955	1959	20.00 – 22.00
Candy jar	3883-TU	1955	1959	50.00 – 60.00
Comport, ftd.	3920-TU	1955	1959	25.00 – 30.00
Comport, ftd. covered	3887-TU	1955	1959	55.00 – 65.00
Creamer and sugar, #3	3906-TU	1955	1957	25.00 – 35.00
Epergne set, miniature 4-pc.	3801-TU	1955	1959	95.00 – 110.00
*Goblet	3845-TU			30.00 – 35.00
Jug, 32 oz. squat	3965-TU	1955	1957	75.00 – 85.00
Lavabo	3867-TU	July 1955	1957	170.00 – 190.00
Oil	3869-TU	1955	1957	30.00 – 40.00
Planter, wall	3836-TU	1956	July 1956	65.00 – 85.00
Puff box	3885-TU	1956	1957	50.00 – 60.00
Salt and pepper, flat	3806-TU	1955	1957	25.00 – 35.00
*Sherbet	3825-TU			22.00 – 25.00
Slipper	3995-TU	1955	1957	20.00 – 25.00
Tumbler, 5 oz.	3945-TU	1955	1957	14.00 – 16.00
Vanity set, 3-pc.	3805-TU	1955	1957	170.00 – 195.00
Vase, 4" ftd. DC	3952-TU	1955	1959	14.00 – 16.00
Vase, 4" ftd. fan	3953-TU	1955	1959	16.00 – 18.00
Vase, 4½" DC	3854-TU	1955	1959	25.00 – 32.00
Vase, 5" DC	3850-TU	1955	1957	40.00 – 45.00

*Not in regular line.

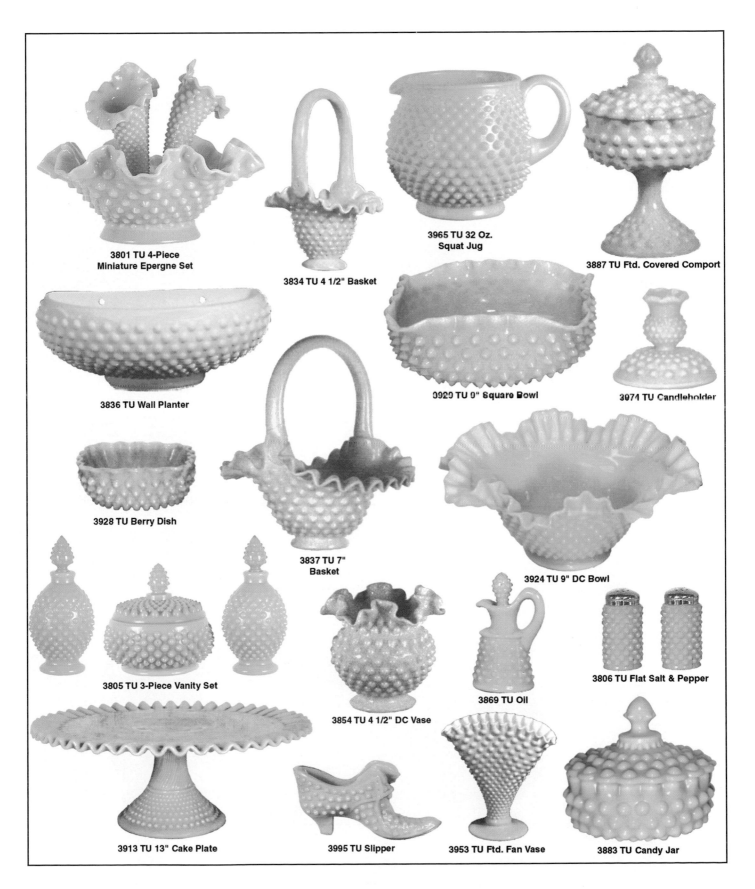

3801 TU 4-Piece
Miniature Epergne Set

3834 TU 4 1/2" Basket

3965 TU 32 Oz.
Squat Jug

3887 TU Ftd. Covered Comport

3836 TU Wall Planter

0929 TU 0" Square Bowl

3974 TU Candleholder

3928 TU Berry Dish

3837 TU 7"
Basket

3924 TU 9" DC Bowl

3805 TU 3-Piece Vanity Set

3854 TU 4 1/2" DC Vase

3869 TU Oil

3806 TU Flat Salt & Pepper

3913 TU 13" Cake Plate

3995 TU Slipper

3953 TU Ftd. Fan Vase

3883 TU Candy Jar

Wild Rose Hobnail

Wild Rose is a deep Cranberry over Opal cased color Fenton introduced in 1961. This color, Apple Green Overlay, and Coral were used briefly on a few early 1960s patterns. Seven pieces of the Hobnail pattern are listed in the catalogs in Wild Rose. The color was discontinued at the end of 1962. Due to the short production period, not much of this color of Hobnail is seen on the secondary market. The lavabo is especially elusive.

Other patterns made in this color during this time period include Jacqueline, Bubble Optic, and Wild Rose with Bowknot.

Wild Rose Hobnail	Ware No.	Introduced	Discontinued	Value
Jug, 12 oz. syrup	3762-WR	1961	1963	40.00 – 50.00
Lavabo	3867-WR	1962	1963	200.00 – 225.00
Vase, 5" DC	3850-WR	1961	1963	40.00 – 50.00
Vase, 5½" DC	3656-WR	1961	1963	45.00 – 55.00
Vase, 6"	3856-WR	1961	1963	45.00 – 55.00
Vase, 8"	3858-WR	1961	1963	70.00 – 80.00
Vase, 11"	3752-WR	1961	1963	120.00 – 150.00

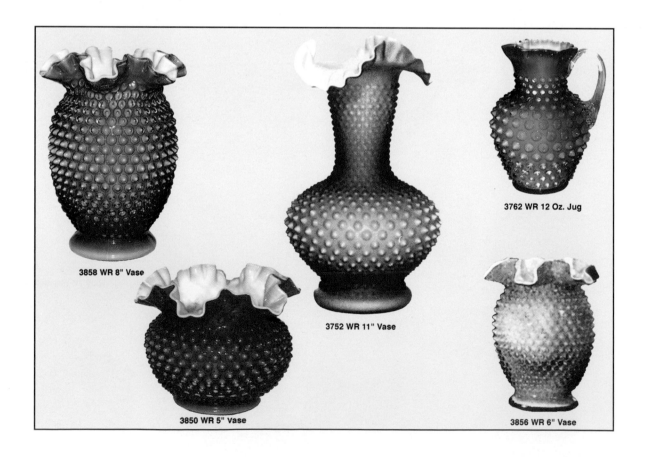

3858 WR 8" Vase

3850 WR 5" Vase

3752 WR 11" Vase

3762 WR 12 Oz. Jug

3856 WR 6" Vase

Miscellaneous Hobnail

Through the years, Fenton has produced many Hobnail lamps, lamp parts, and sample items. Some of this type of product and a few more regular line items are pictured on the following pages.

Hobnail Item	Value
1. Peach Blow Hobnail No. 3752-11" sample vase	140.00 – 160.00
2. Orange Opalescent Hobnail No. 3752-11" sample vase	200.00 – 225.00
3. Orange Opalescent No. 324-9" bowl made as a sample	140.00 – 160.00
4. Orange Opalescent No. 3850-5" vase	90.00 – 110.00
5. Green Opalescent Hobnail 4½" basket with looped handle	250.00 – 285.00
This piece has also been found in blue opalescent.	250.00 – 275.00
6. & 7. Topaz Opalescent early 1940s candy boxes with two different style knobs	200.00 – 225.00
8. Topaz Overlay No. 3853-3" bowl made as a sample	50.00 – 55.00
9. Cranberry Hobnail 10" lamp shade-style vase	175.00 – 200.00
10. Blue Opalescent Hobnail No.3759-18" vase from the regular line	90.00 – 125.00

Hobnail Lamps

Lamps in Photo Above:

Hobnail Lamp	Value
1. Cranberry Hobnail 20" student lamp	300.00 – 325.00
2. Cranberry Hobnail lamp	280.00 – 310.00
3. Cranberry Hobnail lamp	350.00 – 400.00
4. Cranberry Hobnail handled lamp	150.00 – 175.00
5. Cranberry Hobnail lamp made from a No. 3967-80 oz. pitcher	160.00 – 180.00
6. Cranberry Hobnail made from a No. 3870 candleholder	80.00 – 90.00

Lamps in the Photo on Page 239:

Hobnail Lamp	Value
1. Cranberry Opalescent Hobnail 20" student lamp	300.00 – 325.00
2. Cranberry Opalescent Hobnail double student lamp	425.00 – 475.00
3. Blue opalescent Hobnail 20" student lamp	375.00 – 425.00
4. Ruby Overlay Hobnail courting lamp	150.00 – 200.00
5. Cranberry Opalescent Hobnail No. 3907 – 26" lamp in the regular line	275.00 – 325.00
6. Blue Opalescent Hobnail No. 3907 – 26" lamp in the regular line	360.00 – 400.00
7. Milk Glass Hobnail No. 3807-19" lamp in the regular line	200.00 – 225.00
8. Cranberry Opalescent Hobnail lamp made with No. 389 special rose bowl and shade from the hurricane lamp	275.00 – 300.00
9. Milk Glass Hobnail No. 3808-22" lamp in the regular line	200.00 – 225.00

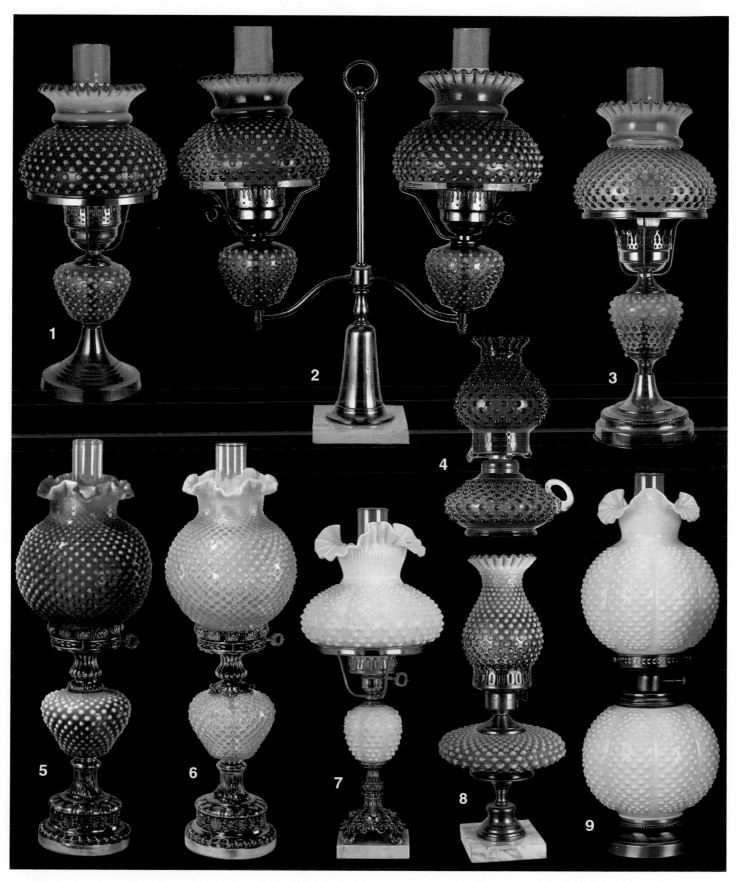

Lamps in Photo Above:

Hobnail Lamp	Value
1. Amber Hobnail double student lamp	100.00 – 125.00
2. Blue Opalescent Hobnail 15" lamp made from a No. 389-8" flared vase	125.00 – 150.00
3. Blue Opalescent Hobnail 13" lamp made from a No. 389-10" flared vase	125.00 – 150.00
4. Blue Opalescent Hobnail 6" lamp base may be found as a vase if not drilled	45.00 – 55.00
5. Blue Opalescent Hobnail lamp made for E. P. Paul from the No. 289 cologne mould with the original label shown to the right (6)	45.00 – 55.00

Lamps in Photo Above:

Hobnail Lamp	Value
1. French Opalescent Hobnail 10" diameter ceiling fixture	125.00 – 150.00
2. French Opalescent Hobnail lamp made for Edward P. Paul	35.00 – 45.00
3. Topaz Opalescent Hobnail 5" vase from lamp base mould (flared crimp)	55.00 – 65.00
4. Green Opalescent Hobnail 6" lamp made for E. P. Paul from the No. 289 cologne mould	55.00 – 65.00
5. White Milk Hobnail lamp adapted from the No. 3998 hurricane lamp	70.00 – 80.00
6. Green Opalescent and brass lamp made with a Hobnail cologne	100.00 – 125.00
7. French Opalescent Hobnail cologne used as a base for a miniature oil lamp	40.00 – 45.00
8. Topaz Oøpalescent 8" vase drilled for use as a lamp	140.00 – 160.00
9. Honey Amber Overlay Hobnail student lamp	100.00 – 125.00
10. Topaz Opalescent Hobnail lamp produced from a 5" vase (triangular crimp)	55.00 – 65.00
11. Topaz Overlay Hobnail footed vase/lamp base	60.00 – 80.00

Hobnail Floor Lamps

Hobnail Floor Lamps	Value
1. Peach Blow Hobnail double floor lamp with milk glass fount	200.00 – 225.00
2. Cranberry Opalescent Hobnail floor lamp	150.00 – 170.00
3. Cranberry Opalescent Hobnail double floor lamp with Cranberry Opalescent fount	400.00 – 450.00

Hobnail in Unusual Shapes and Colors

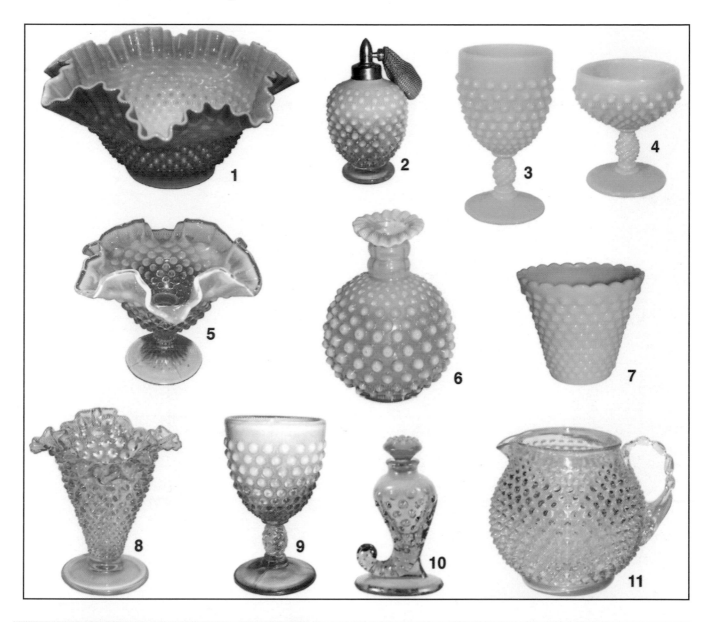

Hobnail Item	Value
1. Coral Hobnail No. 3924-9" DC bowl	40.00 – 45.00
2. Green Opalescent Hobnail atomizer made for DeVilbiss	90.00 – 110.00
3. Turquoise Hobnail No. 3845 water goblet	30.00 – 35.00
4. Turquoise Hobnail No. 3825 sherbet	22.00 – 25.00
5. Blue Opalescent Hobnail candleholder made from No. 3728 footed comport	175.00 – 200.00
6. Green Opalescent Hobnail 5" vase	40.00 – 50.00
7. Pastel Green Hobnail 4½" jardiniere made for florist supply wholesaler A. L. Randall of Chicago, was in the regular line for six months in 1955	30.00 – 35.00
8. Blue non-Opalescent Hobnail No. 3956-6¼" footed vase	18.00 – 22.00
9. Cameo Opalescent Hobnail No. 3845 water goblet	N. D.
10. Blue Opalescent cornucopia-shaped cologne bottle made from No. 3971 cornucopia candle	N. D.
11. Blue non Opalescent Hobnail No. 3965 squat jug	55.00 – 65.00

Jonquil Yellow and Pekin Blue II Hobnail

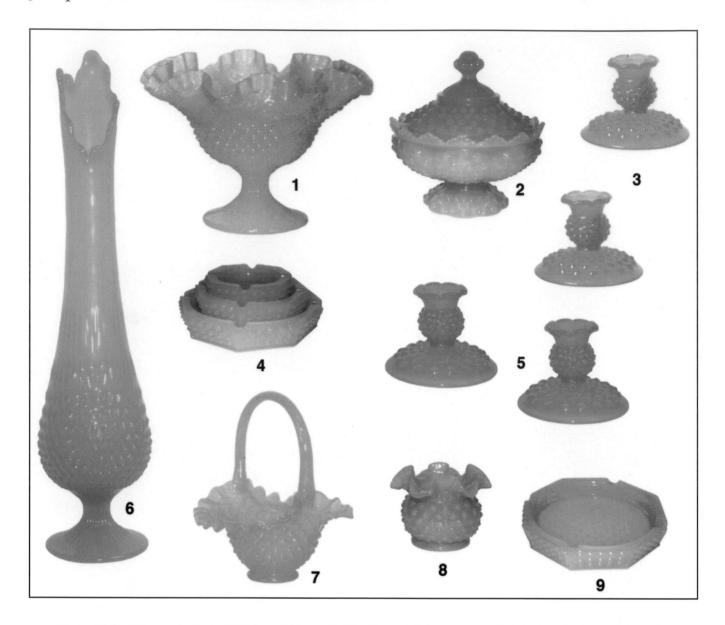

These Hobnail items in Jonquil Yellow (JO) and Pekin Blue II (JB) were sampled during the late 1960s. The items in these colors were not included in the regular line. However, there are enough examples on the secondary market to indicate that at least some of the product was sold through the Gift Shop.

Hobnail Item	Ware No.	Value
1. Bowl, 10" footed	3731-JO	90.00 – 110.00
2. Candy and cover	3886-JB	65.00 – 85.00
3. Candleholder, ea.	3974-JO	20.00 – 25.00
4. Ashtray set, 3-piece	3810–JB	40.00 – 50.00
5. Candleholder, ea.	3974-JB	20.00 – 25.00
6. Vase, 12" ftd. swung	3753-JB	75.00 – 90.00
7. Basket, 7" handled	3837-JO	7500 – 95.00
8. Vase, 3"	3853-JB	15.00 – 20.00
9. Ashtray, #3 octagonal	3878-JO	22.00 – 25.00

Unusual Milk Glass Hobnail

Milk Glass Hobnail Item	Value
1. Milk Glass Hobnail No. 3867 Lavabo on wooden mount with advertising mirror	200.00 – 225.00
2. Milk Glass No. 3926-6" bonbon with hand painted floral decoration	22.00 – 27.00
3. Milk Glass Hobnail 6½" vase	40.00 – 45.00
4. Milk Glass Hobnail 4-piece condiment set on wooden Lazy susan	100.00 – 125.00
5. Milk Glass Hobnail No. 3928 berry dishes on wooden server	40.00 – 45.00
6. Milk Glass Hobnail candleholder from a No. 3728 comport	45.00 – 55.00
7. Milk Glass Hobnail 9" footed basket	140.00 – 160.00

Hobnail Candle Arrangements

Although the No. 3872 candle bowl entered the line in July 1968, it was not until floral arrangements were added in July 1970, that sales began to soar. Candle bowls were boxed with a scented candle and an attractive floral arrangement that changed with the spring and fall seasons. New assortments of floral arrangements were introduced each January and July through 1976. In July 1973 four and six-piece centerpiece arrangements were added. The listing for January 1975 included vase arrangements. The vase arrangements for July 1975 were the same as the ones introduced in January. The last period, July 1976, only lists a single candle bowl arrangement. Some of the arrangements are shown on the following pages. The candle bowls and vases are priced with their respective colors.

Descriptions, ware numbers, and dates of availability of the candle arrangements and floral centerpieces are on the next few pages.

and you have 9 of the best fall & Christmas gift & decorative ideas we've ever thought of... and at only $10.00 retail–

3615

3616

3613

3614

3617

3618

3612

3611

3619

As all good Fenton dealers know– order early. Christmas is almost here!

Packed 4 to a carton but in any combination you wish.

July 1970	Ware No.	January 1971	Ware No
Candle bowl arr.	3611-CA	Candle bowl arr.	3611-CA
Candle bowl arr.	3612-CA	Candle bowl arr.	3612-CB
Candle bowl arr.	3613-MI	Candle bowl arr.	3613-CG
Candle bowl arr.	3614-MI	Candle bowl arr.	3614-MI
Candle bowl arr.	3615-MI	Candle bowl arr.	3615-MI
Candle bowl arr.	3616-MI	Candle bowl arr.	3616-MI
Candle bowl arr.	3617-CG	Candle bowl arr.	3617-MI
Candle bowl arr.	3618-CG	Candle bowl arr.	3618-MB
Candle bowl arr.	3619-BK		

July 1971	Ware No.	January 1972	Ware No.
Candle bowl arr.	0301-CA	Candle bowl arr.	0320-MI
Candle bowl arr.	0302-CA	Candle bowl arr.	0321-MI
Candle bowl arr.	0303-MI	Candle bowl arr.	0322-MI
Candle bowl arr.	0304-MI	Candle bowl arr.	0323-MI
Candle bowl arr.	0305-CB	Candle bowl arr.	0324-MI
Candle bowl arr.	0306-MI	Candle bowl arr.	0325-MI
Candle bowl arr.	0307-CG	Candle bowl arr.	0326-MI
Candle bowl arr.	0308-MI	Candle bowl arr.	0327-MI
Candle bowl arr.	0309-MI	Candle bowl arr.	0328-MI
Candle bowl arr.	0310-MB	Candle bowl arr.	0329-MI
Candle bowl arr.	0311-MI	Candle bowl arr.	0330-MI
Candle bowl arr.	0312-MI		

July 1972	Ware No.	January 1973	Ware No.
Candle bowl arr.	0331-CB	Candle bowl arr.	0350-MI
Candle bowl arr.	0332-CA	Candle bowl arr.	0351-MI
Candle bowl arr.	0333-MI	Candle bowl arr.	0352-MI
Candle bowl arr.	0334-MI	Candle bowl arr.	0353-MI
Candle bowl arr.	0335-MI	Candle bowl arr.	0354-MI
Candle bowl arr.	0337-MB	Candle bowl arr.	0355-MI
Candle bowl arr.	0338-MI	Candle bowl arr.	0356-MI
Candle bowl arr.	0339-MI	Candle bowl arr.	0357-CT
Candle bowl arr.	0340-CG		
Candle bowl arr.	0341-MI		

July 1973	Ware No.	January 1974	Ware No.
Candle bowl arr.	0360-MI	Candle bowl arr.	0370-MI
Candle bowl arr.	0361-CB	Candle bowl arr.	0371-MI
Candle bowl arr.	0362-MI	Candle bowl arr.	0372-MI
Candle bowl arr.	0363-CA	Candle bowl arr.	0373-MI
Candle bowl arr.	0364-CT	Candle bowl arr.	0374-MI
Candle bowl arr.	0365-MI	Candle bowl arr.	0375-MI
Candle bowl arr.	0366-MI	Candle bowl arr.	0376-MI
Candle bowl arr.	0367-MI	Candle bowl arr.	0377-MI
Candle bowl arr.	0368-MI	Centerpiece arr., 6-pc.	3744-PF
Candle bowl arr.	0369-MI	Centerpiece arr., 6-pc.	3744-DA
Centerpiece arr., 6-pc.	3744-MI	Centerpiece arr., 6-pc.	3744-YF
Centerpiece arr., 6-pc.	3744-DA	Centerpiece arr., 4-pc.	3747-DA
Centerpiece arr., 6-pc.	3744-XG	Centerpiece arr., 4-pc.	3747-PF
Centerpiece arr., 6-pc.	3744-XR	Centerpiece arr., 4-pc.	3747-YF
Centerpiece arr., 4-pc.	3747-MI		
Centerpiece arr., 4-pc.	3747-XG		
Centerpiece arr., 4-pc.	3747-XR		

Catalog Reprint July, 1971

Courtesy Of:

The Fenton Art Glass Museum

0307 CG

0308 MI

0312 MI

0310 MB

0302 CA

0304 MI

0305 CB

0301 CA

0306 MI

0311 MI

0303 MI

0309 MI

A Dozen Tested Arrangements

A consumer survey was done on a large variety of new arrangements featuring different rings, different candles and different color bowls. The dozen shown here proved to be most popular. Each set is attractively boxed as illustrated.

The Fenton Candle Bowl

July 1974	Ware No.
Candle bowl arr.	0380-CB
Candle bowl arr.	0381-CA
Candle bowl arr.	0382-CT
Candle bowl arr.	0383-MI
Candle bowl arr.	0384-MI
Candle bowl arr.	0385-CT
Candle bowl arr.	0386-MI
Candle bowl arr.	0387-LM
Candle bowl arr.	0388-LM

January 1975	Ware No.
Candle bowl arr.	0380-CB
Candle bowl arr.	0381-CA
Candle bowl arr.	0382-CT
Candle bowl arr.	0383-MI
Candle bowl arr.	0384-MI
Candle bowl arr.	0390-MI
Candle bowl arr.	0391-MI
Candle bowl arr.	0392-MI
Candle bowl arr.	0393-MI
Candle bowl arr.	0394-MI
Centerpiece arr., 6-pc.	3744-DA
Centerpiece arr., 6-pc.	3744-YF
Vase arrangement	0251-BG
Vase arrangement	0252-LM
Vase arrangement	0253-MI
Vase arrangement	0254-CT
Vase arrangement	0255-CT
Vase arrangement	0256-BG
Vase arrangement	0257-LM

July 1975	Ware No.
Candle bowl arr.	0380-CB
Candle bowl arr.	0381-CA
Candle bowl arr.	0382-CT
Candle bowl arr.	0384-MI
Candle bowl arr.	0385-CT
Candle bowl arr.	0386-MI
Candle bowl arr.	0387-MI
Candle bowl arr.	0388-MI
Candle bowl arr.	0389-MI
Centerpiece arr., 6-pc.	3744-XH

Vase arrangements are the same as January 1975 arrangements.

January 1976	Ware No.
Candle bowl arr.	0400-MI
Candle bowl arr.	0401-MI
Candle bowl arr.	0402-MI
Candle bowl arr.	0403-MI
Candle bowl arr.	0404-MI
Candle bowl arr.	0405-MI
Vase arrangement	0260-MI
Vase arrangement	0261-MI
Vase arrangement	0262-MI
Vase arrangement	0263-MI
Vase arrangement	0264-MI
Vase arrangement	0265-MI

July 1976	Ware No.
Candle bowl arr.	0388-MI

Four and Six Piece Centerpiece Arrangements for Spring and Summer

Catalog Reprint Circa 1974
Courtesy Of:
The Fenton Art Glass Museum

3744 PF

3744 YF

3747 DA

3747 PF

3747 YF

Spring and Summer Candle Bowl Arrangements Complete with candles and rings.

In display-gift box.

0373 MI

0372 MI

0370 MI

0376 MI

0374 MI

0375 MI

0371 MI

0377 MI

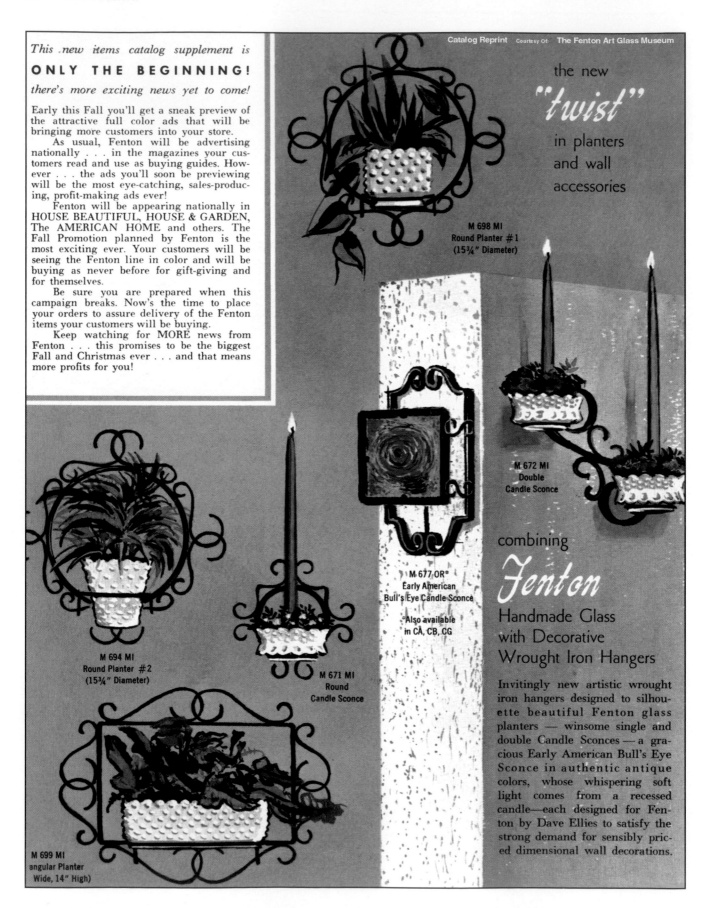

This new items catalog supplement is

ONLY THE BEGINNING!

there's more exciting news yet to come!

Early this Fall you'll get a sneak preview of the attractive full color ads that will be bringing more customers into your store.

As usual, Fenton will be advertising nationally . . . in the magazines your customers read and use as buying guides. However . . . the ads you'll soon be previewing will be the most eye-catching, sales-producing, profit-making ads ever!

Fenton will be appearing nationally in HOUSE BEAUTIFUL, HOUSE & GARDEN, The AMERICAN HOME and others. The Fall Promotion planned by Fenton is the most exciting ever. Your customers will be seeing the Fenton line in color and will be buying as never before for gift-giving and for themselves.

Be sure you are prepared when this campaign breaks. Now's the time to place your orders to assure delivery of the Fenton items your customers will be buying.

Keep watching for MORE news from Fenton . . . this promises to be the biggest Fall and Christmas ever . . . and that means more profits for you!

the new

"twist"

in planters and wall accessories

M 698 MI
Round Planter #1
(15¾" Diameter)

M 672 MI
Double
Candle Sconce

M 677 OR*
Early American
Bull's Eye Candle Sconce

*Also available
in CA, CB, CG

M 694 MI
Round Planter #2
(15¾" Diameter)

M 671 MI
Round
Candle Sconce

M 699 MI
angular Planter
Wide, 14" High)

combining

Fenton

Handmade Glass with Decorative Wrought Iron Hangers

Invitingly new artistic wrought iron hangers designed to silhouette beautiful Fenton glass planters — winsome single and double Candle Sconces — a gracious Early American Bull's Eye Sconce in authentic antique colors, whose whispering soft light comes from a recessed candle—each designed for Fenton by Dave Ellies to satisfy the strong demand for sensibly priced dimensional wall decorations.

Fenton's Spiral Optic Pattern

Spiral Optic Colors and Shapes

Inventory records from 1938 list the four sizes of top hats in opalescent colors. This is the first written indication of the Spiral Optic pattern which was produced in French Opalescent, Green Opalescent, Cranberry Opalescent, Stiegel Blue, Topaz Opalescent, and Blue Ridge. Blue Ridge items have a French Opalescent Spiral Optic Pattern with an accenting dark blue trim. For more information on the Blue Ridge pattern see the Blue Ridge pattern in the Crest chapter. By 1940, Spiral Optic was no longer in the price listing and all traces of Spiral Optic had disappeared from Fenton's inventory records.

Complete catalog records of all the shapes are not available for Spiral Optic. The following listings are from inventory records and price lists from 1938 and 1939. These listings have been enhanced with additional items known to exist in collections.

The milk glass nymph could be purchased at this time as part of a four-piece set — the nymph, a white block, a 9" flared or 10" crimped #1522 bowl, and either a white or colored base for the bowl.

Lamps may also be found made with Spiral Optic parts. In 1946, Fenton began selling the No. 201 Spiral Optic special rose bowl in Cranberry, French Opalescent, and Blue Opalescent to Quoizel for use as a lamp part. Later, after Spiral Optic returned to the line in the mid-1980s lamps were also produced for the regular Fenton line.

In 1950, four different Spiral Optic vases in Cranberry returned to the line. Three of these were discontinued by the end of 1951. Seven other vases were brought into the line in Cranberry during the mid-1950s. Most of these remained in production until about 1960.

In the fall of 1950, several Snowcrest shapes that were produced from Spiral Optic moulds were introduced into the Fenton line. Bowls, vases, and hats in green, blue, and ruby were made with opal crests. In 1951, shapes in amber with opal crests replaced items in blue.

In 1979, Spiral Optic returned again to the Fenton line for a very limited time. Six different pieces were made in Cameo Opalescent (amber opalescent) and Blue Opalescent. All of the pieces from this production were discontinued by June 1980.

Other later productions of opalescent Spiral Optic include:

1985
The No. 3138-7" basket was made in Green Opalescent for special accounts (former Levay customers).

1985 – 1986
The following vases were made in French Opalescent (FO), Minted Cream (EO), and Peaches 'n Cream (UO) Spiral Rib Optic:

3195-7" vase	3196-13" vase	3197-14" vase

In addition these pieces were made in Periwinkle Blue Overlay in Spiral Optic:

Basket, 8½"	3132-OP	Vase, 11"	3161-OP
Vase, 7½"	3140-OP		

French Opalescent Spiral Optic items with blue crests and trim returned to the line as part of Fenton's 80th anniversary celebration. For details see the Blue Ridge section of the Crest chapter.

The June catalog supplement featured several pieces of opalescent Spiral Optic as part of the Connoisseur Collection. A puff box in French Royale (KF) was used as part of a four-piece Blue Ridge vanity set. In addition two other Spiral Optic pieces were included. A No. 3194-13" two-handled urn was made in French Cranberry Satin (ZS) and a No. 3190-7" handled vase was made in French Royale. Both items were limited in production to 1000 pieces.

1988
The following limited edition cruets and cream pitchers were opalescent Spiral Optic productions:

No 3172-KF cruet (French Royale)	No. 3178-KF pitcher (French Royale)
No. 3176-EO cruet (Minted Cream)	No. 3177-EO pitcher (Minted Cream)
No. 3174-FO cruet (French Opalescent)	

1990 – 1991
Cranberry opalescent Spiral Optic returned to the line with the introduction of the following:

3161-CR-13" vase	3163-CR-16 oz. pitcher	133-CR-6" basket

1992 – 1993
The No. 3161-13" vase was the only remaining piece of Cranberry Opalescent Spiral Optic in the regular line.

1994

An assortment of Rib Optic Autumn Gold (AO) also included the No. 1217-11" Spiral Optic basket inscribed with the signature of Frank M. Fenton.

1996

A large water pitcher returned to the line in Cranberry Opalescent with the introduction of the No. 3064-8" pitcher. The No. 3103-20" Spiral Optic Cranberry Opalescent lamp also entered the line.

1997

The following hand-painted Spiral Optic pieces in the hand-painted Meadow Beauty (PD) decoration with Sea Mist Green crests and handles appeared in the 1997 catalog:

Basket, 7½"	1219-PD	Vase, 6"	3055-PD
Lamp, 20" student	2719-PD	Vase, 9" Jack-in the-pulpit	3058-PD
Pitcher, 7"	1212-PD		

In addition to the above opalescent production, some pitchers, lamps, and vases were made in non-opalescent colors such as Country Cranberry, Dusty Rose Overlay, Periwinkle Blue, and Mulberry.

1998

The hand-painted floral Meadow Beauty pattern continued in production on French opalescent Spiral Optic blanks. The same pieces remained in the line except for the No. 3058 vase, which was discontinued. The No. 3161-11" vase was in the line in Cranberry (CC).

1999

The Family Signature Series included a clear Crest-trimmed hand-painted Martha's Rose on French Opalescent No. 3070-8½" Jack-in the Pulpit vase with the Shelley Fenton Ash signature. Fenton's new floral hand-painted Martha's Rose pattern included the following pieces on an Aquamarine-trimmed French Opalescent background:

Basket, 8½"	3131-AZ	Vase, 5"	3050-AZ
Lamp, 18" student	2791-AZ	Vase, 11"	3054-AZ
Pitcher, 7¼"	3072-AZ		

2000

Fenton's new hand-painted Lavender Petals decoration was featured on a Violet-trimmed French Opalescent Spiral Optic background. Spiral Optic items included:

Basket, 8½"	3131-ON	Vase, 5"	3050-ON
Lamp, 18" student	2791-ON	Vase, 11"	3054-ON
Pitcher, 7¼"	3072-ON		

An Aquamarine with Cobalt Crest No. 1548-8½" Spiral Optic vase was included in the Tranquility (AK) offering. The No. 3080-8" vase and the No. 3076-8" basket were a part of the Cranberry (CC) assortment.

2001

The above items in Lavender Petals continued in production, with the exception of the No. 3072 pitcher, which was discontinued. It was replaced with the No. 3081-6½" pitcher, and the No. 1585-5½" covered box was also added to this pattern. The No. 3070-8½" Jack-in-the-Pulpit vase returned to the line in Cranberry to complement the two vases from last year, which were still in production. The No. 3076 basket in Cranberry was also decorated with hand-painted White Poppies.

2002

The No. 3131-8½" basket was made in the Dotted Swiss on Willow Green Satin (GB) pattern. The Lavender Petals items from last year continued in production. The No. 3080-CC basket was discontinued, but the other Cranberry pieces remained in the line.

2003

The No. 3054-11" vase was in the line in Violet (OE). The No. 3131 Dotted Swiss on Willow Green Satin basket remained in production. New Lavender Petals pieces included the No. 3102-23" Gone with the Wind lamp and the No. 3091-5½" pitcher.

Blue Opalescent Spiral Optic (1939)

Stiegel Blue was Fenton's name for their early blue opalescent color. This early version of Stiegel Blue Spiral was produced only during 1939. Catalogs indicate this color of Spiral Optic has not been made since that time. The lamp base in the photo below was made from the No. 201 special rose bowl mould.

There are no records to indicate the #187 pitcher was made in this color. However, the #1353 pitcher was made and it was combined with the 9 ounce tumbler to produce a beverage set. The hurricane shade was available with a crystal, milk, or crystal satin base. The milk glass nymph could be purchased at this time as part of a four-piece set — the nymph, a white block, a 9" flared or 10" crimped #1522 bowl, and either a white or colored base for the bowl.

Stiegel Blue Spiral Optic (1939)	Value	Stiegel Blue Spiral Optic (1939)	Value
Basket, #1924-4½"	80.00 – 90.00	Tumbler, #1353-9 oz.	35.00 – 40.00
Basket, #1923-6"	100.00 – 125.00	Vase, #183-10" flared, regular, special,	
Bowl, #1522-9" flared	55.00 – 65.00	square, triangle	85.00 – 125.00
Bowl, #1522-10" crimped, 10" oval, 10"		Vase, #186-8" crimped, flared, square,	
square, triangle	70.00 – 80.00	triangle, tulip	65.00 – 85.00
Bowl, #1522-A-10" crimped	70.00 – 80.00	Vase, #201-6" cupped, crimped; cupped,	
Ginger jar, #893 with base and cover	250.00 – 350.00	flared	55.00 – 65.00
Hurricane lamp, #170 w/base	180.00 – 210.00	Vase, #894-10" flared, triangle, tulip	200.00 – 225.00
Pitcher, #1353-9" ice lip	280.00 – 310.00	Vase, #895-10" flared	200.00 – 225.00
Rose bowl, #201 crimped	55.00 – 65.00	Vase, #1922-8" flared, square, triangle	120.00 – 145.00
Rose bowl, #201 special	60.00 – 70.00	Vase, #1923-6" crimped, flared, square,	
Top hat, #1920-12"	250.00 – 350.00	tulip	55.00 – 65.00
Top hat, #1921-10"	200.00 – 250.00	Vase, #1924-4" crimped, flared, square,	
Top hat, #1922-9"	100.00 – 150.00	tulip	40.00 – 50.00
Top hat, #1923-6"	60.00 – 70.00		
Top hat, #1924-4"	45.00 – 55.00		

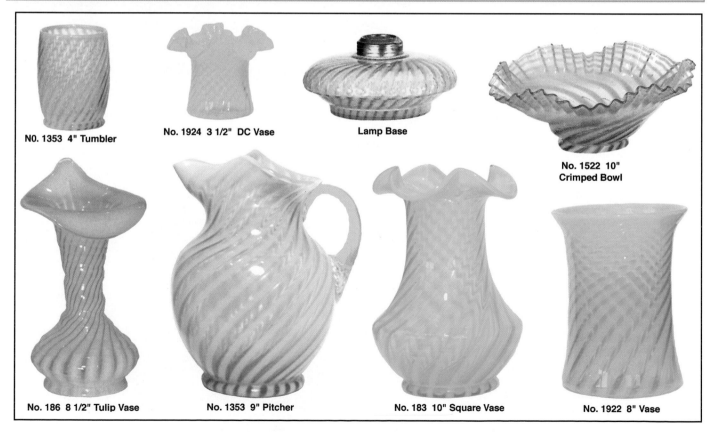

NO. 1353 4" Tumbler

No. 1924 3 1/2" DC Vase

Lamp Base

No. 1522 10" Crimped Bowl

No. 186 8 1/2" Tulip Vase

No. 1353 9" Pitcher

No. 183 10" Square Vase

No. 1922 8" Vase

Blue Opalescent Spiral Optic (1979)

After a long absence, Blue Opalescent Spiral Optic returned to the Fenton line again in January 1979, with an assortment of all new shapes. However, of the six pieces in the pattern, only the basket, fairy light, and vase remained in production after the first year. None of these items were listed in the mid-1980 price list and they are not easily found today.

Blue Opalescent Spiral Optic (1979)	Ware No.	Introduced	Discontinued	Value
Basket	3137-BO	1979	July 1980	55.00 – 65.00
Candy box	3180-BO	1979	1980	75.00 – 85.00
Fairy light	3100-BO	1979	July 1980	47.00 – 55.00
Pitcher, 10 oz.	3166-BO	1979	1980	35.00 – 45.00
Pitcher, 44 oz.	3164-BO	1979	1980	100.00 – 135.00
Vase, 6½"	3157-BO	1979	July 1980	25.00 – 30.00

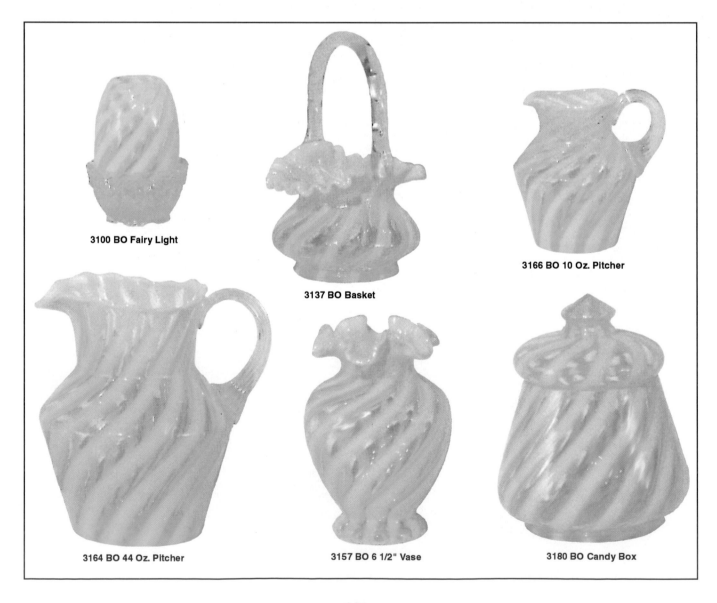

3100 BO Fairy Light

3137 BO Basket

3166 BO 10 Oz. Pitcher

3164 BO 44 Oz. Pitcher

3157 BO 6 1/2" Vase

3180 BO Candy Box

Cameo Opalescent Spiral Optic

This amber opalescent pattern was not in the Fenton line for very long. This color and the same items in Blue Opalescent were introduced in January 1979. The two pitchers and the candy box were discontinued by December, 1979, but the other three pieces remained in the catalog through mid-1980.

Amber opalescent glassware with a new name — Autumn Gold (AO) — in the form of the Rib Optic and Spiral Optic patterns returned to the Fenton line in 1994. The new color was a little more yellow than the older version. Autumn Gold pieces included a No. 1217-11" Spiral Optic basket with the signature of Frank M. Fenton.

Cameo Opalescent Spiral Optic	Ware No.	Introduced	Discontinued	Value
Basket	3137-CO	1979	July 1980	45.00 – 55.00
Candy box	3180-CO	1979	1980	50.00 – 65.00
Fairy light	3100-CO	1979	July 1980	30.00 – 35.00
Pitcher, 10 oz.	3166-CO	1979	1980	27.00 – 32.00
Pitcher, 44 oz.	3164-CO	1979	1980	75.00 – 90.00
Vase, 6½"	3157-CO	1979	July 1980	30.00 – 35.00

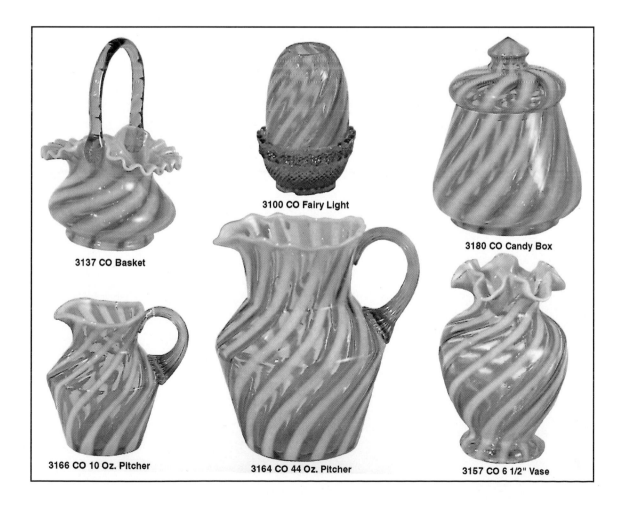

3137 CO Basket

3100 CO Fairy Light

3180 CO Candy Box

3166 CO 10 Oz. Pitcher

3164 CO 44 Oz. Pitcher

3157 CO 6 1/2" Vase

Cranberry Spiral Optic

Original production of Cranberry Spiral Optic began late in 1938 and was discontinued by early 1940. There was no longer any mention of any Spiral items in the 1940 inventory records at the end of the year.

Price lists indicate the #187 pitcher and the #1352 pitcher were sold with both the 9 ounce and 12 ounce tumblers as either a seven-piece or nine-piece beverage set. The hurricane shade was available with a crystal, milk, or crystal satin base. The milk glass nymph was sold with this pattern as a four-piece set — the nymph, a white block, a 9" flared or 10" crimped #1522 bowl, and a base for the bowl.

The first reappearance of Cranberry Spiral Optic was in 1950 when four vases — #3001-5", #3001-7", #3003-6", #3003-7" — were produced. Although these four vases were listed in January 1950, all but the #3001-5" vase were discontinued by January 1952. The #3001-5" vase continued in production and assumed the 3160-CR ware number in July 1952. Production of this vase continued until the end of the Cranberry Spiral Optic era in 1960. Three new shapes — No. 3252-8" pinch, No. 3253-6", and No. 3255-5" — joined the No. 3160 vase in July 1954. Although the pinch vase was discontinued by 1956, other shapes were added to the Cranberry Spiral Optic line and most were made until 1959 or 1960. A few more shapes were later added to finish out the fifties. For more information, see the section following this listing.

Almost three decades later, in 1986, Fenton made the No. 3194-13" French Cranberry handled urn as part of the Connoisseur Collection. In 1990, Fenton added a few pieces of Cranberry Opalescent Spiral Optic which had not been made earlier. Included in this issue were a No. 3133-6" basket, a No. 3163 pitcher, and a No. 3161-11" vase. In addition, in 1996, new Cranberry Opalescent items in this pattern included a No. 3103-20" lamp and a No. 3064-8" pitcher. Other items which may be found are lamp shades. These will sometimes be seen in the form of vases if the bottoms have not been cut off.

The wine bottle and shakers shown in the catalog reprint are actually Rib Optic in the New World shape. These were introduced in January 1952, but were sometimes advertised with Spiral Optic. The shakers were discontinued by 1960 but the wine bottle was made until 1963. For prices, see the New World pattern.

Cranberry Spiral Optic	Value
Basket, #1924-4½"	95.00 – 110.00
Basket, #1923-6"	125.00 – 140.00
Basket, #201-9"	200.00 – 250.00
Basket, #1922-10"	300.00 – 375.00
Basket, #1921-11"	400.00 – 475.00
Bowl, #1522-9" flared	65.00 – 85.00
Bowl, #1522-10" crimped, 10" oval, 10" square, triangle	85.00 – 100.00
Bowl, #1522-A-10" crimped	85.00 – 100.00
Bowl, #1523-12" flared	90.00 – 120.00
Candleholder, #1523	75.00 – 90.00
Decanter	450.00 – 550.00
Ginger jar, #893 with base and cover	350.00 – 395.00
*Hurricane lamp, #170 w/base	190.00 – 220.00
Pitcher, #187	400.00 – 500.00
Pitcher, #1353-9" ice lip	300.00 – 350.00
Pitcher, #1923 cream	185.00 – 200.00
Rose bowl, #201 crimped	75.00 – 85.00
Rose bowl, 4" #201 special	75.00 – 85.00
Top hat, #1924-4"	60.00 – 80.00
Top hat, #1923-6"	95.00 – 115.00
Top hat, #1922-9"	200.00 – 250.00
Top hat, #1921-10"	300.00 – 400.00
Top hat, #1920-12"	350.00 – 450.00
Tumbler, #187-9 oz.	50.00 – 55.00
Tumbler, #187-12 oz.	55.00 – 65.00
Tumbler, #1353-9 oz.	35.00 – 45.00
Tumbler, #1353-12 oz.	55.00 – 60.00
Vase, #183-6" special	65.00 – 75.00
Vase, #186-8" crimped, flared, square, triangle, tulip	75.00 – 90.00
Vase, #187-7" crimped, flared, triangle	100.00 – 125.00

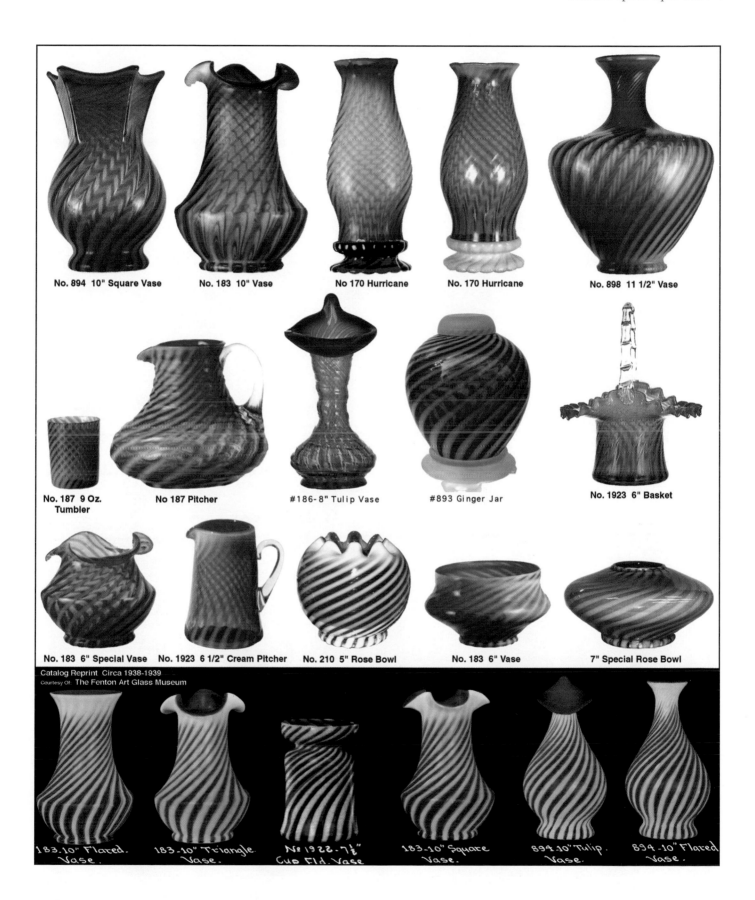

No. 894 10" Square Vase   No. 183 10" Vase   No 170 Hurricane   No. 170 Hurricane   No. 898 11 1/2" Vase

No. 187 9 Oz. Tumbler   No 187 Pitcher   #186-8" Tulip Vase   #893 Ginger Jar   No. 1923 6" Basket

No. 183 6" Special Vase   No. 1923 6 1/2" Cream Pitcher   No. 210 5" Rose Bowl   No. 183 6" Vase   7" Special Rose Bowl

Catalog Reprint Circa 1938-1939
Courtesy Of: The Fenton Art Glass Museum

183-10" Flared Vase.   183-10" Triangle Vase.   No 1922-7½" Cud Fld. Vase   183-10" Square Vase.   894-10" Tulip Vase.   894-10" Flared Vase.

Cranberry Spiral Optic (1938 – 1940)	Value
Vase, #188-7" flared	125.00 – 150.00
Vase, #188-7½" cupped	125.00 – 150.00
Vase, #188-9½" flared	150.00 – 170.00
Vase, #183-10" flared, regular, special, square, triangle	150.00 – 185.00
Vase, #201-6" cupped, crimped, cupped, flared	65.00 – 75.00
Vase, #894-10" flared, triangle, tulip	175.00 – 200.00
Vase, #895-10" flared	225.00 – 250.00
Vase, #898-11½"	200.00 – 250.00
Vase, #1922-8" cupped flared, flared, square, triangle	225.00 – 250.00
Vase, #1923-6" crimped, flared, square, tulip	60.00 – 70.00
Vase, #1924-4" crimped, flared, square, tulip	50.00 – 65.00
*With blue base 200.00 – 225.00	

Cranberry Spiral Optic (Circa 1950s)	Ware No.	Introduced	Discontinued	Value
Ivy vase	3248-CR	1956	1959	100.00 – 125.00
Vase, 5"	3255-CR	July 1954	1959	75.00 – 95.00
Vase, 6"	3256-CR	1956	1959	75.00 – 95.00
Vase, 6"	3253-CR	July 1954	1960	75.00 – 95.00
Vase, #3001-5"	3160-CR	1950	1960	75.00 – 85.00
Vase, #3001-7"		1950	1952	85.00 – 90.00
Vase, #3003-6"		1950	1952	80.00 – 85.00
Vase, #3003-7"		1950	1952	80.00 – 90.00
Vase, 8" pinch	3252-CR	July 1954	1956	125.00 – 150.00
Vase, 12"	3261-CR	1956	1959	185.00 – 200.00
Vase, 11½"	3264-CR	1956	1960	185.00 – 220.00

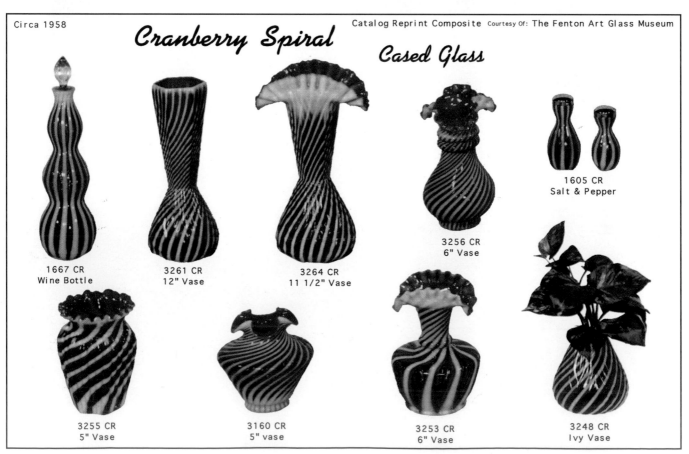

Circa 1958

Cranberry Spiral

Catalog Reprint Composite Courtesy Of: The Fenton Art Glass Museum

Cased Glass

1667 CR
Wine Bottle

3261 CR
12" Vase

3264 CR
11 1/2" Vase

3256 CR
6" Vase

1605 CR
Salt & Pepper

3255 CR
5" Vase

3160 CR
5" vase

3253 CR
6" Vase

3248 CR
Ivy Vase

French Opalescent Spiral Optic

French Opalescent Spiral Optic appeared in Fenton's line for a short period — only during 1939. Since then, the only piece of French Opalescent Spiral to appear in the regular line has been a tumbler which was made in 1985, to accompany the Blue Ridge pitcher. The tumbler to this water set does not have blue trim. Another item which may be found is a lamp shade from the mid-1950s. Some of these escaped from the plant before the bottoms were cut off and will be found masquerading as a vase.

Early records indicate both the #187 pitcher and the #1353 pitcher were sold with the 9 ounce and 12 ounce tumblers as either a seven-piece or nine-piece beverage set. The hurricane shade was available with a crystal, milk, or crystal satin base.

French Opalescent Spiral Optic (1939)	Value
Basket, #1923-6"	50.00 – 55.00
Basket, #201-9"	75.00 – 85.00
Bowl, #1522-9" flared	45.00 – 55.00
Bowl, #1522-10" crimped, 10" oval, 10" square, triangle	50.00 – 60.00
Bowl, #1522-A-10" crimped	50.00 – 60.00
Candleholder, #1523	22.00 – 25.00
Ginger jar, #893 with base and cover	200.00 – 225.00
Hurricane lamp, #170 w/base	75.00 – 95.00
Pitcher, #187	175.00 – 200.00
Pitcher, #1353-9" ice lip	175.00 – 200.00
Rose bowl, #201 crimped	22.00 – 27.00
Rose bowl, 7" #201 special	25.00 – 30.00
Top hat, #1920-12"	100.00 – 150.00
Top hat, #1921-10"	85.00 – 100.00
Top hat, #1922-9"	65.00 – 75.00
Top hat, #1923 6"	30.00 – 35.00
Top hat, #1924-4"	22.00 – 27.00
Tumbler, #187-9 oz.	18.00 – 20.00
Tumbler, #187-12 oz.	25.00 – 30.00
Tumbler, #1353-9 oz.	18.00 – 20.00
Tumbler, #1353-12 oz.	25.00 – 30.00
Vase, #187-7" crimped, flared, triangle	45.00 – 55.00
Vase, #188-7" flared	45.00 – 55.00
Vase, #188-7½" cupped	45.00 – 55.00
Vase, #186-8" crimped, flared, square, triangle, tulip	40.00 – 45.00
Vase, #188-9½" flared	45.00 – 55.00
Vase, #183-10" flared, regular, special, square, triangle	50.00 – 60.00
Vase, #201-6" cupped, crimped, cupped, flared	25.00 – 35.00
Vase, #894-10" flared, triangular, tulip	75.00 – 90.00
Vase, #1523 cornucopia	75.00 – 95.00
Vase, #1922-8" flared, square, triangle	65.00 – 75.00

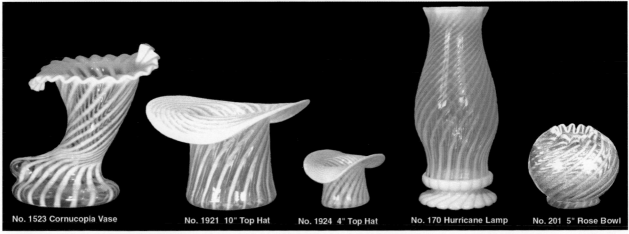

No. 1523 Cornucopia Vase   No. 1921 10" Top Hat   No. 1924 4" Top Hat   No. 170 Hurricane Lamp   No. 201 5" Rose Bowl

Green Opalescent Spiral Optic

Green Opalescent Spiral Optic appeared in Fenton's line for a short period — only during 1939. Since then, no Green Opalescent Spiral Optic has been produced. Green has the smallest variety of pieces listed of all the opalescent Spiral Optic colors. It also appears as if the quantities of these items made were very limited, since today's collectors are having a difficult time finding examples in this color.

An early price list indicates the #1353 pitcher was sold with 12 ounce tumblers as a seven-piece #1353 beverage set. There is no record of the #187 pitcher having been made in this color. The hurricane shade was available with a crystal, milk, or crystal satin base.

Green Opalescent Spiral Optic (1939)	Value	Green Opalescent Spiral Optic (1939)	Value
Basket, #1922-10"	275.00 – 300.00	Top hat, #1924-4"	45.00 – 55.00
Basket, #1924-4½"	90.00 – 100.00	Tumbler, #1353-9 oz.	30.00 – 40.00
Bowl, #1522-9" flare	55.00 – 65.00	Tumbler, #1353-12 oz.	45.00 – 55.00
Bowl, #1522-10" crimped, oval,		Vase, #1924-4" crimped, flared,	
square, triangle	70.00 – 90.00	square, tulip	45.00 – 55.00
Bowl, #1522-A-10" crimped	70.00 – 90.00	Vase, #1923-6" crimped, flared,	
Candleholder, #1523	65.00 – 75.00	square, tulip	60.00 – 70.00
Hurricane lamp, #170 w/base	200.00 – 225.00	Vase, #201-6" cupped, crimped,	
Pitcher, #1353-9" ice lip	300.00 – 325.00	cupped, flared	60.00 – 70.00
Rose bowl, #201 crimped	65.00 – 75.00	Vase, #186-8" crimped, flared, square,	
Rose bowl, #201 special	65.00 – 75.00	triangle, tulip	80.00 – 120.00
Top hat, #1920-12"	275.00 – 300.00	Vase, #1922-8" flared, square, triangle	200.00 – 225.00
Top hat, #1921-10"	250.00 – 275.00	Vase, #1351-9"	200.00 – 225.00
Top hat, #1922-9"	200.00 – 225.00		
Top hat, #1923-6"	60.00 – 70.00		

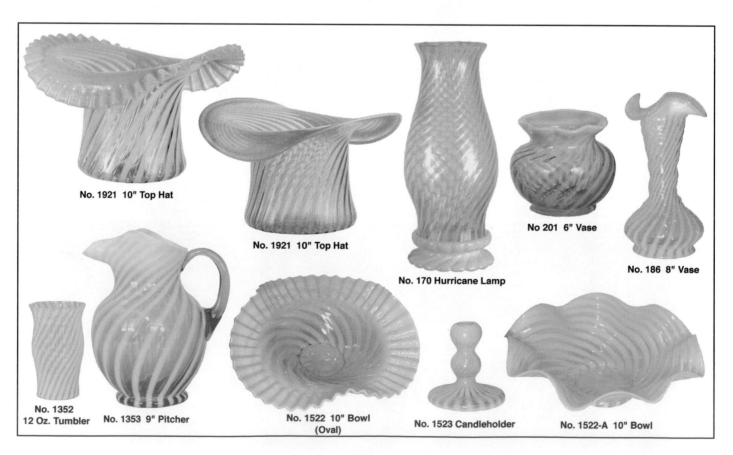

No. 1921 10" Top Hat

No. 1921 10" Top Hat

No. 170 Hurricane Lamp

No 201 6" Vase

No. 186 8" Vase

No. 1352 12 Oz. Tumbler

No. 1353 9" Pitcher

No. 1522 10" Bowl (Oval)

No. 1523 Candleholder

No. 1522-A 10" Bowl

Topaz Opalescent Spiral Optic

Topaz Opalescent is the most elusive of the Spiral Optic opalescent colors. This color does not appear in the Fenton price lists for 1939 and the color is not listed in the 1939 inventory records. It appears that Spiral Optic pattern pieces in this color were made in early 1940. The listing below is limited to the shapes that are known to exist in this color. However, most of the shapes listed in Green Opalescent should also be found in topaz.

Topaz Opalescent Spiral Optic	Value
Barber bottle	350.00 – 375.00
Basket, #1922-10"	325.00 – 350.00
Basket, #1923-6"	125.00 – 145.00
Bowl, #1522-9" flared	80.00 – 100.00
Bowl, #1522-10" crimped, oval, square, triangle	80.00 – 100.00
Bowl, #1522-A-10" crimped	90.00 – 120.00
Candleholder, #1523	75.00 – 90.00
Pitcher, #1353-9" ice lip	300.00 – 375.00
Rose bowl, #201 crimped	75.00 – 85.00
Top hat, #1920-12"	300.00 – 350.00
Top hat, #1921-10"	200.00 – 250.00
Top hat, #1922-9"	150.00 – 200.00
Top hat, #1923-6"	110.00 – 140.00
Top hat, #1924-4"	90.00 – 110.00
Tumbler, #1353-9 oz.	40.00 – 50.00
Tumbler, #1353-12 oz.	50.00 – 60.00
Vase, #183-6"	80.00 – 90.00
Vase, #1925-6"	65.00 – 80.00
Vase, #1924-4" crimped, flared, square, tulip	55.00 – 65.00
Vase, #1923-6" crimped, flared, square, tulip	80.00 – 90.00
Vase, #201-6" cupped, crimped, cupped, flared	70.00 – 80.00
Vase, #186-8" crimped, flared, square, triangle, tulip	100.00 – 130.00
Vase, #1922-8" flared, square, triangle	200.00 – 225.00

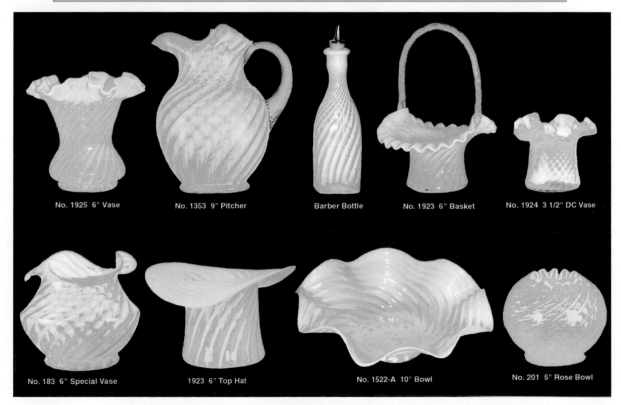

No. 1925 6" Vase   No. 1353 9" Pitcher   Barber Bottle   No. 1923 6" Basket   No. 1924 3 1/2" DC Vase

No. 183 6" Special Vase   1923 6" Top Hat   No. 1522-A 10" Bowl   No. 201 5" Rose Bowl

Spiral Optic Above:

Item	Value
1. Cranberry Opal Satin No. 183-6" vase	80.00 – 90.00
2. French Opalescent No. 183-10" vase in ormolu mount	75.00 – 85.00
3. Cranberry Opalescent DeVilbiss No. S-550 atomizer	140.00 – 165.00
4. Topaz Opalescent DeVilbiss atomizer	85.00 – 100.00
5. Green Opalescent DeVilbiss No. CS-200 atomizer	125.00 – 140.00
6. Cranberry Opalescent Satin No. 170 hurricane lamp	220.00 – 240.00
7. Green Opalescent electric lamp with No. 170 hurricane shade	250.00 – 290.00
8. Cranberry Opalescent No. 3252-8" vase	125.00 – 150.00
9. Blue Opalescent No. 1923-6" basket	100.00 – 125.00
10. Cranberry Opalescent No. 187-9 oz. tumbler	50.00 – 55.00
11. Cranberry Opalescent No. 18 pitcher	400.00 – 500.00

Spiral Optic Photo on Page 265:

Spiral Optic	Value
1. Cranberry Opal No. 1438-8½" bowl	200.00 – 225.00
2. Cranberry Opalescent lamp from No. 894-10" flared vase	150.00 – 175.00
3. French Opal lamp from No. 894-10" flared vase and 6" bonbon	120.00 – 140.00
4. Cranberry Opalescent lamp (Wright)	300.00 – 325.00
5. Blue Opalescent No. 192-8" jug	140.00 – 160.00
6. Cranberry Opalescent No. 192-A 9" jug	200.00 – 225.00
7. Cranberry Opalescent 10" uncut lamp shade vase	225.00 – 250.00
Items 8 through 16 were made for L. G. Wright:	
8. Cranberry Opalescent syrup	300.00 – 325.00
9. Cranberry Opalescent cruet	200.00 – 225.00
10. Cranberry Opalescent short milk jug	110.00 – 130.00
11. Cranberry Opalescent sugar shaker	225.00 – 250.00
12. Cranberry Opalescent Satin tall milk jug	120.00 – 140.00
13. Blue Opalescent barber bottle	250.00 – 275.00
14. Cranberry Opalescent barber bottle	260.00 – 290.00
15. Cranberry Opal tankard-style vase	200.00 – 225.00
16. Blue Opalescent water pitcher	250.00 – 275.00

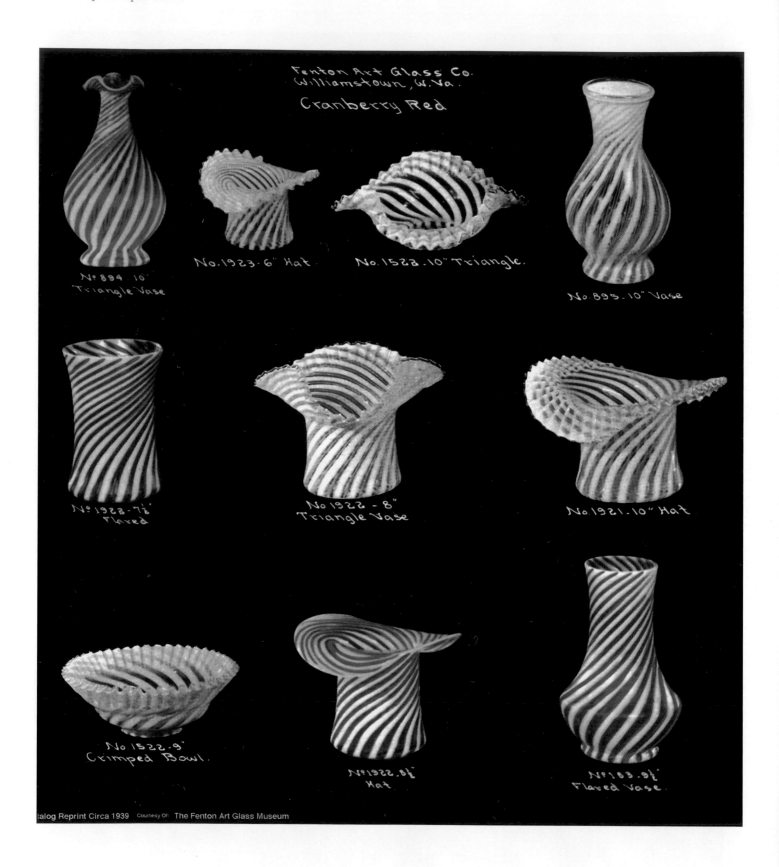

Fenton Art Glass Co.
Williamstown, W. Va.

Cranberry Red

No. 894. 10"
Triangle Vase

No. 1923. 6" Hat

No. 1523. 10" Triangle.

No. 895. 10" Vase

No. 1928. 7½"
Flared

No. 1922 - 8"
Triangle Vase

No. 1921. 10" Hat

No. 1522. 9"
Crimped Bowl.

No. 1922. 8½"
Hat

No. 183. 8½"
Flared Vase.

Catalog Reprint Circa 1939   Courtesy Of: The Fenton Art Glass Museum

266

Supplemental Patterns and Shapes

Block Optic

Fenton's Block Optic is an opalescent pattern that features elongated horizontal blocks of opalescence arranged in vertical rows. Two of the three pieces of Block Optic shown below were listed in a late 1930s catalog in French Opalescent as part of an unusual opalescent assortment along with items in the Ring Optic and Wide Rib Optic patterns. These pieces were probably only made for one year since they do not appear in later catalogs. At this time there is no complete catalog listing of the pieces available. Items in the listing below are known to exist, but more shapes will probably be found.

Block Optic	Value
Ginger jar, #893	300.00 – 350.00
Top hat, #1922-9"	145.00 – 160.00
Vase, #1354-10" crimped top	80.00 – 110.00

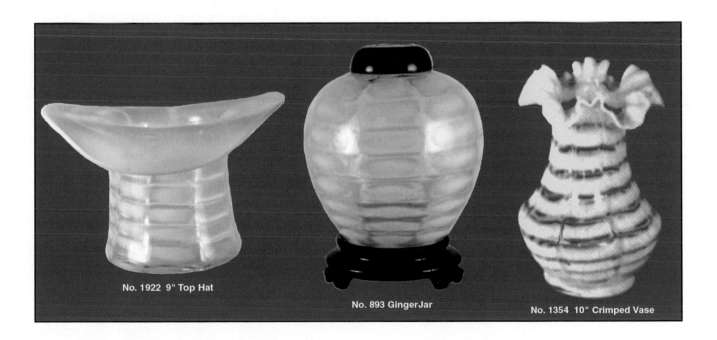

No. 1922 9" Top Hat

No. 893 GingerJar

No. 1354 10" Crimped Vase

Block and Star

The Block and Star pattern was introduced in January 1955. Although some pieces were sampled in other colors, items in the regular line were produced in Fenton's milk and turquoise colors. By July 1956 only three pieces were still in production in turquoise — the bonbon, 10" cupped bowl, and handled candleholders. The turquoise color was discontinued by the end of 1957 and most of the milk glass pieces were out of production by the end of the next year. All pieces of Block and Star except the salt and pepper were discontinued by December 1958. The shaker set in milk remained in the line through December 1965.

The following individual pieces were combined and sold as sets:

No. 5601 console set: No. 5624-9" square bowl and 2 No. 5671 square candleholders
No. 5605 flared console set: No. 5625-11" flared bowl and 2 No. 5672 flared candleholders
No. 5608 cupped console set: No. 5626-10" cupped bowl and 2 No. 5673 cupped candleholders
No. 5600 console set: No. 5626-10" cupped bowl and 2 No. 5670 handled candleholders
No. 5607-7-pc. ice tea set: No. 5667-70 oz. jug and 6 No. 5647-12 oz., tumblers

The sugar and creamer were sold as a set using the 5604 ware number. The salt and pepper combination was Ware Number 5606. A covered condiment jar with a clear glass ladle was sold as the No. 5609 mayonnaise set. The mayonnaise sets were used in combination with glass trays to produce two different condiment sets. The No. 5602 buffet set was made by placing two mayonnaise sets on an elevated glass tray with a glass center handle. The same glass tray, without the base, was inverted for use with the jam and jelly set. A metal handle was used in place of the glass handle.

Most items in the turquoise color are becoming hard to find. This is especially true for sets such as the buffet set and the jam and jelly set. The basket was only made for six months and is elusive in both colors.

Block and Star	Ware No.	Introduced	Discontinued	Value
Basket, handled	5637-MI	July 1955	1956	30.00 – 35.00
Bonbon	5635-MI	1955	1959	10.00 – 12.00
Bowl, 9" square	5624-MI	1955	July 1956	20.00 – 25.00
Bowl, 10" cupped	5626-MI	1955	1959	25.00 – 35.00
Bowl, 11" flared	5625-MI	1955	July 1956	35.00 – 45.00
Buffet set	5602-MI	1955	July 1956	140.00 – 160.00
Candleholder, cupped	5673-MI	1955	1959	15.00 – 20.00
Candleholder, flared	5672-MI	1955	July 1956	15.00 – 20.00
Candleholder, handled	5670-MI	1955	1959	15.00 – 20.00
Candleholder, square	5671-MI	1955	July 1956	16.00 – 20.00
Creamer	5661-MI	1955	1957	12.00 – 14.00
Dessert, cupped	5622-MI	1955	July 1956	12.00 – 14.00
Dessert, flared	5621-MI	1955	July 1956	12.00 – 14.00
Dessert, square	5620-MI	1955	July 1956	12.00 – 14.00
Jam and jelly with tray	5603-MI	1955	1957	85.00 – 100.00
Jug, 70 oz.	5667-MI	1955	1958	100.00 – 125.00
Mayonnaise set	5609-MI	1955	1957	20.00 – 28.00
Relish	5623-MI	1955	July 1956	12.00 – 16.00
Salt and pepper	5606-MI	1955	1966	35.00 – 45.00
Sugar	5627-MI	1955	1957	14.00 – 16.00
Tumbler, 9 oz.	5649-MI	1955	1957	10.00 – 15.00
Tumbler, 12 oz.	5647-MI	1955	1958	15.00 – 22.00
Vase, 8½"	5658-MI	1955	1956	30.00 – 45.00
Vase, 9"	5659-MI	1955	1956	30.00 – 45.00

Scale approximately one-seventh actual size

BLOCK and STAR

FINEST GLASS FOR FIFTY YEARS

A. No. 5671-MI Square Candleholder	**J.** No. 5604-MI Sugar & Cream	**S.** No. 5605-MI Flared Console Set
B. No. 5624-MI 9" Square Bowl	**K.** No. 5661-MI Creamer	**T.** No. 5673-MI Cupped Candleholder
C. No. 5601-MI Square Console Set	**L.** No. 5620-MI Square Dessert	**U.** No. 5608-MI Cupped Console Set
D. No. 5603-MI Jam & Jelly	**M.** No. 5622-MI Cupped Dessert	**V.** No. 5626-MI 10" Cupped Bowl
E. No. 5635-MI Bonbon	**N.** No. 5621-MI Flared Dessert	**W.** No. 5600-MI 3 pc. Console Set
F. No. 5658-MI 8½" Vase	**O.** No. 5659-MI 9" Vase	**X.** No. 5670-MI Handled Candleholder
G. No. 5609-MI Mayonnaise Set	**P.** No. 5602-MI Buffet Set	**Y.** No. 5649-MI 9 oz. Tumbler
H. No. 5606-MI Salt & Pepper	**Q.** No. 5672-MI Flared Candleholder	**Z.** No. 5647-MI 12 oz. Tumbler
I. No. 5627-MI Sugar Bowl	**R.** No. 5625-MI 11" Flared Bowl	**AA.** No. 5667-MI 70 oz. Jug

269

Block and Star	Ware No.	Introduced	Discontinued	Value
Basket, handled	5637-TU	July 1955	1956	70.00 – 90.00
Bonbon	5635-TU	1955	1957	20.00 – 25.00
Bowl, 10" cupped	5626-TU	1955	1957	55.00 – 65.00
Buffet set	5602-TU	1955	July 1956	250.00 – 300.00
Candleholder, cupped	5673-TU	1955	July 1956	20.00 – 25.00
Candleholder, handled	5670-TU	1955	1957	20.00 – 25.00
Creamer	5661-TU	1955	July 1956	20.00 – 25.00
Dessert, cupped	5622-TU	1955	July 1956	15.00 – 18.00
Jam and jelly with tray	5603-TU	1955	July 1956	150.00 – 175.00
Jug, 70 oz.	5667-TU	July 1955	July 1956	200.00 – 225.00
Mayonnaise set	5609-TU	1955	July 1956	50.00 – 60.00
Relish	5623-TU	1955	July 1956	25.00 – 30.00
Salt and pepper	5606-TU	1955	July 1956	65.00 – 75.00
Sugar	5627-TU	1955	July 1956	20.00 – 25.00
Tumbler, 9 oz.	5649-TU	July 1955	July 1956	20.00 – 25.00
Tumbler, 12 oz.	5647-TU	July 1955	July 1956	30.00 – 35.00

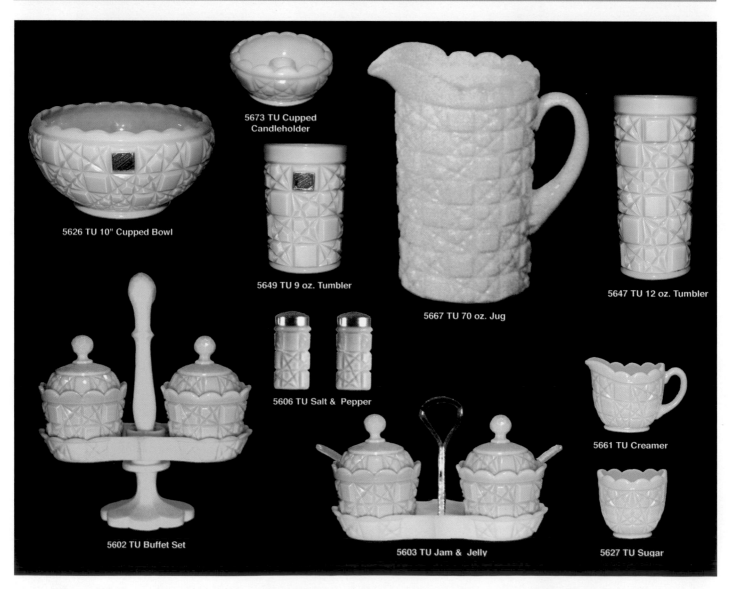

5673 TU Cupped Candleholder

5626 TU 10" Cupped Bowl

5649 TU 9 oz. Tumbler

5667 TU 70 oz. Jug

5647 TU 12 oz. Tumbler

5606 TU Salt & Pepper

5661 TU Creamer

5602 TU Buffet Set

5603 TU Jam & Jelly

5627 TU Sugar

Bubble Optic/Honeycomb

In January 1952, Fenton introduced two different sizes of pinch vases with a Honeycomb pattern. The vases were made in 7½" and 8½" sizes in green overlay and blue overlay colors. Satin finished versions of both vases were also sold. The 7½" vases were discontinued after one year, but the larger vases were made until the end of 1953.

Almost ten years later, in January 1961, Fenton introduced four vases in a similar pattern called Bubble Optic. These new vases were produced in Fenton's new overlay colors — Apple Green (AG), Coral (CL), Honey Amber (HA), Wild Rose (WR), and Powder Blue Overlay (BV). The following year, three of the vases were produced in Fenton's cased dark blue over milk color — Opaque Blue (OB). Fenton's No. 1306-20" Satin Blue Overlay (SB) lamp was introduced in the Bubble Optic pattern in the July 1976 catalog supplement. The lamp was discontinued at the end of 1977. A large Honey Amber jug may also be found. Fenton produced this piece for the B and P Lamp Company of McMinnville, Tennessee.

The price ranges below are for items with good color. The Coral and Wild Rose colors were heat sensitive. If conditions were not exactly right during production, numerous examples turned out with poor color.

Bubble Optic Apple Green	Ware No.	Introduced	Discontinued	Value
Vase, 5"	1350-AG	1961	1962	50.00 – 55.00
Vase, 7½"	1356-AG	1961	1962	55.00 – 60.00
Vase, 8" pinch	1358-AG	1961	1962	75.00 – 85.00
Vasc, 11½"	1359 AG	1961	1962	160.00 – 180.00
Powder Blue Overlay	**Ware No.**	**Introduced**	**Discontinued**	**Value**
Vase, 5"	1350-BV	1961	1962	50.00 – 60.00
Vase, 7½"	1356-BV	1961	1962	60.00 70.00
Vase, 8" pinch	1358-BV	1961	1962	75.00 – 90.00
Vase, 11½"	1359-BV	1961	1962	160.00 – 180.00
Coral	**Ware No.**	**Introduced**	**Discontinued**	**Value**
Vase, 5"	1350-CL	1961	1962	45.00 – 55.00
Vase, 7½"	1356-CL	1961	1962	55.00 – 60.00
Vase, 8" pinch	1358-CL	1961	1962	75.00 – 85.00
Vase, 11½"	1359-CL	1961	1962	185.00 – 210.00

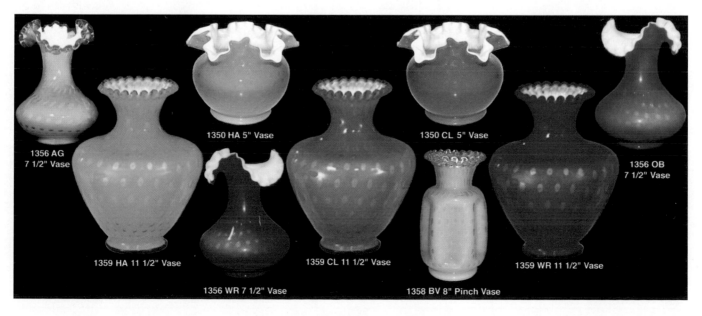

1356 AG 7 1/2" Vase
1350 HA 5" Vase
1350 CL 5" Vase
1356 OB 7 1/2" Vase
1359 HA 11 1/2" Vase
1359 CL 11 1/2" Vase
1359 WR 11 1/2" Vase
1356 WR 7 1/2" Vase
1358 BV 8" Pinch Vase

Honey Amber	Ware No.	Introduced	Discontinued	Value
Vase, 5"	1350-HA	1961	1962	35.00 – 45.00
Vase, 7½"	1356-HA	1961	July 1962	35.00 – 45.00
Vase, 8" pinch	1358-HA	1961	July 1962	45.00 – 50.00
Vase, 11½"	1359-HA	1961	1965	100.00 – 120.00
Satin Blue Overlay	Ware No.	Introduced	Discontinued	Value
Lamp, 20"	1306-SB	July 1976	1978	190.00 – 200.00
Wild Rose	Ware No.	Introduced	Discontinued	Value
Vase, 5"	1350-WR	1961	1962	45.00 – 65.00
Vase, 7½"	1356-WR	1961	1963	65.00 – 70.00
Vase, 8" pinch	1358-WR	1961	July 1962	80.00 – 95.00
Vase, 11½"	1359-WR	1961	1963	200.00 – 250.00
Opaque Blue Overlay	Ware No.	Introduced	Discontinued	Value
Vase, 7½"	1356-OB	1962	1963	60.00 – 80.00
Vase, 8" pinch	1358-OB	1962	1963	60.00 – 80.00
Vase, 11½"	1359-OB	1962	1965	225.00 – 275.00
Honeycomb	Ware No.	Introduced	Discontinued	Value
Vase, #1720-7½" pinch (blue)	1357-BV	1952	1953	50.00 – 60.00
Vase, #1720-7½" pinch (blue satin)	1357-BA	1952	1953	50.00 – 60.00
Vase, #1720-7½" pinch (green)	1357-GV	1952	1953	50.00 – 60.00
Vase, #1720-7½" pinch (green satin)	1357-GA	1952	1953	50.00 – 60.00
Vase, #1721-8½" pinch (blue)	1352 BV	1952	1954	60.00 – 80.00
Vase, #1721-8½" pinch (blue satin)	1352-BA	1952	1954	60.00 – 70.00
Vase, #1721-8½" pinch (green)	1352-GV	1952	1954	60.00 – 80.00
Vase, #1721-8½" pinch (green satin)	1352-GA	1952	1954	60.00 – 70.00

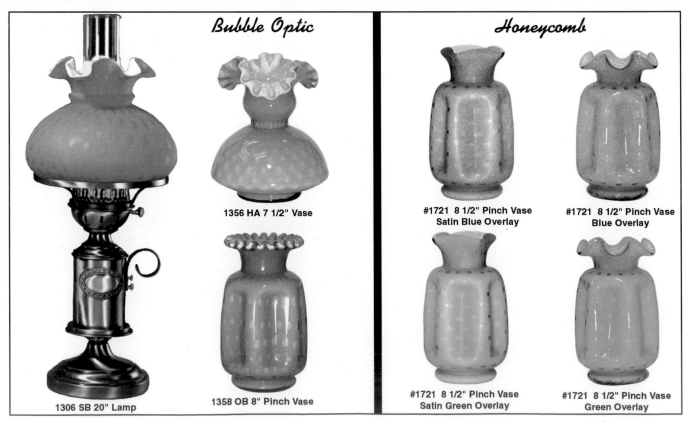

Bubble Optic

1356 HA 7 1/2" Vase

1306 SB 20" Lamp

1358 OB 8" Pinch Vase

Honeycomb

#1721 8 1/2" Pinch Vase
Satin Blue Overlay

#1721 8 1/2" Pinch Vase
Blue Overlay

#1721 8 1/2" Pinch Vase
Satin Green Overlay

#1721 8 1/2" Pinch Vase
Green Overlay

Burred Hobnail

The Burred Hobnail pattern is a minor adaptation of Fenton's regular Hobnail pattern. Burred Hobnail pieces have small burrs at the base of each hob. The original line number of this small pattern was 489.

Only three different pieces were made in Burred Hobnail. All three pieces are listed initially in the price list in three colors — Blue Opalescent, French Opalescent, and milk glass. However, only the witch's kettle was still being made in French Opalescent and Blue Opalescent by the end of 1950. This kettle later entered the line in Blue Pastel, Green Pastel, and Rose Pastel. The kettle is 2½" high and comes with a wire handle. The small child's cup is 2¾" high and 2½" in diameter. This small cup was discontinued after only two years and is not easy to find today. The small hat is 2¾" tall. It was made with burred hobs through December 1956. Then, in the late 1980s, the hat returned for a short time. This last version of the hat will be marked with the Fenton logo.

Milk Glass Burred Hobnail	Ware No.	Introduced	Discontinued	Value
Cup, #489 child's		1950	1952	35.00 – 45.00
Hat, 2¾"	3991-MI	1950	1957	14.00 – 16.00
Witch's kettle	3990-MI	1950	1969	12.00 – 14.00
Opalescent Burred Hobnail	**Blue Opalescent**	**French Opalescent**		
Cup, #489 child's	60.00 – 80.00	45.00 – 55.00		
Hat, #489	25.00 – 30.00	22.00 – 27.00		
Witch's kettle, #489	25.00 – 30.00	14.00 – 18.00		

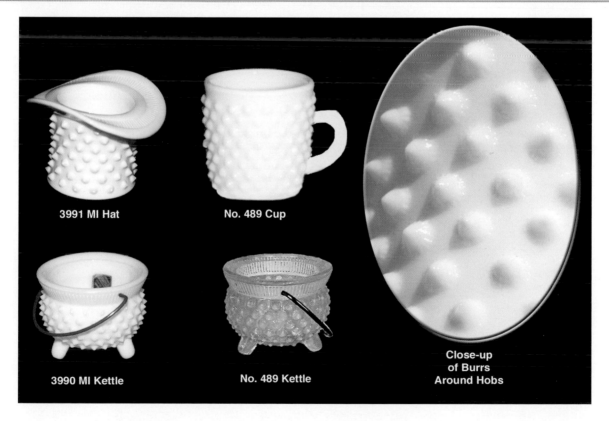

3991 MI Hat   No. 489 Cup

3990 MI Kettle   No. 489 Kettle

Close-up of Burrs Around Hobs

Cactus

Fenton's Cactus pattern, which was inspired from the old Greentown Cactus, was introduced in January 1959 in Topaz Opalescent and milk glass colors. Topaz Opalescent did not sell as well as the milk glass. Therefore, it was discontinued at the end of 1960, but pieces in milk glass continued to be made. All the items in milk glass were discontinued by the end of 1962, with the exception of the No. 3450 bud vase which remained in the line through 1964. Pieces in this pattern were originally made in the early 1900s in a chocolate color by the Greentown plant of the Indiana Tumbler and Goblet Company. Fenton items included new original designs and reproductions of old Greentown pieces. Fenton's early milk glass color was relatively translucent. Beginning in 1959, Cactus was one of the first patterns to experience the use of the new denser white color of milk glass.

The creamer and sugar were listed as the No. 3404 set without a lid. The same sugar and creamer were sold with a lid using No. 3408 as the ware number for the set. The No. 3445 goblet was also made in Colonial Amber, Colonial Blue, and Colonial Pink in 1962.

Cactus was also marketed through Fenton's catalog house sales division masquerading as Desert Tree. More information about Desert Tree will be contained in the Olde Virginia Glass section of the forthcoming book *Fenton Art Glass Colors and Hand-Painted Decorations 1939 – 1980.*

LeVay Distributing Company marketed a 400 set limited edition seven-piece water set in Aqua Opalescent Carnival in 1980. These sets, which were made by Fenton, consisted of a large pitcher and six 10-ounce goblets.

In 1982, the Cactus pattern reappeared in Red Sunset Carnival and Chocolate. The No. 3480 covered cracker jar was made in Chocolate as a part of an assortment produced for the LeVay Distributing Company. Fenton produced the following items in Red Carnival for LeVay:

Basket, 7½" DC w/ribbed looped handle	3436-RN	Cruet	3463-RN
Basket, 10" DC cracker	3431-RN	Cuspidor, ladies'	3426-RN
Basket, 10" DC	3433-RN	Cuspidor, gentlemen's	3427-RN
Basket, 10½" banana w/looped handle	3432-RN	Toothpick	3495-RN
		Vase, DC Jack in Pulpit	3441-RN
Compote, ftd., DC	3429-RN	Vase, 9" swung	3483-RN
Cracker jar, covered	3480-RN	Vase, 10" basket	3434-RN
Cream & covered sugar	3408-RN	Water set (pitcher & 6-10 oz. goblets)	3407-RN

A Topaz Opalescent Cactus water set was offered as part of the limited edition Collector's Extravaganza series for 1988. The set was composed of six 10-ounce goblets and a large water jug. Items from this issue will bear the Fenton logo.

The No. 3488 candy box also reappeared in the line in 1995 and was still being made as late as 1997, in Fenton's popular Dusty Rose color. The candy box was also made in Spruce Green for the 1995 holiday season. In 1997, the No. 3429 comport was issued in a light pink iridescent color called Champagne Satin (PQ) by Fenton.

Cactus	Ware No.	Introduced	Discontinued	Value
Basket, 10"	3430-MI	1959	1960	45.00 – 55.00
Basket, 7" handled	3437-MI	1959	1960	25.00 – 35.00
Basket, 9" handled	3439-MI	1959	1960	45.00 – 55.00
Bonbon, handled	3435-MI	1959	1961	8.00 – 10.00
Bowl, 8"	3424-MI	1959	July 1959	20.00 – 22.00
Bowl, 8" ftd.	3422-MI	1959	1961	25.00 – 30.00
Bowl, 9" oval	3429-MI	1959	July 1960	25.00 – 35.00
Bowl, banana	3425-MI	1959	1960	35.00 – 40.00
Butter, ¼ lb.	3477-MI	1959	1961	20.00 – 30.00
Candleholder	3474-MI	1959	July 1960	18.00 – 22.00
Candy box	3488-MI	1959	1963	25.00 – 30.00
Candy jar	3480-MI	1959	1961	30.00 – 40.00
Creamer and sugar	3404-MI	1959	1960	20.00 – 25.00
Creamer and sugar with lid	3408-MI	1959	1961	38.00 – 47.00

Cactus in Milk

All Cactus items are made in both
Milk Glass and Topaz Opalescent.

Catalog Reprint Courtesy Of: **The Fenton Art Glass Museum**

3401 MI
Epergne Set

3463 MI
Cruet

3439 MI
9" Basket

3408 MI
Cov'd Sugar & Cream

3477 MI
1/4 lb. Cov. Butter

3437 MI
7" Basket

3480 MI
Candy Jar

3445 MI
Goblet

3435 MI
Hdl. Bonbon

3474 MI
Candleholder
Priced per dozen pieces

3406 MI
Salt & Pepper

3424 MI
8" Bowl

3459 MI
6" Fan Vase

3460 MI
Ftd. Vase

3458 MI
9" Vase

3457 MI
7" Vase

3454 MI
5" Vase

3455 MI
5" Vase

3488 MI
Candy Box

Cactus	Ware No.	Introduced	Discontinued	Value
Cruet	3463-MI	1959	1961	30.00 – 32.00
Epergne set	3401-MI	1959	1960	45.00 – 65.00
*Goblet	3445-MI	1959	1963	10.00 – 12.00
Nut dish, ftd.	3428-MI	1959	1963	10.00 – 12.00
Plate, 11"	3411-MI	1959	1960	12.00 – 14.00
Salt and pepper	3406-MI	1959	1963	20.00 – 25.00
Vase, 5"	3454-MI	1959	1961	6.00 – 8.00
Vase, 5"	3455-MI	1959	July 1959	6.00 – 8.00
Vase, 6" fan	3459-MI	1959	1960	15.00 – 20.00
Vase, 7"	3457-MI	1959	1961	10.00 – 12.00
Vase, 7" flared	3456-MI	1959	July 1959	10.00 – 12.00
Vase, 8" bud	3450-MI	July 1959	1965	10.00 – 12.00
Vase, 9"	3458-MI	July 1959	1961	14.00 – 16.00
Vase, medium	3461-MI	July 1959	1961	18.00 – 22.00
Vase, ftd	3460-MI	July 1959	1963	22.00 – 25.00
Vase, tall swung	3452-MI	July 1959	1960	40.00 – 50.00

*Made in Colonial Amber, Colonial Blue, Colonial Pink (1962)

Cactus	Ware No.	Introduced	Discontinued	Value
Basket	3430-TO	1959	1960	140.00 – 180.00
Basket, 7" handled	3437-TO	1959	1960	140.00 – 160.00
Basket, 9" handled	3439-TO	1959	1960	225.00 – 250.00
Bonbon, handled	3435-TO	1959	1961	30.00 – 40.00
Bowl, 8"	3424-TO	1959	July 1959	100.00 – 110.00
Bowl, 8" ftd.	3422-TO	1959	1960	160.00 – 175.00
Bowl, 9" oval	3429-TO	1959	July 1960	165.00 – 185.00
Bowl, banana	3425-TO	1959	1960	185.00 – 200.00
Butter, ¼ lb.	3477-TO	1959	1960	175.00 – 200.00
Candleholder	3474-TO	1959	July 1960	60.00 – 70.00
Candy box	3488-TO	1959	1960	110.00 – 130.00
Candy jar	3480-TO	1959	1960	180.00 – 220.00
Creamer and sugar	3404-TO	1959	1960	100.00 – 120.00
Creamer and sugar with lid	3408-TO	1959	1960	130.00 – 150.00
Cruet	3463-TO	1959	1960	165.00 – 185.00
Epergne set	3401-TO	1959	1960	270.00 – 290.00
Goblet	3445-TO	1959	1961	40.00 – 50.00
Nut dish, ftd.	3428-TO	1959	1961	55.00 – 60.00
Plate, 11"	3411-TO	1959	1960	75.00 – 80.00
Salt and pepper, pr.	3406-TO	1959	1960	100.00 – 125.00
Vase, 5"	3454-TO	1959	1960	60.00 – 70.00
Vase, 5"	3455-TO	1959	July 1959	60.00 – 70.00
Vase, 6" fan	3459-TO	1959	1960	150.00 – 180.00
Vase, 7"	3457-TO	1959	1960	90.00 – 110.00
Vase, 7" flared	3456-TO	1959	July 1959	90.00 – 110.00
Vase, 8" bud	3450-TO	July 1959	July 1960	75.00 – 90.00
Vase, 9"	3458-TO	July 1959	1960	150.00 – 175.00
Vase, medium	3461-TO	July 1959	July 1960	160.00 – 180.00
Vase, ftd.	3460-TO	July 1959	July 1960	160.00 – 180.00
Vase, tall swung	3452-TO	July 1959	1960	225.00 – 250.00

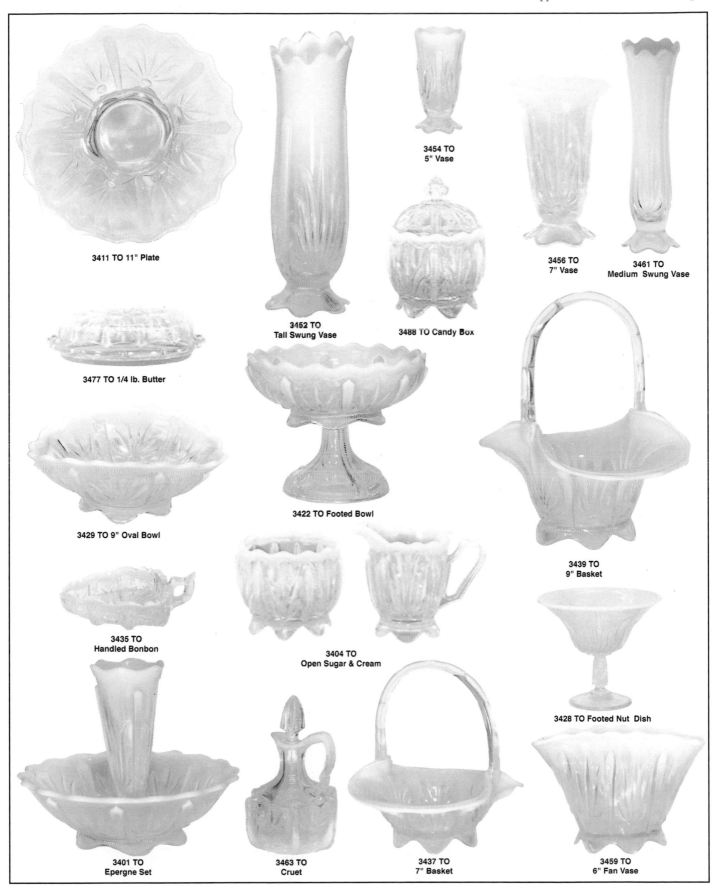

3411 TO 11" Plate

**3454 TO
5" Vase**

**3456 TO
7" Vase**

**3461 TO
Medium Swung Vase**

3477 TO 1/4 lb. Butter

**3452 TO
Tall Swung Vase**

3488 TO Candy Box

3429 TO 9" Oval Bowl

3422 TO Footed Bowl

**3439 TO
9" Basket**

**3435 TO
Handled Bonbon**

**3404 TO
Open Sugar & Cream**

3428 TO Footed Nut Dish

**3401 TO
Epergne Set**

**3463 TO
Cruet**

**3437 TO
7" Basket**

**3459 TO
6" Fan Vase**

Daisy and Button

Fenton's Daisy and Button pattern was originally introduced in 1937 as the No. 1900 Cape Cod Crystal Line. The pattern was offered in crystal and transparent colors between 1937 and 1939. For more information on this early issue of Daisy and Button see page 234 of *Fenton Art Glass 1907 – 1939*.

The Daisy and Button pattern was brought back into the line in July 1953, with the introduction of new pieces in milk glass. Later, other colors and new shapes were added. Various pieces continued to appear in the Fenton catalogs through the 1980s and into the 1990s. Dating pieces can generally be accomplished by noting color and checking for a Fenton logo. Items made after 1970 will have the Fenton logo embossed on the bottom. The color and shape information below will also be useful in helping to date the more recent productions.

The No. 1904-MI three-piece console set was in the catalog from July 1953 through December 1954. The console set was composed of a No. 1920-10½" square bowl and a pair of No. 1974 candleholders.

A few items in this pattern may be in short supply. Note the leaf ashtray was only made for a short time and the candy box in orange was only available for a year. The entire assortment of Blue Pastel Daisy and Button was only made for one year. Items in Green Pastel, Rose Pastel, and Turquoise are not found very often either. In 1968 Fenton made an attempt to revive their 1930s Pekin Blue color. Production problems forced this attempt to make Peking Blue II (BJ) to be abandoned, but a number of items were sampled in Daisy and Button and other patterns. At the same time, a new bright yellow opaque color called Jonquil Yellow (JO) was also sampled. Pieces of both colors may sometimes be found in the secondary market. A later attempt at Pekin Blue in 1980, called Peking Blue (PK), did not include items from this pattern.

During the 1970s Daisy and Button was an important pattern of the Olde Virginia Glass line. More information about the colors and shapes of this pattern that Fenton made for the catalog houses will be forthcoming in the Olde Virginia glass section of the supplemental book for this era: *Fenton Art Glass Colors and Hand-Painted Decorations 1939 – 1980*. Not all of the Daisy and Button items on the secondary market were made by Fenton. Early pieces were made by Hobbs, Brockunier and Company of Wheeling, West Virginia, in the late 1800s. Later, other companies such as Imperial, Mosser, and L. G. Wright also made or sold this pattern.

Fenton items and colors available after 1979 include:

1980

Colored items in Daisy and Button were discontinued by 1980, except for the Custard and Blue Satin bells which continued to be made into the early 1980s. A crystal assortment including the following items appeared in the January 1980 catalog supplement. These items will be marked with the embossed Fenton logo and most should have a tiny "8" included at the base of the logo.

Bell	1967-CY		Bowl, oval	1921-CY
Bowl, 8½" covered	1981-CY		Candleholder	1970-CY
Bowl, 10½"	1925-CY		Slipper	1995-CY

1981

An expanded crystal assortment appeared in the 1981 – 82 general catalog. The offering consisted of the following:

Basket, oval	1939-CY		Candy, covered	1980-CY
Bell	1967-CY		Hat, #1 small	1991-CY
Boot	1990-CY		Hat, #2	1992-CY
Bowl, 10½"	1925-CY		Leaf tray	1976-CY
Bowl, oval	1921-CY		Slipper	1995-CY
Candleholder	1970-CY			

1982

Crystal pieces continued in production and the No. 1939 oval basket and No. 1980 covered candy box were also made in carnival (CN). The No. 1967 bell and No. 1939 oval basket were also made in Ruby from 1982 through 1984.

1983

The two small hats and the leaf tray in crystal were no longer included in the 1983 – 84 general catalog. However, the No. 1760 petite bell was added to the continuing crystal assortment. New items included in this catalog are the No. 1967 bell, the No. 1995 slipper, and the No. 1980 candy in Federal Blue (FB).

1984

The No. 1995 slipper and No. 1939 oval basket were made in Dusty Rose (DK).

1985

The No. 1995 slipper was continued in Dusty Rose (DK). The slipper was also available in Periwinkle Blue (PW) and Sunset Peach (PH) colors. The crystal offering was reduced to the No. 1995 slipper, the No. 1967 bell, and the No. 1980 covered candy.

1986

The only remaining pieces listed in the 1986 general catalog were the No. 1967 bell, the No. 1980 covered candy in crystal, and the No. 1995 slipper in the following colors:

Burmese	1995-BR	Minted Cream	1995-EO
Crystal	1995-CY	Peaches 'n Cream	1995-UO
Dusty Rose	1995-DK	Periwinkle Blue Transparent	1995-PW

1987

The No. 1995 slipper continued to be listed in the 1987 – 88 general catalog in Burmese, Dusty Rose, Minted Cream, and Peaches 'n Cream. The slipper was also made in Colonial Amber (CA) and in the newly introduced Provincial Blue Opalescent (OO) color.

1988

The No. 1995 slipper was made in pearlized opal Shell Pink (PE), greenish blue Teal Royale (OC), cobalt Blue Royale (KK), Provincial Blue Opalescent (OO), Peaches 'n Cream (UO), Dusty Rose, and carnival Teal Marigold (OI) colors.

1989

The No. 1990-4" boot was included in Fenton's carnival Teal Marigold (OI) assortment.

1990 – 99

The No. 1995 slipper was available in Blue Royale (KK) and Dusty Rose in 1900 and 1991. The No. 1990 boot was made for the 1992 Christmas season in Holiday Green (GH). In 1993, the No. 1992-2½" top hat and the slipper were produced in Rose Pearl (DN). The Christmas supplement also included the following items in Holiday Green: No. 1967-5½" bell, No. 1990-6" boot, No. 1925-10" bowl and No. 1975-12" cake plate. Production for the regular line in 1994 was limited to the No. 1995 slipper in Autumn Gold (AM). In 1995, the No. 1936-8" basket was made in Red Carnival (RN). The No. 1995 slipper returned to the line in 1998 in Aquamarine (AA) and Champagne Satin (PQ).

2000 – 03

In 2000, the No. 1995 slipper was made in Aquamarine, Empress Rose Satin (CP) and Cobalt (KN). The No. 1980-6" candy, No. 1967-5½" bell, No. 1931-7½" basket, and the slipper were made in Ice Blue Pearl (L9). Except for the slipper, these same pieces were continued in this color through 2001. In 2001, the slipper was made in Willow Green (GR), Cobalt, Pink Chiffon (PS), and hand-painted Violet (L1). The No. 1980 candy and No. 1967 bell were also made in Empress Rose (CP). In 2002, the slipper was made in Blue Topaz (SY), Pink Chiffon, Willow Green, and Violet (OE). Numerous items returned to the line in 2003 in new colors. The slipper continued in Blue Topaz and was made in a new Rose (N3) color. The No. 1985 covered comport was introduced in Amethyst Carnival (CN). Other items entering the line in French Opalescent (FS) included the No. 1980 candy, No. 1970 candle, No. 1906 salt and pepper, No. 1928-11" bowl and the No. 1903 sugar and creamer. With the exception of the candy, theses pieces were also made in Sunset Stretch (SD).

Amber/Colonial Amber

Daisy and Button	Ware No.	Introduced	Discontinued	Value
Basket, oval	1939-CA	1965	1973	10.00 – 12.00
Bowl, 10½" square	1920-AR	1959	July 1959	25.00 – 30.00
Boot	1990-CA	1967	1975	12.00 – 14.00
Candy box	1980-CA	1968	1974	25.00 – 35.00
Leaf ashtray	1976-CA	1968	1970	8.00 – 10.00

Blue Satin Daisy and Button	Ware No.	Introduced	Discontinued	Value
Bell	1966-BA	1973	1980+	25.00 – 35.00
Boot	1990-BA	1973	1977	20.00 – 22.00

Blue Pastel Daisy and Button	Ware No.	Introduced	Discontinued	Value
Bootee	1994-BP	1954	1955	30.00 – 35.00
Vase, 8" ftd. cupped	1957-BP	1954	1955	50.00 – 60.00
Vase, 9" ftd. fan	1959-BP	1954	1955	50.00 – 60.00

Carnival Daisy and Button	Ware No.	Introduced	Discontinued	Value
Bell	1966-CN	1971	1976	27.00 – 35.00
Boot	1990-CN	1970	1975	20.00 – 22.00

Colonial Blue Daisy and Button	Ware No.	Introduced	Discontinued	Value
Basket, oval	1939-CB	1965	1970	12.00 – 15.00
Boot	1990-CB	1967	1975	20.00 – 25.00
Candy box	1980-CB	1968	1971	45.00 – 50.00
Leaf ashtray	1976-CB	1968	1970	12.00 – 14.00

Colonial Green Daisy and Button	Ware No.	Introduced	Discontinued	Value
Basket, oval	1939-CG	1965	1973	10.00 – 12.00
Boot	1990-CG	1967	1975	18.00 – 20.00
Candy box	1980-CG	1968	1974	35.00 – 40.00
Leaf ashtray	1976-CG	1968	1970	8.00 – 10.00

Colonial Pink Daisy and Button	Ware No.	Introduced	Discontinued	Value
Boot	1990-CP	1967	1969	18.00 – 20.00

Custard Daisy and Button	Ware No.	Introduced	Discontinued	Value
Bell	1966-CU	1972	1980+	20.00 – 22.00
Boot	1990-CU	1972	1977	12.00 – 15.00

French Opalescent Satin

Daisy and Button	Ware No.	Introduced	Discontinued	Value
Candleholder, 2-light	1974-FA	1954	1955	45.00 – 50.00

Green Pastel Daisy and Button	Ware No.	Introduced	Discontinued	Value
Bootee	1994-GP	1954	1955	30.00 – 35.00
Vase, 8" ftd. cupped	1957-GP	1954	1956	50.00 – 60.00
Vase, 9" ftd. fan	1959-GP	1954	1956	50.00 – 60.00

Scale approximately one-seventh actual size

Catalog Reprint Circa 1955   Courtesy Of: **The Fenton Art Glass Museum**

DAISY and BUTTON

FINEST GLASS FOR FIFTY YEARS

A. No. 1959-MI 9" Ftd. Fan Vase
B. No. 1994-MI Bootee
C. No. 1995-MI Slipper
D. No. 1957-MI 8" Ftd. Vase
E. No. 1903-MI Sugar & Cream
F. No. 1958-MI 8" Ftd. Vase
G. No. 1929-MI 9" Oval Bowl
H. No. 1974-MI 2-Lt. Candleholder

I. No. 1927-MI 7" Cupped Bowl
J. No. 1953-MI 3" Vase
K. No. 1954-MI 4" Vase
L. No. 1920-MI 10½" Square Bowl
M. No. 1993-MI #3 Hat
N. No. 1992-MI #2 Hat
O. No. 1935-MI 5" Basket
P. No. 1922-MI Ftd. Bowl

Q. No. 1937-MI 5½" Bonbon
R. No. 1956-MI 6" Vase
S. No. 1936-MI 6" Basket
T. No. 1926-MI Ftd. Bowl
U. No. 1924-MI Ftd. Bowl
V. No. 1955-MI Ftd. Vase

281

Lime Sherbet Daisy and Button	Ware No.	Introduced	Discontinued	Value
Bell	1966-LS	1973	1980	20.00 – 25.00
Boot	1990-LS	1973	1977	15.00 – 20.00

Milk Glass Daisy and Button	Ware No.	Introduced	Discontinued	Value
Basket, 4"	1934-MI	July 1953	1955	18.00 – 20.00
Basket, 5"	1935-MI	July 1953	1956	20.00 – 25.00
Basket, 6"	1936-MI	July 1953	1958	25.00 – 30.00
Basket, oval	1939-MI	1965	1974	12.00 – 14.00
Bonbon, 5½"	1937-MI	July 1953	July 1956	6.00 – 8.00
Boot	1990-MI	1967	1975	10.00 – 12.00
Bootee	1994-MI	July 1953	July 1956	25.00 – 30.00
Bowl, round ftd.	1922-MI	1954	1960	27.00 – 32.00
Bowl, crimped, ftd.	1924-MI	1954	1961	27.00 – 32.00
Bowl, cupped, ftd.	1926-MI	1954	July 1956	28.00 – 35.00
Bowl, 7" cupped	1927-MI	July 1953	1959	20.00 – 25.00
Bowl, 9" oval	1929-MI	July 1953	1959	25.00 – 30.00
Bowl, 10½" square	1920-MI	July 1953	1963	25.00 – 30.00
Candleholder, 2-light	1974-MI	July 1953	1963	18.00 – 20.00
Candy box	1980-MI	1969	1974	30.00 – 35.00
Creamer and sugar	1903-MI	July 1953	July 1956	20.00 – 25.00
Hat, #1	1991-MI	July 1953	1955	10.00 – 12.00
Hat, #2	1992-MI	July 1953	1956	12.00 – 14.00
Hat, #3	1993-MI	July 1953	July 1956	18.00 – 20.00
Vase, 3"	1953-MI	July 1953	1956	8.00 – 10.00
Vase, 4"	1954-MI	July 1953	1965	10.00 – 12.00
Vase, ftd.	1955-MI	1954	July 1959	35.00 – 40.00
Vase, 6"	1956-MI	July 1953	July 1956	18.00 – 22.00
Vase, 8" ftd. cupped	1957-MI	July 1953	1959	20.00 – 25.00
Vase, 9" flared, ftd.	1958-MI	July 1953	1961	25.00 – 30.00
Vase, 9" ftd. fan	1959-MI	July 1953	1962	28.00 – 30.00

Orange Daisy and Button	Ware No.	Introduced	Discontinued	Value
Basket, oval	1939-OR	1965	1970	12.00 – 14.00
Boot	1990-OR	1967	1975	15.00 – 18.00
Candy box	1980-OR	1969	1970	30.00 – 35.00
Leaf ashtray	1976-OR	1969	1970	6.00 – 8.00

Orange Carnival Daisy and Button	Ware No.	Introduced	Discontinued	Value
Bell	1966-CO	July 1971	1974	30.00 – 35.00
Boot	1990-CO	1972	1974	25.00 – 28.00

Rose Pastel Daisy and Button	Ware No.	Introduced	Discontinued	Value
Bootee	1994-RP	1954	1955	30.00 – 35.00
Vase, 8" ftd. cupped	1957-RP	1954	July 1956	45.00 – 55.00
Vase, 9" ftd. fan	1959-RP	1954	July 1956	45.00 – 55.00

Turquoise Daisy and Button	Ware No.	Introduced	Discontinued	Value
Bowl, 7" cupped	1927-TU	1955	July 1956	35.00 – 40.00
Bowl, 9" oval	1929-TU	1955	July 1956	45.00 – 55.00
Vase, 8" ftd. cupped	1957-TU	1955	July 1956	50.00 – 60.00
Vase, 9" ftd. fan	1959-TU	1955	July 1956	50.00 – 60.00

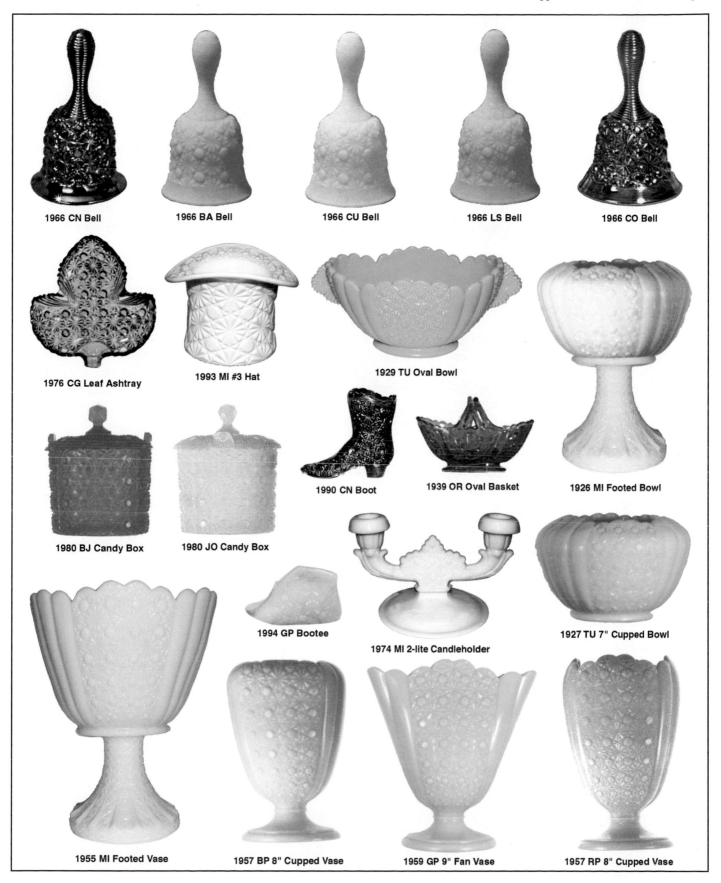

1966 CN Bell   1966 BA Bell   1966 CU Bell   1966 LS Bell   1966 CO Bell

1976 CG Leaf Ashtray

1993 MI #3 Hat

1929 TU Oval Bowl

1980 BJ Candy Box

1980 JO Candy Box

1990 CN Boot

1939 OR Oval Basket

1926 MI Footed Bowl

1994 GP Bootee

1974 MI 2-lite Candleholder

1927 TU 7" Cupped Bowl

1955 MI Footed Vase

1957 BP 8" Cupped Vase

1959 GP 9" Fan Vase

1957 RP 8" Cupped Vase

Diamond Lace

The Diamond Lace pattern was introduced in 1948 as the No. 1948 line. Bowls and epergne sets were produced in French Opalescent and Blue Opalescent colors with either an aqua or silver crest. The 12" bowl was made with and without holes. The version with holes was used with the epergne set.

Starting in 1949, the epergne set, 12" bowl with the plain bottom, and the cornucopia candle were offered in French Opalescent with an Emerald crest. Production of the 12" epergne set in this color combination continued until January 1955. As indicated in the listing below, a number of items were also introduced in French Opalescent and in Blue Opalescent.

In 1950, the cornucopia candle was replaced by the low candle. Also in 1950, the 10" apartment-size epergne set was introduced into the line in milk glass. It had appeared in the A. L. Randall catalog the previous year. Production of this color continued through 1956. This size epergne set was also made in Opaque Turquoise from 1955 through 1956. Production of this size epergne set in Blue Opalescent was discontinued after 1954, but the set was still made in French Opalescent until 1956.

The No. 4802 two-piece epergne set was discontinued in Blue Opalescent after 1954, but production of this set continued in French Opalescent until July 1956. Starting in 1957, this set was made in milk glass. Production in milk glass continued until the end of 1964.

A number of items have been made in the Diamond Lace pattern in recent years. Included are new colors and shapes which were not a part of the original production.

The No. 4801-10" apartment-size epergne set was made in Topaz Opalescent during the late 1960s for the A. A. Importing Company of St. Louis, Missouri. This production of the epergne set is not marked with the Fenton logo.

The No. 4801 4-piece epergne set reappeared in the Fenton line in 1981 in the soft, iridescent pink pastel Velva Rose (VR) color. Topaz Opalescent was the color of choice for this epergne set in the limited edition Collector's Extravaganza offering for 1988. This same 4-piece epergne set made an appearance in the Elizabeth Collection with the revival of Silver Crest in January 1989. That same year, the set was included in Fenton's iridescent Teal Marigold and Persian Blue Opalescent assortments. Later, this epergne set was also included as part of the limited edition Historical Collection in 1992. The new color for this piece was an iridescent topaz opalescent color called Gold Pearl. Also, from 1990 through 1992, the No. 4801 epergne was produced for the regular line in milk glass with a silver crest.

A new 4-piece epergne set in Green Opalescent — No. 4809 — was made in 1985 as part of the Connoisseur Collection. This set was limited in production to 1,000 pieces. In 1986, this epergne set was made in Burmese (BR).

In 1987, the 2-piece epergne set was produced exclusively for Fenton's Gracious Touch division in Sapphire Blue Opalescent with Mother-of-Pearl iridescence. The ware number for this item was Q4805-IA.

The Diamond Lace pattern has also appeared in the 1990s in the popular Dusty Rose color. The 1995 and 1996 catalogs display the No. 4835-DK 9½" basket and the No. 4854-DK 6½" comport in this color.

Some new shapes in the Diamond Lace pattern were created and produced as part of the 1996 Historical Collection. The five pieces made as part of this collection in the Opaline (TG) color include:

Basket, 6"	No. 4833-TG	Epergne set, mini 2-pc	No. 4806-TG
Basket, 9½"	No. 4835-TG	Epergne set, 10" 4-pc.	No. 4808-TG
Comport, 6½"	No. 4854-TG		

The No. 4833 basket reappeared in the line again in 1998 in the Empress Rose (CP) color. It was joined by a basket in the Aquamarine (AA) color in 1999. Both colors were discontinued at the end of 1999. During 2001 and 2002, this basket was made in Daisy Lane (YW). Fenton's Daisy Lane color is French Opalescent with a Pink Chiffon crest and handle. Ware numbers for items made after July 1952 are as follows:

Item	Ware No.	Item	Ware No.
Bowl, 9½"	4824	Console set, (9½" bowl and 2 low candles)	4804
Candlestick, low	4874	Epergne set, 10" apartment size	4801
Comport, covered	4881	Epergne set, 2-pc.	4802
Comport, ftd. double crimped	4825	Epergne set, 12"	4808

Diamond Lace	Introduced	Discontinued	French Opal w/ Aqua Crest	Blue Opal w/Silver Crest
Basket, #1948-12" handled	1948	1950	200.00 – 225.00	250.00 – 300.00
Bowl, #1948-12" crimped w/plain btm.	1948	1951	75.00 – 85.00	85.00 – 95.00
Cake plate, #1948-14"	1948	1951	100.00 – 125.00	100.00 – 125.00
Candlestick, #1948 cornucopia	1949	1950	42.00 – 47.00	45.00 – 50.00
Comport, #1948 ftd. double crimped	1949	1954	65.00 – 85.00	75.00 – 95.00

No. 1948 4-Piece Epergne Set

No. 1948 6 1/2"
DC Vase

No. 1948 4-Piece Epergne Set

No. 1948 Low
Candlestick

No. 1948 9 1/2" Bowl

No. 1948 Low
Candlestick

No. 1948 A
Cornucopia Candlestick

No. 1948 8 1/2" Footed Plate

No. 1948 Footed
DC Comport

No. 1948 Low
Candlestick

No. 1948 14" Cakeplate

No. 1948 2-Piece Epergne Set

No. 1948 4-Piece Epergne Set

Diamond Lace	Introduced	Discontinued	French Opal w/ Aqua Crest	Blue Opal w/Silver Crest
Comport, #1948 ftd. rolled edge	1949	1950	75.00 – 90.00	100.00 – 125.00
Epergne set, #1948 4-pc. (12" bowl)	1948	1955	185.00 – 200.00	200.00 – 225.00

Diamond Lace	Introduced	Discontinued	Blue Opalescent	French Opalescent
Bowl, #1948-9½"	1950	1954	60.00 – 75.00	30.00 – 45.00
Bowl, #1948-A-10" double crimped	1949	1951	75.00 – 80.00	30.00 – 45.00
Cake plate, #1948-A-11"	1949	1951	70.00 – 90.00	40.00 – 45.00
Candlestick, 1948-A cornucopia	1949	1950	35.00 – 45.00	25.00 – 35.00
Candlestick, #1948 low	1950	1954	25.00 – 30.00	15.00 – 18.00
Comport, #1948 ftd. covered	1949	1953	100.00 – 125.00	65.00 – 85.00
*Epergne set, #1948 2-pc. ftd.	1950	1957	100.00 – 125.00	75.00 – 90.00
**Epergne set, #1948-A (10" apartment size)	1949	1957	165.00 – 190.00	100.00 – 125.00
Plate, #1948-8½" ftd. (cake plate)	1949	1952	125.00 – 145.00	60.00 – 110.00
Salver, 10" #1948-A	1949	1950	75.00 – 85.00	35.00 – 45.00
Vase, #1948-6½" ftd. fan	1949	1951	65.00 – 85.00	35.00 – 45.00
Vase, #1948-6½" ftd. double crimped	1949	1951	45.00 – 55.00	30.00 – 35.00

*Milk glass 30.00 – 40.00
**Milk glass 35.00 – 40.00; Turquoise 45.00 – 55.00

French Opalescent w/Emerald Crest

Diamond Lace	Introduced	Discontinued	Value
Bowl, #1948-12" crimped w/plain bottom	1949	1952	75.00 – 85.00
Cake plate, #1948-14"	1950	1952	125.00 – 145.00
Candlestick, #1948 cornucopia	1949	1950	40.00 – 45.00
Epergne set, #1948 4-pc. (12" bowl)	1949	1955	225.00 – 275.00

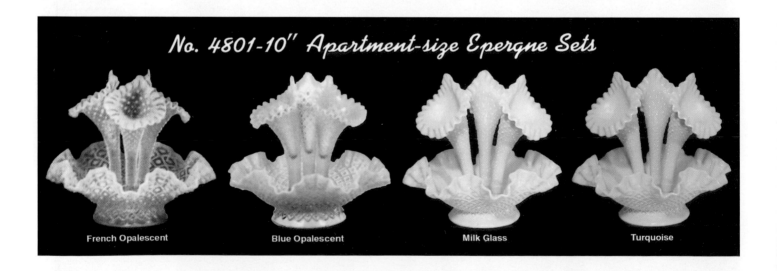

No. 4801-10" Apartment-size Epergne Sets

French Opalescent   Blue Opalescent   Milk Glass   Turquoise

Computer Colorized Catalog Reprint
Courtesy Of
The Fenton Art Glass Museum

No. 1948
6 1/2" Footed Fan Vase

No. 1948A
Cornucopia Candlestick

No. 1948A
Epergne Set
(Apartment size)

No. 1948A
Cornucopia Candlestick

No. 1948
6 1/2" Footed DC Vase

No. 1948A
10" Salver

No. 1948
Footed Comport Rolled Edge

No. 1948
10" DC Bowl

No. 1948
Footed DC Comport

No. 1948
Footed Covered Comport

No. 1948 14" Cake Plate

No. 1948
12" Bowl

No. 1948
8 1/2" Footed Plate

287

Diamond Optic in Mulberry

Fenton first introduced glassware in the Diamond Optic pattern in 1927. Various shapes were made in iridescent. opaque, and transparent colors through the late 1930s. For more information on this early version of Diamond Optic, see page 250 of *Fenton Art Glass 1907 – 1939*.

Although interest in the traditional colors in Diamond Optic began to diminish by the late 1930s, the pattern was not forgotten. In 1942, the Diamond Optic pattern made a comeback in Fenton's new mold-blown cased Mulberry color. The same light blue color that was used for the trim on Aqua Crest was used for the exterior layer. The interior layer was Gold Ruby. Diamond Optic in Mulberry was discontinued by the end of 1942.

When the Mulberry color returned to the line almost 50 years later in 1989, Fenton announced the reintroduction with the following colorful description: "Mulberry is a blend of gold ruby and azure blue skillfully combined to bring you an exciting lavender glass which shades to a lustrous cranberry edge."

New pieces from the January 1989 supplement included:

Basket, 8" Coin Dot	1434-MG	Vase, 11½" Diamond Quilted	9139-MG
Basket, 10½" Jacqueline	9139-MG	Vase, 7¾" Daffodil	9752-MG
Bowl, 9½" Jacqueline	9165-MG	Vase, 6" Caprice	9754-MG
Lamp, 20" Rose	9218-MG	Vase, 6" Beaded Melon	2557-MG
Pitcher, 32 oz. Coin Dot	1432-MG	Vase, 7½"	9655-MG

The June 1989 supplement added:

Bowl, 9½" Jacqueline	9442-MG	Vase, 4½" Jacqueline	9452-MG
Jug, Daisy	2556-MG	Vase, 10" tulip Fine Dot	1353-MG
Lamp, 34" Coin Dot	1415-MG		

Mulberry was continued in 1990 with the following pieces:

Vase, tulip	1353-MG	Vase, Coin Dot	1432-MG
Vase	3161-MG		

In 1992, Mulberry was used in Fenton Family Signature series for the No. CV021 8T-11" Spiral vase with Don Fenton's signature.

Four pieces of the Mulberry color returned to the line in 2003 as part of the limited edition Honor Collection. The No. 3284-M5 7½" hand-painted basket and the No. 3244-M5 9" vase were limited to 1950 each. Limits of 2500 were placed on a No. 6341-6" Drapery pitcher signed by George Fenton and a hand-painted No. 3087-5½" vase signed by Bill Fenton.

Mulberry (1942)	Value	Mulberry (1942)	Value
Basket, #192-10½" handled	300.00 – 350.00	Lamp base, #192-4" handled	300.00 – 325.00
Basket, #203-7" handled	200.00 – 225.00	Puff box, #192-A	200.00 – 225.00
Basket, #1924-4" handled	100.00 – 125.00	Top hat, #1924-4"	125.00 – 150.00
Bottle, #192 squat cologne	115.00 – 135.00	Tumbler, #1353-10 oz.	75.00 – 90.00
Bottle, #192-5½"	115.00 – 135.00	Vanity set, #192-A 3-pc.	430.00 – 495.00
Bottle, #192-7"	170.00 – 190.00	Vase, #192-5" cupped flared,	
Bottle, #192-A cologne	115.00 – 135.00	double crimped	70.00 – 90.00
Bowl, #192-10½" DC	125.00 – 150.00	Vase, #192-5" DC, oval, square,	
Bowl, #203-7" DC	75.00 – 95.00	triangle	70.00 – 80.00
Candlestick, #192 squat	75.00 – 90.00	Vase, #192-6" regular	65.00 – 85.00
Creamer, #1924-5"	90.00 – 110.00	Vase, #192-6" DC, square	65.00 – 85.00
Decanter, #192 large	800.00 – 900.00	Vase, #192-6" triangle, tulip	65.00 – 75.00
Hand vase, #193-11"	550.00 – 600.00	**Vase, #192-8" DC, square,	
Jug, #192 squat	185.00 – 225.00	triangle, tulip	140.00 – 185.00
Jug, #192-6" handled	100.00 – 125.00	Vase, #192-9" crimped	150.00 – 175.00
Jug, #192-8" handled	200.00 – 225.00	Vase, #1353-9" DC, triangle	250.00 – 300.00
*Jug, #192-A-9" handled	200.00 – 250.00		
Jug, #1353-70 oz.	500.00 – 550.00		

*with Charleton Enameled Roses decoration $225.00 – 275.00
**with Charleton Enameled Roses decoration $200.00 – 225.00

No. 1924 5" Top Hat

No. 203 7" Basket

No. 192 10 1/2" Basket

No. 193 11" Hand Vase

No. 192 4" Lamp

No. 192 8" Triangle Vase

No. 192 8" Crimped Vase

No. 1924 5" Top Hat

No. 1353 4" Tumbler

No. 1353 70 Oz. Jug

No. 192 5 1/2" Squat Jug

No. 192 6" Tulip Vase

No. 192 6" Crimped Vase

No. 192 9" Vase

No. 192 9" Jug

No. 192 Decanter

No. 192 5 1/2" Bottle

No. 192 7" Bottle

No. 192 6" Jug

No. 1924 Creamer

Diamond Optic in Ruby Overlay

Fenton's Diamond Optic pattern was introduced in a cased ruby color called Ruby Overlay in 1942. Ruby Overlay is Fenton's name for a non-opalescent cranberry color that combines an interior layer of Gold Ruby with an exterior layer of crystal. In early catalogs Fenton refers to this color as a "cased glass of coin gold cranberry and crystal." Numerous pieces were made in the original production period from 1942 through the end of 1948.

A few other shapes of Ruby Overlay Diamond Optic were made in the early 1950s. One of these pieces was the No. 170 hurricane lamp. The hurricane lamps had a ruby overlay shade and a milk glass base.

Various other shapes including a number of pieces in the Dot Optic and Polka Dot patterns were made in Ruby Overlay beginning in July 1956 when the color was reintroduced into the line. Manufacture of items in this second era of Ruby Overlay production continued through the mid-1970s. Items made in the Dot Optic pattern will be found listed in the Dot Optic and Polka Dot sections later in this book. More information about other pieces of this later issue of Ruby Overlay will be found in the forthcoming book, *Fenton Art Glass: Colors and Hand-Decorated Patterns 1939 – 1980*.

The No. 1353-70 oz. jug and No. 1353 tumblers were often combined and offered as sets. Fenton sold these sets in two different assortments. One included six tumblers with the pitcher and a larger set was bundled with eight tumblers.

Ruby Overlay Diamond Optic vanity sets made an appearance with the introduction of this color in 1942. Several combinations of vanity sets may be found. The original No. 192-A vanity sets appeared in the catalog with two small cologne bottles and the puff box. Two squat cologne bottles were also sold in combination with this same puff box as a No. 192 vanity set. The squat cologne bottle is shaped like the small round colognes; however, it is larger. The squat cologne was also sold without a stopper for use as a candleholder. The opening of the candleholder is slightly larger to fit a candle and is not ground to fit a stopper. The 5½" tall cologne bottles were also used with the small puff box to form a vanity set. The larger 7" bottle may sometimes be found used in sets with the large No. 192 bath salts or candy box. These larger types of bottles and puff box combinations are sometimes found in hand-decorated vanity sets that were decorated by other companies.

Diamond Optic (Ruby Overlay)	Introduced	Discontinued	Value
Basket, #192-10½" handled	1942	1949	125.00 – 150.00
Basket, #192-7" handled	1942	1943	55.00 – 75.00
Basket, #201-10" handled	1946	1947	125.00 – 165.00
Basket, #203-7" handled	1942	1949	55.00 – 75.00
Basket, #1924-4" handled	1942	1949	65.00 – 75.00
Bottle, #192-5½"	1942	1949	55.00 – 65.00
Bottle, #192-7"	1942	1949	65.00 – 70.00
Bottle, #192 squat cologne	1942	1949	60.00 – 70.00
Bottle, #192-A cologne or vanity bottle	1942	1949	50.00 – 70.00
Bowl, #192-10½" double crimped	1942	1949	55.00 – 65.00
Bowl, #203-7" double crimped	1942	1949	25.00 – 35.00
Candleholder, #192 squat	1942	1949	30.00 – 35.00
Creamer, #1924 with crystal handle	1942	1946	35.00 – 40.00
Decanter			350.00 – 400.00
Hurricane lamp, #170	1951		130.00 – 175.00
Jar, #192 covered candy or bath powder	1943	1949	80.00 – 100.00
Jug, #192 squat	1942	1946	60.00 – 70.00
Jug, #192-5½" handled	1943	1949	35.00 – 45.00
Jug, #192-6" handled	1942	1949	45.00 – 55.00
Jug, #192-8" handled	1942	1949	50.00 – 65.00
Jug, #192-A-9" handled	1943	1949	85.00 – 125.00
Jug, #1353-70 oz.	1942	1949	200.00 – 250.00
Lamp base, #192-4" handled	1942	1943	100.00 – 125.00
Puff box, #192-A	1942	1949	30.00 – 40.00
Top hat, #1924-4"	1942	1949	30.00 – 35.00
Tumbler, #1353-10 oz.	1942	1949	25.00 – 27.00
Vanity set, #192-A 3-pc.	1942	1949	130.00 – 180.00
Vase, #192-5" square, triangular	1942	1949	30.00 – 35.00
Vase, #192-5" cupped flared, double crimped	1942	1949	30.00 – 35.00
Vase, #192-5½" double crimped, square	1943	1949	25.00 – 30.00
Vase, #192-5½" triangular, tulip	1943	1949	25.00 – 30.00

No. 192-A 9" Jug

No. 192-A 9" Vase

No. 1353 70 Oz. Jug

No. 1353 10 Oz. Tumbler

No. 1924 5" Basket

No. 170 Hurricane Lamp

No. 192 8" Vase

No. 192 8" Jug

No. 192 6" Vase

No. 192 6" Jug

No. 192 5 1/2" Vase

No. 192 5 1/2" Jug

No. 203 7" DC Bowl

No. 192 5" Top Hat

No. 1924 5" Vase

No. 1924 Creamer

No. 192 Squat Jug

No. 203 7" Basket

1771 RO Barber Bottle

No. 192 5" Vase

No 192 Squat Candleholder

No. 192 6" Regular Vase

No. 192 Decanter

No. 192 10 1/2" Basket

Diamond Optic (Ruby Overlay)	Introduced	Discontinued	Value
Vase, #192-6" regular	1942		30.00 – 35.00
Vase, #192-6" double crimped	1942	1949	25.00 – 30.00
Vase, #192-6" square, triangular, tulip	1942	1949	30.00 – 35.00
Vase, #192-8" double crimped, square	1942	1949	45.00 – 55.00
Vase, #192-8" triangular, tulip	1942	1949	45.00 – 55.00
Vase, #192-9½" regular	1942		65.00 – 85.00
Vase, #192-A-9" double crimped, square	1943	1949	65.00 – 85.00
Vase, #192-A-9" triangular, tulip	1943	1949	65.00 – 85.00
Vase, #192-10" double crimped, square	1943	1946	75.00 – 100.00
Vase, #192-10" triangular, tulip	1943	1946	75.00 – 100.00
Vase, #1353-9" double crimped, triangular	1942	1945	125.00 – 145.00
Vase, #1924-5"	1946	1947	27.00 – 32.00

Later Ruby Overlay	Ware No.	Introduced	Discontinued	Value
Barber bottle	1771-RO	1957	1959	170.00 – 190.00

Photo below:

Diamond Optic (Ruby Overlay)	Value
1. Lamp produced from mould No. 1353-9" vase	100.00 – 125.00
2. Miniature oil lamp made from mould No.192 squat cologne	80.00 – 100.00
3. Mould No. 192-A-9" jug with Charleton Enameled Roses decoration	150.00 – 175.00
4. Lamp produced for L. G. Wright	185.00 – 200.00

No. 192 Vanity Set

No. 192 Squat Cologne Bottle

No. 192-A Vanity Set

Diamond Optic in Opalescent Colors

Fenton introduced opalescent glassware with a diamond optic pattern in January 1952. The glossy opalescent pieces were called Diamond Optic and the satin items were referred to as Diamond Satin. Satin colors produced were Rose Satin (RA) and Blue Satin (BA). During the same time period, an ivy ball was made in glossy Cranberry (CR) and Lime Opalescent (LO). The base for the ivy ball was milk glass for the Cranberry color and either milk glass or dark green for the Lime Opalescent version. Diamond Satin pieces in the regular line were made in Rose Satin (called Cranberry Satin by today's collectors) and Blue Opalescent Satin. Cranberry Satin was a heat sensitive color and the hue could vary from a light peach to a rich cranberry.

An egg-shaped Diamond Satin cookie canister was introduced in January 1952 in Blue Opalescent and Cranberry Red. The cookie canister came in two sizes — #63-2½ quart and #62-1½ quart. These cookie jars were also made in Amber Frost and Green Frost. The jars were discontinued by July 1952.

Some of the items that were made an the regular line in Diamond Satin will also be found without the satin finish. In most cases these were seconds that were never satinized and may have been sold through the Fenton gift shop.

Additional items shown in the accompanying photograph include lamps and other items made in the opalescent Diamond pattern for other firms. These items are numbered in the picture and will be discussed immediately below the price list for the items that were made for the regular Fenton line.

Later, in the 1980s and 1990s different shapes were made in the Diamond Optic pattern in opalescent colors.

1985

The No. 1738- 5½" basket was made in Green Opalescent (GO) for Fenton's special customers (former Levay customers).

1988

The No. 1778 pitcher was available in the soft opalescent Peaches 'n Cream (UO) color.

1990 – 91

The No. 1799-6" vase, the No. 1739-7" basket, and the No. 1726-10" bowl were in the line in Cranberry Opalescent.

1992 – 93

The following items were made in Cranberry Opalescent:

Basket, 7"	1739-CR	Vase, 4"	1784-CR
Bowl, 10"	1726-CR		

1995

The 1995 catalog showcased Diamond Optic in French Opalescent with Dusty Rose handles and crests featuring a hand-painted pink floral decoration on a French Opalescent Trellis background designed by Martha Reynolds. Pieces included:

*Basket, 5½"	1131-DX	Pitcher, 7"	1132-DX
Lamp, 18"	2793-DX	Vase, 7"	1129-DX

*Family Signature piece inscribed with the signature of Lynn Fenton.

1996

Eight items in the opalescent Diamond Optic pattern in the Teal Opaline color with a hand-painted Blush Rose decoration were incorporated into Fenton's 1996 Historical Collection. The pieces are as follows:

Cruet & stopper, 7"	7701-TE	Vase, 7" pinch	1146-TE
Lamp, 24"	1705-TE	*Vase, 8½"	5357-TE
Pitcher, 6½"	5367-TE	Vase, 11" Feather	1795-TE

*Family Signature piece inscribed with the signature of George Fenton.

The hand-painted floral pattern on a French Opalescent Diamond Optic Trellis accented with Dusty Rose trim that was introduced in 1995 continued with the addition of several new pieces. The No. 1131-DX basket was discontinued, but the following items were added:

Basket, 8" Lily	1144-DX	Hurricane Lamp, 11"	7608-DX
Bell, 6½"	1145-DX	Lamp, 24" Gone with the Wind	1703-DX

1997

The hand-painted Trellis decoration in the 1997 catalog featured several new opalescent Diamond Optic pieces. The pattern, designed by Martha Reynolds, incorporates a pink floral pattern on a French Opalescent Diamond Optic Trellis background. Attractiveness is enhanced with the addition of a spun Dusty Rose trim. All the pieces introduced in 1996 were continued this year. All items introduced in years prior to 1996 were discontinued. In addition, new pieces in the pattern included:

Lamp, 18" student	2793-DX	Vase, 4½"	4755-DX
Pitcher, 7"	1132-DX	Vase, 7"	1129-DX

1998 – 99

The hand-painted pink floral pattern on French Opalescent Trellis was now trimmed in Fenton's new pink Empress Rose color although the floral design remained the same. A special item with this decoration was the No. 4830-9" basket as a Family Signature piece with Tom Fenton's signature. Last year's pitcher was replaced by the new No. 4767-7½" pitcher, and the No. 5585-5½" covered box was added to the line. All of the other items from 1997 and 1996 remained in production. In 1999 the Gone with the Wind lamp was dropped, along with the No. 4830-9" hat-shaped basket. These items were replaced with the No. 4803-6" perfume bottle and the No. 6587-7" basket.

2000

Discontinued items included the No. 1144-8" basket and the No. 4767 pitcher. These pieces were replaced with the No. 4780-7½" basket and the No. 4761-7" pitcher. All of the items with the Reynolds floral decoration were discontinued at the end of 2000.

2001 – 2002

A new hand painted pink floral pattern on French Opalescent Trellis trimmed in Fenton's pink Pink Chiffon color entered the line. The new pattern was called Daisy Lane and consisted of the following Diamond Optic hand painted pieces:

Basket, 7"	4775-UC	Pitcher, 5½"	4768-UC
Basket, 8½"	1147-UC	Vase, 5"	4757-UC
Bell, 6½"	1145-UC	Vase, 9"	4752-UC
Lamp, 18" student	6850-UC		

These same pieces were offered again in the general catalog in 2002.

Diamond Optic	Ware No.	Introduced	Discontinued	Value*
Ivy ball and base, #705	1722-CR	1952	1954	140.00 – 160.00
Ivy ball and base, #705	1722-LO	1952	1954	160.00 – 180.00
Diamond Satin				
Cruet, #815	1763-BA	1952	1954	275.00 – 325.00
Vase, 1925-6"	1756-BA	1952	1955	90.00 – 110.00
Vase, #1720-7½" pinch	1757-BA	1952	1955	90.00 – 110.00
Vase, #510-8"	1758-BA	1952	1954	150.00 – 160.00
Cruet, #815	1763-RA	1952	1954	275.00 – 325.00
Vase, 1925-6"	1756-RA	1952	1955	85.00 – 100.00
Vase, #1720-7½" pinch	1757-RA	1952	1954	85.00 – 110.00
Vase, #510-8"	1758-RA	1952	1954	150.00 – 185.00
*Light color variations up to 30% less.				

Cookie Canister	Amber Frost	Blue Opalescent	Cranberry Red	Green Frost
No. 62-1½ quart	200.00 – 225.00	650.00 – 725.00	750.00 – 950.00	200.00 – 250.00
No. 63-2½ quart	200.00 – 225.00	650.00 – 725.00	750.00 – 950.00	200.00 – 250.00

Numbered items in the photo on page 295 include:

	Value
1. Blue Opalescent pitcher in Quilted pattern made for L. G. Wright	250.00 – 300.00
2. Cranberry Opalescent miniature lamp	300.00 – 350.00

Value

3. Blue Opalescent Quilted pattern 10" vase made for L. G. Wright .... 200.00 – 225.00
4. Cranberry Opalescent 10" vase .... 200.00 – 225.00
5. Cranberry Opalescent handled lamp base .... 75.00 – 90.00
6. Cranberry Opalescent lamp .... 450.00 – 500.00
7. Cranberry Opalescent handled lamp .... 150.00 – 175.00
8. Cranberry Opalescent tall cream pitcher made for L.G. Wright .... 100.00 – 125.00
9. Uncut Cranberry lamp part used as a vase .... 90.00 – 120.00

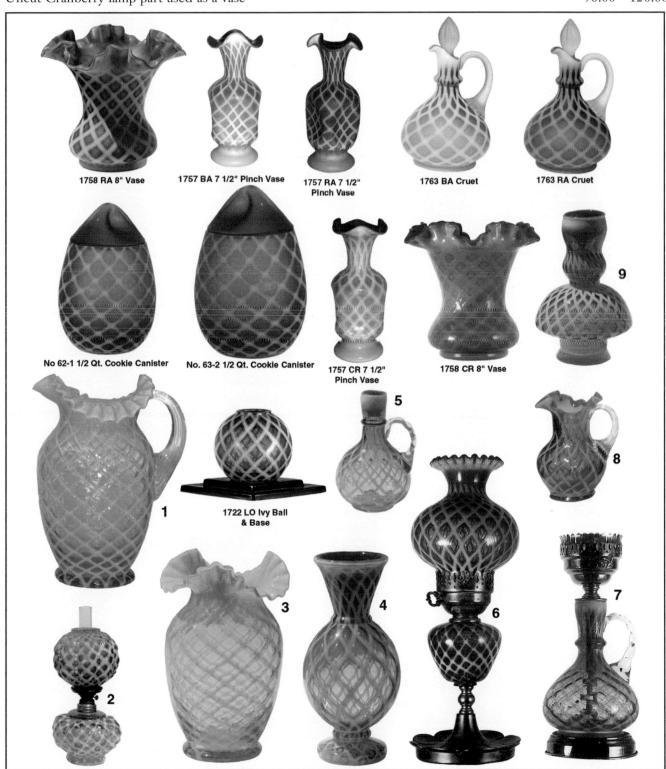

1758 RA 8" Vase

1757 BA 7 1/2" Pinch Vase

1757 RA 7 1/2" Pinch Vase

1763 BA Cruet

1763 RA Cruet

No 62-1 1/2 Qt. Cookie Canister

No. 63-2 1/2 Qt. Cookie Canister

1757 CR 7 1/2" Pinch Vase

1758 CR 8" Vase

9

1

1722 LO Ivy Ball & Base

5

8

2

3

4

6

7

Diamond Optic in Transparent Colors

A non-opalescent version of the Diamond Optic pattern was introduced in transparent Colonial Blue and Colonial Amber colors in 1962. This new issue used the same diamond shape pattern as the 1950s opalescent pieces, and is reminiscent of the Diamond Optic pattern produced in the late 1920s and early 1930s. However, none of the older shapes was reissued in these new colors. The original offering included the following ten pieces in Colonial Amber (CA) and Colonial Blue (CB):

Basket, 7" deep	1737	Pitcher, 44 ounce	1764
Candy jar & cover	1780	Pitcher, 64 ounce	1766
Courting lamp, electric	1791	Tumbler, 10 ounce	1740
Courting lamp, oil	1790	Vase, 10½"	1750
Pitcher, 10 ounce	1761	Vase, 7"	1751

A few additional items were added to the line the next year and some pieces were made in orange beginning in 1963. A few pieces were discontinued at the end of 1963 and the entire line was discontinued by the end of 1965.

Although all of the old colors and many of the old shapes had been discontinued, for almost two decades, some special items in the transparent Diamond Optic pattern were made during the 1980s and 1990s.

1982

The popular No. 1760 Diamond Optic petite bells appeared in Ruby (RU), Crystal (CY), and Transparent Green (KG) colors in the July catalog supplement. These bells were also sold in these colors with hand-painted holly decorations for the Christmas season. This catalog also featured these bells in three different colors with a hand-painted Daisies and Butterfly decoration. A special 12 piece hand-painted petite bell assortment was also offered in a mid-year supplement. Decorations included hand-painted roses, butterflies, and attractive decorative bands. An assortment of Diamond Optic petite bells was made in various pastel colors with hand-painted decorations with the words "Mom" or "Mother" for that special day.

1983

Bells in the Diamond Optic pattern continued to be in strong demand. The 1983 general catalog states "The success of our petite bells in 1982 has influenced the introduction of a 6½" bell in assorted patterns." This year's catalog included a spring assortment of both 6½" and petite bells featuring hand-painted butterflies and roses decorations. The catalog also offered a No. 1760 petite bell assortment that was hand-painted especially for Mother's Day. The Christmas edition of the No. 1760 petite bell came in Ruby, Crystal, and milk glass. Hand-painted decorations included a small decorated Christmas tree, an angel, or a white rose.

1984

The No. 1752-5½" footed vase in Dusty Rose was included as part of a special Valentine's Day assortment. The Dusty Rose vase was hand painted with a pink hearts and blue floral sprig decoration. The 1984 supplement included numerous transparent and opaque color bells with hand-painted decorations. This year's Mother's Day petite bell assortment also included a bell for grandmother. The No. 1760 petite bell with ruby decorated roses (RD) was available in the July supplement for Christmas season. The No. 1775-6½" bell was made in ruby with hand-painted white snowflakes (SR). It featured a musical insert that played *White Christmas*. Also for Christmas, the No. 1776- 4½" petite bell was made in ruby with hand-painted snowflakes and a music box insert.

1985

The design of the 6½" bell shifted from round to oval with the introduction of the No. 1774-6½" oval bell. This bell was the center of the Barnyard Buddies series which featured three different animal scenes on either a Blue Satin or Pink Satin bell. The No. 1774 oval bell was also made with the Country Bouquet (FX) hand-painted decoration in Dusty Rose. The petite bell and the new No. 8637-7½ oval basket and the No. 1759-6½" vase with a Diamond Optic interior were also made in Dusty Rose with the Country Bouquet decoration. Hand-painted No. 1173-6½" bells and No. 1760 petite bells decorated in pastel colors were included in an 18-piece "Festi-bell" Christmas assortment. The new decorations included the Autumn Leaves (LB), Berries and Blossoms (RK), and Meadow Blooms (JU) decorations.

1986

A 42-piece bell assortment was offered in the general catalog. Included in the assortment were the same bells available in 1985 with the exception of the Barnyard Buddies bells. Also various hand-painted floral decorations were available on the round and oval 6½" bells in Dusty Rose (DK) and Periwinkle Blue (PW).

1987

The No. 1796-7¼" vase in Cranberry with Blossoms and Bows (BY) hand-painted decoration was a part of the Connoisseur Collection in a limited edition of 950. The No. 1760 petite bell and No. 1765-6½" bell in crystal with hand-painted Floral Spray and Lovely Lilies decorations were included in Fenton's religious assortments. The No. 1773-6½" Autumn Leaves (LB) hand-decorated bell could be selected as a free gift by a hostess of a Gracious Touch party.

1988

The 1988 general catalog included several assortments of hand-decorated round and oval 6½" bells and numerous petite bells. New colors providing a background for the decorations this year included Country Cranberry (CC), Blue Royale (KK), and Teal Royale (OC). The No. 1726-10" bowl became a part of the regular Fenton line offering starting with the June 1988 catalog supplement.

1989

Production of the bells from 1988 continued with only minor changes. A 2500 piece limited edition No. 7060 pitcher was made in Rosalene as part of the Connoisseur Collection. Diamond Optic in the Mulberry (MG) color returned to the line with the production of the No. 1797-11½" vase in that color. Other Diamond Optic pieces were also made in Mulberry over the next few years. The No. 1798-10½" vase was added to the line in Ruby beginning with the June catalog supplement.

1990 – 1991

The No. 1726-10" bowl in Country Cranberry (CC) remained in the line and the No. 1798-10½" vase was made in Ruby.

1992

Diamond Optic in Mulberry was featured in the form of the No. 1705-21" lamp with prisms and the No. 1738-6" basket. Also, the No. 1726-10" bowl was still in the line in Country Cranberry.

1993

Fenton's Diamond Optic pattern was an inviting setting for the newly created Plum (PL) color. The following five different shapes were made in this color. Some pieces were also hand painted with Frances Burton's Vintage (PV) pattern grape clusters.

Lamp, 17"	1706-PV	Vase, 10" Melon	1786-PL
Vase, 6"	1789-PL	Vase, 11"	1792-PL
Vase, 8" Melon	1785-PL		

A hand-painted version of the 10" Melon vase, No. 1786-PV, was inscribed with the signature of Don Fenton. This vase was a part of the first edition of Family Signature pieces. Family Signature items in this series were limited to the quantity sold through April, 30, 1993.

The following pieces were made in Country Cranberry (CC):

Basket, 6"	1731-CC	Vase, 9" pinch, hand painted	1749-CI
Bowl, 13"	1728-CC		

1994

Diamond Optic in Plum remained in the line with only a few minor changes from last year. The 10" Melon vase was no longer in production and the No. 1785-8" vase was also offered decorated with the Vintage (PV) pattern.

1995

A new Diamond Optic lamp, No. 1706-17½" made an appearance in Cobalt (KN).

The following pieces were still available in Country Cranberry:

Basket, 6"	1731-CC	Bowl, 13"	1728-CC

Production of the No. 1785-8" vase and No. 1706-17" lamp continued in Plum with the Vintage (PV) hand-painted decoration.

A new shape, the No, 1133-7" basket with hand-painted Vining Garden decoration on Sea Mist Green was introduced. This basket was still in the line in 1996.

1996

The No. 1706-17" lamp continued to be made in Plum and Cobalt. The No. 1133-7" Diamond Optic basket with hand-painted Golden Flax on Cobalt was also made.

1998

The No. 4758-8½" vase entered this line in Fenton's Country Cranberry color. The vase was discontinued at the end of the year.

Colonial Amber Diamond Optic	Ware No.	Introduced	Discontinued	Value
Basket, 7" deep	1737-CA	1962	1965	20.00 – 25.00
Candy jar	1780-CA	1962	1965	25.00 – 35.00
Lamp, courting (electric)	1791-CA	1962	1966	85.00 – 90.00
Lamp, courting (oil)	1790-CA	63	1966	85.00 – 90.00
Pitcher, 10 oz.	1761-CA	1962	1965	12.00 – 15.00
Pitcher, 44 oz.	1764-CA	1962	1964	35.00 – 45.00
Pitcher, 64 oz.	1766-CA	1962	1964	50.00 – 75.00
Tumbler, 10 oz.	1740-CA	1962	1964	10.00 – 12.00
Tumbler, 14 oz.	1742-CA	1963	1964	12.00 – 14.00
Vase, 7"	1751-CA	1962	1965	10.00 – 12.00
Vase, 10½"	1750-CA	1962	1964	25.00 – 28.00
Colonial Blue Diamond Optic	**Ware No**	**Introduced**	**Discontinued**	**Value**
Basket, 7" deep	1737-CB	1962	1965	50.00 – 55.00
Candy jar	1780-CB	1962	1965	45.00 – 50.00
Lamp, courting (electric)	1791-CB	1962	1966	100.00 – 125.00
Lamp, courting (oil)	1790-CB	63	1966	100.00 – 125.00
Pitcher, 10 oz.	1761-CB	1962	1965	18.00 – 20.00
Pitcher, 44 oz.	1764-CB	1962	1964	45.00 – 50.00
Pitcher, 64 oz.	1766-CB	1962	1964	75.00 – 85.00
Tumbler, 10 oz.	1740-CB	1962	1964	14.00 – 16.00
Tumbler, 14 oz.	1742-CB	1963	1964	18.00 – 20.00
Vase, 7"	1751-CB	1962	1965	14.00 – 16.00
Vase, 10½"	1750-CB	1962	1964	45.00 – 55.00

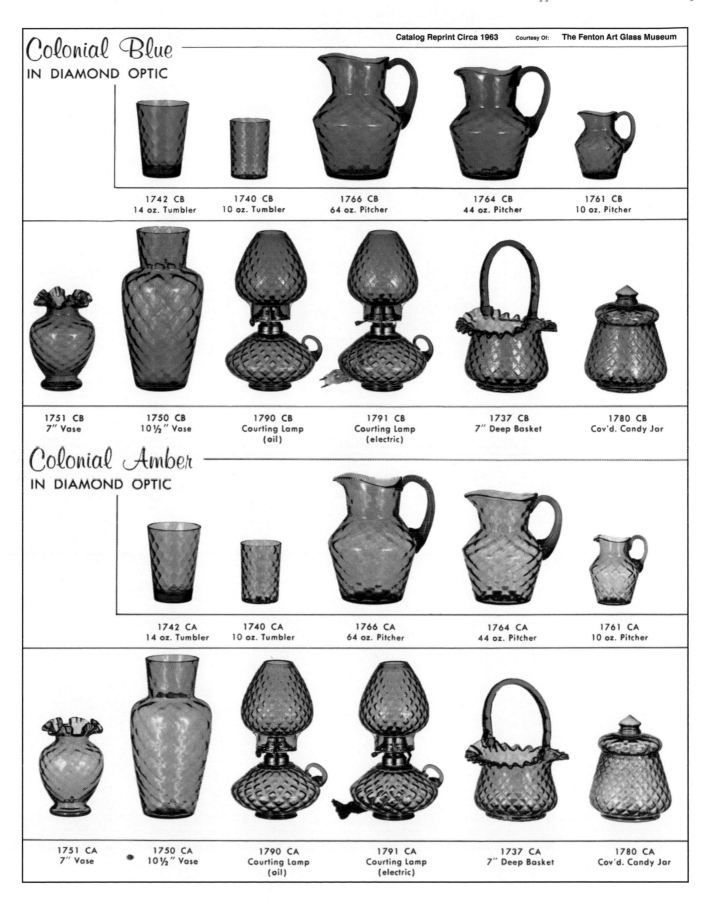

Colonial Blue
IN DIAMOND OPTIC

Catalog Reprint Circa 1963   Courtesy Of: **The Fenton Art Glass Museum**

1742 CB	1740 CB	1766 CB	1764 CB	1761 CB
14 oz. Tumbler	10 oz. Tumbler	64 oz. Pitcher	44 oz. Pitcher	10 oz. Pitcher

1751 CB	1750 CB	1790 CB	1791 CB	1737 CB	1780 CB
7" Vase	10½" Vase	Courting Lamp (oil)	Courting Lamp (electric)	7" Deep Basket	Cov'd. Candy Jar

Colonial Amber
IN DIAMOND OPTIC

1742 CA	1740 CA	1766 CA	1764 CA	1761 CA
14 oz. Tumbler	10 oz. Tumbler	64 oz. Pitcher	44 oz. Pitcher	10 oz. Pitcher

1751 CA	1750 CA	1790 CA	1791 CA	1737 CA	1780 CA
7" Vase	10½" Vase	Courting Lamp (oil)	Courting Lamp (electric)	7" Deep Basket	Cov'd. Candy Jar

Orange Diamond Optic	Ware No.	Introduced	Discontinued	Value
Basket, 7" deep	1737-OR	1963	1965	45.00 – 50.00
Candy jar	1780-OR	1963	1965	40.00 – 50.00
Lamp, courting (electric)	1791-OR	1963	1966	100.00 – 125.00
Lamp, courting (oil)	1790-OR	1963	1966	100.00 – 125.00
Pitcher, 10 oz.	1761-OR	1963	1965	18.00 – 20.00
Vase, 7"	1751-OR	1963	1965	12.00 – 15.00

Catalog Reprint Circa 1963

Courtesy Of:

The Fenton Art Glass Museum

1790 OR Courting Lamp   1791 OR Courting Lamp   1737 OR 7" Basket   1780 OR Candy Jar

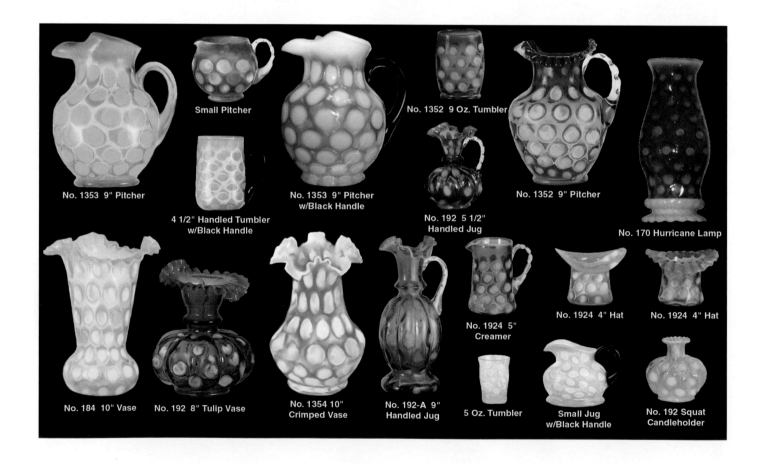

No. 1353 9" Pitcher

Small Pitcher

4 1/2" Handled Tumbler w/Black Handle

No. 1353 9" Pitcher w/Black Handle

No. 1352 9 Oz. Tumbler

No. 192 5 1/2" Handled Jug

No. 1352 9" Pitcher

No. 170 Hurricane Lamp

No. 184 10" Vase

No. 192 8" Tulip Vase

No. 1354 10" Crimped Vase

No. 192-A 9" Handled Jug

No. 1924 5" Creamer

5 Oz. Tumbler

Small Jug w/Black Handle

No. 1924 4" Hat

No. 1924 4" Hat

No. 192 Squat Candleholder

Dot Optic

Dot Optic, or Coin Spot as this pattern is commonly called by collectors, made its first appearance in the Fenton line about 1908. These early pieces included a pitcher and tumbler combining to form a water set in French Opalescent, Blue Opalescent, and Green Opalescent. These pieces were made intermittently through Fenton's early years. In the early 1930s several different styles of lamps were produced in the Dot Optic pattern. In the late 1930s and early to mid-1940s, numerous other pieces were made in this pattern in French Opalescent, Green Opalescent, Blue Opalescent, and Topaz Opalescent. A complete listing of pieces produced is not available from Fenton catalogs or inventory records. The items included in the listing below are those we have seen and ones that have been confirmed by collectors.

In addition to producing Dot Optic pieces for the regular line, Fenton also made numerous pieces for private companies in colors and moulds similar to those used by Fenton. Dot, a pattern made for L. G. Wright, is one of more frequently found patterns. For examples of pieces made in this pattern, see page 302. In addition to making its own lamps in this pattern, Fenton also produced lamp parts for use by other lamp companies. Examples of both categories of lamps are shown at the bottom of the photo on page 302.

Pieces made more recently in Dot Optic include:

1985

A Green Opalescent No. 1353-10" tulip vase was made for Fenton's special accounts customers (former LeVay customers).

1986

A limited edition miniature boudoir lamp, No. 7802-CZ, and a cruet with a stopper, No. 7863-CZ, were part of the Connoisseur Collection. The lamp was limited to 750 pieces and the cruet had a production limit of 1000. The color code "CZ" represents the color Cranberry Pearl.

1990 91

The No. 1354-7" wheat sheaf vase was made in Cranberry Opalescent.

1992 – 93

The wheat sheaf vase was joined in the line by a Cranberry Opalescent 10" vase.

Vase, 7"	1354-CR	Vase, 10" tulip	1353-CR

Dot Optic	French Opalescent	Topaz Opalescent	Blue Opalescent Green Opalescent Cranberry
Basket		190.00 – 250.00	
Bottle, cologne			N.D.
Bowl, #203-10"	25.00 – 30.00		55.00 – 65.00
Bowl, #1522-10" crimped, triangle	45.00 – 55.00	85.00 – 100.00	85.00 – 100.00
Candleholder, #192 squat	25.00 – 35.00		
Creamer, #1924-4"	25.00 – 35.00		80.00 – 90.00
Decanter			350.00 – 450.00
Hurricane lamp, #170			
w/base			150.00 – 200.00
Jug, 5" syrup			55.00 – 65.00
Jug, #192-5½" handled			65.00 – 75.00
Jug, #192-A-9" handled			100.00 – 125.00
Pitcher, #1352-9"	100.00 – 150.00		200.00 – 300.00
Pitcher, #1353-9"	100.00 – 150.00		200.00 – 300.00
Top hat, #1924-4"	25.00 – 30.00		35.00 – 45.00
Top hat, #1923-6"	30.00 – 35.00		45.00 – 55.00
Tumbler, #1353-4"	18.00 – 22.00		30.00 – 40.00
Tumbler, 4½" handled	35.00 – 40.00		45.00 – 55.00
Vase, #203-5" crimped	25.00 – 35.00		40.00 – 50.00
Vase, #184-6"	45.00 – 55.00	85.00 – 95.00	85.00 – 95.00
Vase, #186-8"	55.00 – 65.00	90.00 – 110.00	90.00 – 100.00

Dot Optic	French Opalescent	Topaz Opalescent	Blue Opalescent Green Opalescent Cranberry
Vase, #192-5"			40.00 – 50.00
Vase, #192-8" tulip			110.00 – 135.00
Vase, #183-8"	60.00 – 70.00		95.00 – 110.00
Vase, #184-10"			150.00 – 185.00
Vase, #1354-10" crimped	110.00 – 125.00		190.00 – 225.00

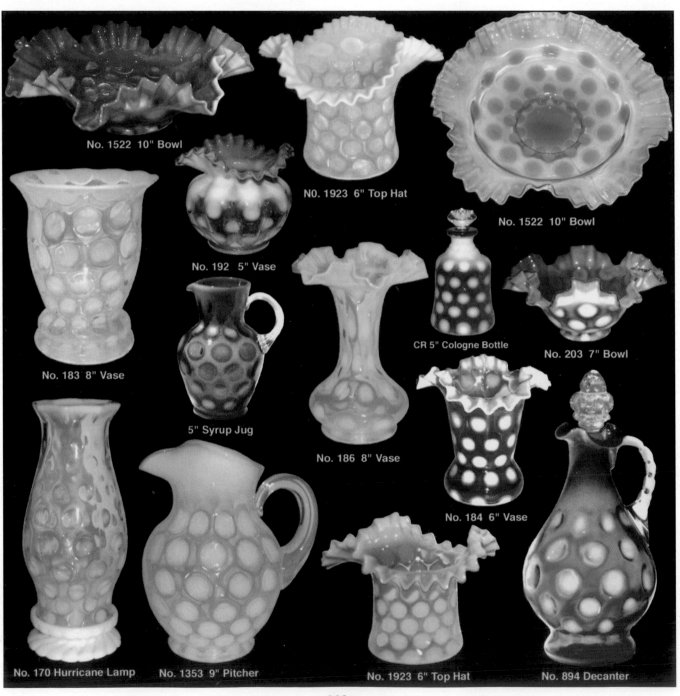

No. 1522 10" Bowl

N0. 1923 6" Top Hat

No. 1522 10" Bowl

No. 192 5" Vase

No. 183 8" Vase

5" Syrup Jug

No. 186 8" Vase

CR 5" Cologne Bottle

No. 203 7" Bowl

No. 184 6" Vase

No. 170 Hurricane Lamp

No. 1353 9" Pitcher

No. 1923 6" Top Hat

No. 894 Decanter

Many of the items in the photo below were made for L. G. Wright by Fenton. L. G. Wright's Dot pattern was similar to Fenton's Dot Optic pattern. In addition to producing lamps for the regular line in this pattern during the 1930s, Fenton made many lamp parts for various manufacturers.

Item	Value	Item	Value
1. Cranberry pitcher (Wright)	250.00 – 300.00	9. Blue Opalescent sugar shaker	125.00 – 150.00
2. Cranberry tumbler (Wright)	35.00 – 40.00	10. Blue Opalescent lamp base	45.00 – 55.00
3. Topaz Opalescent pitcher		11. Cranberry round cruet	125.00 – 145.00
(Wright)	275.00 – 325.00	12. Topaz Opalescent lamp	85.00 – 90.00
4. Blue Opalescent vase	165.00 – 180.00	13. Satin Blue Opalescent lamp	250.00 – 300.00
5. Cranberry Opalescent		14. French Opalescent lamp	150.00 – 200.00
milk pitcher (Wright)	125.00 – 140.00	15. French Opalescent double	
6. Green Opalescent lamp	85.00 – 90.00	student lamp	100.00 – 150.00
7. Blue Opalescent tall		16. French Opalescent lamp	85.00 – 100.00
cream pitcher	60.00 – 75.00	17. French Opalescent lamp base	65.00 – 75.00
8. Cranberry miniature lamp	300.00 – 325.00		

Blue Fern

89-2
Rd.
Barber
Bottle

88-2
Fluted
Barber
Bottle

84-2
Water Pitcher

98-2-404
Pickle Jar
Ft. Frame

725
Hurricane Lamp

97-2
Tumbler

98-8
11" Wedding Bowl

85-2
Milk Pitcher

98-6
Small Rose Bowl

98-7
Lg. Rose Bowl

98-2
Pickle Jar with/cov.

96A-2
Syrup Pitcher

96-2
Sugar Shaker

95-2
Round Cruet

94-2
Oval Cruet

90-2
Tall Cream

age 2

304

Fern/Fern Satin

Fenton's Fern pattern was introduced into the regular line in July 1952. A cruet and two sizes of vases were made in Blue Satin (BA) and Rose Satin (RA). Both of these colors are opalescent colors that have been frosted with acid to produce a satin finish. The cruet made an early departure at the end of 1953 and all the remainder of these satin Fern items were discontinued by the end of 1954. The Fern pattern ivy ball in the photo is a sample from the Fenton museum. This item was not a production item.

Fenton also made an opalescent pattern for L. G. Wright called Fern, but the L. G. Wright pattern differed from the Fenton pattern in that it also included a daisy-like flower in the design. Most collectors now refer to this L. G. Wright pattern as "Daisy and Fern." See the photo for examples and a pattern comparison of L. G. Wright's Daisy and Fern pattern. In 1990 Fenton produced pieces in the Daisy and Fern pattern in Sapphire Blue Opalescent for inclusion in their Collector's Extravaganza series. Only recently, with the appearance of new Cranberry Opalescent shapes in the early 1990s, a redesigned Fern pattern, with an added Daisy has entered the regular Fenton line.

Highlights of later production include:

1982

The No. 1866-16 oz. pitcher was made in Amethyst (AY), Forget-Me-Not Blue (KL), Country Cranberry (CC), and Glacier Blue (BB). The No. 1824-4½" vase also entered the line in Country Cranberry. The July catalog supplement also featured the No. 1892 Country Cranberry fairy light and the No. 1835-5" hat basket in Country Cranberry.

1983

Production of the No. 1866-16 oz. pitcher continued in Amethyst and light blue transparent Forget-Me-Not Blue. New hues for the pitcher this year included the newly introduced overlay colors: Yellow Overlay (OY), Federal Blue Overlay (OF), and Heritage Green Overlay (OH).

1984

The No. 1866-16 oz pitcher continued in the line in Country Cranberry and Heritage Green Overlay — a pastel green overlay — and was introduced in a new overlay color — Dusty Rose Overlay (OD).

1985

Production of the No. 1866-16 oz. pitcher continued in Country Cranberry. This pitcher remained in the line in this color through 1992. Fenton's No. 1803 three-piece fairy light was made in Green Opalescent for special accounts (former Levay customers).

1988

The June catalog supplement included the No. 2065-16 oz. pitcher as part of the Connoisseur Collection. This Cranberry Opalescent Fern optic jug had a teal spun top edge. This pitcher with the ware number 2056-ZC was limited to 3500 pieces.

1989

The following items were made in the Fern pattern as a part of Fenton's Persian Blue Opalescent (XC) assortment:

Basket, 5½" DC	1830-XC	Fairy light, 3-piece	1803-XC
Cruet	1865-XC		

1990 – 91

In 1990, the No. 1866-16 oz. pitcher was made in Ocean Blue Opalescent (XN) with a Cobalt Blue crest and handle for QVC. The ware number for this item was C1866-XN. The No. 1844 vase in Cranberry was also made for QVC. This vase, with the ware number C1844-CR, was inscribed with the signature of Bill Fenton.

The new No. 1852-11" vase entered the line in Cranberry Opalescent. This vase continued in production through 1993 and was the first of several items in the redesigned Fern pattern that would soon appear in Cranberry Opalescent.

1992

Several items were made in Persian Pearl in the Fern pattern as a part of the 1992 Historical Collection. Sales were limited to items sold by May 31, 1993, and included:

Lamp, 23" w/prisms	1801-XV	Tumbler	1876-XV
Pitcher, 8½"	1875-XV		

The pitcher and four tumblers were sold as a water set with the ware number 1870.

1992 – 1993

The following pieces were made in Cranberry Opalescent (CR):

Lamp, 23½" Gone with the Wind	1800-CR	Tumbler, 9 oz.	1840-CR
Pitcher, 70 oz.	1874-CR	Vase, 11"	1852-CR
Pitcher, 32 oz.	3562-CR		

A combination of the No. 1874 pitcher and four tumblers produced a five-piece water set that Fenton promoted with the No. 1804 ware number.

1995

Fern returned to the line in Cranberry Opalescent with the introduction of four new shapes.

Lamp, 21" w/prisms	1801-CR	Vase, 4"	1869-CR
Pitcher, 10"	1873-CR	Vase, 9½"	1854-CR

1996 – 1997

In the 1996 catalog, the No. 1873-10" pitcher was discontinued and the No. 1843-7" vase was added. The other items in the Fern pattern remained the same as in 1995. In 1997, the only item remaining in the regular catalog was the No. 1801-21" lamp in Cranberry Opalescent.

2003

Cranberry opalescent Fern returned to the regular Fenton line in the form of the No. 1808-21" handkerchief-style lamp.

Fern	Ware No.	Introduced	Discontinued	Value
Ivy ball and base, #705	1822-GO	not in the line		150.00 – 160.00
Fern Satin Blue				
Cruet, #815	1863-BA	July 1952	1954	250.00 – 300.00
Vase, #1720-7½" pinch	1857-BA	July 1952	1955	65.00 – 85.00
Vase, #510-8"	1858-BA	July 1952	1954	90.00 – 110.00
Fern Satin Rose				
Cruet, #815	1863-RA	July 1952	1954	300.00 – 325.00
Vase, #1720-7½" pinch	1857-RA	July 1952	1955	90.00 – 100.00
Vase, #510-8"	1858-RA	July 1952	1955	100.00 – 125.00

L. G. Wright Daisy and Fern shapes made by Fenton:	Value
1. Cranberry Satin 5" rose bowl	60.00 – 80.00
2. Cranberry Satin small bowl	125.00 – 140.00
3. Cranberry Satin milk pitcher	175.00 – 200.00
4. Cranberry Satin tall cream pitcher	125.00 – 145.00
5. Topaz Opalescent large pitcher	250.00 – 300.00
6. Cranberry Satin large pitcher	250.00 – 300.00
7. Blue Opalescent large pitcher	200.00 – 250.00
8. Cranberry Satin tumbler	50.00 – 60.00
9. Cranberry Opalescent large pitcher	200.00 – 250.00
10. Cranberry Opalescent tankard style jug	300.00 – 350.00
11. Blue Opalescent barber bottle	190.00 – 210.00
12. Cranberry Opalescent sugar shaker	190.00 – 220.00
13. Cranberry Opalescent cruet	150.00 – 175.00
14. Blue Opalescent tumbler	45.00 – 55.00
15. Blue Opalescent 4" rose bowl	35.00 – 45.00
16. Topaz Opalescent cruet	175.00 – 200.00
17. Cranberry Opalescent canister	350.00 – 400.00

1863 BA Cruet

1863 RA Cruet

1863 BO Cruet

1858 BA 8" Vase

1857 BA 7 1/2" Pinch Vase

1822 Ivy Ball

Daisy & Fern Examples Made For L. G. Wright

1

2

3

4

5

6

7

8

9

10

11

12

13

14

15

16

17

Hanging Heart

Mould-blown Hanging Heart pieces, inspired by the off-hand production of Robert Barber the previous year, entered the Fenton line in January 1976. Ten assorted items were produced in Custard Iridescent and Turquoise Iridescent colors. Some, but not all of the shapes were made in both colors. The hearts and vines were carefully inlaid by hand into the hot glass after the pieces were formed. High production costs and less than spectacular sales resulted in the removal of these items from production at the end of the year.

The items listed below were offered as part of the regular line. Other items were also sampled. Coverage of other off-hand items made by Robert Barber will be provided in the "Special Items" chapter of the accompanying book, *Fenton Art Glass Colors and Hand-Painted Decorations: 1939 – 1980*, which will provide additional coverage for these years. The black amethyst vase with white hanging hearts to the bottom right of the photo below was a special item made in 1981 for the Fenton Art Glass Collectors of America, Inc.

Custard Iridescent	Ware No.	Value
Barber bottle	8960-CI	175.00 – 200.00
Basket, handled	8939-CI	190.00 – 220.00
Cruet	8969-CI	125.00 – 150.00
Lamp, 20¼"	8900-CI	450.00 – 500.00
Pitcher, 70 oz.	8964-CI	280.00 – 300.00
Rose bowl, 5"	8925-CI	40.00 – 50.00
Tumbler, 10 oz.	8940-CI	45.00 – 55.00
Vase, 5"	8955-CI	65.00 – 80.00
Vase, 6"	8956-CI	90.00 – 125.00
Vase, 8"	8958-CI	125.00 – 150.00
Turquoise Iridescent	**Ware No.**	**Value**
Basket, handled	8937-TH	150.00 – 170.00
Bottle	8961-TH	190.00 – 225.00
Cruet	8969-TH	175.00 – 195.00
Lamp, 20¼"	8900-TH	600.00 – 700.00
Pitcher, 70 oz.	8964-TH	400.00 – 450.00
Rose bowl, 4"	8924-TH	45.00 – 65.00
Tumbler, 10 oz.	8940-TH	55.00 – 65.00
Vase, 4"	8954-TH	75.00 – 85.00
Vase, 7"	8957-TH	75.00 – 85.00
Vase, 8"	8958-TH	150.00 – 175.00

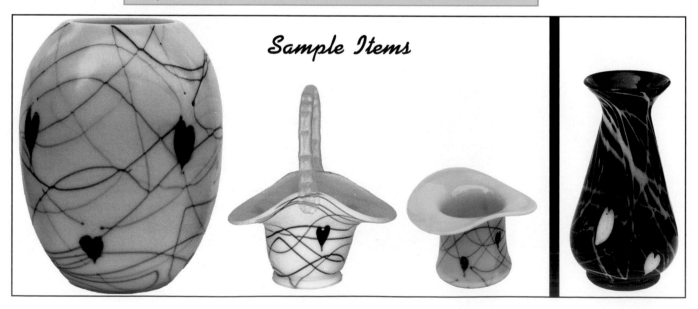

Sample Items

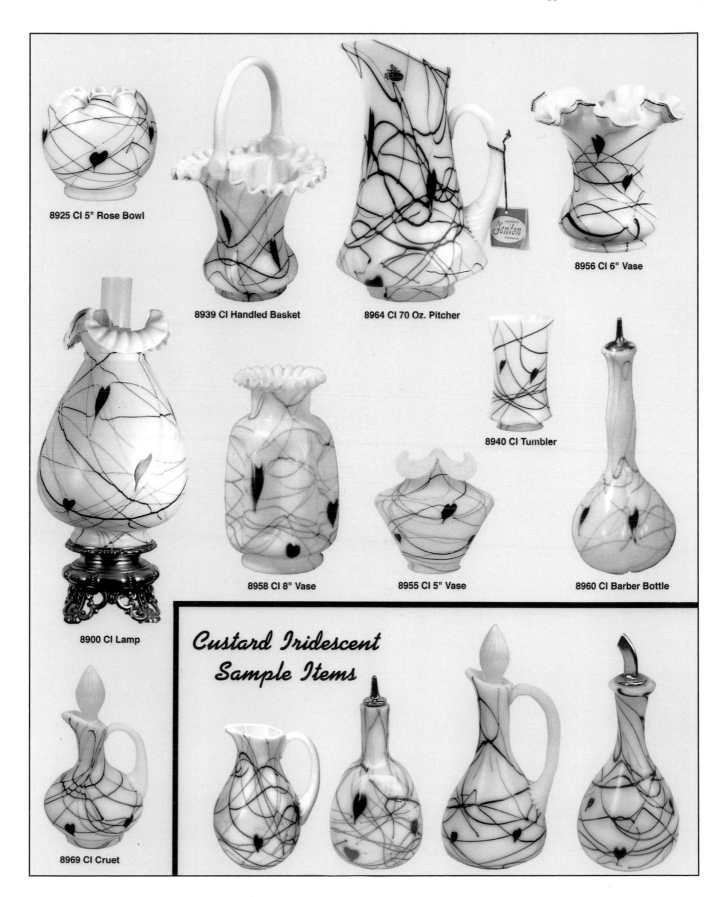

8925 CI 5" Rose Bowl

8939 CI Handled Basket

8964 CI 70 Oz. Pitcher

8956 CI 6" Vase

8940 CI Tumbler

8900 CI Lamp

8958 CI 8" Vase

8955 CI 5" Vase

8960 CI Barber Bottle

Custard Iridescent Sample Items

8969 CI Cruet

Turquoise Hanging Heart
by Fenton

Last year Fenton presented some Hanging Heart pieces in each of the first two Robert Barber Collections.* They were so well received at the "high" limited edition prices that it was decided to see if techniques could be developed to permit bringing this unusual glass of the early 20's into a more moderate price range. Some of the strictly offhand shaping has been adapted to our more conventional forming processes with a considerable reduction in costs. Still it takes as many as 27 persons on a shop to make a single Hanging Heart basket. The intertwined vines and hanging hearts must be skillfully hand inlaid while the very hot glass is being finished.

*A third collection will be presented in a few months.

8964 TH
70 oz. Pitcher

8940 TH
10 oz. Tumbler

8958 TH
8" Vase

8961 TH
Bottle

8937 TH
Handled Basket

8957 TH
7" Vase

8900 TH
20¼" Mariner's Lamp

8954 TH
4" Vase

8969 TH
Cruet

8924 TH
4" Rose Bowl

Catalog Reprint   Courtesy Of: The Fenton Art Glass Museum

Custard Hanging Heart

Here is glassmaking at its zenith. Here is a uniquely beautiful glassware brought within manageable price range.

Since the samples of Hanging Heart shown on these pages were photographed, we have perfected a new technique for softly iridizing these Hanging Heart pieces which makes them even more beautiful than shown. We feel sure Hanging Heart will be one of the biggest pluses in your sales for '76. It will provide a home decoration and gift sought after by a very active new market segment.

8939 CI
Handled Basket

8900 CI
20¼" Mariner's Lamp

8964 CI
70 oz. Pitcher

8940 CI
10 oz. Tumbler

8925 CI
5" Rose Bowl

8958 CI
8" Vase

8956 CI
6" Vase

8955 CI
5" Vase

8960 CI
Barber Bottle

8969 CI
Cruet

Catalog Reprint Circa 1976 Courtesy Of The Fenton Art Glass Museum

311

Historic America

Beginning in 1937, the eight-piece Historic America line was made for Macy's department store as an accompanying pattern to a line of English dinnerware of the same name that was produced by Johnson Brothers.

Pieces not shown include the underplate for the finger bowl and the 4" plate. The center pattern of the finger bowl underplate is The Rockies. The scene shows mountains in the background with four oxen pulling a covered wagon up the rugged terrain. The focal point of the 4" plate is Mount Vernon.

This pattern was discontinued in the early 1940s and the moulds were retooled in 1942 to produce the Butterfly Net pattern.

Historic America	Scene	Value
Bowl, finger	Prairie Schooner	30.00 – 35.00
Goblet, 4½" wine	Fort Dearborn	35.00 – 45.00
Goblet, 6"	Capitol in Washington	45.00 – 55.00
Liner, finger bowl	The Rockies with a covered wagon	30.00 – 35.00
Plate, 4" cup	Mount Vernon	20.00 – 25.00
Plate, 8"	Niagara Falls	25.00 – 35.00
Sherbet, 4½"	Independence Hall	20.00 – 30.00
Tumbler, 5½"	Broadway, New York	35.00 – 45.00

"Prairie Schooner" Finger Bowl
"The Rockies" Finger Bowl Liner

"Independence Hall" 4 1/2" Sherbet

"Broadway, New York" 5 1/2" Tumbler

"Fort Dearborn" 4 1/2" Goblet

"Capitol at Washinton" 6" Goblet

"Niagara Falls" 8" Plate

HORIZON

designed by Michael Lax for

PLATE 2

A	8176	FO	Candleholder with Insert
B	8126	FO	10½" Bowl with Base
C	8157	FO	8½" Vase
D	8101	FO	Sugar & Cream Set
E	8162	FO	Oil
F	8106	FO	Salt & Pepper

PLATE 1

A	8175	AR	5" Candleholder with Insert
B	8176	JT	6½" Candleholder with Insert
C	8177	AR	8" Candleholder with Insert
D	8123	AR	Bowl
E	8123	JT	Bowl
F	8121	JT	Nut Dish
G	8122	AR	Bowl
H	8122	JT	Bowl
I	8121	AR	Nut Dish

Catalog Reprint Circa 1960
Courtesy Of:
The Fenton Art Glass Museum

For well over a half a century Fenton has specialized in Early American designs — and very successfully too!

However, knowing that you have a number of contemporary minded customers we have had Michael Lax, a young inspirational contemporary designer, develop the "Horizon" line as shown on the front and back covers. "Horizon" is a marriage of beautiful Fenton colors, rubbed walnut wood tops, porcelain candle cups and bases, and rawhide thongs — as new as tomorrow; functional and beautiful, truly a pace setting achievement that has long been our forte — and always with you our customers in mind.

8103 Hangers needed with 8104 & 8105

Horizon

Fenton entered into an agreement for the design of contemporary style glassware with designer Michael Lax in 1957. Although the designs were ready by 1958, Fenton was doing well with its traditional type glassware at the time and declined to introduce the new line. Since part of the agreement included a five percent royalty on each item sold, Lax continued to press Fenton to produce his products and a new line, called Horizon, consisting of 23 different items, was finally introduced in July 1959.

Pieces made included bowls, candles, nut dishes, oil bottles, shakers, and vases. The colors offered were Amber, Jamestown Blue, and French Opalescent. Glass was used in combination with other items to form the finished product. Hanging bowls and vases included rawhide thongs and the oils, sugars, and shakers were combined with rubbed walnut wood tops. Porcelain cups and bases were used with the candleholders.

Unfortunately, for both Lax and Fenton, this new style of glassware did not sell well. As a result, Horizon was not included in the 1960 Fenton line.

Horizon	Ware No.	Amber	Jamestown Blue	French Opalescent
Bowl	8122	20.00 – 25.00	30.00 – 35.00	
Bowl	8123	35.00 – 40.00	45.00 – 55.00	
Bowl, 10½" w/walnut base	8126	20.00 – 25.00	40.00 – 50.00	45.00 – 55.00
Bowl, hanging w/thong	8105	65.00 – 75.00	75.00 – 85.00	
Candleholder, 5" w/insert	8175	10.00 – 12.00	12.00 – 15.00	12.00 – 15.00
Candleholder 6½" w/insert	8176	11.00 – 13.00	15.00 – 18.00	35.00 – 45.00
Candleholder 8" w/insert	8177	12.00 – 15.00	20.00 – 22.00	20.00 – 25.00
Epergne	8102	75.00 – 85.00	125.00 – 150.00	150.00 – 175.00
Nut dish	8121	20.00 – 25.00	30.00 – 35.00	
Oil with walnut stopper	8162	22.00 – 25.00	40.00 – 45.00	40.00 – 50.00
Salt and pepper, pr	8106	25.00 – 28.00	40.00 – 45.00	35.00 – 45.00
Sugar and cream set	8101	22.00 – 25.00	45.00 – 55.00	55.00 – 65.00
Vase, 8½"	8157	20.00 – 22.00	35.00 – 40.00	45.00 – 55.00
Vase, hanging w/thong	8104	65.00 – 75.00	75.00 – 85.00	

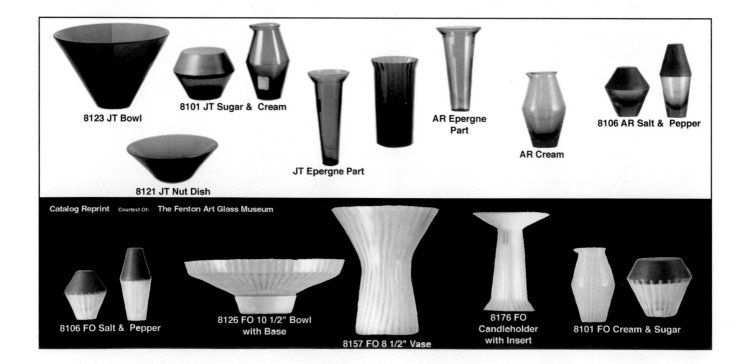

8123 JT Bowl

8101 JT Sugar & Cream

8121 JT Nut Dish

JT Epergne Part

AR Epergne Part

AR Cream

8106 AR Salt & Pepper

Catalog Reprint Courtesy Of: The Fenton Art Glass Museum

8106 FO Salt & Pepper

8126 FO 10 1/2" Bowl with Base

8157 FO 8 1/2" Vase

8176 FO Candleholder with Insert

8101 FO Cream & Sugar

A	8105	JT	Hanging Bowl with Thong
B	8105	AR	Hanging Bowl with Thong
C	8104	AR	Hanging Vase with Thong
D	8104	JT	Hanging Vase with Thong
E	8102	JT	Epergne

Catalog Reprint Circa 1960 Courtesy Of: **The Fenton Art Glass Museum**

Jacqueline

Fenton's Jacqueline pattern, which was named for the first lady of the era, Jacqueline Kennedy, was introduced in 1960. Two vases, the No. 9152-7" tulip and the No. 9153-5", were made in special opaline colors in 1960. These opaline colors were blue, pink, and yellow. The next year the opaline colors were discontinued, but the line was continued with the addition of several new shapes. New colors for 1961 included milk glass and Fenton's new overlay colors — Apple Green, Powder Blue Overlay, Coral, Honey Amber, and Wild Rose. Production of items in Coral and Wild Rose was limited to the No. 9156-6" vase. With the exception of the salt and pepper shakers in milk glass, the pattern was discontinued at the end of 1961. The milk glass shakers were made through June 1962.

During the 1980s and 1990s original shapes in the Jacqueline pattern have been made in other colors and some new shapes have been added to the pattern. These newer pieces have the embossed Fenton logo and include:

1982

The No. 9166-48 oz. pitcher was made in Ruby (RU).

1989

In January 1989, the following were in the line in both Mulberry (MG) and Country Cranberry (CC):

Basket, 10½"	9139-MG	Bowl, 9½"	9442-CC
Basket, 8¼"	9434-CC	Bowl, 9½"	9165-MG
Basket, 8½"	9464-CC	Vase, 4½"	9452-CC

The following items were listed in the June 1989 supplement in Mulberry (MG):

| Bowl, 9½" | 9442-MG | Vase, 4½" | 9452-MG |

The Mulberry No. 9139-10½" basket and the No. 9452-4½" vase were still listed in the 1900 – 1991 catalog. The No. 9464-8½" basket was in the line in Mulberry in 1992 and the No. 9442-9½" bowl was also still being made. These items were no longer shown in the 1993 catalog.

Some pieces in the Jacqueline pattern were also made in Country Cranberry (CC) during the 1990s.

1990

Starting in January 1990, the following were made in Country Cranberry (CC):

| Bowl, 9½" | 9442-CC | Basket, 8½" | 9464-CC |

The bowl was discontinued in 2000, but the basket was still in the line in 2003. The No. 9434-8¼" basket and the No. 9452-4½" vase were also in the 1990 – 1991 catalog in Country Cranberry.

The No. 6569 miniature vase was made in pearlized colors in 1992 and 1993. Colors produced were Rose (DN), Twilight (TZ), Jade (EZ), and Blue (SM). In 1993, Blue (SM) was replaced by Ocean Blue (OB).

Blue Opaline	Ware No	Introduced	Discontinued	Value
Vase, 5"	9153-BN	1960	1961	55.00 – 65.00
Vase, 7" tulip	9152-BN	1960	1961	85.00 – 95.00
Pink Opaline	**Ware No.**	**Introduced**	**Discontinued**	**Value**
Vase, 5"	9153-PN	1960	1961	65.00 – 75.00
Vase, 7" tulip	9152-PN	1960	1961	85.00 – 100.00
Yellow Opaline	**Ware No.**	**Introduced**	**Discontinued**	**Value**
Vase, 5"	9153-YN	1960	1961	55.00 – 65.00
Vase, 7" tulip	9152-YN	1960	1961	75.00 – 85.00
Apple Green Overlay	**Ware No.**	**Introduced**	**Discontinued**	**Value**
Pitcher, 48 oz.	9166-AG	1961	1962	110.00 – 125.00
Salt and pepper	9106-AG	1961	1962	45.00 – 50.00
Sugar and creamer	9100-AG	1961	1962	45.00 – 55.00
Vase, 6"	9156-AG	1961	1962	55.00 – 65.00
Vase, pansy	9150-AG	1961	1962	35.00 – 40.00

Powder Blue Overlay	Ware No.	Introduced	Discontinued	Value
Pitcher, 48 oz.	9166-BV	1961	1962	110.00 – 125.00
Salt and pepper	9106-BV	1961	1962	45.00 – 50.00
Sugar and creamer	9100-BV	1961	1962	45.00 – 55.00
Vase, 6"	9156-BV	1961	1962	55.00 – 65.00
Vase, pansy	9150-BV	1961	1962	35.00 – 40.00
Honey Amber	**Ware No.**	**Introduced**	**Discontinued**	**Value**
Pitcher, 48 oz.	9166-HA	1961	1962	50.00 – 60.00
Salt and pepper	9106-HA	1961	1962	25.00 – 30.00
Sugar and creamer	9100-HA	1961	1962	25.00 – 30.00
Vase, 6"	9156-HA	1961	1962	35.00 – 40.00
Vase, pansy	9150-HA	1961	1962	25.00 – 30.00
Milk Glass	**Ware No.**	**Introduced**	**Discontinued**	**Value**
Pitcher, 48 oz.	9166-MI	1961	1962	45.00 – 55.00
Salt and pepper	9106-MI	1961	July 1962	20.00 – 25.00
Sugar and creamer	9100-MI	1961	1962	25.00 – 30.00
Vase, 6"	9156-MI	1961	1962	25.00 – 30.00
Vase, pansy	9150-MI	1961	1962	15.00 – 17.00
Coral	**Ware No.**	**Introduced**	**Discontinued**	**Value**
Vase, 6"	9156-CL	1961	1962	65.00 – 70.00
Wild Rose	**Ware No.**	**Introduced**	**Discontinued**	**Value**
Vase, 6"	9156-WR	1961	1962	65.00 – 75.00

9100 BV Sugar & Creamer

9106 BV Salt & Pepper

9100 HA Creamer

9150 WR Pansy Vase (Sample)

9153 YN 5" Vase

9153 PN 5" Vase

9150 AG Pansy Vase

9156 BV 6" Vase

9166 AG 48 Oz. Pitcher

9152 BN Tulip Vase

9152 PN 7" Tulip Vase

9152 YN Tulip Vase

Lacy Edge

Lacy Edge is a general term for a group of items consisting of several open edge patterns made by Fenton in the mid-1950s that were made in milk glass and opaque pastel colors.

Milk	Ware No.	Introduced	Discontinued	Value
Bowl, banana	9024-MI	1955	1959	40.00 – 50.00
Bowl, 8" "C"	9026-MI	1954	1959	18.00 – 22.00
Bowl, Scroll & Eye	9025-MI	1955	1957	15.00 – 18.00
Comport	9028-MI	1953	July 1961	35.00 – 40.00
Comport, ftd.	9029-MI	July 1952	1965	35.00 – 40.00
Comport, Scroll & Eye	9021-MI	1955	1959	25.00 – 35.00
Plate, Scroll & Eye	9015-MI	1955	July 1959	7.00 – 9.00
Plate, #360-8"	9018-MI	1952	1956	8.00 – 10.00
Plate, 9" "C"	9019-MI	July 1952	July 1961	10.00 – 12.00
Plate, 11"	9011-MI	1953	1960	14.00 – 16.00
Plate, 12"	9012-MI	1954	1958	20.00 – 25.00
Plate, ftd.	9017-MI	1954	1959	40.00 – 50.00
Plate planter, 9" "C"	9099-MI	July 1952	1960	15.00 – 18.00
Shell	9030-MI	1955	1966	8.00 – 10.00
Lattice bowl	9031-MI	1957	1960	25.00 – 28.00
Lattice bowl, flared	9023-MI	1957	1970	25.00 – 28.00
Blue Pastel	**Ware No.**	**Introduced**	**Discontinued**	**Value**
Bowl, 8" "C"	9026-BP	1954	1955	25.00 – 30.00
Comport	9028-BP	1954	1955	40.00 – 50.00
Comport, ftd.	9029-BP	1954	1955	40.00 – 50.00
Plate, #360-8"	9018-BP	1954	1955	14.00 – 16.00
Plate, 9" "C"	9019-BP	1954	1955	18.00 – 22.00
Plate, 11"	9011-BP	1954	1955	20.00 – 25.00
Plate planter, 9" "C"	9099-BP	1954	1955	20.00 – 25.00
Green Pastel	**Ware No.**	**Introduced**	**Discontinued**	**Value**
Bowl, banana	9024-GP	1955	1956	50.00 – 55.00
Bowl, 8" "C"	9026-GP	1954	1956	25.00 – 30.00
Bowl, Scroll & Eye	9025-GP	1955	1956	20.00 – 25.00
Comport	9028-GP	1954	1956	40.00 – 50.00
Comport, ftd.	9029-GP	1954	1956	40.00 – 50.00
Comport, Scroll & Eye	9021-GP	1955	1956	35.00 – 45.00
Plate, Scroll & Eye	9015-GP	1955	1956	12.00 – 14.00
Plate, #360-8"	9018-GP	1954	1956	14.00 – 16.00
Plate, 9" "C"	9019-GP	1954	1956	18.00 – 22.00
Plate, 11"	9011-GP	1954	1956	20.00 – 25.00
Plate planter, 9" "C"	9099-GP	1954	1956	20.00 – 25.00
Rose Pastel	**Ware No.**	**Introduced**	**Discontinued**	**Value**
Bowl, banana	9024-RP	1955	July 1956	50.00 – 55.00
Bowl, 8" "C"	9026-RP	1954	1957	20.00 – 25.00
Bowl, Scroll & Eye	9025-RP	1955	1957	20.00 – 25.00
Comport	9028-RP	1954	July 1956	40.00 – 50.00
Comport, ftd.	9029-RP	1954	July 1956	40.00 – 50.00
Comport, Scroll & Eye	9021-RP	1955	July 1956	35.00 – 45.00
Plate, Scroll & Eye	9015-RP	1955	July 1956	12.00 – 14.00
Plate, #360-8"	9018-RP	1954	1955	12.00 – 14.00
Plate, 9" "C"	9019-RP	1954	1957	18.00 – 22.00

LACY EDGE *Milk Glass* Fenton

Catalog Reprint   Courtesy Of: The Fenton Art Glass Museum

A. 9012 MI   12″ Plate
B. 9024 MI   Banana Bowl
C. 9011 MI   11″ Plate
D. 9028 MI   Comport
E. 9015 MI   Scroll & Eye Plate

F. 9019 MI   9″ C Plate
G. 9021 MI   Scroll & Eye Comport
H. 5196 MI   Leaf Tidbit
I. 5116 MI   8″ Leaf Plate
J. 5118 MI   11″ Leaf Plate

K. 9017 MI   Ftd. Plate
L. 9025 MI   Scroll & Eye Bowl
M. 9030 MI   Lacy Edge Shell
N. 9026 MI   8″ C Bowl
O. 9029 MI   Ftd. Comport

Rose Pastel	Ware No.	Introduced	Discontinued	Value
Plate, 11"	9011-RP	1954	1955	20.00 – 25.00
Plate, 12"	9012-RP	1955	1957	20.00 – 25.00
Plate planter, 9" "C"	9099-RP	1954	1957	20.00 – 25.00
Turquoise	**Ware No.**	**Introduced**	**Discontinued**	**Value**
Bowl, banana	9024-TU	1955	July 1956	50.00 – 55.00
Bowl, 8" "C"	9026-TU	1955	July 1956	25.00 – 30.00
Bowl, Scroll & Eye	9025-TU	1955	1957	20.00 – 25.00
Comport	9028-TU	1955	July 1956	40.00 – 50.00
Comport, ftd.	9029-TU	1955	July 1956	40.00 – 50.00
Comport, Scroll & Eye	9021-TU	1955	July 1956	35.00 – 45.00
Plate, Scroll & Eye	9015-TU	1955	1957	12.00 – 14.00
Plate, 9" "C"	9019-TU	1955	July 1956	18.00 – 22.00
Plate, #360-8"	9018-TU	1955	1956	14.00 – 16.00
Plate, 11"	9011-TU	1955	July 1956	20.00 – 25.00
Plate planter, 9" "C"	9099-TU	1955	July 1956	20.00 – 25.00
Shell	9030-TU	1955	July 1956	12.00 – 15.00

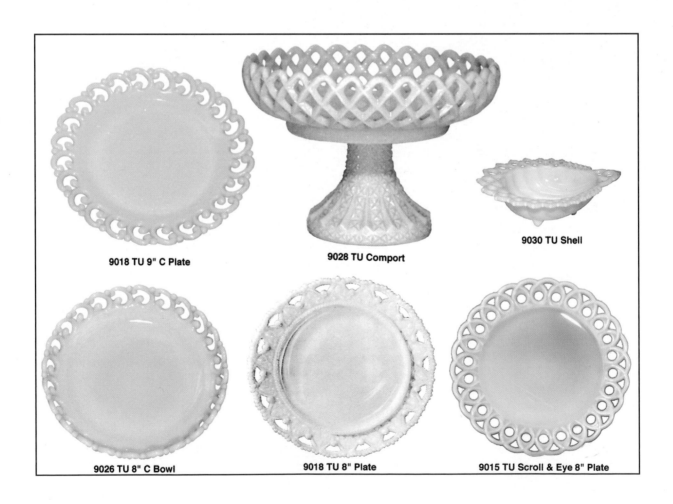

9018 TU 9" C Plate

9028 TU Comport

9030 TU Shell

9026 TU 8" C Bowl

9018 TU 8" Plate

9015 TU Scroll & Eye 8" Plate

Lamb's Tongue

Five different pieces in the Lamb's Tongue pattern were made during the mid-1950s. Milk (MI) glass and the popular pastel colors — Blue Pastel (BP), Green Pastel (GP), and Rose Pastel (RP) — were chosen to portray this pattern. The candy was also made in Turquoise (TU) for a year toward the end of the production.

A No. 2731-6" basket in the Lamb's Tongue pattern has been made recently in the following colors:

Rose Pearl (DN)	(Dusty Rose with an iridescent finish)	1993
Plum (PL)		1993 through 1996
Autumn Gold (AM) (Fenton's new name for Amber)		1994
Rose Magnolia Opalescent (RV)		1994
Sea Mist Green (LE)		1996 & 1997
Champagne Satin (PQ) (light pink opalescent)		1996 & 1997
Sea Green Satin (GE)		1998

Lamb's Tongue	Ware No.	Introduced	Discontinued	Value
Candy jar	4381-BP	July 1954	1955	90.00 – 110.00
Creamer and sugar	4301-BP	July 1954	1955	60.00 – 65.00
Mayonnaise set	4303-BP	July 1954	1955	70.00 – 80.00
Oil bottle	4369-BP	July 1954	1955	130.00 – 145.00
Salt and pepper	4306-BP	July 1954	1955	50.00 – 75.00
Candy jar	4381-GP	July 1954	July 1955	90.00 – 110.00
Creamer and sugar	4301-GP	July 1954	1955	60.00 – 65.00
Mayonnaise set	4303-GP	July 1954	1955	70.00 – 80.00
Oil bottle	4369-GP	July 1954	1955	130.00 – 145.00
Salt and pepper	4306-GP	July 1954	1955	50.00 – 75.00
Candy jar	4381-MI	July 1954	July 1956	60.00 – 70.00
Creamer and sugar	4301-MI	July 1954	1955	45.00 – 55.00
Mayonnaise set	4303-MI	July 1954	1956	25.00 – 30.00
Oil bottle	4369-MI	July 1954	1955	120.00 – 135.00
Salt and pepper	4306-MI	July 1954	July 1956	50.00 – 75.00
Candy jar	4381-RP	July 1954	1955	90.00 – 100.00
Creamer and sugar	4301-RP	July 1954	1955	60.00 – 65.00
Mayonnaise set	4303-RP	July 1954	1955	65.00 – 75.00
Oil bottle	4369-RP	July 1954	1955	120.00 – 135.00
Salt and pepper	4306-RP	July 1954	1955	50.00 – 75.00
Candy jar	4381-TU	1955	July 1956	90.00 – 100.00

4381 TU
Candy Jar

4303 GP Mayonnaise Set

4306 BP Salt & Pepper

No. 4369
Oil Bottle

No. 4301
Sugar & Cream Set

Lily of the Valley

The Lily of the Valley pattern was introduced into the Fenton line in January 1979 in the Cameo Opalescent (CO) and Carnival (CN) colors. There were five shapes in the carnival assortment and nine different pieces were included in the Cameo Opalescent color. The carnival Lily of the Valley pieces were discontinued at the end of 1979, but many of the Cameo Opalescent pieces were made through 1982.

In later years, other items were also made in this pattern.

1980

Cameo Opalescent production continued and Topaz Opalescent Lily of the Valley appeared in January 1980, catalog supplement. The bell and candleholders and handkerchief vase were also available in Blue Opalescent.

Basket, 6"	8437-TO	Bell, 6"	8265-BO
Candleholder	8475-TO	Candleholder	8475-BO
Vase, handkerchief	8450-TO	Vase, handkerchief	8450-BO

1981

The following pieces were in the catalog in Blue Opalescent, French Opalescent, and Cameo Opalescent:

Basket, 6"	8437	Fairy light	8404	Vase, handkerchief	8450
Bell, 6"	8265	Rose bowl	845		
Candy box	8489	Vase, 10" bud	8458		

1987

Some pieces in the Lily of the Valley pattern were made for the Fenton's Gracious Touch collectibles division. The following items appeared in Dusty Rose Velvet (VO) and Sapphire Blue Opalescent (BX) during 1987:

Basket, 6"	Q8437	Rose bowl	Q8453
Bell, 6"	Q8265	Candy box	Q8489
Vase, 10" bud	Q8458	Vase, handkerchief	Q8450

1993

The No. 8489 candy & cover was made in Red Carnival (RN).

1994

The following items were made in Rose Magnolia Opalescent (RV):

| Bell | 8265-RV | Rose bowl | 8453-RV | Vase, handkerchief | 8450-RV |

1995

The No. 8450 handkerchief vase was made in Cobalt (KN), Petal Pink (PN), and Sea Mist Green (LE).

1996

Old moulds were used with a newly introduced color to create an interesting assortment. The new color was Champagne Satin (PQ) and the old shapes were as follows:

Basket, 8" oval	8437-PQ	Rose bowl, 5½"	8453-PQ
Bell,	8265-PQ	Vase, handkerchief	8450-PQ
Candy & cover, 9"	8484-PQ		

Production of the No. 8450 vase also continued in Sea Mist Green and Cobalt.

1997 – 98

Four Lily of the Valley shapes were utilized with Fenton's new Misty Blue Satin (LR) color. Included in the assortment were the following:

| Bell, 6" | 8265-LR | Rose bowl, 5½" | 8453-LR |
| Candy & cover, 9" | 8484-LR | Vase, handkerchief | 8450-LR |

The above pieces were also made in a light pink opalescent color that Fenton called Champagne Satin (PQ). In addition, the No. 8437 oval basket and the No. 8475 candleholders were made in this color.

In 1998, all of the preceding pieces were still in the line in their respective colors. In addition, the No. 8450 handkerchief vase was made in Sea Green Satin (GE). In 1999, the only items remaining in these colors were the rose bowl, bell, and handkerchief vase in Misty Blue Satin and the bell and the basket in Champagne Satin.

2000 – 03

During the year 2000, the bell and the 8" basket from the preceding decade remained in the line in Champagne Satin. Additionally, the No. 8404 fairy light was made in Ice Blue Pearl (L9). These pieces were all discontinued at the end of the year. In 2001, the No. 8484 candy was made in Topaz Opalescent Satin (TS). Numerous items entered the line in new colors in 2003. The No. 8450 handkerchief vase was made in Ruby Amberina Stretch (RL) and in Amethyst Carnival (CN). The No. 8437 oval basket and the No. 8363 bell were made in Willow Green Opalescent (GR). The No. 8489 candy and the No. 8404 fairy light were in the line in Blue Topaz Opalescent (S7).

Carnival Lily of the Valley	Ware No.	Introduced	Discontinued	Value
Basket	8437-CN	1979	1980	40.00 – 50.00
Bell	8265-CN	1979	1980	30.00 – 35.00
Candy, ftd.	8484-CN	1979	1980	45.00 – 50.00
Rose bowl	8453-CN	1979	1980	25.00 – 27.00
Vase, bud	8458-CN	1979	1980	20.00 – 25.00
Cameo Opalescent Lily of the Valley	**Ware No.**	**Introduced**	**Discontinued**	**Value**
Basket	8437-CO	1979	1980+	40.00 – 50.00
Bell	8265-CO	1979	1980+	35.00 – 40.00
Bowl, ftd.	8451-CO	1979	1980+	45.00 – 55.00
Cake plate, ftd.	8411-CO	1979	1980+	45.00 – 65.00
Candy	8489-CO	1979	1980+	40.00 – 45.00
Candy, ftd.	8484-CO	1979	1980+	45.00 – 50.00
Fairy light	8404-CO	1979	1980+	40.00 – 47.00
Rose bowl	8453-CO	1979	1980+	18.00 – 25.00
Vase, bud	8458-CO	1979	1980+	18.00 – 25.00

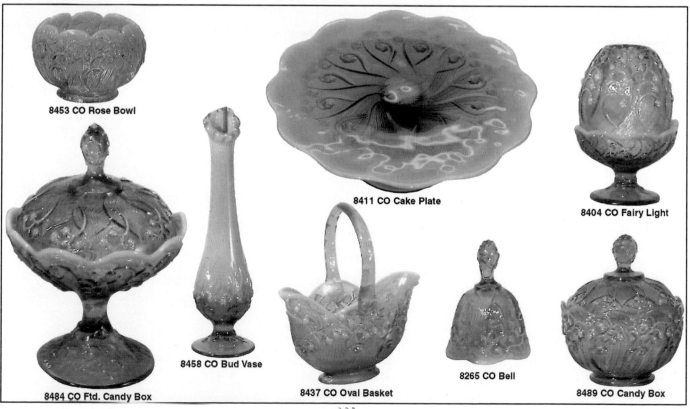

8453 CO Rose Bowl

8411 CO Cake Plate

8404 CO Fairy Light

8458 CO Bud Vase

8484 CO Ftd. Candy Box

8437 CO Oval Basket

8265 CO Bell

8489 CO Candy Box

New World

Fenton's distinctly modern entry into the line in 1953 was described in the January catalog supplement as a pattern "designed by Stan Fistick to adapt to our particular skills and distinctive processes to contemporary living. The beautiful color effects and new feeling in modern of the wine bottle (No. 1667) and wine glass (No. 1647), cruet, salt and pepper, sugar and cream, and others will stimulate your sales of Fenton. These are made in Cranberry and Lime. The spell of Dusk is captured by the same shapes made in the very smart color combination of black and gray. The cruet (No. 7369) is made in solid gray with black handle and black stopper. The wine bottle (No. 7367) is gray with black stopper, while the wine glass is black on the outside and gray on the inner surfaces. Plates and bowls are all gray on the upper surface and black on the underside except the 8" plate (No. 7318) which is solid black."

Public acceptance of this contemporary style glassware was slow to develop. Sales of the gray and black items were particularly sluggish; therefore, this color combination was discontinued by the end of 1953. As a result of this very short period of production, all Dusk (KV) items are in short supply on the secondary market. Some items in the more popular rib optic colors remained in production for several more years. The wine bottle in Cranberry was especially popular and stayed in the line for ten years. The wine bottle may also be found in Topaz Opalescent, but this color is so elusive many collectors are unaware of its existence.

Hard-to-find pieces in the opalescent colors include the two large bowls, the plates, cruets, and the wines. Generally, items in Lime Opalescent are more elusive than the same pieces in Cranberry.

New World	Ware No.	Introduced	Discontinued	Value
Bowl, 12" salad	7323-KV	1953	Sept. 1953	140.00 – 180.00
Bowl, 14" floater	7324-KV	1953	Sept. 1953	180.00 – 200.00
Creamer and sugar	7304-KV	1953	Sept. 1953	150.00 – 175.00
Cruet	7369-KV	1953	Sept. 1953	150.00 – 200.00
Plate, 8" salad	7318-BK	1953	Sept. 1953	45.00 – 55.00
Plate, 9" salad	7319-KV	1953	Sept. 1953	45.00 – 55.00
Plate, 14" torte	7314-KV	1953	Sept. 1953	125.00 – 150.00
*Salt and pepper	7305-KV	1953	Sept. 1953	90.00 – 125.00
**Wine	7347-KV	1953	Sept. 1953	100.00 – 125.00
**Wine bottle	7367-KV	1953	Sept. 1953	175.00 – 225.00

*Shakers were also made with a black exterior.
**Also sold as a 7-piece wine set with the ware number 7307.

Cranberry Rib Optic	Ware No.	Introduced	Discontinued	Value
Bowl, 12" salad	1623-CR	1953	1955	150.00 – 200.00
Bowl, 14" floater	1624-CR	1953	1955	200.00 – 225.00
Creamer and sugar	1604-CR	1953	1955	200.00 – 225.00
Cruet, cry handle	1669-CR	1953	1955	**200.00 – 225.00
Plate, 9" salad	1619-CR	1953	July 1954	70.00 – 80.00
Plate, 16" torte	1614-CR	1953	1955	150.00 – 170.00
Salt and pepper	1605-CR	1953	July 1959	110.00 – 140.00
*Wine	1647-CR	1953	1955	140.00 – 160.00
*Wine bottle	1667-CR	1953	1963	#200.00 – 225.00

*Also marketed as a 7-piece wine set with the ware number 1607.

**With black handle 350.00 – 400.00.

#Topaz 450.00 – 500.00.

Lime Opalescent Rib Optic	Ware No.	Introduced	Discontinued	Value
Bowl, 12" salad	1623-LO	1953	1954	150.00 – 200.00
Bowl, 14" floater	1624-LO	1953	1954	200.00 – 225.00
Creamer and sugar	1604-LO	1953	1954	200.00 – 225.00
Cruet	1669-LO	1953	1954	200.00 – 230.00
Plate, 9" salad	1619-LO	1953	1954	75.00 – 85.00
Plate, 16" torte	1614-LO	1953	1954	145.00 – 185.00
Salt and pepper	1605-LO	1953	1955	125.00 – 140.00
*Wine	1647-LO	1953	1954	140.00 – 160.00
*Wine bottle	1667-LO	1953	1954	275.00 – 325.00

*Also marketed as a 7-piece wine set with the ware number 1607.

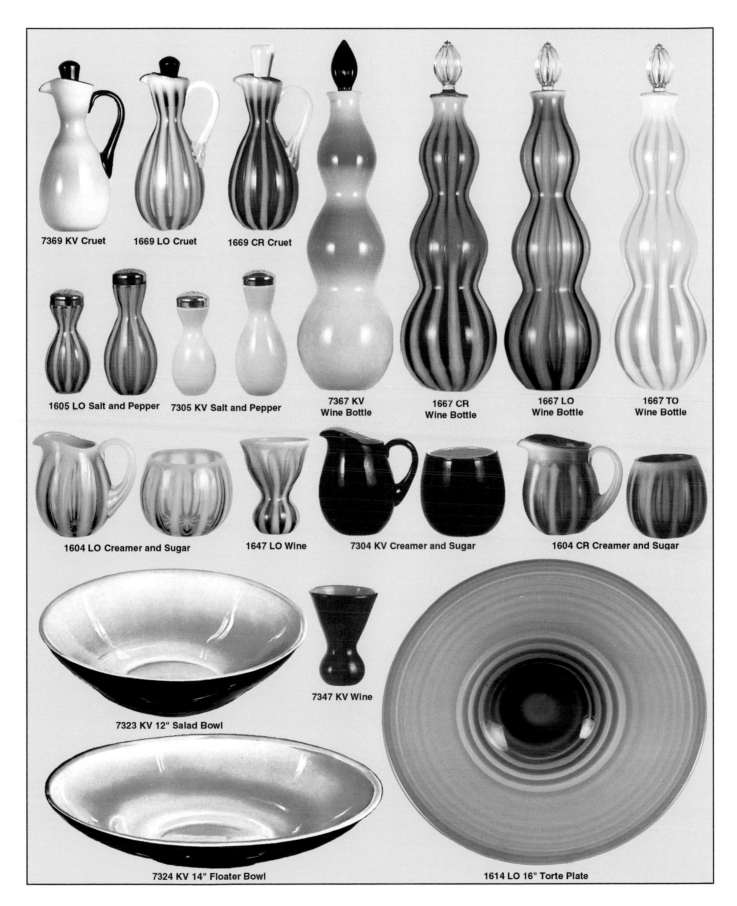

7369 KV Cruet

1669 LO Cruet

1669 CR Cruet

1605 LO Salt and Pepper

7305 KV Salt and Pepper

7367 KV
Wine Bottle

1667 CR
Wine Bottle

1667 LO
Wine Bottle

1667 TO
Wine Bottle

1604 LO Creamer and Sugar

1647 LO Wine

7304 KV Creamer and Sugar

1604 CR Creamer and Sugar

7323 KV 12" Salad Bowl

7347 KV Wine

7324 KV 14" Floater Bowl

1614 LO 16" Torte Plate

Polka Dot in Cranberry

Fenton introduced Cranberry Polka Dot into the regular line in January 1955. It featured glassware with a Cranberry background that was interwoven with tiny uniformly spaced French Opalescent dots. Unfortunately, the opalescent version of this pattern did not sell well and was discontinued by July 1956. The Polka Dot pattern was continued in a new color — Ruby Overlay. Some of the old shapes were continued and other new shapes were introduced. A barber bottle was made in transparent Jamestown Blue in 1957. Other shapes were placed into the line in the following year in this color. In 1960, three different shapes of vases were made in amber. However, the experiment with amber was not very successful and this color was quickly discontinued.

Sets were sold in the following forms:

Set	Ware No.
Creamer and sugar: consisted of a sugar shaker and creamer	2204-CR
Ice tea set: 1 No. 2267 jug and 6 No. 2247 tumblers	2207-CR

The No. 2221-CR footed ivy ball was made with a crystal base. Unusual items for the regular Fenton line included the butter or cheese dish and the sugar shaker. The cheese dish had a Polka Dot top and a milk glass underplate.

Polka Dot is the inverse of a pattern that Fenton made for L. G. Wright. Wright's Honeycomb pattern had an opalescent background with small Cranberry dots. During the 1990s Fenton also used this reverse coloration for a Cranberry Opalescent pattern called Fine Dot.

A cruet with a stopper and a small basket were made in Topaz Opalescent Polka Dot for the LeVay Distributing Company in 1979.

Polka Dot	Ware No.	Introduced	Discontinued	Value
Basket, 7" handled	2237-CR	1955	1956	200.00 – 225.00
Bowl, 7"	2227-CR	1955	July 1956	85.00 – 95.00
Butter or cheese	2277-CR	1955	July 1956	400.00 – 500.00
Creamer	2261-CR	1955	July 1956	60.00 – 80.00
Cruet	2273-CR	1955	July 1956	200.00 – 250.00
Ivy ball, ftd.	2221-CR	1955	July 1956	200.00 – 225.00
Jug, 70 oz.	2267-CR	1955	July 1956	450.00 – 500.00
Rose bowl, 4"	2224-CR	1955	July 1956	60.00 – 80.00
Rose bowl, 5"	2225-CR	1955	July 1956	85.00 – 100.00
Salt and pepper	2206-CR	1955	July 1956	140.00 – 160.00
Sugar shaker	2293-CR	1955	July 1956	225.00 – 250.00
Tumbler, 12 oz.	2247-CR	1955	July 1956	65.00 – 85.00
Vase	2255-CR	1955	July 1956	95.00 – 110.00
Vase, 6"	2256-CR	1955	July 1956	125.00 – 135.00
Vase, 7½"	2257-CR	1955	July 1956	125.00 – 145.00
Vase, 8" tulip	2250-CR	1955	July 1956	185.00 – 200.00
Vase, 8" DC	2251-CR	1955	July 1956	150.00 – 200.00
Vase, 8"	2258-CR	1955	July 1956	250.00 – 290.00
Vase, 8½"	2259-CR	1955	1956	300.00 – 325.00

2221 CR Footed Ivy Ball

2251 CR 8" DC Vase

2250 CR 8" Tulip Vase

2258 CR 8" Vase

2237 CR 7" Basket

2256 CR 6" Vase

2257 CR 7 1/2" Vase

2255 CR Vase

2261 CR Creamer

2224 CR 4" Rose Bowl

2277 CR Butter
or Cheese Dish

2293 CR Sugar Shaker

2273 CR Cruet

2206 CR Salt & Pepper

2267 CR 70 Oz. Jug

2247 CR 12 Oz. Tumbler

2259 CR 8 1/2" Vase

2227 CR 7" Bowl

Polka Dot in Ruby Overlay

Ruby Overlay is a cased glass with Gold Ruby as the interior layer and crystal on the outside. When opalescent Polka Dot failed to perform as well as expected, Fenton switched production to Ruby Overlay with a Fine Dot Optic pattern. The first pieces were introduced in July 1956, and some pieces of this color lasted through the late 1960s. A few pieces such as the pitcher, tumblers, and sugar shaker were only made for a short time. Expect these items to be slightly elusive.

Fenton used the No. 2458 ware number for two different vases. The first piece was a 7½" vase made from 1956 through December 1957. Later, from 1960 through 1964, an 8½" vase was produced with this ware number. When pieces of this pattern were made in Country Cranberry in the late 1980s, the pattern was referred to as Fine Dot Optic.

Ruby Overlay Polka Dot	Ware No.	Introduced	Discontinued	Value
Creamer	2461-RO	July 1956	1969	25.00 – 35.00
Cruet	2473-RO	July 1956	1967	125.00 – 135.00
Decanter	2478-RO	1960	1965	200.00 – 225.00
Pitcher, 2 quart	2467-RO	July 1956	1957	240.00 – 270.00
Rose bowl, 4"	2424-RO	July 1956	1969	25.00 – 30.00
Salt and pepper	2406-RO	July 1956	1960	40.00 – 50.00
Sugar shaker	2493-RO	July 1956	1957	100.00 – 125.00
Tumbler, 12 oz.	2447-RO	July 1956	1957	20.00 – 25.00
Vase, 6"	2450-RO	1958	1960	35.00 – 45.00
Vase, 6"	2454-RO	1958	1963	35.00 – 40.00
Vase, 6"	2456-RO	July 1956	1969	30.00 – 35.00
*Vase, 7"	2442-RO	1959	1960	45.00 – 60.00
Vase, 7" pinch	2451-RO	1958	1969	40.00 – 45.00
Vase, 7"	2455-RO	1958	1960	35.00 – 45.00
Vase, 7½"	2457-RO	July 1956	1969	40.00 – 50.00
Vase, 8" pinch	2452-RO	1958	1963	55.00 – 65.00
Vase, 8½"	2458-RO	1960	1965	50.00 – 55.00
*Vase, 8½"	2448-RO	1959	1960	85.00 – 100.00
Vase, 8½"	2459-RO	1960	1963	55.00 – 65.00
*Vase, 10"	2440-RO	1959	1960	140.00 – 160.00
Vase, 10"	2453-RO	1958	1963	100.00 – 125.00
*Also made in Amber 25.00 – 35.00				

Polka Dot in Transparent Jamestown Blue

Jamestown Blue	Ware No.	Introduced	Discontinued	Value
Barber bottle	2471-JT	1957	July 1959	150.00 – 185.00
Creamer	2461-JT	1958	July 1959	35.00 – 40.00
Cruet	2473-JT	1958	1960	135.00 – 155.00
Rose bowl, 4"	2424-JT	1958	1960	25.00 – 35.00
Salt and pepper	2406-JT	1958	July 1959	55.00 – 65.00
Vase, 6"	2450-JT	1958	July 1959	45.00 – 55.00
Vase, 6"	2454-JT	1958	July 1959	30.00 – 35.00
Vase, 7" pinch	2451-JT	1958	July 1959	45.00 – 50.00
Vase, 7"	2455-JT	1958	July 1959	40.00 – 55.00
Vase, 8" pinch	2452-JT	1958	July 1959	65.00 – 85.00
Vase, 10"	2453-JT	1958	July 1959	100.00 – 145.00

Ruby Overlay

2493 RO Sugar Shaker

2448 RO 8 1/2" Vase

2478 RO Decanter

2456 RO 6" Vase

2447 RO 12 Oz. Tumbler

2467 RO 2 Quart Pitcher

2424 RO 4" Rose Bowl

2442 RO 7 " Vase

2440 RO 10" Vase

2458 RO 7" Vase

2452 RO 8" Pinch Vase

2453 RO 10" Vase

2457 RO 7 1/2" Vase

2458 RO 8 1/2" Vase

2459 RO 8 1/2" Vase

Transparent Jamestown Blue

2406 JT Salt & Pepper

2455 JT 7" Vase

2424 JT 4" Rose Bowl

2461 JT Creamer

2451 JT 7" Pinch Vase

2450 JT 6" Vase

2453 JT 10" Vase

2471 JT Barber Bottle

2454 JT 6" Vase

2473 JT Cruet

Priscilla

Fenton attempted to bring back a tableware line in January 1950, with the introduction of the No. 1890 Priscilla luncheon set. Priscilla was made in crystal, green, and light blue. The primary focus of this pattern was on tableware, but a large 12" basket was also included in the line. The pattern was not highly successful in gaining market share. Therefore, all items in all colors were discontinued by the end of June 1952.

A few selected items in this pattern were later revived. The 11" plate was reissued in 1992 in Holiday Green (GH) and Ruby (RU). The Christmas catalog listed this piece as the No. 9679-11½" tray. The 12" No. 9036 basket was made in Salem Blue (SR) in 1990 and in Dusty Rose (DK) from 1990 through 1992. The No. 9068-10½" flared bowl was also made from 1990 through 1992 in Salem Blue.

Priscilla	Crystal	Blue	Green
Basket, 12" handled	75.00 – 85.00	125.00 – 150.00	145.00 – 200.00
Bonbon, 6" 2-handled	10.00 – 12.00	18.00 – 22.00	18.00 – 22.00
Bowl, 9" cupped	20.00 – 25.00	32.00 – 37.00	35.00 – 40.00
Bowl, 10½" flared	25.00 – 35.00	45.00 – 50.00	45.00 – 55.00
Creamer	8.00 – 10.00	20.00 – 25.00	20.00 – 25.00
Goblet, cocktail	8.00 – 10.00	25.00 – 27.00	25.00 – 27.00
Goblet, water	14.00 – 18.00	27.00 – 30.00	27.00 – 35.00
Goblet, wine	10.00 – 12.00	20.00 – 25.00	27.00 – 30.00
Plate, 6"	5.00 – 6.00	8.00 – 10.00	10.00 – 12.00
Plate, 8"	8.00 – 12.00	20.00 – 22.00	20.00 – 22.00
Plate, 11" rolled edge	14.00 – 16.00	40.00 – 45.00	40.00 – 45.00
Plate, 12½"	15.00 – 18.00	50.00 – 55.00	50.00 – 55.00
Sherbet	8.00 – 12.00	16.00 – 18.00	16.00 – 18.00
Sugar	8.00 – 10.00	20.00 – 25.00	20.00 – 25.00
Tumbler, 12 oz. ftd.	10.00 – 12.00	30.00 – 35.00	30.00 – 35.00

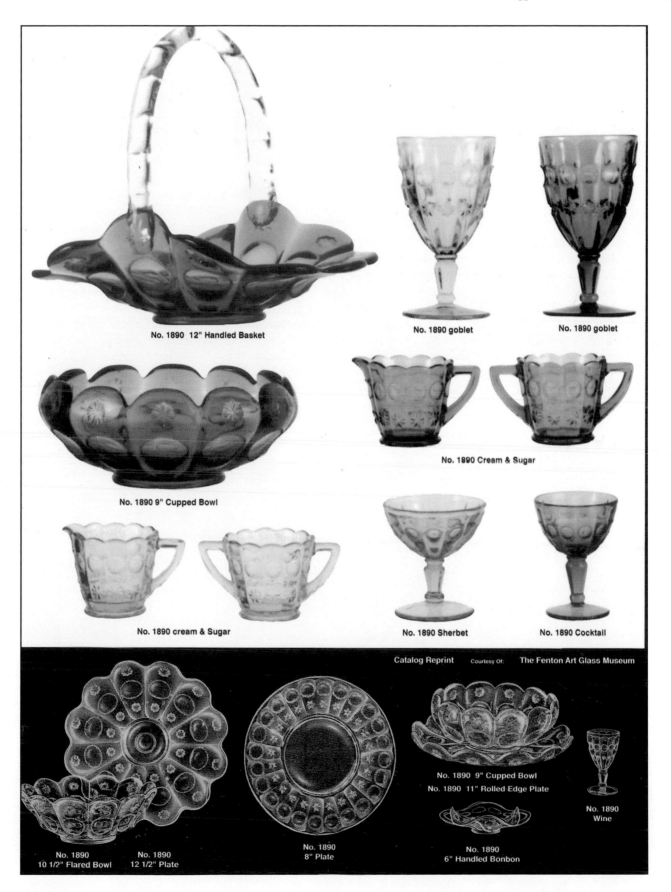

No. 1890 12" Handled Basket

No. 1890 goblet

No. 1890 goblet

No. 1890 9" Cupped Bowl

No. 1890 Cream & Sugar

No. 1890 cream & Sugar

No. 1890 Sherbet

No. 1890 Cocktail

Catalog Reprint   Courtesy Of: The Fenton Art Glass Museum

No. 1890
10 1/2" Flared Bowl

No. 1890
12 1/2" Plate

No. 1890
8" Plate

No. 1890 9" Cupped Bowl
No. 1890 11" Rolled Edge Plate

No. 1890
6" Handled Bonbon

No. 1890
Wine

Rib Optic/Rib Satin

Fenton has made vertical ribbed opalescent glassware since the early years of production. Opalescent and iridized Ribbed Optic water and lemonade sets in several colors were made through the 1920s and production of opalescent beverage sets and vases continued through the late 1930s. Lamps, handled guest sets, and night sets were also among the items made during that era. For more information on these items, see *Fenton Art Glass 1907 – 1939*.

During the late 1930s Fenton made water sets, vases, and top hats in the Rib Optic pattern in French Opalescent, Blue Opalescent, Green Opalescent, and Cranberry colors. These shapes in Rib Optic appear to have been discontinued by 1940.

In 1952 Fenton introduced four new Rib Optic pieces in satin colors. The cranberry opalescent color was called Rose Satin and the blue opalescent color was called Blue Satin. The next year an ivy ball was introduced in Green Opalescent and Cranberry. The Cranberry ivy ball was sold with a white diamond-shaped base. The Green Opalescent ivy ball may be found with a white or dark green base. At this same time Fenton's New World shapes were introduced in Green Opalescent and Cranberry Rib Optic. Most of these shapes were discontinued by 1955, but the wine decanter remained in the line through the early 1960s. The 8" pinch vase has also been found in Green Opalescent. This vase has not been found in the regular line listings, but was probably made in the late 1950s. Also not in the regular line, but generally available are glossy versions of all the Rib Satin pieces. These pieces are shown in the top section of the photo to the right.

Today, Rib Optic is still in the Fenton line. Recent production has included the No. 1531-8" basket, No. 3053-11½" tulip vase, No. 1599-5" vase, and the No. 1554-9" vase in Cranberry. Eight different Rib Optic shapes were also made in Autumn Gold Opalescent (AO) — Fenton's latest name for amber opalescent — in 1994.

In 2002, Fenton revived Rib Optic in French Opalescent as a background for the hand-painted Cottage Roses decoration. The design was created by Frances Burton as a re-creation of a spray of old-fashioned fuchsia roses overlying the French Opalescent glass in a manner that created a romantic cottage garden. The decoration remained in the line in 2003.

Fenton made several opalescent Rib pattern items for L. G. Wright. Included in this selection were a small rose bowl, barber bottle, cruet, and small jug in Cranberry. Barber bottles were also made in Topaz Opalescent and Green Opalescent. Some of these L. G. Wright items are pictured in the bottom right area of the photo.

Rib Optic (1950s)	French Ware No.	Green Introduced	Blue Discontinued	Value
Ivy ball and base	1622-CR	1952	1954	100.00 – 150.00
Ivy ball and base	1622-GO			100.00 – 150.00
Wine	1647-CR	1953	1955	100.00 – 125.00
Wine bottle	1667-CR	1953	1963	225.00 – 240.00
Blue Satin Rib Optic	**Ware No.**	**Introduced**	**Discontinued**	**Value**
Cruet, #815	1663-BA	1952	1955	200.00 – 250.00
Vase, #1925-6"	1656-BA	1952	1955	75.00 – 85.00
Vase, #1720-7½" pinch	1657-BA	1952	1953	75.00 – 85.00
Vase, #510-8"	1658-BA	1952	1954	75.00 – 85.00
Rose Satin Rib Optic	**Ware No.**	**Introduced**	**Discontinued**	**Value**
Cruet, #815	1663-RA	1952	1955	250.00 – 275.00
Vase, #1925-6"	1656-RA	1952	1955	90.00 – 110.00
Vase, #1720-7½" pinch	1657-RA	1952	1953	85.00 – 95.00
Vase, #510-8"	1658-RA	1952	1954	90.00 – 100.00
L. G. Wright Items	**Blue Opalescent**	**Topaz Opalescent**	**Cranberry**	
Barber Bottle	140.00 – 160.00	185.00 – 200.00	185.00 – 200.00	
Jug	90.00 – 110.00	100.00 – 150.00	100.00 – 125.00	
Rose Bowl	40.00 – 50.00	45.00 – 60.00	50.00 – 60.00	

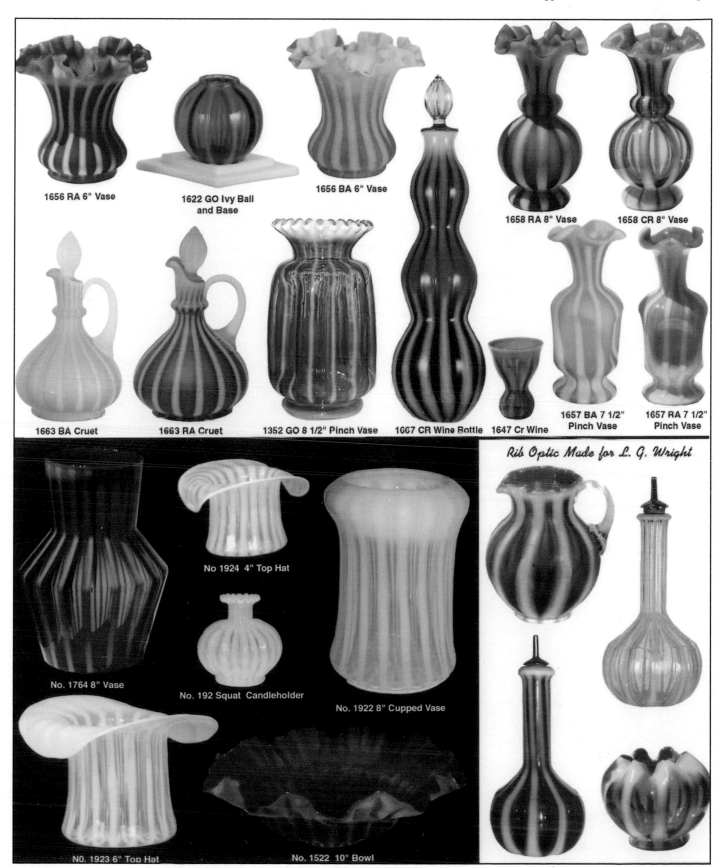

1656 RA 6" Vase

1622 GO Ivy Ball and Base

1656 BA 6" Vase

1658 RA 8" Vase

1658 CR 8" Vase

1663 BA Cruet

1663 RA Cruet

1352 GO 8 1/2" Pinch Vase

1607 CR Wine Bottle

1647 Cr Wine

1657 BA 7 1/2" Pinch Vase

1657 RA 7 1/2" Pinch Vase

No 1924 4" Top Hat

No. 1764 8" Vase

No. 192 Squat Candleholder

No. 1922 8" Cupped Vase

No. 1923 6" Top Hat

No. 1522 10" Bowl

Rib Optic Made for L. G. Wright

Ring Optic

Ring is an opalescent Fenton pattern that was listed in a circa 1939 catalog. The pattern consists of alternating opalescent and transparent concentric rings. Colors made include French Opalescent, Stiegel Blue Opalescent, and Cranberry. Ring is similar to another opalescent pattern made during the same time period called Block. However, the Block pattern also has vertical transparent separations which create blocks in the opalescent rings.

Catalog listings from this era are incomplete. Therefore it is difficult to determine exactly what shapes may be found in this pattern. However, the pattern was made during the same time period as Spiral Optic, and many pieces with those same shapes should be expected to be found.

The large handled bottle was also used as a lamp base.

Ring Optic	Stiegel Blue Opalescent	French Opalescent	Cranberry
Bottle, 6" handled	60.00 – 75.00	40.00 – 45.00	75.00 – 80.00
Bottle, 8" handled	75.00 – 85.00	45.00 – 55.00	80.00 – 90.00
Bowl, #1522-10" crimped	60.00 – 70.00	35.00 – 45.00	100.00 – 125.00
Bowl, #1523-11" crimped	90.00 – 110.00	45.00 – 55.00	125.00 – 150.00
Candlestick, #1523	60.00 – 80.00	35.00 – 50.00	75.00 – 95.00
Pitcher, #201-7"	240.00 – 280.00	150.00 – 185.00	275.00 – 300.00
Pitcher, #1353	290.00 – 325.00	180.00 – 200.00	300.00 – 350.00
Tumbler, #201 8 oz.	20.00 – 25.00	18.00 – 20.00	25.00 – 35.00
Tumbler, 10 oz.	30.00 – 35.00	20.00 – 25.00	30.00 – 40.00
Vase, #184-10" tulip, crimped	100.00 – 125.00	80.00 – 95.00	200.00 – 225.00
Vase, #510-8"	75.00 – 95.00	45.00 – 55.00	100.00 – 125.00

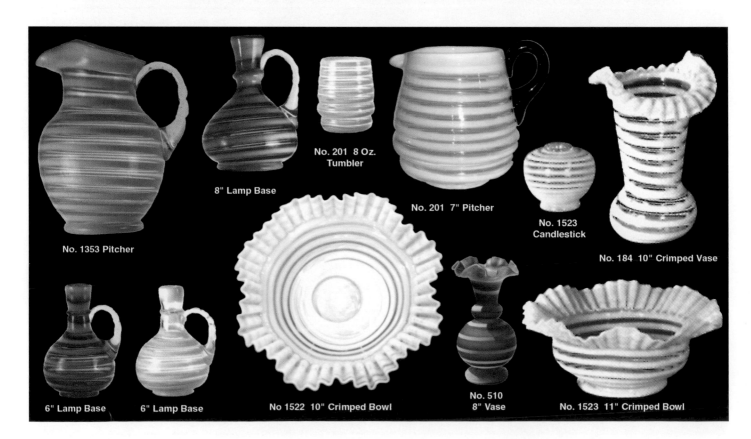

No. 1353 Pitcher

8" Lamp Base

No. 201 8 Oz. Tumbler

No. 201 7" Pitcher

No. 1523 Candlestick

No. 184 10" Crimped Vase

6" Lamp Base

6" Lamp Base

No 1522 10" Crimped Bowl

No. 510 8" Vase

No. 1523 11" Crimped Bowl

Rose

The idea for Fenton's Rose pattern was spawned when Frank Fenton purchased a Tiffin "Roses" comport at an antique show. Fenton's replica of this piece, the No. 9222 high footed comport, was introduced into the line in the January 1964 catalog supplement in Colonial Amber, Colonial Blue, Colonial Green, Colonial Pink, and milk glass. Due to the popularity of this first piece, more items were created in this pattern over the next few years. Roses also appeared in new colors. Orange was added to the line in 1965 and Blue Marble appeared in 1970. The high footed comport and several lamps were made in other colors, too. The comport was made in Blue Satin (BA), Carnival (CN), Custard (CU), and Lime Sherbet (LS). In 1967, three different Roses lamps were made in overlay colors. Three of the lamps were made in Honey Amber (HA), Blue Overlay (OB), and Wild Rose (WR). One of the lamps was made in an additional overlay color — Shelley Green Overlay (OG).

Production of the Rose pattern after 1980 was quite extensive. Pieces of the Rose pattern were included in many of Fenton's later opalescent, overlay, and transparent colors. These later pieces will have the Fenton logo embossed on the bottom.

Colonial Amber Rose	Ware No.	Introduced	Discontinued	Value
Ashtray	9271-CA	1966	1970	4.00 – 5.00
Ashtray set (4) individual	9210-CA	1968	1970	18.00 – 20.00
Basket, 9"	9235-CA	1967	1973	25.00 – 35.00
Bowl, 9½" DC	9225-CA	1967	1970	14.00 –16.00
Candleholder	9270-CA	1967	1969	5.00 – 10.00
Candy box (oval)	9282-CA	1965	1967	20.00 – 22.00
Candy box, ftd.	9284-CA	1967	1975	25.00 – 28.00
Comport, high ftd.	9222-CA	1964	1974	14.00 – 16.00
Comport, DC	9223-CA	1966	1975	12.00 – 14.00
Creamer, sugar, and lid	9203-CA	1967	1969	20.00 – 25.00
Goblet, 9 oz.	9246-CA	1967	1969	6.00 – 8.00
Lamp, 19" student	9208-CA	1967	1973	85.00 – 100.00
Ring tree	9299-CA	1967	1969	12.00 – 18.00
Salt and pepper	9206-CA	1967	1969	18.00 – 22.00
Soap dish	9216-CA	1967	1969	10.00 – 12.00
Tumbler, bathroom	9242-CA	1967	1969	12.00 – 14.00
Vase, 4½" oval	9251-CA	1967	1969	12.00 – 14.00
Vase, handkerchief	9254-CA	1968	1970	10.00 – 12.00
Vase, 9" bud	9256-CA	1968	1972	10.00 – 12.00
Colonial Blue Rose	**Ware No.**	**Introduced**	**Discontinued**	**Value**
Ashtray	9271-CB	1966	1969	6.00 – 8.00
Ashtray set (4) individual	9210-CB	1968	1969	25.00 – 30.00
Basket, 9"	9235-CB	1967	1970	45.00 – 50.00
Bowl, 9½" DC	9225-CB	1967	1969	20.00 – 25.00
Candleholder	9270-CB	1967	1969	12.00 – 15.00
Candy box (oval)	9282-CB	1965	1967	25.00 – 30.00
Candy box, ftd.	9284-CB	1967	1975	35.00 – 45.00
Comport, high ftd.	9222-CB	1964	1974	20.00 – 25.00
Comport, DC	9223-CB	1966	1975	18.00 – 20.00
Creamer, sugar, and lid	9203-CB	1967	1969	30.00 – 35.00
Goblet, 9 oz.	9246-CB	1967	1969	18.00 – 20.00
Lamp, 19" student	9208-CB	67	1973	150.00 – 175.00
Ring tree	9299-CB	1967	1969	20.00 – 22.00
Salt and pepper	9206-CB	1967	1969	35.00 – 40.00
Soap dish	9216-CB	1967	1969	18.00 – 20.00
Tumbler, bathroom	9242-CB	1967	1969	18.00 – 20.00
Vase, 4½" oval	9251-CB	1967	1969	14.00 – 16.00
Vase, handkerchief	9254-CB	1968	1970	20.00 – 22.00
Vase, 9" bud	9256-CB	1968	1970	14.00 – 16.00

Colonial Green Rose	Ware No.	Introduced	Discontinued	Value
Ashtray	9271-CG	1966	1970	4.50 – 5.50
Ashtray set (4) individual	9210-CG	1968	1970	18.00 – 20.00
Basket, 9"	9235-CG	1967	1973	25.00 – 35.00
Bowl, 9½" DC	9225-CG	1967	1970	14.00 – 18.00
Candleholder	9270-CG	1967	1969	5.00 – 8.00
Candy box (oval)	9282-CG	1965	1967	18.00 – 22.00
Candy box, ftd.	9284-CG	1967	1975	25.00 – 30.00
Comport, high ftd.	9222-CG	1964	1974	14.00 – 16.00
Comport, DC	9223-CG	1966	1975	12.00 – 14.00
Creamer, sugar, and lid	9203-CG	1967	1969	22.00 – 27.00
Goblet, 9 oz.	9246-CG	1967	1969	7.00 – 9.00
Lamp, 19" student	9208-CG	1967	1973	90.00 – 110.00
Ring tree	9299-CG	1967	1969	12.00 – 18.00
Salt and pepper	9206-CG	1967	1969	18.00 – 22.00
Soap dish	9216-CG	1967	1969	12.00 – 14.00
Tumbler, bathroom	9242-CG	1967	1969	12.00 – 14.00
Vase, 4½" oval	9251-CG	1967	1969	12.00 – 14.00
Vase, handkerchief	9254-CG	1968	1970	12.00 – 14.00
Vase, 9" bud	9256-CG	1968	1972	10.00 – 12.00

Colonial Pink Rose	Ware No.	Introduced	Discontinued	Value
Ashtray	9271-CP	1966	1969	6.00 – 8.00
Ashtray set (4) individual	9210-CP	1968	1969	20.00 – 25.00
Candy box (oval)	9282-CP	1965	1967	25.00 – 30.00
Comport, high ftd.	9222-CP	1964	1969	20.00 – 25.00
Comport, DC	9223-CP	1966	1969	15.00 – 17.00
Vase, 4½" oval	9251-CP	1968	1969	15.00 – 17.00
Vase, handkerchief	9254-CP	1968	1969	15.00 – 17.00
Vase, 9" bud	9256-CP	1968	1969	10.00 – 15.00

Orange Rose	Ware No.	Introduced	Discontinued	Value
Ashtray	9271-OR	1966	1969	6.00 – 8.00
Ashtray set (4) individual	9210-OR	1968	1969	25.00 – 30.00
Candy box (oval)	9282-OR	1965	1967	30.00 – 35.00
Candy box, ftd.	9284-OR	1967	1975	25.00 – 30.00
Comport, high ftd.	9222-OR	1965	1970	18.00 – 22.00
Comport, DC	9223-OR	1966	1975	15.00 – 17.00
Vase, 4½" oval	9251-OR	1967	1969	14.00 – 16.00
Vase, handkerchief	9254-OR	1968	1970	14.00 – 16.00
Vase, 9" bud	9256-OR	1968	1970	10.00 – 15.00

Milk Glass Rose	Ware No.	Introduced	Discontinued	Value
Ashtray	9271-MI	1966	1972	3.00 – 4.00
Ashtray set (4) individual	9210-MI	1968	1970	18.00 – 20.00
Basket, 9"	9235-MI	1967	1977	20.00 – 25.00
Bowl, 7"	9224-MI	1967	1973	12.00 – 14.00
Bowl, 9½" DC	9225-MI	1967	1972	14.00 – 16.00
Candleholder	9270-MI	1967	1973	4.00 – 5.00
Candy box (oval)	9282-MI	1965	1967	18.00 – 20.00
Candy box, ftd.	9284-MI	1967	1977	20.00 – 25.00
Comport, high ftd.	9222-MI	1964	1977	11.00 – 13.00
Comport, DC	9223-MI	1966	1977	12.00 – 14.00
Creamer, sugar, and lid	9203-MI	1967	1974	20.00 – 25.00
Goblet, 9 oz.	9246-MI	1967	1969	8.00 – 10.00

9222 MB High Footed Comport

9284 MB Footed Candy Box

9223 MB DC Comport

9210 MI Ash Tray Set

9224 MB 7" Bowl

9246 CG 9 Oz. Goblet

9254 MI Handkerchief Vase

9222 OR High Footed Comport

9216 CA Soap Dish

9256 CA 9" Bud Vase

9254 CG Handkerchief Vase

9299 CG Ring Tree

9251 OR 4 1/2" Oval Vase

9203 CA Creamer Sugar & Lid

9206 CB Salt & Pepper

9207 MI 21 1/2" Ball Lamp

9270 CA Candleholder

9242 CB Bathroom Tumbler

9271 CA Ash Tray

9271 CP Ash Tray

9282 CP Oval Candy Box

9205 HA 20 1/2" Buffet Lamp

9235 CA 9" Basket

9204 WR 24" Double Ball Lamp

9225 CB 9 1/2" Bowl

9208 CB 19" Student Lamp

Milk Glass Rose	Ware No.	Introduced	Discontinued	Value
Lamp, 24"	9204-MI	1967	1969	120.00 – 150.00
Lamp, 20½"	9205-MI	1967	1969	85.00 – 100.00
Lamp, 21½" ball	9207-MI	1967	1976	100.00 – 125.00
Lamp, 19" student	9208-MI	1967	1977	85.00 – 100.00
Ring tree	9299-MI	1967	1969	10.00 – 12.00
Salt and pepper	9206-MI	1967	1974	18.00 – 22.00
Soap dish	9216-MI	1967	1969	7.00 – 10.00
Tumbler, bathroom	9242-MI	1967	1969	10.00 – 12.00
Vase, 4½" oval	9251-MI	1967	1970	9.00 – 11.00
Vase, handkerchief	9254-MI	1968	1972	12.00 – 14.00
Vase, 9" bud	9256-MI	1968	1977	10.00 – 12.00

Blue Marble Rose	Ware No.	Introduced	Discontinued	Value
Ashtray	9271-MB	1970	1972	10.00 – 12.00
Basket, 9"	9235-MB	1970	1974	55.00 – 65.00
Bowl, 7"	9224-MB	1970	1974	25.00 – 35.00
Bowl, 9½" DC	9225-MB	1970	1974	40.00 – 45.00
Candleholder	9270-MB	1970	1973	16.00 – 18.00
Candy box, ftd.	9284-MB	1970	1974	35.00 – 45.00
Comport, high ftd.	9222-MB	1970	1974	25.00 – 28.00
Comport, DC	9223-MB	1970	1974	20.00 – 22.00
Vase, handkerchief	9254-MB	1970	1974	20.00 – 22.00
Vase, 9" bud	9256-MB	1970	1974	20.00 – 22.00

Comport, No. 9222 high footed	Color	Introduced	Discontinued	Value
	Blue Satin	1974	1977	20.00 – 22.00
	Carnival (CN)	1971	1976	22.00 – 25.00
	Custard (CU)	1973	1977	12.00 – 14.00
	Lime Sherbet (LS)	1973	1977	20.00 – 22.00

Lamps	Color	Introduced	Discontinued	Value
9204-HA	Honey Amber	1967	1969	120.00 – 140.00
9204-OB	Opaque Blue	1967	1968	150.00 – 175.00
9204-WR	Wild Rose	1967	1968	175.00 – 200.00
9205-HA	Honey Amber	1967	1969	100.00 – 115.00
9205-OB	Opaque Blue	1967	1968	140.00 – 160.00
9205-OG	Shelley Green	1967	1969	110.00 – 130.00
9205-WR	Wild Rose	1967	1968	160.00 – 185.00
9207-HA	Honey Amber	1967	1969	120.00 – 140.00
9207-OB	Opaque Blue	1967	1968	170.00 – 190.00
9207-WR	Wild Rose	1967	1969	190.00 – 210.00

Swirl

Fenton's Swirl pattern entered the line in January 1954 in Blue Pastel, Green Pastel, Rose Pastel, and milk. All pieces of Blue Pastel and Rose Pastel, except the 6" vase in Rose Pastel, were discontinued by the end of the year. Later in the decade, the 6" vase was also made in Turquoise and Jamestown Blue overlay.

The No. 7021-11" bowl and a pair of candleholders were combined to form the No. 7003 three-piece console set in Green Pastel and milk during 1955. The puff box and a pair of cologne bottles produced the vanity set. These latter two pieces were not marketed individually. Later editions of Swirl included:

1980

The No. 7056-6" vase was made in shiny Custard, shiny Cameo, Blue Opalescent, and Cameo Opalescent.

1982 – 1983

The No. 7063 cruet was in the line in amethyst (AY) and Country Cranberry (CC). The amethyst cruet continued to be listed in the 1983 – 84 general catalog.

A few pieces of the Swirl pattern were revived for production in the 1990s. A similar Swirl vase, Ware No. 1222-6", with a DC top was made in Country Cranberry. The colognes and puff boxes were recently in the Fenton gift shop in Rosalene.

Blue Pastel Swirl	Ware No.	Introduced	Discontinued	Value
Bowl, 11"	7021-BP	1954	1955	55.00 – 65.00
Bowl, 11" deep	7025-BP	1954	1955	55.00 – 65.00
Candleholder	7073-BP	1954	1955	18.00 – 24.00
Cologne		1954	1955	45.00 – 50.00
Creamer and sugar	7006-BP	1954	1955	45.00 – 55.00
Cruet	7063-BP	1954	1955	45.00 – 55.00
Mayonnaise set	7004-BP	1954	1955	30.00 – 35.00
Puff box		1954	1955	35.00 – 37.00
Salt and pepper	7001-BP	1954	1955	35.00 – 40.00
Vanity set, 3-pc.	7005-BP	1954	1955	125.00 – 137.00
Vase, 6"	7056-BP	1954	1955	25.00 – 27.00

Green Pastel Swirl	Ware No.	Introduced	Discontinued	Value
Bowl, 11"	7021-GP	1954	1956	50.00 – 60.00
Bowl, 11" deep	7025-GP	1954	1955	50.00 – 60.00
Candleholder	7073-GP	1954	1956	18.00 – 24.00
Cologne		1954	1956	45.00 – 50.00
Creamer and sugar	7006-GP	1954	1955	45.00 – 55.00
Cruet	7063-GP	1954	1956	45.00 – 55.00
Mayonnaise set	7004-GP	1954	1956	30.00 – 35.00
Puff box		1954	1956	35.00 – 37.00
Salt and pepper	7001-GP	1954	1956	35.00 – 40.00
Vanity set, 3-pc.	7005-GP	1954	1956	125.00 – 137.00
Vase, 6"	7056-GP	1954	1956	25.00 – 27.00

Rose Pastel Swirl	Ware No.	Introduced	Discontinued	Value
Bowl, 11"	7021-RP	1954	1955	40.00 – 45.00
Bowl, 11" deep	7025-RP	1954	1955	40.00 – 45.00
Candleholder	7073-RP	1954	1955	18.00 – 24.00
Creamer and sugar	7006-RP	1954	1955	40.00 – 45.00
Cologne		1954	1955	30.00 – 35.00
Cruet	7063-RP	1954	1955	35.00 – 40.00
Mayonnaise set	7004-RP	1954	1955	30.00 – 35.00
Puff box		1954	1955	25.00 – 35.00
Salt and pepper	7001-RP	1954	1955	35.00 – 40.00

Rose Pastel Swirl	Ware No.	Introduced	Discontinued	Value
Vanity set, 3-pc.	7005-RP	1954	1955	85.00 – 105.00
*Vase, 6"	7056-RP	1954	1957	18.00 – 22.00
Milk Glass Swirl	**Ware No.**	**Introduced**	**Discontinued**	**Value**
Bowl, 11"	7021-MI	1954	1956	20.00 – 25.00
Bowl, 11" deep	7025-MI	1954	1955	20.00 – 25.00
Candleholder	7073-MI	1954	1956	15.00 – 18.00
Creamer and sugar	7006-MI	1954	1955	30.00 – 35.00
Cologne		1954	1957	20.00 – 28.00
Cruet	7063-MI	1954	1956	30.00 – 32.00
Mayonnaise set	7004-MI	1954	1956	30.00 – 35.00
Salt and pepper	7001-MI	1954	1957	18.00 – 20.00
Puff box		1954	1957	18.00 – 22.00
Vanity set, 3-pc.	7005-MI	1954	1957	78.00 – 86.00
Vase, 6"	7056-MI	1954	July 1959	9.00 – 12.00
Turquoise Swirl	**Ware No.**	**Introduced**	**Discontinued**	**Value**
*Vase, 6"	7056-TU	1955	1958	25.00 – 30.00
Jamestown Blue Swirl	**Ware No.**	**Introduced**	**Discontinued**	**Value**
Vase, 6"	7056-JB	1957	1959	45.00 – 55.00

*With Charleton Roses decoration   40.00 – 50.00

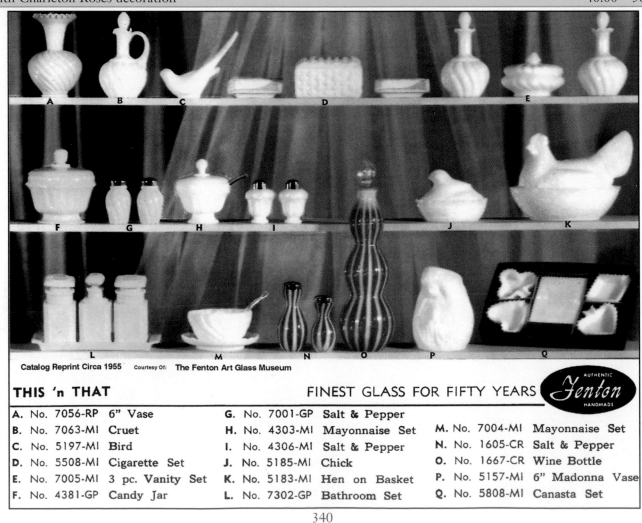

Catalog Reprint Circa 1955   Courtesy Of: The Fenton Art Glass Museum

THIS 'n THAT   FINEST GLASS FOR FIFTY YEARS   *Fenton* AUTHENTIC HANDMADE

A. No. 7056-RP 6" Vase
B. No. 7063-MI Cruet
C. No. 5197-MI Bird
D. No. 5508-MI Cigarette Set
E. No. 7005-MI 3 pc. Vanity Set
F. No. 4381-GP Candy Jar

G. No. 7001-GP Salt & Pepper
H. No. 4303-MI Mayonnaise Set
I. No. 4306-MI Salt & Pepper
J. No. 5185-MI Chick
K. No. 5183-MI Hen on Basket
L. No. 7302-GP Bathroom Set

M. No. 7004-MI Mayonnaise Set
N. No. 1605-CR Salt & Pepper
O. No. 1667-CR Wine Bottle
P. No. 5157-MI 6" Madonna Vase
Q. No. 5808-MI Canasta Set

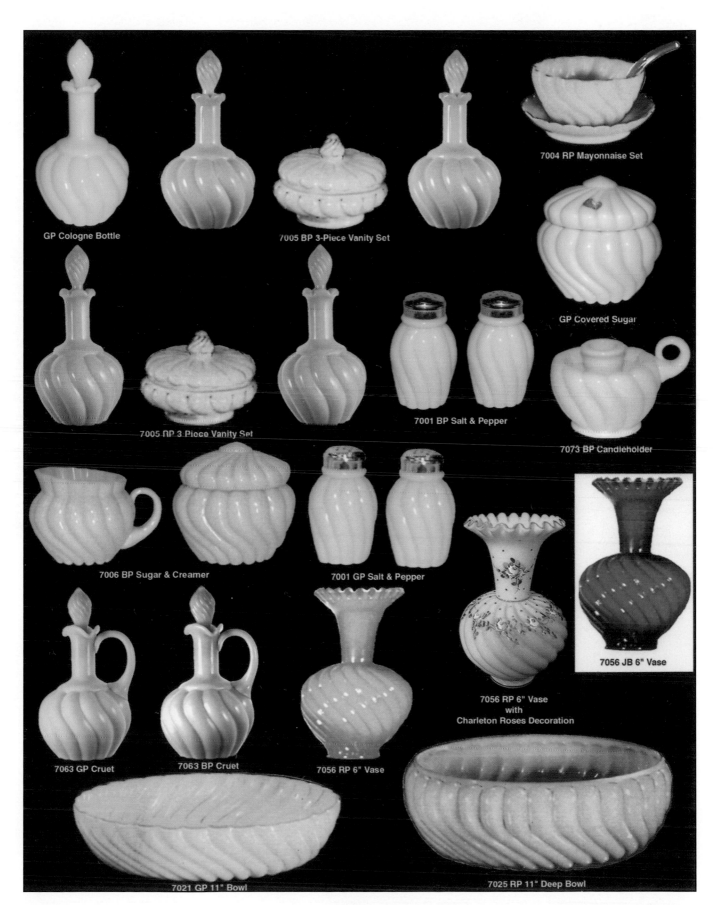

GP Cologne Bottle

7005 BP 3-Piece Vanity Set

7004 RP Mayonnaise Set

GP Covered Sugar

7005 RP 3-Piece Vanity Set

7001 BP Salt & Pepper

7073 BP Candleholder

7006 BP Sugar & Creamer

7001 GP Salt & Pepper

7056 JB 6" Vase

7056 RP 6" Vase
with
Charleton Roses Decoration

7063 GP Cruet

7063 BP Cruet

7056 RP 6" Vase

7021 GP 11" Bowl

7025 RP 11" Deep Bowl

Swirled Feather

Swirled Feather was introduced in 1953. This pattern was made in satinized Blue Opalescent, Cranberry, French Opalescent, and Green Opalescent colors. However, some glossy pieces of this pattern were probably sold through the gift shop.

Included in the Swirled Feather pattern was Fenton's first fairy lamp. Catalogs describe this new item as "an authentic reproduction of an early Victorian night light." It was sold both as a candleholder and electrified.

DeVilbiss of Toledo, Ohio, bought this cologne bottle from Fenton in 1954, and fitted it with an adapter for use as an atomizer. The confirmed colors of atomizers available are French Satin, Green Satin, Blue Satin and Rose Satin. An example of a Blue Satin atomizer is shown in the top right of the photo.

Blue Satin Swirled Feather	Ware No.	Introduced	Discontinued	Value
Candy jar	2083-BA	1953	1955	350.00 – 450.00
Cologne		1953	1955	200.00 – 250.00
Cruet	2063-BA	1953	1954	450.00 – 500.00
Fairy lamp (candle)	2990-BA	1953	1955	350.00 – 400.00
Fairy lamp (electric)	2092-BA	1953	1955	350.00 – 425.00
Hurricane lamp	2098-BA	1953	1955	350.00 – 400.00
Puff box		1953	1955	185.00 – 225.00
Vanity set	2005-BA	1953	1955	565.00 – 775.00
French Satin Swirled Feather	Ware No.	Introduced	Discontinued	Value
Candy jar	2083-FA	1953	1955	250.00 – 300.00
Cologne		1953	1955	150.00 – 175.00
Fairy lamp (candle)	2090-FA	1953	1955	175.00 – 200.00
Fairy lamp (electric)	2092-FA	1953	1955	175.00 – 200.00
Hurricane lamp	2098-FA	1953	1955	250.00 – 275.00
Puff box		1953	1955	100.00 – 140.00
Vanity set	2005-FA	1953	1955	400.00 – 490.00
*Atomizer		1954	1955	150.00 – 200.00
Green Satin Swirled Feather	Ware No.	Introduced	Discontinued	Value
Candy jar	2083-GA	1953	July 1954	400.00 – 475.00
Cologne		1953	1955	200.00 – 250.00
Fairy lamp (candle)	2090-GA	1953	1955	350.00 – 425.00
Fairy lamp (electric)	2092-GA	1953	1955	400.00 – 450.00
Hurricane lamp	2098-GA	1953	1955	350.00 – 425.00
Puff box		1953	1955	185.00 – 225.00
Vanity set	2005-GA	1953	1955	565.00 – 775.00
*Atomizer		1954	1955	250.00 – 275.00
Cranberry Satin Swirled Feather	Ware No.	Introduced	Discontinued	Value
Candy jar	2083-RA	1953	July 1954	500.00 – 600.00
Cologne		1953	1955	200.00 – 250.00
Cruet	2063-RA	1953	1954	450.00 – 500.00
Fairy lamp (candle)	2090-RA	1953	1955	400.00 – 450.00
Fairy lamp (electric)	2092-RA	1953	1955	400.00 – 450.00
Hurricane lamp	2098-RA	1953	1955	350.00 – 425.00
Puff box		1953	1955	185.00 – 225.00
Vanity set	2005-RA	1953	1955	585.00 – 775.00
*Atomizer		1954	1955	250.00 – 300.00
Cologne				

*Fitted with the atomizer parts and marketed by DeVilbiss.

2098 BA Hurricane Lamp

2098 GA Hurricane Lamp

2098 RA Hurricane Lamp

BA Atomizer For DeVilbiss

2005 CR 3-piece Vanity Set

2005 BA 3-piece Vanity Set

2080 GA Candy Jar

GA Cologne

GA Puff Box

2005 RA 3-piece Vanity Set

2083 RA Candy Jar

2063 RA Cruet

2090 FA Fairy Lamp

Insert for Lamp

2092 GA Electric Lamp

Teardrop

Fenton's Teardrop pattern entered the line with the introduction of the mustard in January 1955 in milk glass and Turquoise colors. In July 1955, a flat candy, salt and pepper, and condiment set joined the mustard in the same colors. The condiment set was formed by combining the salt and peppers and mustard with a chrome handled tray. A year later this condiment set was made in Fenton's new Goldenrod color. Today, all items in Goldenrod are elusive. The color was discontinued at the end of 1956, after only six months of production. Pieces of Turquoise Teardrop are not easy to find either. All of the items in this color were in the line for two years or less. Different pieces were made in milk and most of these shapes were made for a longer period. The shakers and the condiment set were sold into the 1960s. The mustard, which was a part of the condiment set, was not listed in the catalogs as a separate item after the end of June 1959.

Notice there are two different styles of No. 6985 flat candy jars. One style has teardrops that form a pointed knob on the lid and the other style has a teardrop knob formed into a more rectangular shape. Milk and Turquoise candy jars have been found in both styles. A more elusive tall footed candy was made in milk during 1957. The shape of this candy is similar to the Hobnail No. 3885 footed candy.

Fenton catalogs listed the sugar and creamer as a set with the ware number 6901. The ware number for the condiment set was 6909.

Milk Glass Teardrop	Ware No.	Introduced	Discontinued	Value
Bowl, 9"	6929-MI	1957	1959	20.00 – 25.00
Cake plate, ftd.	6913-MI	1957	1959	40.00 – 50.00
Candleholder	6974-MI	1957	1959	14.00 – 16.00
Candy box, ftd.	6983-MI	1957	1958	45.00 – 55.00
Candy box, flat	6985-MI	July 1955	July 1959	25.00 – 35.00
Condiment set	6909-MI	July 1955	1962	65.00 – 85.00
Creamer		1957	1959	14.00 – 16.00
Mustard & spoon	6989-MI	1955	July 1959	22.00 – 24.00
Oil cruet	6963-MI	1957	1959	30.00 – 35.00
Salt and pepper	6906-MI	July 1955	1967	18.00 – 20.00
Sugar		1957	1959	20.00 – 25.00
Tray, sandwich	6997-MI	1957	1959	30.00 – 35.00
Goldenrod Teardrop	**Ware No.**	**Introduced**	**Discontinued**	**Value**
Condiment set	6909-GD	July 1956	1957	200.00 – 225.00
Mustard & spoon	6989-GD	July 1956	1957	45.00 – 55.00
Salt and pepper	6906-GD	July 1956	1957	45.00 – 55.00
Turquoise Teardrop	**Ware No.**	**Introduced**	**Discontinued**	**Value**
Candy box, flat	6985-TU	July 1955	July 1956	70.00 – 75.00
Condiment set	6909-TU	July 1955	July 1956	160.00 – 185.00
Mustard & spoon	6989-TU	1955	1957	35.00 – 40.00
Salt and pepper	6906-TU	July 1955	1957	35.00 – 40.00

6963 MI Oil Cruet

6909 MI Condiment Set

6909 GD Condiment Set

6909 TU Condiment Set

6989 TU Mustard
and Spoon

6901 MI Cream and Sugar

6997 MI Sandwich Tray

6906 TU Salt and Pepper

6985 TU Flat Candy Box

6929 MI 9" Bowl

6974 MI Candleholder

6913 MI Footed Cake Plate

6985 MI Flat Candy Box

6983 MI Footed Candy Box

Thumbprint

The Thumbprint pattern was introduced into the Fenton line in July 1962, in Colonial Amber, Colonial Blue, and Colonial Pink. Orange Thumbprint was added with the introduction of a single piece — the bud vase — in 1963. Colonial Green also came along in 1963, Ruby was added in 1966, and Black debuted in 1968. A hand-painted White Daisies decoration, on black, was available on four Thumbprint shapes from 1972 through 1976. In addition, two other shapes — an egg and a candy — were hand painted with this white floral decoration. These are also priced in the listing below. Individual pieces are signed by the various artists. Add about 40 percent to the listed prices for any items signed by Louise Piper.

Pieces were constantly added to expand the line through 1968. After that time, the number of pieces of Thumbprint in the line began to decrease. The last remaining item in the line was the No. 4438-8½" basket. It was still available in 1980.

In some early catalogs, the cocktail goblet was listed as a small sherbet or wine. The ware number for this item was No. 4441. Later, when Fenton introduced a regular sherbet into the line, the ware number for this piece was No. 4443. Ware numbers for sets included No. 4402 for a combination of a No. 4495 cigarette lighter with a No. 4469-6½" ashtray. This set was originally sold to Sears beginning in March 1969. It entered the regular Fenton line in January 1970, and was discontinued by the end of the year. The creamer, sugar, and lid were marketed as one item using Ware Number 4403.

In addition to the Thumbprint colors and shapes that were made for the regular line, Fenton also made Thumbprint in milk. All of that production was for the Old Virginia Line during the 1950s, before Thumbprint entered the regular Fenton line. Later production also included:

1985

The No. 4401 four-piece epergne set reappeared in mid 1985. At this time Fenton made this set in Red Slag (RX). It was included as part of an assortment of various items in that color and was marketed to customers previously served by the LeVay Distributing Company.

In late 1985, Fenton made five items in the Thumbprint pattern as part of an assortment of items in Green Opalescent with a Cobalt Crest (GK). The following pieces were made in Thumbprint and were intended for dealers formerly serviced by LeVay:

Basket, 8½" handled	4438-GK	Epergne set, 4-pc.	4401-GK
Bowl, 8"	4426-GK	Salt jar, 5"	4452-GK
Comport, ftd.	4429-GK		

1999

A small No. 4460-4½" Cranberry pitcher with a clear ribbed handle was in the line for one year.

Colonial Amber Thumbprint	Ware No.	Introduced	Discontinued	Value
Ashtray, oval	4476-CA	1963	1968	4.00 – 6.00
Ashtray, 6½"	4469-CA	1967	1970	6.00 – 8.00
Ashtray, 7"	4479-CA	1964	1967	9.00 – 11.00
Basket, 8" handled	4434-CA	1969	1971	20.00 – 25.00
Basket, 8½" handled	4438-CA	1963	1977	25.00 – 30.00
Bonbon, 8" DC	4435-CA	1964	1970	4.00 – 6.00
Bowl, candy and nut	4433-CA	1964	1966	5.00 – 7.00
Bowl, anniversary	4484-CA	1963	1971	20.00 – 22.00
Bowl, ftd.	4423-CA	1963	1967	18.00 – 20.00
Bowl, 8"	4426-CA	1965	1971	11.00 – 13.00
Bowl, 12"	4427-CA	1964	1970	18.00 – 20.00
Bowl, royal wedding	4488-CA	1964	1969	35.00 – 40.00
Butter, ¼ lb. covered	4477-CA	1965	1968	20.00 – 25.00
Cake plate, ftd.	4411-CA	1964	1968	16.00 – 20.00
Candleholder, 4"	4470-CA	July 1964	1970	4.00 – 6.00
Candleholder, 8¼"	4473-CA	1964	1968	10.00 – 12.00
Candy box, oval	4486-CA	1963	1969	12.00 – 15.00

4426 CA 8" DC Bowl

4435 CA 8" DC Bonbon

4411 CA Ftd. Cake Plate

4488 CA
Royal Wedding Bowl

4454 CA 8" Ftd. Vase

4459 CA 7" Ftd. Vase

4401 CA 4-Piece
Epergne Set

4477 CA Covered Butter

4469 CA 6 1/2" Ash Tray

4495 CA
Cigarette Lighter

4466 CA 60 Oz. Pitcher

449 CA
13 Oz. Ftd. Tumbler

4445 CA 10 Oz. Goblet

4442 CA 12 Oz.
Tumbler

4444 CA
Wine Goblet

4409 CA Ftd.
Salt & Pepper

4416 CA 8 1/2"
Divided Relish

4425 CA Ftd. DC Comport

4425 CA Ftd. Comport

Colonial Amber Thumbprint	Ware No.	Introduced	Discontinued	Value
Chalice, 8" tall	4448-CA	1965	1967	10.00 – 12.00
Chip 'n Dip	4404-CA	1963	1967	45.00 – 50.00
Cigarette lighter	4495-CA	1967	1969	8.00 – 10.00
Comport, ftd. DC	4425-CA	1965	1974	8.00 – 10.00
Comport, ftd.	4429-CA	July 1962	1975	8.00 – 10.00
Creamer, sugar and lid	4403-CA	1963	1969	15.00 – 18.00
Epergne set, 4-pc.	4401-CA	1964	1968	45.00 – 65.00
Goblet, cocktail	4441-CA	July 1962	1965	10.00 – 12.00
Goblet, 5 oz. wine	4444-CA	1964	1971	6.00 – 8.00
Goblet, 10 oz.	4445-CA	July 1962	1973	8.00 – 10.00
Jug, 34 oz.	4465-CA	1965	1967	20.00 – 25.00
Jug, 2 qt. ice lip	4464-CA	1964	1967	30.00 – 40.00
Pitcher, 64 oz.	4466-CA	1968	1969	65.00 – 85.00
Plate, 8½"	4417-CA	1964	1970	7.00 – 8.00
Relish, 8½" divided	4416-CA	1966	1968	8.00 – 12.00
Salt and pepper	4408-CA	1963	1968	18.00 – 22.00
Salt and pepper, ftd.	4409-CA	1968	1969	60.00 – 75.00
Sherbet	4443-CA	1963	1971	5.00 – 8.00
Tumbler, 6 oz. juice	4446-CA	1965	1967	6.00 – 8.00
Tumbler, 12 oz.	4442-CA	July 1962	1970	10.00 – 12.00

Colonial Blue

Catalog Reprint Circa 1964   Courtesy Of: The Fenton Art Glass Museum

4423 CB
Ftd. Bowl

4484 CB
Anniversary Bowl

4438 CB
8 ½" Basket

4476 CB
Oval Ash Tray

4479 CB
7" Ash Tray

4486 CB
Oval Candy Box

4408 CB
Salt & Pepper Set

4445 CB
Thumbprint
Goblet

4429 CB
Thumbprint
Ftd. Comport

4453 CB
Tall Bud Vase

4441 CB
Small Sherbet
or Wine

4443 CB
Sherbet

4442 CB
11 oz. Tumbler

4403 CB
Cov'd. Sugar & Cream

Colonial Amber Thumbprint	Ware No.	Introduced	Discontinued	Value
Tumbler, 13 oz. ftd.	4449-CA	1966	1972	12.00 – 14.00
Vase, bud	4455-CA	1965	1977	4.00 – 6.00
Vase, tall bud	4453-CA	1963	1975	6.00 – 10.00
Vase, 7" ftd.	4459-CA	1966	1969	8.00 – 10.00
Vase, 8" ftd.	4454-CA	1964	1974	10.00 – 12.00

Colonial Blue Thumbprint	Ware No.	Introduced	Discontinued	Value
Ashtray, oval	4476-CB	1963	1968	10.00 – 12.00
Ashtray, 6½"	4469-CB	1967	1969	14.00 – 16.00
Ashtray, 7"	4479-CB	1964	1967	18.00 – 20.00
Basket, 8" handled	4434-CB	1969	1971	35.00 – 45.00
Basket, 8½" handled	4438-CB	1963	1977	45.00 – 55.00
Bonbon, 8" DC	4435-CB	1964	1969	10.00 – 15.00
Bowl, candy and nut	4433-CB	1964	1966	10.00 – 15.00
Bowl, anniversary	4484-CB	1963	1969	45.00 – 65.00
Bowl, ftd.	4423-CB	1963	1967	35.00 – 40.00
Bowl, 8"	4426-CB	1965	1971	20.00 – 25.00
Bowl, 12"	4427-CB	1964	1969	35.00 – 45.00
Bowl, royal wedding	4488-CB	1964	1967	90.00 – 110.00
Butter, ¼ lb. covered	4477-CB	1965	1967	35.00 – 45.00
Cake plate, ftd.	4411-CB	1964	1967	35.00 – 40.00
Candleholder, 4"	4470-CB	July 1964	1969	12.00 – 15.00
Candleholder, 8¼"	4473-CB	1964	1965	25.00 – 27.00
Candy box, oval	4486-CB	1963	1969	35.00 – 40.00
Chalice, 8" tall	4448-CB	1965	1967	18.00 – 20.00
Chip 'n Dip	4404-CB	1963	1966	50.00 – 60.00
Cigarette lighter	4495-CB	1967	1969	20.00 – 25.00
Comport, ftd. DC	4425-CB	1965	1974	10.00 – 12.00
Comport, ftd.	4429-CB	1962	1975	10.00 – 12.00
Creamer, sugar and lid	4403-CB	1963	1969	35.00 – 45.00
Epergne set, 4-pc.	4401-CB	1964	1967	75.00 – 100.00
Goblet, cocktail	4441-CB	July 1962	1965	12.00 – 14.00
Goblet, 5 oz. wine	4444-CB	1964	1969	12.00 – 14.00
Goblet, 10 oz.	4445-CB	1962	1973	15.00 – 18.00
Jug, 34 oz.	4465-CB	1965	1967	60.00 – 75.00
Jug, 2 qt. ice lip	4464-CB	1964	1967	75.00 – 95.00
Pitcher, 64 oz.	4466-CB	1968	1969	125.00 – 150.00
Plate, 8½"	4417-CB	1964	1969	14.00 – 16.00
Relish, 8½" divided	4416-CB	1966	1968	14.00 – 16.00
Salt and pepper	4408-CB	1963	1968	35.00 – 45.00
Salt and pepper, ftd.	4409-CB	1968	1969	90.00 – 110.00
Sherbet	4443-CB	1963	1969	8.00 – 10.00
Tumbler, 6 oz. juice	4446-CB	1965	1967	12.00 – 14.00
Tumbler, 12 oz.	4442-CB	July 1962	1969	16.00 – 18.00
Tumbler, 13 oz. ftd.	4449-CB	1966	1969	20.00 – 22.00
Vase, bud	4455-CB	1965	1977	10.00 – 12.00
Vase, tall bud	4453-CB	1963	1975	12.00 – 14.00
Vase, 7" ftd.	4459-CB	1966	1970	15.00 – 18.00
Vase, 8" ftd.	4454-CB	1964	1974	20.00 – 25.00

Colonial Green Thumbprint	Ware No.	Introduced	Discontinued	Value
Ashtray, oval	4476-CG	1963	1968	4.00 – 6.00
Ashtray, 6½"	4469-CG	1967	1970	6.00 – 8.00
Ashtray, 7"	4479-CG	1964	1967	9.00 – 11.00
Basket, 8" handled	4434-CG	1969	1971	25.00 – 30.00
Basket, 8½" handled	4438-CG	1963	1977	30.00 – 35.00
Bonbon, 8" DC	4435-CG	1964	1970	6.00 – 8.00
Bowl, candy and nut	4433-CG	1964	1966	7.00 – 9.00
Bowl, anniversary	4484-CG	1963	1971	30.00 – 35.00
Bowl, ftd.	4423-CG	1963	1967	20.00 – 25.00
Bowl, 8"	4426-CG	1965	1971	11.00 – 15.00
Bowl, 12"	4427-CG	1964	1970	25.00 – 30.00
Bowl, royal wedding	4488-CG	1964	1967	55.00 – 65.00
Butter, ¼ lb. covered	4477-CG	1965	1968	20.00 – 25.00
Cake plate, ftd.	4411-CG	1964	1968	18.00 – 20.00
Candleholder, 4"	4470-CG	July 1964	1970	4.00 – 6.00
Candleholder, 8¼"	4473-CG	1964	1968	12.00 – 15.00
Candy box, oval	4486-CG	1963	1969	10.00 – 12.00
Chalice, 8" tall	4448-CG	1965	1967	10.00 – 12.00
Chip 'n Dip	4404-CG	1963	1967	45.00 – 50.00
Cigarette lighter	4495-CG	1967	1969	8.00 – 10.00
Comport, ftd. DC	4425-CG	1965	1974	8.00 – 10.00
Comport, ftd.	4429-CG	1963	1975	8.00 – 10.00
Creamer, sugar and lid	4403-CG	1963	1969	15.00 – 18.00
Epergne set, 4-pc.	4401-CG	1964	1968	50.00 – 65.00
Goblet, cocktail	4441-CG	1963	1965	10.00 – 12.00
Goblet, 5 oz. wine	4444-CG	1964	1971	6.00 – 8.00
Goblet, 10 oz.	4445-CG	1963	1973	8.00 – 10.00
Jug, 34 oz.	4465-CG	1965	1967	20.00 – 25.00
Jug, 2 qt. ice lip	4464-CG	1964	1967	30.00 – 40.00
Pitcher, 64 oz.	4466-CG	1968	1969	65.00 – 85.00
Plate, 8½"	4417-CG	1964	1970	7.00 – 8.00
Relish, 8½" divided	4416-CG	1966	1968	8.00 – 11.00
Salt and pepper	4408-CG	1963	1968	18.00 – 22.00
Salt and pepper, ftd.	4409-CG	1968	1969	60.00 – 75.00
Sherbet	4443-CG	1963	1971	5.00 – 8.00
Tumbler, 6 oz. juice	4446-CG	1965	1967	6.00 – 8.00
Tumbler, 12 oz.	4442-CG	1963	1970	10.00 – 12.00
Tumbler, 13 oz. ftd.	4449-CG	1966	1972	6.00 – 9.00
Vase, bud	4455-CG	1965	1977	4.00 – 6.00
Vase, tall bud	4453-CG	1963	1975	6.00 – 10.00
Vase, 7" ftd.	4459-CG	1966	1969	8.00 – 10.00
Vase, 8" ftd.	4454-CG	1964	1974	10.00 – 12.00

Catalog Reprint Composite Circa 1965   Courtesy Of: The Fenton Art Glass Museum

4465 CG
34 oz. Jug

4464 CG
2 qt. Ice Lip Jug

4448 CG
8" Chalice

4484 CG
Anniversary Bowl

4488 CG
Royal Wedding Bowl

4408 CG
Salt & Pepper Set

4403 CG
Cov'd. Sugar & Cream

4442 CG
12 oz. Tumbler

4446 CG
Juice Tumbler

4477 CG
Oval ¼ lb. Cov'd. Butter

4429 CG
Ftd. Comport

4433 CG
Candy & Nut Bowl

4455 CG
Bud Vase

4486 CG
Oval Candy Box

4401 CG
4 pc. Epergne Set

4423 CG
Ftd. Bowl

4453 CG
Tall Bud Vase

4454 CG
8" Ftd. Vase

4435 CG
8" DC Bonbon

4425 CG
Ftd. Comport DC

4411 CG
Ftd. Cakeplate

4426 CG
8" Bowl

4473 CG
8 ¾" Candleholder

4404 CG
Chip 'n Dip

4427 CG
12" Bowl

4479 CG
7" Ash Tray

Colonial Pink Thumbprint	Ware No.	Introduced	Discontinued	Value
Ashtray, oval	4476-CP	1963	1967	10.00 – 12.00
Ashtray, 7"	4479-CP	1964	1967	14.00 – 16.00
Basket, 8½" handled	4438-CP	1963	1969	45.00 – 55.00
Bonbon, 8" DC	4435-CP	1964	1969	10.00 – 15.00
Bowl, candy and nut	4433-CP	1964	1966	10.00 – 15.00
Bowl, anniversary	4484-CP	1963	1967	55.00 – 65.00
Bowl, ftd.	4423-CP	1963	1967	35.00 – 40.00
Bowl, 8"	4426-CP	1965	1969	20.00 – 25.00
Bowl, 12"	4427-CP	1964	1969	40.00 – 45.00
Bowl, royal wedding	4488-CP	1964	1967	95.00 – 110.00
Butter, ¼ lb. covered	4477-CP	1965	1967	35.00 – 45.00
Cake plate, ftd.	4411-CP	1964	1967	35.00 – 40.00
Candleholder, 4"	4470-CP	July 1964	1969	12.00 – 15.00
Candleholder, 8¼"	4473-CP	1964	1965	25.00 – 27.00
Candy box, oval	4486-CP	1963	1967	35.00 – 40.00
Chalice, 8" tall	4448-CP	1965	1967	18.00 – 20.00
Chip 'n Dip	4404-CP	1963	1966	50.00 – 60.00
Creamer, sugar and lid	4403-CP	1963	1968	35.00 – 45.00
Comport, ftd. DC	4425-CP	1965	1969	10.00 – 12.00
Comport, ftd.	4429-CP	1962	1969	10.00 – 12.00
Goblet, cocktail	4441-CP	July 1962	1965	12.00 – 14.00
Goblet, 5 oz. wine	4444-CP	1964	1968	12.00 – 14.00
Goblet, 10 oz.	4445-CP	1962	1969	15.00 – 18.00
Jug, 34 oz.	4465-CP	1965	1967	60.00 – 75.00
Jug, 2 qt. ice lip	4464-CP	1964	1967	140.00 – 160.00
Plate, 8½"	4417-CP	1964	1968	14.00 – 16.00
Salt and pepper	4408-CP	1963	1968	35.00 – 45.00
Sherbet	4443-CP	1963	1968	8.00 – 10.00
Tumbler, 6 oz. juice	4446-CP	1965	1967	12.00 – 14.00
Tumbler, 12 oz	4442-CP	July 1962	1968	16.00 – 18.00
Vase, bud	4455-CP	1965	1969	10.00 – 12.00
Vase, tall bud	4453-CP	1963	1969	12.00 – 14.00
Vase, 8" ftd.	4454-CP	1964	1969	20.00 – 22.00

Orange Thumbprint	Ware No.	Introduced	Discontinued	Value
Ashtray, 6½"	4469-OR	1967	1970	5.00 – 8.00
Basket, 8" handled	4434-OR	1969	1971	35.00 – 40.00
Basket, 8½" handled	4438-OR	1964	1977	38.00 – 45.00
Bowl, 8"	4426-OR	1965	1971	18.00 – 22.00
Candleholder, 4"	4470-OR	July 1964	1969	10.00 – 12.00
Chalice (8" tall)	4448-OR	1965	1967	14.00 – 16.00
Cigarette lighter	4495-OR	1967	1969	15.00 – 18.00
Comport, ftd. DC	4425-OR	1965	1974	10.00 – 12.00
Comport, ftd.	4429-OR	1964	1975	12.00 – 14.00
Vase, bud	4455-OR	1965	1977	9.00 – 12.00
Vase, tall bud	4453-OR	1963	1974	11.00 – 14.00
Vase, 7" ftd.	4459-OR	1966	1969	10.00 – 12.00
Vase, 8" ftd.	4454-OR	1964	1974	18.00 – 20.00

4484 CP
Anniversary Bowl

4488 CP
Royal Wedding Bowl

4433 CP
Candy & Nut Bowl

4477 CP Butter

4435 CP 8" DC Bonbon

4486 CP
Oval Candy Box

4411 CP Cake Plate

4465 CP 34 Oz. Jug

4442 CP
12 Oz. Tumbler

4446 CP
6 Oz. Tumbler

4427 CP 12" Bowl

4464 CP 2 Qt.
Ice Lip Jug

4476 CP Oval Ash Tray

4408 CP Salt & Pepper

4403 CP Covered
Sugar & Creamer

4423 CP Ftd. Bowl

4404 CP
Chip 'n Dip

4438 OR 8 1/2" Basket

4426 OR 8" Bowl

4425 OR Ftd. DC
Comport

4470 OR 4"
Candleholder

4469 OR 6 1/2"
Ash Tray

4429 OR Ftd. Comport

4454 OR 8" Ftd. Vase

4448 OR 8" Chalice

4434 OR 8" Basket

4455 OR
Bud Vase

4453 OR
Tall Bud Vase

Ruby Thumbprint	Ware No.	Introduced	Discontinued	Value
Basket, 8½" handled	4438-RU	1969	1980+	50.00 – 60.00
Comport, ftd.	4429-RU	1966	1976	18.00 – 20.00
Goblet, 5 oz. wine	4444-RU	1966	1974	14.00 – 18.00
Goblet, 10 oz.	4445-RU	1966	1974	14.00 – 18.00
Plate, 8½"	4417-RU	1966	1970	18.00 – 20.00
Sherbet	4443-RU	1966	1974	8.00 – 10.00
Tumbler, 13 oz. ftd.	4449-RU	1966	1974	20.00 – 25.00
Vase, tall bud	4453-RU	1966	1974	20.00 – 22.00

Black Thumbprint	Ware No.	Introduced	Discontinued	Value
Ashtray, 6½"	4469-BK	1968	1970	12.00 – 14.00
Basket, 8" handled	4434-BK	July 1968	1977	45.00 – 50.00
Cigarette lighter	4495-BK	July 1968	1970	30.00 – 35.00
Comport, ftd. DC	4425-BK	July 1968	1975	18.00 – 20.00
Comport, ftd.	4429-BK	July 1968	1976	18.00 – 20.00
Vase, bud	4455-BK	1968	1977	15.00 – 18.00
Vase, 8" ftd.	4454-BK	1968	1975	16.00 – 20.00
Vase, tall bud	4453-BK	July 1968	1976	20.00 – 22.00

White Daisies Decoration	Ware No.	Introduced	Discontinued	Value*
Ashtray, 6½"	4469-WD	1972	1975	14.00 – 18.00
Candy box, ftd.	7380-WD	1973	1976	45.00 – 55.00
Egg	5140-WD	1973	1974	25.00 – 30.00
Vase, bud	4455-WD	1972	1977	18.00 – 25.00
Vase, 8" ftd.	4454-WD	1972	1977	18.00 – 25.00
Vase, tall bud	4453-WD	1972	1977	25.00 – 30.00

*If decorated by Louise Piper, add 30% to 50%.

4444 RU 5 Oz. Wine Goblet

TO Comport (Sample)

4417 RO 8 1/2" Plate

TO Candy Box (Sample)

4455 WD Bud Vase

4454 WD 8" Footed Vase

4445 RU 10 Oz. Goblet

4453 WD Tall Swung Bud Vase

4469 WD 6 1/2" Ash Tray

4438 RU 8 1/2" Basket

4434 BK 8" Basket

Valencia

Fenton's Valencia pattern, designed by Anthony Rosena, was adapted from a Czechoslovakian Moser piece obtained at an antique show by Frank M. Fenton. This piece was reproduced as the No. 8380 candy box and was part of an assortment of ten items which debuted in the line in 1969. The line was expanded considerably in 1970, but no new moulds were created in the following years. The pattern was well received, but production problems greatly hindered Fenton's ability to produce this pattern. Only two items — the No. 8356 bud vase and the No. 8380 candy — remained in the 1972 – 1973 catalog, and these were discontinued at the end of 1974.

Later production of Valencia included:

1987 – 1988

The No. 8304 trinket box was made in Provincial Blue Opalescent (OO). The No. 8376 hurricane lamp base appeared in Dusty Rose (DK), Colonial Amber (CA), Provincial Blue Opalescent, and Ruby (RU).

1988

A Valencia hurricane lamp base, No. 8376, was made in Shell Pink (PE), Dusty Rose (DK), Provincial Blue Opalescent (OO), and Teal Royale (OC). These hurricane lamps were sold with a crystal shade. The No. 8356 bud vase and No. 8327 nut/soap dish were available in Colonial Amber and the No. 8304 trinket box was made in Provincial Blue Opalescent (OO).

1990s

A miniature footed candy box was made with a hand-painted decoration in Holiday Green Carnival for the International Carnival Glass Association. This piece was made by combining the regular footed sherbet with the sugar lid. The regular 1900 – 1991 catalog featured the No. 8342-6" basket in Lilac (LX). This basket was also made in Salem Blue (SR) in 1992. From 1992 through 1994 the basket was made in Dusty Rose (DK) and Twilight Blue (TB). An additional color for this basket was Sea Mist Green from 1992 through 1995. The No. 8379-6" comport was made in the following colors:

Dusty Rose (DK)	1992 – 1993	Twilight Blue(TB)	1992 – 1994
Petal Pink (PN)	1992 – 1993	Plum (PL)	1994

Colonial Amber Valencia	Ware No.	Introduced	Discontinued	Value
Ashtray	8377-CA	1969	1973	6.00 – 8.00
Basket, 8"	8338-CA	1970	1973	20.00 – 25.00
Bowl, 8"	8328-CA	1970	1972	10.00 – 12.00
Bowl, flared ftd.	8320-CA	1969	1972	14.00 – 16.00
Cake plate, ftd.	8313-CA	1970	1972	22.00 – 25.00
Candleholder	8374-CA	1970	1972	6.00 – 8.00
Candy box, flat	8380-CA	1969	1975	18.00 – 20.00
Candy box, ftd.	8386-CA	1969	1972	25.00 – 30.00
Cigarette box	8398-CA	1969	1973	14.00 – 18.00
Cigarette lighter	8399-CA	1969	1972	10.00 – 12.00
Creamer, sugar and lid	8306-CA	1970	1972	14.00 – 20.00
Goblet, wine	8344-CA	1970	1972	6.00 – 7.00
Goblet, water	8345-CA	1970	1972	6.00 – 7.00
Salt and pepper	8309-CA	1970	1972	10.00 – 12.00
Sherbet	8343-CA	1970	1972	4.00 – 6.00
Vase, small bud	8356-CA	1969	1975	10.00 – 12.00
Vase, medium bud	8353-CA	1969	1973	10.00 – 14.00
Vase, handkerchief	8359-CA	1969	1972	12.00 – 15.00
Vase, large swung	8352-CA	1969	1973	22.00 – 25.00

Colonial Blue Valencia	Ware No.	Introduced	Discontinued	Value
Ashtray	8377-CB	1969	1973	10.00 – 12.00
Basket, 8"	8338-CB	1970	1973	35.00 – 40.00
Bowl, 8"	8328-CB	1970	1972	20.00 – 22.00
Bowl, flared ftd.	8320-CB	1969	1972	30.00 – 35.00
Candleholder	8374-CB	1970	1972	12.00 – 14.00
Candy box, flat	8380-CB	1969	1975	20.00 – 25.00
Candy box, ftd.	8386-CB	1969	1972	35.00 – 40.00
Cigarette box	8398-CB	1969	1973	20.00 – 25.00
Cigarette lighter	8399-CB	1969	1972	14.00 – 16.00
Vase, small bud	8356-CB	1969	1975	14.00 – 18.00
Vase, medium bud	8353-CB	1969	1973	18.00 – 20.00
Vase, handkerchief	8359-CB	1969	1973	25.00 – 30.00
Vase, large swung	8352-CB	1969	1973	35.00 – 40.00

Colonial Green Valencia	Ware No.	Introduced	Discontinued	Value
Ashtray	8377-CG	1969	1973	6.00 – 8.00
Basket, 8"	8338-CG	1970	1973	25.00 – 30.00
Bowl, 8"	8328-CG	1970	1972	16.00 – 18.00
Bowl, flared ftd.	8320-CG	1969	1972	18.00 – 22.00
Cake plate, ftd.	8313-CG	1970	1972	28.00 – 30.00
Candleholder	8374-CG	1970	1972	8.00 – 10.00
Candy box, flat	8380-CG	1969	1975	22.00 – 25.00
Candy box, ftd.	8386-CG	1969	1972	28.00 – 32.00
Cigarette box	8398-CG	1969	1973	18.00 – 20.00
Cigarette lighter	8399-CG	1969	1972	12.00 – 14.00
Creamer, sugar and lid	8306-CG	1970	1972	20.00 – 25.00
Goblet, wine	8344-CG	1970	1972	8.00 – 9.00
Goblet, water	8345-CG	1970	1972	8.00 – 9.00
Salt and pepper	8309-CG	1970	1972	15.00 – 18.00
Sherbet	8343-CG	1970	1972	6.00 – 8.00
Tumbler, ftd. ice tea	8349-CG	1970	1972	9.00 – 10.00
Vase, small bud	8356-CG	1969	1975	10.00 – 12.00
Vase, medium bud	8353-CG	1969	1973	10.00 – 12.00
Vase, handkerchief	8359-CG	1969	1973	18.00 – 20.00
Vase, large swung	8352-CG	1969	1973	25.00 – 30.00

Crystal Valencia	Ware No.	Introduced	Discontinued	Value
Ashtray	8377-CY	1969	1971	4.00 – 6.00
Basket, 8"	8338-CY	1970	1972	10.00 – 14.00
Bowl, 8"	8328-CY	1970	1972	8.00 – 10.00
Bowl, flared ftd.	8320-CY	1969	1971	10.00 – 12.00
Cake plate, ftd.	8313-CY	1970	1972	14.00 – 18.00
Candleholder	8374-CY	1970	1971	4.00 – 5.00
Candy box, flat	8380-CY	1969	1973	10.00 – 12.00
Candy box, ftd.	8386-CY	1969	1971	10.00 – 12.00
Cigarette box	8398-CY	1969	1971	8.00 – 10.00
Cigarette lighter	8399-CY	1969	1971	3.00 – 5.00
Creamer, sugar and lid	8306-CY	1970	1972	10.00 – 12.00
Goblet, wine	8344-CY	1970	1972	3.00 – 4.00
Goblet, water	8345-CY	1970	1972	3.00 – 4.00
Salt and pepper	8309-CY	1970	1972	10.00 – 12.00
Sherbet	8343-CY	1970	1972	2.00 – 3.00
Tumbler, ftd. ice tea	8349-CY	1970	1972	4.00 – 5.00

8328 CA 8" Bowl

8380 CA Flat Candy Box

8399 CA Cigarette Lighter

8398 CA Cigarette Box

8386 Footed Candy Box

8343 CA Sherbet

8344 CA Wine Goblet

8345 CA Water Goblet

8320 CG Footed Flared Bowl

8377 CA Ash Tray

8377 CG Ash Tray

8380 CG Flat Candy Box

8386 CG Footed Candy Box

8374 CG Candleholder

8399 CB Cigarette Lighter

8359 CB Handkerchief Vase

8352 CA Large Swung Vase

8356 CA Small Bud Vase

8320 CB Footed Flared Bowl

8343 CY Sherbet

8353 CY Medium Bud Vase

8352 CG Large Swung Vase

Crystal Valencia	Ware No.	Introduced	Discontinued	Value
Vase, small bud	8356-CY	1969	1975	4.00 – 5.00
Vase, medium bud	8353-CY	1969	1971	6.00 – 8.00
Vase, handkerchief	8359-CY	1969	1971	8.00 – 9.00
Vase, large swung	8352-CY	1969	1971	10.00 – 15.00
Orange Valencia	**Ware No.**	**Introduced**	**Discontinued**	**Value**
Ashtray	8377-OR	1969	1973	8.00 – 10.00
Basket, 8"	8338-OR	1970	1972	30.00 – 35.00
Bowl, 8"	8328-OR	1970	1972	18.00 – 20.00
Bowl, flared ftd.	8320-OR	1969	1972	20.00 – 25.00
Candleholder	8374-OR	1970	1972	14.00 – 16.00
Candy box, flat	8380-OR	1969	1975	20.00 – 25.00
Candy box, ftd.	8386-OR	1969	1972	25.00 – 30.00
Cigarette box	8398-OR	1969	1973	20.00 – 25.00
Cigarette lighter	8399-OR	1969	1972	18.00 – 20.00
Vase, small bud	8356-OR	1969	1975	14.00 – 16.00
Vase, medium bud	8353-OR	1969	1973	14.00 – 16.00
Vase, handkerchief	8359-OR	1969	1973	16.00 – 20.00
Vase, large swung	8352-OR	1969	1973	35.00 – 40.00

8398 OR Cigarette Box   8399 OR Cigarette Lighter   8313 CA Footed Cake Plate   8386 OR Footed Candy Box

8306 CA Creamer, Sugar and Lid   8380 OR Flat Candy Box   8328 OR 8" Bowl

8320 OR Footed Flared Bowl   8390 CA Salt and Pepper   8338 OR 8" Basket   8352 OR Large Swung Vase

Vasa Murrhina

Vasa Murrhina, which means "vessel of gems," is a cased glassware that contains colored crushed glass flakes, called frit, incorporated into the layers of glass. This type of glass was initially made by ancient glassmakers many centuries ago and more recently by the Cape Cod Glass Works during the 1880s. At that time flakes of mica were used since this substance fuses well with the other layers of glass and it has good reflective properties.

Over the years the formula for making this type of glassware was lost. Therefore, when Frank M. Fenton wanted to create glassware similar to a piece he had bought at an antique show, his chemist, Charles Goe, was directed to redevelop the process.

After the technique was reinvented, Vasa Murrhina was introduced into the regular line in 1964 in Blue Mist (BM), Rose Mist (RM), Aventurine Green with Blue (GB), and Rose with Aventurine Green (RG). Blue Mist was discontinued and a new color, Autumn Orange (AO), entered the line in 1965. New shapes in the other existing colors were also added to the line. Rose Mist was discontinued in 1966. No new shapes or colors were developed for the regular line after 1965 and the entire line was discontinued at the end of 1968.

Vasa Murrhina colors included:

Autumn Orange or Gold Aventurine (AO) features brown and orange colored frit rolled in an opal layer and then cased with a crystal exterior.

Aventurine Green with Blue (GB) contains flecks of green and blue caught in opal and cased with a clear exterior layer.

Blue Mist (BM) contains blue and white frit encased in a crystal layer which is then covered by another layer of crystal.

Rose with Aventurine Green (RG) is a combination of a clear exterior layer with an opal interior layer containing pink and green frit combined with flakes of mica.

Rose Mist (RM) contains pink and white frit rolled in crystal and then covered by another layer of crystal.

Three different pieces of Vasa Murrhina were made for Sears in 1967 for use in the Vincent Price National Treasures feature. The special color was designated Cranberry Mist (CM), a color that was similar to Rose Mist, but that had somewhat more intensity. Two vases and a small pitcher were made for this collection. The vases were made in Cranberry Mist Crest (CC) — Cranberry Mist spun with a clear crest. See the photo on page 362.

Later issues of Vasa Murrhina include:

1983

Vasa Murrhina returned in 1983 with the production of two limited edition pieces. A new color variation was made by blending cranberry, cobalt, and milk glass with a crystal background. The No. 6432-IM-9" basket and the No. 6462-IM-7½" cruet that were produced in this color were each limited to 1,000 pieces.

1989

The No. 6453-RG-8" pinch vase in a limited edition of 2,000 was made in 1989 as part of the Connoisseur Collection. Also, an iridescent teal cased Vasa Murrhina No. 3132-8¾" basket was produced as a part of the Connoisseur Collection. This basket was limited to 2,500 pieces.

Blue Mist Vasa Murrhina	Ware No.	Introduced	Discontinued	Value
Basket, 7" handled	6435-BM	1964	1965	60.00 – 70.00
Basket, 11" handled	6437-BM	1964	1965	110.00 – 130.00
Cream pitcher	6464-BM	1964	1965	40.00 – 45.00
Vase, 4"	6454-BM	1964	1965	20.00 – 25.00
Vase, 5½"	6455-BM	1964	1965	27.00 – 29.00
Vase, 7" fan	6457-BM	1964	1965	55.00 – 65.00
Vase, 8"	6456-BM	1964	1965	40.00 – 45.00
Vase, 11"	6458-BM	1964	1965	90.00 – 110.00
Vase, 14"	6459-BM	1964	1965	110.00 – 145.00

Rose Mist Vasa Murrhina	Ware No.	Introduced	Discontinued	Value
Basket, 7" handled	6435-RM	1964	1966	65.00 – 75.00
Basket, 11" handled	6437-RM	1964	1966	120.00 – 140.00
Cream pitcher	6464-RM	1964	1966	40.00 – 45.00
Pitcher	6465-RM	1965	1966	180.00 – 200.00
Vase, 4"	6454-RM	1964	1966	20.00 – 25.00
Vase, 5½"	6455-RM	1964	1966	27.00 – 30.00
Vase, 7" fan	6457-RM	1964	1966	60.00 – 70.00
Vase, 7" square	6452-RM	1965	1966	40.00 – 45.00
Vase, 8"	6456-RM	1964	1966	40.00 – 50.00
Vase, 9" pinch	6450-RM	1965	1966	60.00 – 70.00
Vase, 10"	6451-RM	1965	1966	120.00 – 140.00
Vase, 11"	6458-RM	1964	1966	90.00 – 110.00
Vase, 14"	6459-RM	1964	1966	120.00 – 140.00

Aventurine Green with Blue Vasa Murrhina	Ware No.	Introduced	Discontinued	Value
Basket, 7" handled	6435-GB	1964	1969	65.00 – 75.00
Basket, 11" handled	6437-GB	1964	1969	120.00 – 140.00
Cream pitcher	6464-GB	1964	1967	40.00 – 45.00
Pitcher	6465-GB	1965	1966	180.00 – 200.00
Vase, 4"	6454-GB	1964	1969	20.00 – 25.00
Vase, 5½"	6455-GB	1964	1966	27.00 – 30.00
Vase, 7" fan	6457-GB	1964	1967	60.00 – 70.00
Vase, 7" square	6452-GB	1965	1966	40.00 – 45.00
Vase, 8"	6456-GB	1964	1969	40.00 – 50.00
Vase, 9" pinch	6450-GB	1965	1966	60.00 – 70.00
Vase, 10"	6451-GB	1965	1967	120.00 – 140.00
Vase, 11"	6458-GB	1964	1969	90.00 – 110.00
Vase, 14"	6459-GB	1964	1967	120.00 – 140.00

Rose with Aventurine Green Vasa Murrhina	Ware No.	Introduced	Discontinued	Value
Basket, 7" handled	6435-RG	1964	1969	60.00 – 70.00
Basket, 11" handled	6437-RG	1964	1969	110.00 – 130.00
Cream pitcher	6464-RG	1964	1967	40.00 – 45.00
Pitcher	6465-RG	1965	1966	160.00 – 180.00
Vase, 4"	6454-RG	1964	1969	20.00 – 25.00
Vase, 5½"	6455-RG	1964	1966	25.00 – 30.00
Vase, 7" fan	6457-RG	1964	1967	55.00 – 65.00
Vase, 7" square	6452-RG	1965	1966	40.00 – 50.00
Vase, 8"	6456-RG	1964	1969	40.00 – 45.00
Vase, 9" pinch	6450-RG	1965	1966	60.00 – 65.00
Vase, 10"	6451-RG	1965	1966	100.00 – 110.00
Vase, 11"	6458-RG	1964	1969	90.00 – 100.00
Vase, 14"	6459-RG	1964	1967	110.00 – 120.00

Catalog Reprint Circa 1964 Courtesy Of: **The Fenton Art Glass Museum**

Rose Mist

6437 RM
Hdl. Basket 11" High

6454 RM
4" Vase

6455 RM
5½" Vase

6459 RM
14" Vase

6458 RM
11" Vase

6435 RM
Hdl. Basket 7" High

6457 RM
7" Fan Vase

6464 RM
Cream Pitcher

6456 RM
8" Vase

FENTON PRESENTS

Vasa Murrhina

Blue Mist

6459 BM
14" Vase

6457 BM
7" Fan Vase

6455 BM
5½" Vase

6454 BM
4" Vase

6458 BM
11" Vase

6456 BM
8" Vase

6437 BM
Hdl. Basket 11" High

6464 BM
Cream Pitcher

6435 BM
Hdl. Basket 7" High

361

Autumn Orange Vasa Murrhina	Ware No.	Introduced	Discontinued	Value
Basket, 7" handled	6435-AO	1965	1968	50.00 – 60.00
Basket, 11" handled	6437-AO	1965	1968	90.00 – 100.00
Cream pitcher	6464-AO	1965	1967	22.00 – 25.00
Pitcher	6465-AO	1965	1966	150.00 – 170.00
Vase, 4"	6454-AO	1965	1968	22.00 – 25.00
Vase, 7" fan	6457-AO	1965	1967	50.00 – 60.00
Vase, 7" square	6452-AO	1965	1966	35.00 – 45.00
Vase, 8"	6456-AO	1965	1968	45.00 – 50.00
Vase, 9" pinch	6450-AO	1965	1966	60.00 – 65.00
Vase, 10"	6451-AO	1965	1967	80.00 – 90.00
Vase, 11"	6458-AO	1965	1968	75.00 – 85.00
Vase, 14"	6459-AO	1965	1967	90.00 – 100.00

Sears Vincent Price National Treasures Collection		Value
Pitcher	S6464-CM	40.00 – 50.00
Vase, 6"	S6466-CC	45.00 – 55.00
Vase, 11"	S6468-CC	90.00 – 100.00

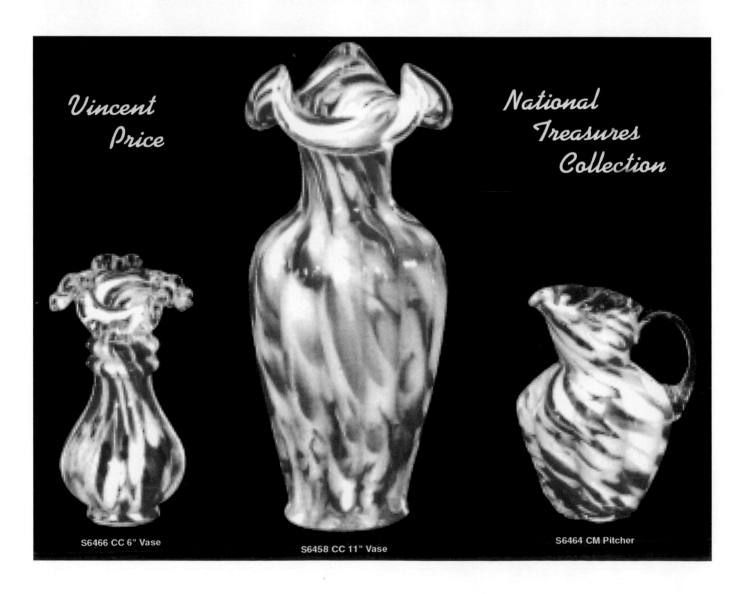

S6466 CC 6" Vase

S6458 CC 11" Vase

S6464 CM Pitcher

362

Catalog Reprint Circa 1964 Courtesy Of The Fenton Art glass Museum

Rose with Aventurine Green

6457 RG
7" Fan Vase

6454 RG
4" Vase

6455 RG
5½" Vase

6458 RG
11" Vase

6459 RG
14" Vase

6437 RG
Hdl. Basket 11" High

6435 RG
Hdl. Basket 7" High

6464 RG
Cream Pitcher

6456 RG
8" Vase

Vasa Murrhina glass was first honored in Roman palaces nearly 2000 years ago. In the nineteenth century it became one of the most desired examples of historically famous Sandwich glass. Now—Fenton brings you Vasa Murrhina—in pleasing Early American designs. Its unusual richness and enchanting color patterns will appeal to all who prize the unique in beauty.

Aventurine Green with Blue

6455 GB
5½" Vase

6454 GB
4" Vase

6457 GB
7" Fan Vase

6456 GB
8" Vase

6464 GB
Cream Pitcher

6435 GB
Hdl. Basket 7" High

6437 GB
Hdl. Basket 11" High

6459 GB
14" Vase

6458 GB
11" Vase

363

Waffle

Fenton's Waffle pattern made its appearance in the regular line in January 1960. The entire offering consisted of four different pieces — a basket, candy box, and two sizes of vases. The pattern was made in Blue Opalescent, Green Opalescent, and milk. All items except the medium vase in milk were discontinued by the end of 1960. This vase was discontinued at the end of 1961.

Blue Opalescent Waffle	Ware No.	Introduced	Discontinued	Value
Basket	6137-BO	1960	1961	100.00 – 125.00
Candy box	6180-BO	1960	1961	85.00 – 90.00
Vase, 4"	6152-BO	1960	1961	35.00 – 45.00
Vase, medium	6158-BO	1960	1961	60.00 – 70.00
Green Opalescent Waffle	Ware No.	Introduced	Discontinued	Value
Basket	6137-GO	1960	1961	100.00 – 125.00
Candy box	6180-GO	1960	1961	75.00 – 85.00
Vase, 4"	6152-GO	1960	1961	35.00 – 45.00
Vase, medium	6158-GO	1960	1961	45.00 – 55.00
Milk Waffle	Ware No.	Introduced	Discontinued	Value
Basket	6137-MI	1960	1961	40.00 – 45.00
Candy box	6180-MI	1960	1961	30.00 – 35.00
Vase, 4"	6152-MI	1960	1961	20.00 – 25.00
Vase, medium	6158-MI	1960	1962	25.00 – 30.00

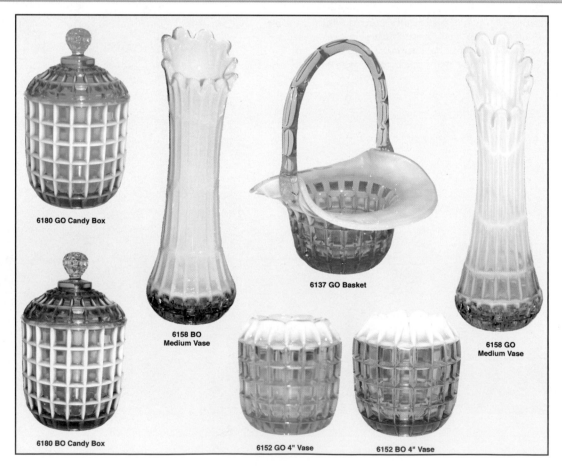

6180 GO Candy Box

6158 BO Medium Vase

6137 GO Basket

6158 GO Medium Vase

6180 BO Candy Box

6152 GO 4" Vase

6152 BO 4" Vase

Wide Rib Optic

Wide Rib Optic is similar to Fenton's other vertical ribbed pattern — Rib Optic. However, just as the name implies, the opalescent ribs of Wide Rib Optic are about two to three times as wide as those of Rib Optic. Several pieces of Fenton's Wide Rib Optic pattern were pictured in an opalescent assortment in a catalog from about 1939. At this time there is no complete catalog listing of the pieces available. Items in the listing below are known to exist, but more shapes will probably be found.

Wide Rib Optic	French Opalescent
Bowl, #1522-10" crimped	35.00 – 45.00
Bowl, #1523-11" crimped	45.00 – 60.00
Ginger jar, #893	200.00 – 225.00
Vase, #184-10" crimped	80.00 – 110.00
Vase, #1523	100.00 – 120.00

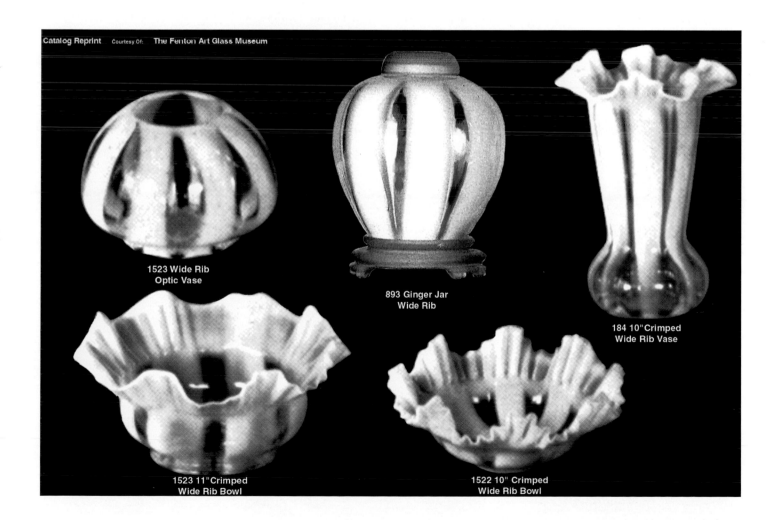

Catalog Reprint   Courtesy Of: The Fenton Art Glass Museum

1523 Wide Rib
Optic Vase

893 Ginger Jar
Wide Rib

184 10"Crimped
Wide Rib Vase

1523 11"Crimped
Wide Rib Bowl

1522 10" Crimped
Wide Rib Bowl

Wild Rose with Bowknot

Fenton's Wild Rose with Bowknot pattern was introduced in January 1961 in milk and the overlay colors — Apple Green, Coral, Honey Amber, Powder Blue Overlay, and Wild Rose. Two different sizes of vases were made in the overlay colors. Additional pieces made in milk included a salt and pepper, a 32 oz. pitcher, and a 7½" vase. All the items in the overlay colors were discontinued at the end of 1961. Milk glass pieces, with the exception of the pitcher and the shakers, were discontinued at the same time. The pitcher was made through June 1962, and production of the shakers continued through 1967.

Lamp shades and lamp founts in this pattern were available in 1962 as stock items for sale to lamp manufacturers. These parts were made in Milk, Honey Amber, and Peach Blow. Sometimes shades that have not been cut will be found on the secondary market masquerading as vases.

1980

New shapes and colors were created in this pattern for marketing by the LeVay Distributing Company. A No. 2805-20" lamp was made in Aqua Opalescent Carnival (IO). This lamp was marketed as a limited edition with a total production of 400.

Six other pieces of Wild Rose with Bowknot were made for LeVay in Celestial Blue Satin. These included:

Basket, 7" DC	2834-ES	Pitcher, ruffled top	2864-ES
Basket, pie crust crimp, looped handle	2836-ES	Rose bowl, 5" crimped	2853-ES
Bowl, Jack-in-the-Pulpit	2824-ES	Vase, 7½" DC	2857-ES
Bowl, 9" DC	2823-ES	Vase, 9" Jack-in-the Pulpit	2854-ES

1992-1994

Miniature No. 6561-3½" baskets appeared in Sea Mist Green (LE) and Twilight Blue (TB).

1995

Although Fenton shortened the name to Wild Rose, the pattern remained the same as the earlier version with the longer name. The No. 2857-7½" vase and No. 2927-6" rose bowl were produced as part of the 1995 Red Carnival assortment.

1997

The No. 2854 handkerchief vase was introduced in Topaz Opalescent (TS).

Wild Rose with Bowknot	Ware No.	Apple Green	Blue Overlay	Coral
Vase, 5"	2855	35.00 – 45.00	35.00 – 45.00	35.00 – 45.00
Vase, 7½"	2857	50.00 – 55.00	55.00 – 65.00	50.00 – 60.00

Wild Rose with Bowknot	Ware No.	Honey Amber	Wild Rose	
Vase, 5"	2855	30.00 – 35.00	40.00 – 50.00	
Vase, 7½"	2857	35.00 – 40.00	55.00 – 65.00	

Milk Glass Wild Rose with Bowknot	Ware No.	Introduced	Discontinued	Value
Pitcher, 32 oz. handled	2865-MI	1961	July 1962	45.00 – 50.00
Salt and pepper	2806-MI	1961	1968	35.00 – 40.00
Vase, 5"	2855-MI	1961	1962	20.00 – 25.00
Vase, 7½"	2857-MI	1961	1962	25.00 – 30.00
Vase, 8"	2858-MI	1961	1962	30.00 – 40.00

2857 BV 7 1/2" Vase

2855 MI 5" Vase

2806 MI Salt & Pepper

2857 AG 7 1/2 Vase

2855 AG 5" Vase

2855 HA 5" Vase

2855 BV 5" Vase

2857 CL 7 1/2" Vase

2865 MI 32 Oz. Pitcher

2858 MI 8" Vase

Bibliography

Books

Ezell, Elaine and George Newhouse. *Cruets, Cruets, Cruets, Volume I*. Marietta, Ohio: Antique Publications, 1991.

Griffith, Shirley. *A Pictorial Review of Fenton's White Hobnail Milk Glass*. Warren, Ohio: Shirley Griffith, 1994.

Heacock, William. *Fenton Glass, The Second Twenty-five Years*. Marietta, Ohio: O-val Advertising Corp., 1980.

Heacock, William. *Fenton Glass, The Third Twenty-five Years*. Marietta, Ohio: O-val Advertising Corp., 1989.

Measell, James. *Fenton Glass, The 1980s Decade*. Marietta, Ohio: Antique Publications, 1996.

Measell, James and W. C. "Red" Roetteis. *The L. G. Wright Glass Company*. Marietta, Ohio: Antique Publications, 1997.

Newbound, Betty and Bill. *The Collector's Encyclopedia of Milk Glass, Identification and Values*. Paducah, Kentucky: Collector Books, 1995.

Palmer, Michael and Lori. *The Charleton Line: AWCO's Decorations on Fenton, Cambridge, Consolidated, Westmoreland, Duncan and Miller, Heisey, Imperial, Limoges, and Others*. Atglen, Pennsylvania: Schiffer Publishing, Ltd., 2002.

Catalogs

DeVilbiss Company. *Devilbiss Perfume Atomizers*. Toledo, Ohio: The Devilbiss Company, 1939 – 1955.

Randall, A. L. *Fenton for Flowers*. Chicago, Illinois: A. L. Randall Company, 1970 – 1980.

Fenton Art Glass Company. *Fenton General Catalogs and Supplements*. Williamstown, West Virginia: Fenton Art Glass Company, 1940 – 1980.

Newsletters

Fenton Art Glass. *Glass Messenger*. Williamstown, West Virginia: Fenton Art Glass Company, 2000 – 2003.

Pacific Northwest Fenton Association. *The Fenton Nor'wester*. Tillamook, Oregon: P. N. W. F. A., 1992 – 2003.